NOV
22

Also by Michael Eddowes
THE MAN ON YOUR CONSCIENCE
(An Investigation of the
Timothy Evans Murder Trail)

Frontispiece Jack Ruby breaks through the cordon of newsmen and shoots Lee Harvey Oswald at point blank range. Picture shows the moment of impact

MICHAEL EDDOWES

NOV
22

How They Killed
KENNEDY

JERSEY
NEVILLE SPEARMAN

First published in Great Britain in 1976 by
Neville Spearman (Jersey) Limited
PO Box 75, Normandy House, St Helier
Jersey, Channel Islands

Distributed by Neville Spearman Ltd.
112 Whitfield Street, London W1P 6DP

ISBN 0 85978 019 8

This book has been produced in some haste so that it may coincide with the hearings of the current Congressional Enquiry into the validity of the Warren Report.

The publishers regret that the following errors, which occurred in production, came to light after the book went to press.

ERRATA

Foreword, page 2, line 22, for Manella Novotny, *read* Mariella Novotny
page 89, line 8, for FBEI *read* FBI; *line 10, for* remarkaele *read* remarkable
page 92, line 4 and page 95, line 5, for Tankin *read* Rankin
page 137, line 27, for Marine *read* Marina
page 175, line 23, for on 13 and 16 September *read* on 17 and 13 September

page 177, line 8, after MVD, *delete remainder of line and all line 9*
page 179, line 24, for much *read* such
page 189, line 3, figure 2. *starts a new paragraph*
page 252, line 13, for from *read* for
page 307, second line of heading, for Hankin *read* Rankin; *last line of page, at left insert* CHAIRMAN
page 346, line 14, for 7 *read* 6

Filmset in 12/13 point Bembo by
Specialised Offset Services Ltd., Liverpool
Printed by Clarke, Doble & Brendon Ltd., Plymouth

FOREWORD

In this book I will discuss the assassination of President John Fitzgerald Kennedy on 22 November 1963, in Dealey Plaza, Dallas, Texas, United States, by a young labourer, describing himself as an ex-Marine, Lee Harvey Oswald. After being arrested later that day he was himself murdered two days later in the basement of Dallas Police Station by a middle-aged underworld figure, Jack Ruby, who was associated with members of Organized Crime (OC), and operated two strip and dance clubs in Dallas, 'The Carousel' and 'The Vagas'. He was immediately arrested, later convicted of premeditated murder, and died in prison in early 1967.

The official report of the assassination and related matters, known as *The Warren Report* and published in September 1964, states that the assassin was ex-Marine Lee Harvey Oswald who had acted alone, that he was not associated with his murderer who too had acted alone, and that there was no available evidence of domestic or international conspiracy.

I will prove beyond reasonable doubt: (1) that material vital to establishing the truth was withheld from the authors of *The Warren Report*, (2) that the assassination was an act of political sabotage, (3) that the assassin was a Russian agent who had impersonated ex-Marine Oswald, (4) that within seven hours of the arrest of the assassin the White House was informed by the federal agencies that the assassin was a Russian impostor, and (5) that it was decided that this fact should not be made public. When Jack Ruby, a Russian-Jewish hoodlum, sacrificed all in silencing the assassin, the authorities realized that the Russians had provided the assassin and that, but for his arrest, the underworld would have provided his means of escape from Dallas.

Commencing in July 1959 and culminating in June 1963, three consecutive and apparently connected attempts at political sabotage were made in Canada, the United States and Britain. In each case the attempt was at first suppressed by the authorities; in each case a different and attractive young woman had been involved; in each case the young woman had been associated with the underworld; in each case a senior and clandestine Russian intelligence officer had been involved.

The sabotages were directed at the character-assassination by sexual compromise of a prominent political figure in each of the three countries; in Canada the Associate Minister of National Defense, Pierre Sevigny, in the United States, President Kennedy, and in Britain, the Secretary for War, John Profumo. In due course, Sevigny and Profumo resigned, and it is difficult to accept that Kennedy would have permitted himself – or been permitted by his security guards – to be involved in a situation that might result in compromise.

The Spence Report (1966) details the Canadian sabotage (1959/60) and states that a 'Major in Russian Intelligence' was involved. There is no official report on the United States sabotage (1960/61), and information is limited to the words of the young woman, Manella Novotny, involved, in *The News of the World* (1961) and in *Saturday Titbits* (1972). In 1972, she wrote *inter alia*, 'Looking back, I now realize that Jack's susceptibility to beautiful women was precisely why I was sent to America. Naively, I believed what I had been told – that the trip (from London) was to find me TV work as a model. I now know the truth. I was groomed specifically to compromise Kennedy on the eve of his inauguration as President. I was a pawn, and the name of the game was espionage'. She claimed an acquaintanceship with Captain Yevgemmi Ivanov, a clandestine Russian intelligence officer stationed at the Russian Embassy in London who occupied the cover position of Naval Attache and who, according to himself, acted directly under the orders of Soviet Premier, Nikita Khrushchev. *The Denning Report* (1963) details the British sabotage (1961/63) and discloses that the operator was Ivanov.

The similarity of the three attempts at political sabotage, their chronology and the presence of the underworld in the basement of Dallas Police Station, led me to suspect that all four political sabotages were ordered by Khrushchev and carried out by his intelligence officers. My eleven years study of *The Warren Report* and its 26 supporting Volumes of Testimony and Exhibits travel to several countries and interviews with hundreds of persons, including a lengthy interview with the FBI in New York at their request, have produced this book which is, in effect, a 'brief for the prosecution' of Khrushchev for the murder of President Kennedy.

My purpose is to disclose the truth and, if the 'brief' is found to be accurate, to contribute to the peace of the world; in the words of President Kennedy on 22 October 1962, 'Aggressive conduct if allowed to go unchecked and unchallenged ultimately leads to war.'

'Our goal is not the victory of might but the vindication of right – not peace at the expense of freedom, but both peace and freedom, here in this hemisphere and, we hope, around the world. God willing, that goal will be achieved.'

John F. Kennedy
('Cuba Crisis')
22 October 1962.

1

On the death of Stalin in 1953, Malenkov became Soviet Premier and First Secretary of the Communist Party of the Soviet Union; within a week Nikita Khrushchev had taken over the position of First Secretary. The oligarchy included Molotov, Bulganin, Kaganovich and Shepilov. They had to ensure their own physical survival and towards this end their first move was to arrest Beria who, next to Stalin, was possibly the most powerful man in Russia and the head of the gigantic State Security Service that had implemented Stalin's policy of terror and mass murder. Beria was charged as a criminal conspirator and as an agent of British Intelligence, and was executed. His name was erased from history books and encyclopedias, and he became a 'non-person'. In 1954, the State Security apparatus was renamed Komitet Gosudarstvennoy Bezopasnosti (KGB).

In 1955, Bulganin succeeded Malenkov as Soviet Premier, and in 1957 Khrushchev eliminated Molotov, Kaganovich and Shepilov, members of the original oligarchy and all of whom in one way or another were his rivals.

In 1956, Khrushchev denounced Stalin whose body was removed from its position beside the body of Lenin in a joint and public tomb.

In 1958, Bulganin was disgraced and Khrushchev became Soviet Premier, a position he was to hold until the autumn of 1964. As undisputed leader of the Russian people and with the KGB under his sole control, Khrushchev and the KGB became in effect a single entity. It was through the KGB that Khrushchev was able not only to control his own people but to implement his foreign policy.

Khrushchev stated to the Russians and to the world that the

'Stalin terror' was over and presented the Soviet Union as an advanced modern state, broadcasting his policy of 'peaceful co-existence'. In reality, his external policy was to conquer the West in a colossal gamble that transcended anything that the mighty Stalin had attempted.

In the 1950s, President of the United States, Dwight Eisenhower, had endeavoured to come to terms with the Malenkov/Bulganin/Khrushchev leaderships. His bitterness over the threats and demands of the Russians – the demands included the dismantling of the North Atlantic Treaty Organisation (NATO) – found expression in his words: 'But to those of us responsible for the conduct of foreign relations, the Soviet duplicity was a grievous disappointment ... The record was established: All could now see the nature of Soviet Diplomatic tactics as contrasted with those of the free world.'

In January 1959, Fidel Castro had overthrown the Batista dictatorship in Cuba and was looking for support to the extreme left; by mid-1959 Cuba had accepted the embrace of Khrushchev and had become a Soviet satellite, and in July 1959 Khrushchev was opposed by Vice President Richard Nixon in Moscow.

In late 1960, John Kennedy defeated Nixon in a close contest for the Presidency and was inaugurated on 20 January 1961. While the character assassination of Kennedy was being attempted in New York in the spring of 1961, the spy/assassin was allegedly being trained in a spy school in or near Minsk (some 450 miles southwest of Moscow) supposedly having arrived from Moscow on 7 January 1961.

In June 1961, Kennedy met Khrushchev in Vienna where the latter reiterated Russian demands over Berlin, giving Kennedy an ultimatum. Kennedy felt that Khrushchev could not be persuaded that the West would fight to support its rights in West Berlin, and it would seem that Khrushchev hoped that the young President might be hectored into a posture of appeasement by threats of global war so early in his Presidency but, like Nixon, Kennedy had exhibited a determination to oppose him.

In July 1961, Kennedy addressed the United States: 'Seven weeks ago tonight I returned from Europe to report on my meeting with Premier Khrushchev and the others. His grim warnings about the future of the world, his aide-memoire on

Berlin, his subsequent speeches and threats which he and his agents have launched, and the increase in the Soviet military budget that he had announced have all prompted a series of decisions by the administration and a series of consultations by members of NATO organisations ... We do not want to fight, but we have fought before. And others in earlier times have made the same dangerous mistake of assuming that the West was too selfish and too soft and too divided to resist invasions of freedom in other lands ... Soviet strategy has long been aimed not merely at Berlin but at dividing and neutralising all of Europe, forcing us back to our own shores. We must meet our oft stated pledge to the free peoples of West Berlin ... The world is not deceived by the Communist attempt to label Berlin as a hot bed of war. There is peace in Berlin today. The source of world tension is Moscow, not Berlin. And if war begins, it will have begun in Moscow and not Berlin. For the choice of peace or war is largely theirs, not ours. It is the Soviets who have stirred up this crisis. It is they who are trying to change. It is they who have opposed free elections. It is they who have rejected an all-German peace treaty and the rulings of international law ... The Atlantic Community, as we know it, has been built in response to challenge: The challenge of European chaos of 1947, of the Berlin Blockade in 1948, the challenge of Communist aggression in Korea in 1950 ... If we do not meet our commitments to Berlin, where will we stand later? If we are not true to our word there, all that we have achieved in collective security, which relies on these words will mean nothing. And if there is one path of all others to war, it is the path of weakness and disunity ... We shall seek peace, but we shall not surrender. That is the central meaning of this crisis and the meaning of your Government's policy ... '

From the end of World War II the Russians had overhauled the West in their military potential and, as this had increased in 1961 to the point of equality, Khrushchev was prepared to challenge Kennedy at a Berlin confrontation. In October 1961, Russian tanks moved up to 'Checkpoint Charlie' which lay between East and West Berlin, but Kennedy faced these tanks with American tanks, and the Russians retreated. It might seem in retrospect that Khrushchev's action may have been taken only in order to satisfy his colleagues and the Russian military that victory over the West could not be achieved in stages and that an all-out offensive would be necessary; after their meeting in Vienna, Khrushchev must have anticipated Kennedy's response to this (comparatively) limited action.

In July 1962, Raul Castro, the brother of Fidel Castro and Cuba's Minister of Defence, visited Moscow where a month later he was joined by Che Guevara, the third member of the ruling triumvirate in Cuba. Early in September 1962, a Russian-Cuban security treaty was announced and, although material for missile sites had begun to arrive in Cuba several months earlier, it was not until 14 October 1962 that a U-2 reconnaisance plane brought back final confirmatory photographs of missile and bomber bases under rapid construction in Cuba. The Russians had selected bad-weather months in Cuba for the erection of their missiles, and clouds had made it difficult for photographs to be taken. The weather, however, improved and Major Anderson, flying the U-2, was able to obtain the definitive photographs. While on another over-flight of Cuba 13 days later he was shot down and killed by a Russian-operated SAM.

On 22 October 1962, Kennedy addressed the United States, and his decisions and his words were to be his death warrant.

Kennedy said: 'Good evening, my fellow citizens. This Government, as promised, has maintained the closest surveillance of the Soviet military build-up on the island of Cuba. Within the past week unmistakable evidence has established the fact that a series of offensive missile sites is now in preparation on that imprisoned island. The purpose of these bases can be none other than to provide a nuclear strike capability against the Western Hemisphere.

'Upon receiving the first preliminary hard information of this nature last Tuesday morning (16 October) at 9.00 a.m., I directed that our surveillance be stepped up. And having now confirmed and completed our evaluation of the evidence and our decision on a course of action, this Government feels obliged to report this new crisis to you in fullest detail.' (Author's note: After two days training, his work sheets disclosed that between 9.45 a.m. and 10.10 a.m. on 16 October the spy/assassin executed photographic work for the *Army Map Service* on the premises of a firm in

Dallas, Jaggars-Chiles-Stovall, who are sometimes entrusted with 'highly secret' work by that Service and other departments of the United States military, such work allegedly being executed in a separate department by specially cleared employees. Using the name Lee Harvey Oswald – being the name under which the man had entered the United States in June 1962 – he had obtained employment in the firm on Friday 12 October, falsely stating that he was just out of the Marines with an honourable discharge. Lee Harvey Oswald had, in fact, left the Marines some three years previously with an honourable discharge, a year later to be changed to an undesirable discharge when it was believed that he had defected to Russia. The purpose of the espionage would have been to discovery what, if anything, the U-2 had photographed of the rapid and aggressive military build-up in Cuba.)

Kennedy continued: 'The characteristics of these new missile sites indicate two distinct types of installations. Several of them include medium-range ballistic missiles capable of carrying a nuclear warhead for a distance of more than 1,000 nautical miles. Each of these missiles, in short, is capable of striking Washington, D.C., the Panama Canal, Cape Canaveral, Mexico City, or any other city in the southeastern part of the United States, in Central America, or in the Caribbean area.

'Additional sites not yet completed appear to be designed for intermediate-range ballistic missiles capable of travelling more than twice as far – and thus capable of striking most of the major cities in the Western Hemisphere, ranging as far north as Hudson Bay, Canada, and as far south as Lima, Peru. In addition, jet bombers, capable of carrying nuclear weapons, are now being uncrated and assembled in Cuba, while the necessary air bases are being prepared.

'This urgent transformation of Cuba into an important strategic base – by the presence of these large, long-range, and clearly offensive weapons of sudden mass destruction – constitutes an explicit threat to the peace and security of all the Americas, in flagrant and deliberate defiance of the Rio Pact of 1947, the traditions of this nation and hemisphere, the Joint Resolution of the 87th Congress, the Charter of the United Nations, and my own public warnings to the Soviets on

September 4 and 13.' (Author's note: By using Cuba, Khrushchev had reduced the 'warning-time' of the firing of missiles from 15 minutes to 30 seconds – thus prohibiting retaliatory response and thus identifying Khrushchev's purpose in selecting Cuba as the base from which could be launched 'sudden mass destruction'. The 42 missiles with thermonuclear warheads and some two weeks short of completed installation could have inflicted damage to the United States estimated to be 1000 times greater than the destruction caused by the Hiroshima or Nagasaki atom bombs. The nuclear bombers could reach any part of the United States, pinpoint and destroy all surviving military installations or cities; the inclusion of bombers in the military build-up suggests that the build-up was not intended for neutralisation as opposed to vapourisation of the United States.)

Kennedy continued: 'This action also contradicts the repeated assurances of Soviet spokesmen, both publicly and privately delivered, that the arms build-up in Cuba would retain its original defensive character and that the Soviet Union had no need or desire to station strategic missiles on the territory of any other nation.

'The size of this undertaking makes clear that it has been planned for some months. Yet only last month, after I had made clear the distinction between any introduction of ground-to-ground missiles and the existence of defensive anti-aircraft missiles, the Soviet Government publicly stated on September 11 that, and I quote, "The armaments and military equipment sent to Cuba are designed exclusively for defensive purposes", and, I quote the Soviet Government, "There is no need for the Soviet Government to shift its weapons for a retaliatory blow to any other country, for instance Cuba", and that, and I quote the Soviet Government, "The Soviet Union has so powerful rockets to carry these nuclear warheads that there is no need to search for sites for them beyond the boundaries of the Soviet Union." That statement was false.

'Only last Thursday (18 October), as evidence of this rapid offensive build-up was already in my hand, Soviet Foreign Minister Gromyko told me in my office that he was instructed to make it clear once again, as he said his Government had already done, that Soviet assistance to Cuba, and I quote "pursued solely the purpose of contributing to the defense capabilities of Cuba", that, and I quote him, "training by Soviet specialists of Cuban nationals in handling defensive armaments was by no means offensive", and that "if it were otherwise", Mr. Gromyko went on, "the Soviet Government would never become involved in rendering such assistance". That statement was false.

'Neither the United States of America nor the world community of nations can tolerate diliberate deception and offensive threats on the part of any nation, large or small ...

'But this secret, swift, and extraordinary build-up of Communist missiles ... is a deliberately provocative and unjustified change in the status quo which cannot be accepted by this country if our courage and our commitments are ever to be trusted again by either friend or foe.

'The 1930s taught us a clear lesson: Aggressive conduct, if allowed to grow unchecked and unchallenged, ultimately leads to war. This nation is opposed to war. We are also true to our word. Our unswerving objective, therefore, must be to prevent the use of these missiles against this or any other country and to secure their withdrawal or elimination from the Western Hemisphere ...

'Acting, therefore, in the defense of our own security and of the entire Western Hemisphere, and under the authority entrusted to me by the Constitution as endorsed by the resolution of the Congress, I have directed that the following initial steps be taken immediately:

'First: To halt this offensive build-up, a strict quarantine on all offensive military equipment under shipment to Cuba is being initiated. All ships of any kind bound for Cuba from whatever nation or port will, if found to contain cargoes of offensive weapons, be turned back. This quarantine will be extended, if needed, to other types of cargo and carriers. We are not at this time, however, denying the necessities of life as the Soviets attempted to do in their Berlin blockade of 1948.

'Second: I have directed the continued and increased close surveillance of Cuba and its military build-up. The Foreign Ministers of the OAS (Organisation of American States) in their communique of October 3 rejected secrecy on such matters in this hemisphere. Should these offensive military preparations continue, thus increasing the threat to the hemisphere, further action will be justified. I have directed the Armed Forces to prepare for any eventualities; and I trust that, in the interests of both the Cuban people and the Soviet technicians at the sites, the hazards to all concerned of continuing this threat will be recognized.

'Third: It shall be the policy of this nation to regard any nuclear missile launched from Cuba against any nation in the Western Hemisphere as an attack by the Soviet Union on the United States, requiring a full retaliatory response upon the Soviet Union.

'Fourth: As a necessary military precaution I have reinforced our base at Guantanamo, evacuated today the dependents of our personnel there, and ordered additional military units to be on a standby alert basis.

'Fifth: We are calling tonight for an immediate meeting of the Organ of Consultation, under the Organization of American States, to consider this threat to hemispheric security and to invoke articles 6 and 8 of the Rio Treaty in support of all necessary action. The United Nations Charter allows for regional security arrangements – and the nations of this hemisphere decided long ago against the military presence of outside powers. Our other allies around the world have also been alerted.

'Sixth: Under the Charter of the United Nations, we are asking tonight that an emergency meeting of the Security Council be convoked without delay to take action against this latest Soviet threat to world peace. Our resolution will call for the prompt dismantling and withdrawal of all offensive weapons in Cuba, under the supervision of U.N. observers, before the quarantine can be lifted.

'Seventh and finally: I call upon Chairman Khrushchev to halt and eliminate this clandestine, reckless and provocative threat to world peace and to stable relations between our two nations. I call upon him further to abandon this course of world domination and to join in an historic effort to end the perilous arms race and transform the history of man. He has an opportunity now to move the world back from the abyss of destruction – by returning to his Government's own words that it had no need to station missiles outside its own territory, and withdrawing these weapons from Cuba – by refraining from any action which will widen or deepen the present crisis – and then by participating in a search for peaceful and permanent solutions …

'My fellow citizens, let no one doubt that this is a difficult and dangerous effort on which we had set out … But the greatest danger of all would be to do nothing.

'The path we have chosen for the present is full of hazards, as all paths are; but it is the one most consistent with our character and courage as a nation and our commitments around the world. The cost of freedom is always high – but Americans have always paid it. And one path we shall never choose, and that is the path of surrender or submission.

'Our goal is not the victory of might but the vindication of right – not peace at the expense of freedom, but both peace and freedom, here in this hemisphere and, we hope, around the world. God willing, that goal will be achieved.'

Kennedy's historic speech was broadcast around the world in 38 languages, and printed and distributed in many more.

After an exchange of notes between Kennedy and Khrushchev beginning on 26 October – those from Kennedy stating his absolute determination not to waver from the course that he had set and those from Khrushchev containing threats and denunciations – on 28 October Khrushchev capitulated and a merchant fleet en route for Cuba carrying additional nuclear warheads from Russian and Russian controlled ports retreated, the missiles already in Cuba were withdrawn and the missile sites destroyed under the supervision of the United Nations.

The record of the days and nights at the White House during the 'Cuba Crisis' show how Kennedy, his brother Robert and those who agreed with them had finally persuaded the advocates of bombing and invasion of Cuba – or even of doing nothing – into agreeing with them upon what turned out to have been the only possible and successful resolution of one of the most difficult diplomatic and military problems in history; the decision of two statesmen that would cost their lives. (When some years later Robert Kennedy announced that he would run for President, I (the author) felt that if my theory was correct he too would be assassinated; shortly thereafter he was shot dead by Sirhan Sirhan, allegedly a member of Al Fatah.)

With the benefit of hindsight, it is possible to speculate upon Khrushchev's 'colossal gamble'. It would seem that if the Cuba plot had matured with all the missiles installed on their launching pads and the nuclear bombers prepared for take-off, 'sudden mass destruction' would have reduced the United States to rubble. After long preparation and under their leader, Mao Tse Tung, the Chinese had invaded India in great strength at the time of the 'Cuba Crisis'. The actual date of the commencement of hostilities is indeterminable, but on 20 October 1962 (being four days *after* the assassin had executed photographic work at Jaggars-Chiles-Stovall in Dallas but two days *before* Kennedy addressed the American people to disclose to the world what had previously been kept secret) the Chinese, although having destroyed three Indian Divisions, having occupied 12,000 square miles of Indian territory, with the Indian armies in disarray and with the plains of India before them, suddenly halted. It would seem that having been informed by the Russians that their spy in Jaggars-Chiles-Stovall had discovered that the Americans were aware of the presence of missiles on Cuba, the Chinese decided to await the outcome of the missile crisis. The territory that they had occupied provided them with a favourable mountain position for a continuance of their invasion should the outcome of the missile crisis favour the Russians, and they called upon the Indians for a cease-fire, but one in which the Chinese would neither withdraw from the territory taken nor give any guarantee against a pursuance of the invasion. Prime Minister Nehru of India asked Krushchev, whom he had always regarded as a friend of the Indian people, to intercede for him, but Khrushchev refused and advised that the Chinese offer be accepted. On 26 October, Nehru turned for help to John Kennedy, and the latter, believing that an overt offer of assistance would be inadvisable, through diplomatic channels made it known to Nehru that assistance would be forthcoming should it be necessary. Although on 28 October the missile crisis was to be resolved in favour of the Americans, the Chinese remained in their positions until 21 November 1962 when, after being informed that American and British assistance would be given to India in view of the demonstrated weakness of the Indian Army, they retreated behind the line of Chinese/Indian border control settled in November 1959. Nehru then told his people that America and Britain were his true friends, and that the Chinese should never again be trusted. It can be seen, therefore, that Kennedy's resolution of the 'Cuba Crisis' had saved not only the Western world from Russian domination, but had saved Asia and most of the southern hemisphere from Chinese domination.

It would appear that Khrushchev's plan had been for Russia to confront a Europe unsupported by the United States, and that after neutralising India the Chinese would have turned West to take over the Arab states and their oil wells. Deprived of support from the United States, faced by Russia and stripped of oil, Europe could do little to resist Russian pressure or invasion and nothing to halt further Chinese aggression. It might be that Khrushchev's gamble had been that the Russians would take over not only Europe and the shores of the Mediterranean but North and South America. In addition to the conquest of the Arab states it might be that the Chinese would have proceeded further west to take over vast and fertile southern Africa for their expanding population, and south to a defenceless Australasia. The Russian and Chinese apparent concert is somewhat reminiscent of the lesser bargain struck between the Germans and the Italians before World War II when the former allocated the latter an African empire.

That the above speculation might be correct appears to be confirmed by the fact that, although the synchronisation of these events greatly disturbed the Kennedys – to the extent that they felt that in the long term the danger of the Chinese adventure might rival that of the 'Cuba Crisis' – no official explanation has been proffered for the contemporaneous actions in Cuba and India, nor indeed for the *ultimate* purpose behind the installation of the missiles in Cuba and the invasion of India. The intended vapourisation of the United States by missiles in Cuba is fact, and the Chinese objectives when invading India appear to be clear. It must be remembered that Mao Tse Tung, politician, diplomat and military leader, had been responsible in the mid-nineteen thirties for much of the conduct of the Long March of 5,000 miles from southeast to northwest China accomplished with a (comparatively) small army. It may be presumed that between this time and 1962, Mao Tse Tung, who had assumed control of all China, would have experienced no great difficulty in a similar march into the Arab States when he could be supported by an army which in 1962 must have been incomparably stronger than that of the Long March. That the Chinese would not have been content with Arab oil but would have proceeded into southern Africa would seem to be confirmed by the fact that for some years since 1962 they have consolidated a foothold in this area through the injection of many tens of thousands of Chinese into Tanzania. It may be, of course, that the Chinese, after destroying the military power of India, instead of advancing only west would have also turned southeast towards Australasia, although the single westward thrust might have appeared at that time to be more attractive; an isolated Australasia could later be absorbed.

It should not, perhaps, be forgotten that Khrushchev, referring to the North American people, once said, 'I will bury you'. Mao Tse Tung once told Premier Nehru of India, 'A third world war is inevitable. There will be two or three hundred million dead in the first few days, but they will soon be born again.' Kennedy once said, 'These Chinese are tough ... and seemed to be prepared to sacrifice 300 million people if necessary to dominate Asia'. An authoritative London newspaper has estimated that the present Chinese military manpower may be in the order of 250 million.

This book is concerned only with the assassination of President Kennedy in November 1963, and I have been more than reluctant to discuss international affairs or even to ascribe a motive for the assassination. All those with whom I have discussed the facts of the assassination, although agreeing with my conclusions, have asked me what the Russians had stood to gain, and it has been necessary, therefore, to endeavour to identify not only the decisions and the words of the Kennedy brothers, but to try to identify the ultimate purpose of the foiled Cuban and Indian adventures in order to indicate a possible motive for the subsequent assassination of the President. If, as the evidence indicates, the KGB organised the assassination, it would seem that it had appeared imperative to remove Kennedy from the area of international relations, for he had captured the ear of the world and had obtained the support of the United Nations over the 'Cuba Crisis'. It might well have been that he would have won world-wide and perhaps United Nations support in opposing the next great Russian-Chinese offensive – the invasion of South Vietnam by North Vietnam in 1964. The new President, Lyndon B. Johnson, was not to be so supported, even by Britain, with the result that the North Vietnamese invasion was to end in a defeat for the United States and the imminent removal of their military influence from the Far East, a lesser success when compared with the possible results of the 'colossal gamble', but partly securing the Russian-Chinese Pacific eastern flank when these countries later contemplate a western and/or southeastern adventure.

If the assassin escaped, investigations by the authorities in the United States would disclose an almost incredible story. It would appear that a Marine, Lee Harvey Oswald, who had been contracted to complete his three years Marine service in December 1959, in July 1959 had applied for an earlier discharge on the ground of family hardship. When nearly twenty years of age, in September 1959 he had been released from the Marines and that same month had apparently travelled to Russia and apparently immediately defected to that country. After marrying a young Russian woman, he had apparently returned to the United States with his wife and infant child in June 1962. Investigation would disclose that Oswald's height in September 1959 had twice been recorded by different Marine officials on two different ocassions as 71″ (5′ 11″) when he left the Marines and that he had travelled to and back from Russia on the same passport which gave his height as 5′ 11″. Furthermore, the Marine had himself recorded in March and again in September 1959 his height as 5′ 11″.

It was essential for the success of the KGB plot that the assassin should escape and that neither the Central Intelligence Agency (CIA) not the Federal Bureau of Investigation (FBI) should discover his or a confederate's contacts with three clandestine KGB officers during the seven weeks prior to the assassination;

one, if not two, of these officers is now believed to have been a member of Department 13, the KGB sabotage and assassination squad deployed abroad.

As it was to transpire, the assassin, who had always given his name as Lee Harvey Oswald, failed to escape and on his arrest in Dallas, Texas, on 22 November 1963 was found to be 5' 9" in height. During September, October and November 1963, through their secret informants installed inside and outside the Russian Embassy in Mexico City and inside the Russian Embassy in Washington D.C., the CIA and the FBI had discovered not only the KGB contacts but also the assassin's association with an 'American male' confederate, approximately 35 years old, approximately 6 feet in height, of athletic build, and with a receding hair-line, who in the name of 'Lee Oswald' had twice (28 September and 1 October) visited the Russian Embassy in Mexico City during the six days (27 September through 2 October 1963) when the assassin was secretly in that city having travelled from the United States on a false document and resided there in a false name. On the long-distance bus journey from the United States to Mexico City, the assassin had been accompanied by another confederate, a 75 years old British citizen also travelling in a false name and on false documents. The existence of the 75 years old confederate was not to be discovered until early 1964, but the 35 years old confederate was observed in the Russian Embassy and covertly photographed by the CIA in Mexico City on more than one occasion some seven weeks prior to the assassination, and it would appear that he must have been a stranger to the Russian Embassy for the CIA informant inside the Embassy and the cameraman or cameramen outside to have been attracted to his presence.

Prior to 22 November 1963, full use had not been made of the covertly obtained information and photographs, and the FBI had not noticed that they *already* had in their file on Oswald two recorded heights, 5' 11" and 5' 9"; the significance was to be realised by the FBI only immediately after the assassination.

Some two hours after the assassination, the Vice President, Lyndon B. Johnson, was sworn in as President and some six hours after the assassination, the assassin's and the American male's contacts with the KGB in Mexico City, the assassin's height of 5′ 9″ and the contents of an incriminating letter posted by the assassin to the Russian Embassy in Washington ten days before the assassination, were known to the United States authorities. About six hours after the assassination, Johnson instructed the FBI to take charge of the necessary investigations. About twenty-four hours after the assassination, it was discovered that the assassin had also been spying at Jaggars-Chiles-Stovall in Dallas during the 'Cuba Crisis' of October 1962.

Some might think that the new President was told by his investigators that the KGB had engineered the assassination and that, apparently recoiling from the horrendous consequences were he then to disclose to the stunned American public that their young President had been assassinated by the Russians, particularly so soon after the terror of the 'Cuba Crisis' – Johnson and his advisers had decided that immediate restraint was necessary.

If Johnson was apprised of all the facts contained in this book he would have been in a difficult position. First, in all conscience, he could not in future confer with Khrushchev and, secondly, were he to do so and were the truth of the assassination ever to emerge, he would be in the indefensible position of having maintained contact with the murderer of his predecessor in office.

Whether or not Johnson was given the totality of the evidence of Russian conspiracy as contained in this book is not known, but this evidence does not appear to have been disclosed to the Commission that a week after the assassination was to be appointed by him to investigate and to report publicly on the assassination and related matters. It would seem that during the 10-month investigation by the President's Commission, the evidence of Russian complicity could have been presented (by the FBI, the CIA or the United States Secret Service) to the Commission in capsulated form, thereby greatly reducing their work. It would also seem that as a result of the failure of the impostor to escape, the Russians realised that the Americans knew the truth and that Khrushchev was probably responsible.

In the event, the problem presented by a trial of the assassin was to be resolved on the morning of 24 November 1963 by Jack

Ruby who, in the basement of Dallas police station, shot dead the handcuffed assassin at point-blank range; this successful murder would have relieved the authorities in Russia and perhaps some in the United States. After the Report of the Commission was published on 24 September 1964, the embarrassment presented by the continued leadership of Khrushchev was also resolved, for in a fanfare of abuse he was deposed in October 1964, but only to live in apparently comfortable retirement. He was to be succeeded by Brezhnev and Kosygin, the latter shortly to visit President Johnson in the United States; Andrei Gromyko remained as Foreign Secretary.

It may well be that Khrushchev knew that even if his plot was discovered by the United States authorities, the latter might choose to conceal the truth; the plot, hidden or uncovered, would have succeeded and the political sabotage would become a "non-event" and the assassin, if not ex-Marine Oswald, a "non-person".

The next Chapter will discuss the formation and conclusions of the President's Commission and direct attention to some of the omissions in their subsequently published Report to the President.

2

On 29 November 1963, being five days after Jack Ruby murdered the assassin, President Johnson appointed his Commission to investigate and report upon the assassination of his predecessor in office. He directed the Commission to evaluate all the facts and circumstances surrounding the assassination and the subsequent killing of the alleged assassin, and to report its findings and conclusions to him. The Commission was given the power to subpoena witnesses and to examine them on oath.

The Chairman of the seven-member Commission was Chief Justice Earl Warren of the United States. At first he had declined the appointment but later accepted having been told by President Johnson that it was in the national interest for him to do so. The other six members were lawyers of distinction and experience; their background is set out in their Report on pages 475 and 476. Their names were: Richard B. Russell, John Sherman Cooper, Hale Boggs, Gerald R. Ford, Allen W. Dulles (for 8 years Director of CIA), and John J. McCloy.

J. Lee Rankin was General Counsel to the Commission and he was aided by 14 assistant counsel and 12 staff members, the latter being lawyers, historians and Internal Revenue officials. In addition, 37 lawyers, clerks and secretaries were engaged.

Their work completed, on 24 September 1964 the Commission submitted an 888 page Report and Appendices to President Johnson; it purports to summarise the contents of 15 Volumes of Testimony given to the Commission by 552 people, and of 11 Volumes of Exhibits received from the FBI, the Secret Service and other agencies; these 26 Volumes of Testimony and Exhibits amounting to some 17,000 pages. The Foreword to the Report, after setting out in detail the formation of the Commission, explains the titanic task undertaken by them, in which they were aided by some 200 FBI, Secret Service and other agents, these agents conducting some 26,500 interviews and re-interviews, and submitting some 30,000 pages of reports to the Commission. Much of the material gathered by the Commission and their assistants has been placed in the National Archives of the United States, and will not be available for public inspection until the year 2039. (In reply to a reporter for *The New York Times*, on 4 February 1964, the day after the taking of testimony commenced, the Chief Justice was alleged to have said that a full report would be made public, 'But it might not be in your lifetime. I am not referring to anything especially but there may be some things that would involve security'.)

The conclusions of the Commission as set out in their Report are, in brief, that the assassin was Lee Harvey Oswald who, after serving for three years in the United States Marines was released from Service in September 1959, defected to Russia in October 1959 and in June 1962 returned disillusioned to the United States, accompanied by his Russian wife, Marina, and their infant daughter; that there was no evidence that either Oswald or Ruby were part of any conspiracy, domestic or foreign; that no direct or indirect relationship between Oswald and Ruby had been discovered, nor that there was any credible evidence that either knew the other; that there was no evidence that Ruby acted with any person in the killing of Oswald; and that, on the basis of the evidence before the Commission, Oswald acted alone.

The Commission could not make any definitive determination of Oswald's motives, but their Report indicates that his resentment of authority, his failure in life, an urge to find a place in history, despair over his failures, his capacity for violence, his avowed commitment to Marxism and Communism and his other varied disappointments contributed to his capacity 'to risk all in cruel and irresponsible actions'.

The Report does not define Ruby's motive in killing the assassin and says only that he, too, acted alone.

The Report says that, because of the difficulty in proving negatives to a certainty, the possibility of others being involved with either Oswald or Ruby could not be established categorically, but if there was any such evidence it had been beyond the reach of all the investigative agencies and resources of the United States and had not come to the attention of the Commission.

In the Report, however, there are omissions vital to the story of the assassination, and I will record these omissions in the Report, and I will indicate that there was powerful evidence of a Russian conspiracy and that this evidence was not only within the reach of but was in the possession of at least one of the investigative agencies, and should have come to the attention of the Commission.

Thirteen of the omissions in the Report may be mentioned briefly in this Chapter:

(1) Height. The Report does not mention that at the time of his release from the Marines in September 1959 Lee Harvey Oswald was 5' 11" in height, whereas on 22 November 1963 the assassin was 5' 9" in height. The Volumes of Exhibits contain six separate documented heights of 5' 11" for Oswald, and contained twelve separate documented heights of 5' 9" for the man calling himself Lee Harvey Oswald who came to the United States from Russia in June 1962. Despite this plethora of evidence that the man who killed the President might not be ex-Marine Lee Harvey Oswald, the Report contents itself by saying that the assassin was Lee Harvey Oswald and that he was 5' 9" in height. By making no reference to the heights the Report consequently does not have to explain this discrepancy between Marine and assassin. Furthermore, nowhere in the 15 Volumes of Testimony are either of these two heights mentioned, none of the witnesses having been asked about the height of the assassin or that of Lee Harvey Oswald.

(2) Fingerprints. When Lee Harvey Oswald enlisted in the Marines in October 1956 his fingerprints were taken and on 22 November 1963 the fingerprints of the arrested assassin were taken by the police. The Commission did not require the chain of evidence to be established to show that the Marine prints, alleged to be those of Oswald and shown on a fingerprint card contained in the Volumes of Exhibits, were those of Oswald, nor did they require the 1956 and the 1963 sets of prints to be compared and identified before them. The Report does not mention the existence of the Marine prints. Later in this book, the fingerprints

of the Marine and the assassin will be discussed at length.

(3) Mastoidectomy. When he was six years old, Lee Harvey Oswald had undergone a mastoidectomy operation which had resulted in a one inch scar behind his left ear, removal of the mastoid bone and a depresssion in the flesh behind the ear. The operation and scar were recorded in the Marine medical records of Oswald, these records being contained in the Volumes of Exhibits. An autopsy performed on the body of the assassin by two doctors on 24 November 1963 did not disclose a mastoidectomy operation, although the post mortem report of the autopsy appearing in the Exhibits records in detail the external and internal examination of the head and neck. The Commission did not call the doctors to testify before them nor did they order an exhumation of the body of the assassin – which had been buried on the day after the autopsy, so that they could ascertain whether or not the post mortem report on the condition of the head and neck was accurate. The Report is silent upon this matter.

(4) Scars. The positions of certain scars on the upper part of the Left arm of the assassin were recorded in the post mortem report, but the number and positions of the scars did not correspond with the number and positions of the scars on the arm of Oswald as recorded in his earlier Marine medical records. Neither the Marine doctors nor the two doctors mentioned above were called to testify about the number and relative positions of the scars. The Report does not mention this matter. There were other physical differences between Lee Harvey Oswald and the assassin that were observed by his relatives which, although not arousing their suspicions at the time nor since, were to be mentioned in their testimony to the Commission after the assassination.

(The evidence supplied by the apparent physical differences powerfully suggests that an impostor who facially resembled Oswald was substituted and, fully briefed in Oswald's background and mannerisms, assumed the identity of Oswald at some time after the latter's release from the Marines on 11 September 1959, the substitution being effected for the purpose of infiltrating an assassin into the United States on 13 June 1962 in the name and identity of Lee Harvey Oswald. In this book the alleged assassin will be referred to as 'Oswald', 'Lee', or 'assassin' as the continuity of the story dictates. All words and actions will be attributed to 'Oswald' for, although the evidence indicates substitution at some time, the date of substitution and the name of the substitute is unknown although his first name may have been 'Alek').

(5) The Assassin and Jaggars-Chiles-Stovall. At the time of the 'Cuba Crisis', the assassin without warning had left his previous employment in Forth Worth, Texas, travelled to Dallas and at once applied for work to the Texas Employment Exchange in Dallas. On 12 October 1962 he obtained employment in Jaggars-Chiles-Stovall, the small firm in Dallas that together with commercial work handled 'highly secret' photographic work for the Armed Forces of the United States. The name of the firm and its commercial aspect, but not its sensitivity, is mentioned in the Report, which therefore does not mention that, after training, on the morning of his first working day, 16 October 1962, the assassin executed work on behalf of the Army Map Service. The Report does not mention that after the assassination there had been found amongst the possessions of the assassin the impedimenta of a spy – a Minox and other cameras, telescope, binoculars, compass, pedometer, films and other apposite material, including a $4\frac{1}{2}''$ blade hunting knife in sheath. The person in the Employment Exchange who had put forward the name of the spy to the firm was not called to testify before the Commission, is not named in the Report and, according to the Volumes of Exhibits, was not interviewed by the FBI or any other agency.

(6) The Assassin and the Texas School Book Depository. It was from a window in the Depository that the assassin fired, and it would seem that his employment in the Depository could not have been accidental, but the persons whose testimony might have illuminated the matter were not called to testify and, according to the Volumes of Exhibits, were not interviewed by the FBI or any other agency. The Report indicates that this employment was happenstance.

(7) The Assassin and the KGB. The assassin had been in contact with two senior Russian officials, one in Mexico city, Mexico and the other in Washington, D.C., during the seven

weeks prior to the assassination. One of these, Valeri Dmitrevich KOSTIN, was a clandestine KGB officer, possibly a member of Department 13 and probably coming to the Russian Embassy in Mexico City from the Russian Embassy in Havana, Cuba, during the assassin's secret visit to Mexico City from 27 September through 2 October 1963. The other Russian official was Consul REZNICHENKO, stationed at the Russian Embassy in Washington, and possibly a clandestine KGB officer. Another senior KGB intelligence officer, Yuri Ivanovich NOSENKO, allegedly defected through Switzerland to the United States in February 1964, bringing with him the alleged Soviet file on Lee Harvey Oswald and saying that, as deputy director of the department of the KGB responsible for operations against American tourists in Russia, he had been in charge of Oswald on the latter's alleged arrival in Russia in October 1959. He later said that he had testified in secret to the Commission. Cf. *KGB* by John Barron. (1974). If this is so, the testimony is not mentioned in the Report and his name does not appear in the list of 552 persons who testified.

(8) The Assassin and his Confederate, the approximately 35 years old American male. This confederate used the name 'Lee Oswald' when visiting the Russian Embassy in Mexico City on 28 September and 1 October 1963, contemporaneously with the presence of the assassin in a false name in that city. On 28 September, the confederate visited the Embassy in order to contact Valeri Vladimirovich KOSTIKOV, a clandestine KGB officer stationed in that Embassy and now believed to have been a member of Department 13, cf. ibid, *KGB*. On 1 October, the confederate again visited the Embassy to enquire if there had been a reply to a telegram sent by that Embassy 'to Washington' – more probably than not to Consul Reznichenko. His two visits to the Embassy had been monitored by a CIA informant inside the building, and his physical description and the purport of the visits was conveyed to CIA headquarters in Washington. On 10 and 18 October, the CIA informed the Bureau of the FBI in Washington of the visits and the physical description of the man. The man was believed by the informant to have been in contact – the evidence is obscure but presumably on 28 September –with Paul Antonvich YATSKOV, another clandestine KGB officer

stationed in the Embassy. Kostikov and Yatskov occupied cover positions as consular officials in the Embassy building that was situated in a secure and guarded compound in which lived all the Russian officials employed at the Embassy and Consulate, and their families. Probably during the assassin's presence in Mexico City and certainly immediately after, CIA surveillance cameras photographed the American male, and the photographs disclose that the CIA informant's description of the man who visited the Embassy was accurate.

The Report of the Commission says that it was the 5' 9" ex-Marine Lee Harvey Oswald who spoke to either Yatskov or Kostikov at the Russian Embassy in Mexico City, and it makes no reference to the American male, referring to him only as an 'unidentified' man at one time thought by the CIA and/or the FBI to have been associated with the assassin, Lee Harvey Oswald.

(9) The Assassin and his other Associates. Apart from his apparent contact with the American male and their contacts with three KGB officers at the Russian Embassy in Mexico City, the youthful and lowly paid assassin's only known male associates for any length of time while he was some 18 months in the United States were: (a) a 52 years old United States citizen, (Baron) George De Mohrenschildt, who had been born in Russia and who, with his Russian-born wife of United States citizenship, had lived in the United States for many years, he at one time having attracted the attention of the FBI and the Immigration and Naturalisation Service. According to his testimony and that of the assassin's Wife, he had become one of the assassin's few friends after the assassin had arrived in Fort Worth, Texas, from Russia in 1962, and they were to remain friends for a period of some ten months before the Baron left the United States to live in Haiti in May or June 1963. He was world-travelled, spoke several languages and was of academic distinction; during his testimony he stated that while living in the United States he had been associated with the French Intelligence Services. After arriving in the United States from Russia in the 1940s, he had become a close friend of the mother of Jacqueline, the wife of the President, and had known her since childhood. After her marriage to Kennedy she had accepted the Presidency of a small charity that he had

helped to found. (b) The 75 years old British confederate, Albert Osborne, who for many years appears to have been a Russian agent and on whom the FBI had an 'Internal Security' file in a false name. He had travelled throughout the United States, Canada and Mexico under both his real and false names, posing as an itinerant Baptist minister, itinerant gardener and a collector of rare books. He gathered old clothes and small sums of money from persons in the United States, the money allegedly for the purpose of buying Bibles for distribution to the natives in Mexico. His permanent residence was a mud and wattle hut in Mexico, and he gave this address, two false addresses in Montreal and an address in England ('The Old Folks Home', Grimsby), to various persons during his some 48 years of travel in the United States, Canada and Mexico. In his alias and using false documents he accompanied the assassin – who was also using a false name and in possession of false documents – on the secret visit paid by the assassin to Mexico City commencing on 27 September 1963. Under their aliases, he and the assassin had occupied a seat for two persons on the long-distance bus journey from the United States to Mexico City. He had been acquainted with the assassin for at least four months prior to the visit to Mexico City, and possibly thereafter. It is not known where he went nor what he did after arriving in Mexico City on 27 September. (c) A 38 years old United States citizen of Italian parentage, John Caesar Grossi – sometimes inmate of El Reno and other penitentiaries – who was an accomplished artist and caricaturist, and on whom the FBI had a 'Criminal' file. He had obtained employment at Jaggars-Chiles-Stovall under an alias shortly before the spy/assassin was dismissed from that firm in April 1963, Grossi ceasing his employment at the firm in August 1963. He had worked in the camera department with the assassin and they had been acquainted for at least four months prior to April 1963 and possibly thereafter.

The Baron returned from Haiti with his wife, both to testify at length to the Commission, but neither Osborne nor Grossi testified. After the assassination, different FBI agents interviewed Albert Osborne in both his real name and his alias at different places in Mexico and the United States, and it was only on the evidence of two old newspaper photographs that the FBI were able to establish that they had been interviewing the same man, Albert Osborne, who at last admitted his double identity but denied untruthfully that he had been sitting beside the assassin on the bus. The Report refers to Albert Osborne as an itinerant Baptist missionary of doubtful veracity but does not mention his double-identity, false documents, the FBI 'Internal Security' file, his apparent espionage activities, lies and other questionable behaviour. The Report does not mention John Caesar Grossi and although the FBI knew of his existence, his work at Jaggars-Chiles-Stovall and his friendship with the assassin, according to the Exhibits he was never interviewed after the assassination by the FBI or any other agency in either his real name or his alias. The alias of the 75 years old Albert Osborne was 'John Howard Bowen' and that of the 38 years old John Caesar Grossi was 'Jack Leslie Bowen'.

(10) The Assassin and Jack Ruby. The movements of the assassin immediately after the assassination and the activities of Ruby from 1 November 1963 until he murdered the assassin on 24 November 1963 indicate that prior to the assassination their existence was known to one another. There is some circumstantial evidence that Ruby was involved for months if not for years in the plot to assassinate. Although the Report states that 52 years old Ruby was a night club operator with extensive contacts in the Dallas police, it does not state that the evidence indicates that as a young man he was associated with Al Capone, that in later years his family was associated with the remnants of the Capone gang and that he was a powerful figure in the Dallas underworld, being connected with narcotics and other illegal or undesirable activities. On 25 November 1963, the FBI in Chicago were to interview John Capone, the brother of Al Capone. The Report mentions evidence that suggests a conspiracy between the assassin and Ruby, but dismisses it as insufficient proof. The Report, however, fails to mention all the evidence pointing to this conspiracy and therefore does not, as it could have done, present this evidence in collated form when it would show beyond reasonable doubt that the two men were associated.

(11) The Assassin as Compromiser. The assassin had left behind considerable evidence that his name was Lee Harvey Oswald and that he was an ex-Marine. He also left behind

evidence provided by his actions and those of others that were to implicate in the assassination (a) Fidel Castro, (b) the CIA, (c) the FBI, (d) Organised Crime (OC), (e) the American Civil Liberties Union (ACLU), (f) a young American married couple, Michael and Ruth Paine, who lived near Dallas and who were members of ACLU, and (g) an ex-Marine, Heindel, who had served with Oswald in the Marines. In disregarding these matters, the Report obscures the fact that, if the assassin escaped, the Russians would know that the American authorities would realise that the skill employed in the assassination and in the disappearance of the impecunious assassin indicated beyond reasonable doubt that he had received the assistance and had acted upon the instructions of others: thus the necessity for the Russians to confound any investigation by supplying evidence of complicity against a diversity of possible suspects. If he had escaped, and if the CIA and the FBI had not discovered his contacts with the KGB officers and others, there would have been no evidence implicating the Russians.

(12) The Assassin as Liar. From the time that the assassin arrived in the United States in June 1962 until he was murdered in Dallas police station, he lied at all times and to all persons, and his lies were, it would appear, for the purpose of deceiving the FBI and others in order to facilitate the exercise of his assignments while in the United States for 18 months. Although referring to the many lies of 'Lee Harvey Oswald', the Report does not assemble, analyse nor indicate how these lies appear to have assisted the assassin.

(13) The Assassin as Impostor. On 3 June 1960, J. Edgar Hoover, the Director of the FBI, sent to the Department of State a memorandum warning against the possibility of an impostor assuming the identity of Lee Harvey Oswald. The report does not mention the memorandum.

All the above is documented fact and it would appear that, whether the assassin was Lee Harvey Oswald or a substitute, his activities while in the United States from 13 June 1962 until 22

November 1963 were unusual and do not correspond with the portrait sketched by the Report of a frustrated young labourer. This is the place, perhaps, to state my view that the Commissioners were unaware of most, if not all, of the above omissions in their Report. It would seem that specific items of information were unknown to them and that deprived of these they could have come to no other than their conclusions. Were it otherwise, it is impossible to conceive of the Commissioners agreeing to avoid asking – amongst the hundreds of questions that were asked by individual Commissioners – any question that might produce an answer that pointed either to domestic or foreign conspiracy.

The Commissioners themselves heard the testimony of only 94 of the 552 witnesses and, with their daily work elsewhere demanding their attention, they would often be available to hear only a part of this testimony. The remaining witnesses testified before Commission Counsel, no Commissioner being present. When, on 3 February 1964, the Commission commenced hearing testimony, they could not have been briefed on the facts and history of the spy/assassin's 18 months residence in the United States, with the result that on occasion a Commissioner would enquire of their Counsel during testimony whether the event about which the witness was being examined had occurred in 1962 or 1963. The Commission had to rely upon their lawyers and the latter had to rely upon the FBI, the overall investigative agency, not only for information but presumably for direction as to whose testimony it would be desirable for the Commissioners to hear. For example, when two officials of Jaggars-Chiles-Stovall and an employee of that firm who had trained Oswald were to testify in April 1964, and were to disclose the 'sensitive' nature of the firm, no Commissioner was present and apparently it did not occur to Counsel when questioning these men and hearing from them that the assassin had no access to secret work, to seek corroboration of their testimony by asking for the production of his work sheets. A Commissioner might well have asked to see the work sheets because two months previously during the testimony of the assassin's wife, Marina, six of the seven Commissioners had heard another of their Counsel refer to the word 'microdots' written in the assassin's notebook, the word being written immediately under the name Jaggars-Chiles-Stovall, although Counsel did not mention this fact. All the Commissioners present must have known of the espionage significance of microdots, and had they heard the testimony of the men from Jaggars-Chiles-Stovall and realised, which apparently they did not, that the firm was 'sensitive' and that spying equipment had been found after the assassination at the assassin's residence, they would have demanded to see his work sheets. (A microdot is a pin-head sized photograph of a plan, document etc., that can be fixed under a postage stamp, hidden in antique books or other material, and despatched.)

When President Johnson appointed the FBI as the overall investigative agency upon whom the Commissioners and their lawyers had to rely, it would seem to have been an unfortunate choice for, as will later be demonstrated, the FBI were responsible for pre-assassination bureaucratic errors that permitted the spy/assassin not only to keep a step ahead of them while he was in the United States, but to kill President Kennedy. For the FBI it must be said, however, that the insignificant labourer and spy/assassin was later accurately to be described as looking like a 'high-school kid' and, accompanied by his younger and pretty wife, might not have appeared even to the eye of an experienced FBI agent as a man who could have been entrusted by the Russians with any assignment. He was, in fact, clever and cunning, and, as a superb actor and deceiver appears to have been trained in 'double-think', the technique of mind training termed and its process analysed by George Orwell in his book, *1984*.

Reference to the Report and its 26 supporting Volumes of Testimony and Exhibits will be as follows: The Report and page as (R.000) and its supporting Volumes by the number of the Volume and page as (XX.000). Where Testimony is mentioned, it will be Testimony before the Commission or their lawyers. Where italics appear (apart from the names of publications) they are used to emphasise a point.

As I do. not know who, if any, of the persons involved in the post-assassination investigation comprehended the story outlined in this book, I am driven to use such words as 'the Commission knew' because, although I believe that they were unaware of the truth, they signed their Report.

If the assassination was the result of a conspiracy, it would seem that the conspiracy would have been known only to a restricted number of people, but the several United States citizens who are named in this book may have been manipulated by the assassin to assist him in carrying through his assignments while he was at large in the United States from 13 June 1962 through 22 November 1963. It must not be thought that any one of them apart from Ruby had knowledge of or was in any way involved in the conspiracy to spy or to assassinate.

The next chapter will discuss the assassination and its immediate aftermath.

3

'If anybody really wanted to shoot the President of the United States it is not a very difficult job – all one has to do is to get on a high building some day with a telescopic rifle, and there is nothing anyone can do to defend against such an attempt'. President Kennedy.

Dallas, Texas – 22 November 1963 – 12.30 p.m.

Proceeding through the city in the motorcade, the President was mortally wounded by two bullets fired from behind – the bullets striking him in the back and the back of the head. Governor Connally of Texas, seated immediately in front of the President, was also gravely wounded from behind by a bullet. Three single bullets had been fired in about seven seconds by a young man who, five weeks earlier in the name of Lee Harvey Oswald, had obtained employment as an order-filler at the Texas School Book Depository, and it was from a window on the sixth floor of this building, overlooking the motorcade, that he fired. Just inside the window stacks of cardboard cartons of books created a 'sniper's nest'. Inside the 'nest' the assassin had placed a carton on the floor, on which he could sit and be scarcely visible from inside and outside the building. He had placed three cartons by the window so that his rifle, resting on the top carton, would be aimed directly at the motorcade. Attached to the rifle was a home-made sling which would be used to wrap round the Left arm to ensure rigidity in the assassin's grip on the forepart of the rifle. Using the sling and resting the rifle on the carton ensured the assassin of a stable position for accurate fire. The weapon was an old Italian military rifle fitted with a telescopic sight and purchased by the assassin in March 1962 from a dealer in Chicago. It has 'an inherent capability of great accuracy under rapid fire conditions' and, having less recoil than the average military rifle (FBI report), was the perfect weapon. The telescopic sight was 4-power and as such was ideal for the distance at which the assassin would have to fire at his slowly moving target, a range of 55 to 88 yards. When the rifle was received by the FBI from the Dallas police and tested by them, it was found to fire slightly high and slightly to the right of a bullseye. This 'defect' was one which would have assisted the assassin when aiming at targets that were moving away and slightly to the right: he would not have to make allowances for the apparent upward movement of the car due to the high elevation of the 'sniper's nest' and for the movement of the car slightly to the right due to a curve in the road; he could aim directly at his targets and be more certain of hitting them.

The choice of the Depository as the assassin's base was an excellent one and finely calculated, not only because the victims appeared 'almost stationary' (FBI report) – minimal movement being corrected by the telescopic sight, but because the Presidential car had passed and was going away from the Depository; almost all eyes were on the President and his wife, and therefore away from the elevated rifleman. So as not to attract attention before firing, the assassin in the window had remained out of sight or motionless, with the result that none of the 14 Secret Service agents accompanying the cars of the President and the Vice President for the purposes of observing the crowds and scanning the buildings saw him.

At the sound of gunfire, the police escorting the motorcade had rushed to the right and to the front of the Presidental car, the direction from which the shots appeared to have come – an instant reaction to the general commotion and panic in the immediate vicinity of the car, aided by the misleading effect of echoes.

After firing, the assassin hid the rifle among some cartons of books and went downstairs to a luncheon room on the second floor.

The immediate attention of one police officer had been drawn to the building because he had seen pigeons fly from the roof at the sound of the shots. He ran to the main entrance where he was joined by a Depository official, and they ran upstairs to search the roof. On reaching the second floor, the officer noticed a man (the assassin, in fact) through a glass panel in the door of the lunch room and, with drawn revolver, he accosted the youthful-looking man who was attired in torn and shabby working clothes. The officer asked the official who the man was, and the official vouched for him as an employee; both to the officer and to the official the man appeared calm and undisturbed. The officer and the official then continued upstairs to search the roof while the assassin, holding a bottle of Coca-Cola, walked down the last flight of stairs and out of the main entrance of the building at approximately 12.33 p.m. It was several minutes before it was to be realised that the shots had been fired from behind, and the Depository was then sealed off at 12.37 p.m.

After leaving the building, the assassin proceeded with his escape by walking northeast for seven blocks where, at 12.40 p.m., he boarded a 'Marsalis' bus, one of a regular local service that ran from the northeast of Dallas to the south through the centre of the city. He purchased a 23c. ticket which would take him to a stop about 350 yards west of Ruby's apartment at 223 South Ewing in suburban Oak Cliff, some $2\frac{1}{4}$ miles from the Depository.

Seated on the bus was one of his former landladies, a Mrs. Bledsoe, who was an old lady and one of the few people in Dallas who knew him by sight *and* by the name of L.H. Oswald, for in that name he had rented for a week a room in a house in Oak Cliff, 621 Marsalis, some six weeks prior to the assassination. After watching the motorcade Mrs. Bledsoe was returning from downtown to 621 Marsalis, which was situated on the southbound Marsalis bus route and about one mile short of the 23c. stop. She recognised him and, as there were only a few people on the bus and he passed in front of her to sit down, it would seem that he must have recognised her. She also noted his attire and later was able to describe it.

When the assassin boarded the bus, it had been approaching the Depository – thereby eliminating the likelihood of a policeman seeking to find a fleeing assassin questioning the occupants of a bus that was proceeding *towards* the scene of the crime. In any event, the assassin had in his wallet a counterfeit identity card in another name. This attempt both to deceive any policeman and to hide the direction of his flight would never have been realised had it not been for the presence of Mrs. Bledsoe on the almost empty bus. If he had escaped from Dallas, in the absence of Mrs. Bledsoe, the direction and means of his flight could never have been discovered.

If by chance one of the twenty or so employees at the Depository had seen and recognised the assassin at the window and had immediately informed the police who would speedily broadcast the name of the wanted man, Lee Harvey Oswald, he could have been 'trapped' on the bus by Mrs. Bledsoe. The bus was now moving very slowly and was to reach the 23c. stop about half an hour late, so that even if Mrs. Bledsoe was to leave the bus before the name of the wanted man was broadcast she would have been able to telephone the police to tell them that he had continued on the Marsalis bus past her house and to describe his attire, thereby perhaps enabling the police to arrest him while still on the bus and, in any event, indicating the direction of the escape and limiting the area to be searched.

Apparently dismayed by her presence and after accepting a transfer ticket the assassin left the bus only four minutes after boarding it; the time was now 12.44 p.m. He then took a taxi southwest to a roominghouse, 1026 North Beckley, also in Oak Cliff and where he had registered in the name of O.H. Lee some five weeks previously. It was served by a different bus route, 'Beckley', which had a stop outside 1026, and a Beckley bus had been immediately behind the Marsalis bus when he had mounted the latter. He arrived at 1026 at 1.00 p.m. and, hurrying inside, collected a .38 snub-nosed Smith and Wesson revolver which he had purchased in March 1962 from a dealer in Los Angeles, and altered his appearance by changing his trousers and putting on a zip-up jacket. After about two minutes he rushed out of the house and walked rapidly southeast in the direction of the 23c. bus stop and Ruby's apartment. The change of clothing had been necessary because he feared that either Mrs. Bledsoe or the police officer in the Depository might have noticed his attire during their brief encounters and could describe it were his name to be quickly broadcast. The need to take a taxi – the only taxi he ever took while in the United States – and his haste at 1026 suggest that he was hurrying to a rendezvous.

Most of the 1,200 Dallas police were surrounding the Depository or searching downtown for the assassin, but at 1.16 p.m., when he had rapidly walked nearly a mile from 1026 North Beckley he was stopped and casually questioned by patrolman Tippit – the only police officer patrolling the large Oak Cliff suburb. The officer must have heard on his police radio a rough description of a wanted man which had been supplied by a man at ground level who had briefly noted a person firing from the window in the Depository, but this description (slender white male, 30, 5′ 10″, 165 lbs.) would have fitted some thousands in Dallas. The officer was apparently unaware that he was speaking to the assassin, for some three minutes earlier he must have heard a remark on his radio that the killer was believed to be 'holed-up' in the Depository. A short conversation ensued between the seated officer and the assassin who was resting his arm on the door of the car. Something appears to have aroused the suspicion of the officer for he got out of his car and was drawing his revolver when he was shot dead by the assassin who fired four rapid and professional shots – stomach, heart and head.

The assassin was now about 350 yards *east* of the point where the 23c. ticket would have dropped him about 350 yards *west* of Ruby's apartment, and therefore at the time of this killing the assassin was about 700 yards from that apartment. The distance from the site of Tippit's murder to Ruby's apartment – roughly a straight line of less than half a mile – was but an infinitesimal fraction of the city area of Dallas which comprised nearly 300 square miles.

Although when leaving the Depository the assassin could have selected any point of the compass and method of transport for his escape, instead of the Beckley bus he had chosen the Marsalis bus that proceeded towards Ruby's apartment and he had paid a fare of 23c. that would carry him to the bus stop some 350 yards west of the apartment. The evidence supplied by the two attempts of the assassin – by bus and later on foot – to approach the vicinity of Ruby's apartment, although in isolation no more than circumstantial, when combined with Ruby's known character, his apparent association with and later murder of the assassin, suggests that the assassin had twice been attempting to reach the apartment or its immediate vicinity.

It would have been dangerous for the assassin – unarmed and wearing the same clothes – to have ordered the taxi driver to drop him at a point nearer to the 23c. bus stop, for the driver might later and rapidly have been able to identify the clothes of his passenger and the area of his escape. The fact that the assassin did not do so but instead went to 1026 to collect his revolver and to change his clothes indicates that it was Mrs. Bledsoe's ability *to identify his area for escape* that had caused him to leave the bus.

After killing the officer, the assassin ran away in the opposite direction to which he had been walking and, as his clothing might have been noted by some people who had observed this killing, he again altered his appearance so far as possible by taking off his zip-up jacket which he hid in a used car lot. He was last observed at about 1.20 p.m., four minutes after killing Tippit.

At about 1.42 p.m. the manager of a shoe shop in Oak Cliff (the shop being about ¾ of a mile west of Ruby's apartment) noticed a man with his back to the street standing near the shop door and apparently attempting to hide his face from a passing police car searching for the killer of the patrolman. The man moved off after the car had gone but the manager, who was the only person in the shop and who had heard on his radio of the killing of the officer, followed him and saw him enter a nearby cinema. The manager spoke to the cashier who had been attracted on to the pavement by the siren of the approaching police car, and she told him that she had noticed a man enter the foyer of the cinema but that she had not appreciated that he must have gone into the cinema without paying. She asked the manager to see if he could find the man in the cinema and to check that the exit doors were closed. The manager did as he was asked but was unable to locate the man he had seen, while the cashier telephoned the police. Some fifteen policemen arrived at the cinema and, after a violent struggle in which the assassin sustained some head injuries, he was arrested at about 1.50 p.m.

The area around the site of Tippit's murder had been rapidly flooded with police cars drawn from downtown Dallas and outer areas to search for the killer. It would have been dangerous for him then to have run towards the apartment of the man upon whom it appears he relied for escape and, although armed and capable of hijacking a car to take him away from Dallas, he had chosen not to flee the city but to hide nearby in a cinema, perhaps to make a third attempt and possibly after dark to approach Ruby's apartment or its vicinity.

Although several people had seen the assassin running away after shooting Tippit, his whereabouts from about 1.20 p.m. until just before he entered the cinema at approximately 1.42 p.m. are unknown and Ruby's whereabouts after about 1.00 p.m. have not been satisfactorily determined. At approximately 1.45 p.m., however, he entered his downtown nightclub. When Ruby testified before the Commission on 7 June and 18 July 1964, he was not asked to account for his movements after 1.00 p.m.

The odds against Mrs. Bledsoe choosing to go downtown to view the motorcade and then to return on the bus that was later to be boarded by the assassin must have been very considerable. The odds against the only officer patrolling a large suburb being in the same street at the same time as the assassin and deciding to speak to him must have been equally considerable. The odds against anyone noticing the assassin in the shop doorway, then being sufficiently alert to follow him, and thereafter for the cashier to decide to call the police must have been fairly considerable. It would seem that but for a series of misadventures – the odds against which must have been substantial – the assassin would have been able to escape from Dallas and ultimately from the United States.

On arrival at Dallas police headquarters at 2.00 p.m., and after having loudly protested to onlookers about 'police brutality' while giving a clenched-fist sign, the assassin was interrogated several times and always vehemently denied the killing of either the officer or the President. He denied that he possessed a rifle but admitted owning the revolver that had been found in his possession on arrest. That evening he was charged with the murder of the officer and early next morning he was charged with the murder of the President. It should be remarked that, during a total of twelve hours interrogation on 22/23/24 November by Captain Fritz, Chief of Homicide in the Dallas police, according to the Report (R.180) no notes, stenographic or tape recordings were made. The representatives of four and sometimes five other investigative agencies were frequently present and they, too, took no notes.

At 2.30 a.m. on Sunday 24 November, the officer of the FBI in Dallas received an anonymous call. The voice of the caller, who apparently was not alone, was 'calm and mature in sound'. The voice said, 'I represent a committee that is neither right nor left wing, and tonight, tomorrow morning or tomorrow night we are going to kill the man that killed the President. There will be no excitement and we will kill him. We wanted to be sure and tell the FBI, the police department and the Sheriff's office, and we will be there and we will kill him ... and there was nothing anyone could do about it'. The caller ' ... did not want any officer hurt, that was the reason for the call'. He then hung up, and the call was reported to the Sheriff's office which had received a similar call, when the voice had added that 'a committee of around 100 people had voted to kill the man ... ' (XXIV.356.429.434). The Dallas police were informed and, taking the threats seriously, arranged for the first time ever for the attendance at the police station of two armoured trucks commissioned from an independent firm, the trucks arriving at the station at about 11.07 a.m.

At 9.25 a.m. on Sunday morning, 24 November, in the Homicide office on the third floor of Dallas police station the last interrogation of the assassin had commenced. Present were Captain Fritz, two senior Secret Service agents, three Dallas police detectives and a senior Postal Inspector, the Inspector being present because the assassin had rented Post Office Boxes during his period in the United States. In due course, the Inspector was to furnish to the FBI a memorandum reflecting his recollections of this last interrogation of the assassin, the memorandum stating *inter alia*, 'Oswald at no time appeared confused or in doubt as to whether or not he should answer a question. On the contrary, he was quite alert and showed no hesitancy in answering those questions which he wanted to answer, and was quite skilful in parrying those questions which he did not wish to answer. I got the impression that he had disciplined his mind and reflexes to a state where I personally doubted if he would ever have confessed'. The memorandum stated that Oswald still denied owning a rifle and killing Tippit or the President, and when questioned about his use of an alias A.J. Hidell and his possession on arrest of counterfeit Marine cards in the name of Hidell, he said that he had never used that name, knew nobody of that name and had not heard of that name before. When asked specifically by Captain Fritz about a counterfeit Marine identification card found in his wallet, Oswald flared up and stated, (XXIV.488-492) 'I've told you all I'm going to tell you about that card. You took notes, just read them for yourself if you want to refresh your memory. You have the card. Now you know as much about it as I do'. (In a memorandum for the Commission, Fritz said that he did make 'rough notes'.)

The interrogation of the assassin ended at 11.15 a.m., and arrangements were made and completed to transfer him from the police jail to the County jail. For this purpose he was to be taken from the third floor down to the basement of the police department and escorted towards a waiting car, it having been decided that the armoured trucks would be deployed as decoys. For security purposes there were over 70 police officers in the basement, and the assassin would be handcuffed to a detective and escorted by other officers during his walk of some twelve yards to the waiting car, with Captain Fritz proceeding the group by some five yards. There were numerous newsmen and television camera crews present who were, or were supposed to have been, screened before being allowed into the basement.

At about 11.15 a.m. Ruby entered a nearby Western Union office and at 11.17 a.m. despatched a money telegram for $25 to one of his employees. He then walked to the police station and arrived in the basement at almost exactly 11.19 a.m.

At 11.20 a.m. the assassin arrived from the third floor by elevator in an area separated from the basement by swing doors. The escorting police waited for a moment to see that all was clear ahead of them and they then passed into the basement to approach the transit car. When the assassin had taken only a few steps and in full view of television cameras, at 11.21 a.m. Ruby — who had been frequenting the police station from the time of the assassin's arrest, mingling with local, national and foreign reporters, photographers and television crews, and pretending to be an Israeli press reporter and carrying a pencil and notebook — lunged through the line of policemen and, thrusting a .38 snub-nosed Cobra revolver close to the assassin's abdomen, with one professional shot murdered him. The assassin collapsed and died shortly afterwards without recovering consciousness, while the murderer was thrown to the ground and overpowered by the police to whom he shouted, 'I'm Jack Ruby, you all know me'.

Ruby had taken his revolver with him into the basement and he had timed his unauthorised entry so that he could murder the assassin in the few seconds left for him to do so. He had been in the basement for not more than two minutes, and it has not been established how he acquired the knowledge of the exact time of the appearance there of the assassin; in the words of defending attorney at Ruby's trial for the murder of 'Lee Harvey Oswald', 'It was the greatest coincidence in history'. Had Ruby entered the basement earlier, he would have risked detection and removal but, as it was, at the time of the arrival of Ruby in the basement the imminent appearance of the assassin had created activity and excitement, and during the time that Ruby was there all present were concentrating their eyes and their cameras upon the swing doors through which it was known the assassin would shortly emerge; such was the timing of Ruby's entry that it passed unnoticed.

After the murder, Ruby was questioned by the police as to how he had penetrated the security screen in the basement. He at first declined to discuss the matter and it was only later that he said he had entered the basement by walking down a police guarded ramp; thereafter he maintained that this had been his means of entry. He told the police that he had shot the assassin because he had been grieving over the assassination for two days and he had wished to save Jacqueline Kennedy the distress of being a witness at the trial of the assassin. At his trial for the murder of the assassin, although Ruby maintained that the killing had been emotionally motivated, he was convicted of premeditated murder.

Ruby's main interests in life had been money, women, physical fitness, gambling and his pet dogs. He had a zest for living and appears to have been able to satisfy his appetites; he sacrificed all

when he silenced the man *who throughout had protested his innocence.*
It is not unreasonable to assume that Ruby *knew* that the man was
guilty and must not be allowed to stand trial.

Following the shooting from the Depository at 12.30 p.m. on 22
November, the car carrying the dying President and the
wounded Governor had rushed to Parkland Hospital, Dallas,
arriving at about 12.35 p.m. Vice President Johnson had been
travelling in the motorcade and arrived at the hospital almost
simultaneously. Secret Service agents who had accompanied the
motorcade and other agents already stationed in Dallas immediately formed a protective circle around Johnson and his wife while
taking further emergency security measures to protect them. They
took similar security measures to protect the families and relatives
of both Johnson and Kennedy. At 1.20 p.m., Johnson was told that
the President was dead, and agents advised him to leave the
hospital for Love Field Airport at once, using an unmarked police
car and being instructed to keep below window level. Security
measures had been taken for the Presidential plane, the airport
terminal and the surrounding area, and agents had worked with
police clearing all the people from the areas adjacent to the aircraft,
including warehouses, other terminal buildings and neighbouring
parking lots.

(When Kennedy was killed and the assassin apparently had
vanished, a Russian conspiracy had been suspected and there was
an official and general fear of imminent missile attack, even to
the extent of some American civilians taking cover.)

For military reasons, a Federal judge was rushed to the airfield
to administer the Presidential oath of office, thereby filling the
vacuum in the Presidency, and at 2.38 p.m. Johnson became
36th President of the United States. Nine minutes later the plane
departed for Washington from where, on arrival at 5.58 p.m.,
the new President went to the White House. Within a few
minutes he was conferring with Heads of Department and
that evening he officially appointed the FBI to investigate
and report upon the assassination. Johnson left the White

House for his own home *at 9.0 p.m.*

After President Kennedy had been pronounced dead, by Texas law the body should not have been removed from the city of Dallas until an autopsy had been performed. Despite the loud protests of Dallas officials and the senior medical staff at Parkland Hospital, the body was almost forcibly removed by the federal agencies from the hospital and taken to Love Field, whence it was to be flown to the National Naval Medical Centre at Bethesda, Maryland, where the autopsy would be performed. The Federal agencies had feared that the Dallas officials might attempt to prevent the plane carrying the body from leaving; this did not occur although the take-off was to be delayed for the more urgent swearing-in of the new President. The removal of the body from Dallas was an illegal act and it would seem that there must have been some purpose in this violation; it might be that the Vice President either ordered or acquiesed in the removal; the autopsy then coming under the control of the authorities in Washington in place of the officials in Dallas.

The next Chapter will discuss the forty-six hours that the assassin was to spend in Dallas police station on 22/23/24 November 1963, for in what occurred on those days lies part of the key to the Report of the Commission, for if the truth was to be suppressed on those days it would later be withheld from the Commission.

4

This Chapter will record chronologically and in detail the information that came into the hands of the intelligence services and probably through them to President Johnson from 2 p.m. on 22 November through 24 November 1963, for the record will show that by the latter date the authorities should have known that (a) the assassin may not have been Lee Harvey Oswald, (b) he had entered the United States from Russia in June 1962 and in the name of Lee Harvey Oswald, accompanied by his Russian wife, Marina, and infant child, (c) he was both spy and assassin, (d) the assassination appeared to be the result of a KGB conspiracy, and (e) after the assassination, on two occasions the assassin had been approaching the vicinity of his murderer's apartment. After 24 November 1963, further information was to be obtained by the FBI that reinforced and in no way detracted from the above, and would disclose (1) that from about the age of 15 Jack Ruby had been part of a group associated with Al Capone in Chicago and forever thereafter associated with criminals and (2) that the assassin was associated with the two 'Bowens', Osborne and Grossi.

The statements made by Dallas officials to the news media on 22/23/24 November 1963, and their subsequent testimony before the Commission, demonstrate that they were under pressure not to disclose information that came into their hands on the arrest of the assassin, such information indicating an international conspiracy to assassinate President Kennedy.

Friday 22 November 1963

At about 2.0 p.m. the assassin had been brought to Dallas police

44

station after his arrest in the cinema at 1.50 p.m. He was wearing a shirt, undershirt, trousers, belt, underpants, socks, shoes, and a cheap silver bracelet inscribed with the name 'Lee'. In his pockets were five revolver cartridges, some $13, a wallet and a Marsalis route bus transfer ticket. During the next few hours, the power of the United States investigative agencies – the Dallas police intelligence department, the FBI, the Secret Service and three local law enforcement agencies (the office of the District Attorney, the office of the Sheriff, and the Texas Rangers) – was brought to bear on the arrested man. The man told a senior FBI agent, sent especially to Dallas police station to obtain 'descriptive and biographical data', that his height was 5′ 9″ and that he had *no permanent scars*: the first statement was true and the second untrue. The FBI agent recorded in his written report that the height of the arrested man was 5′ 9″ and that he had said he had no permanent scars. The agent recorded the contents of the wallet which contained:

1. A Selective Service System notice of classification in the name of Lee Harvey Oswald.
1a. A counterfeit Selective Service System notice of classification in the name of Alek James Hidell recording the height of Hidell as 5′ 9″. (The name Alek James Hidell was later found to be fictitious.)
2. A certificate of service in the United States Marine Corps in the name of Lee Harvey Oswald.
2a. A counterfeit certificate of service in the United States Marine Corps in the name of Alek James Hidell.
3. A Selective Service System registration certificate in the name of Lee Harvey Oswald recording his height as 5′ 11″.
4. A Department of Defence identification card in the name of Lee Harvey Oswald recording his height as 5′ 11″, which card, although genuine, had been materially altered on its face.
5. A United States Forces Japan Identification card issued to Lee H. Oswald on 8 May 1958 (Marine Oswald was on active duty in Japan at that time.)
6. A Social Security card in the name of Lee Harvey Oswald.
7. A Card, 'Compliments GA – JO Enkanko Hotel (A 'special service hotel'), with the telephone number ED 5-0755

handwritten on the reverse side together with another partially legible handwritten number, apparently 92463.

8. A white card with the longhand writing 'Embassy USSR, 1609 Decatur NW, Washington, D.C., Consular Reznichenko'.

9. A slip of paper with longhand writing, 'The Worker, 23 W. 26th St., New York 10, NY. The Worker, Box 28 Madison Sq. Station, New York 10, NY'.

10. A card for the 'Fair Play for Cuba Committee' with a New York address and issued to Lee H. Oswald and filed by V.T. Lee as Executive Secretary. (This was the true address, name and signature of the then secretary of the FPCC. The FPCC was known to the intelligence agencies to be subversive and financed by Fidel Castro.)

11. A card for the 'Fair Play for Cuba, New Orleans Chapter', issued to L.H. Oswald and signed by the Chapter President, A.J. Hidell. (This card later was found to have been printed for the assassin in New Orleans in June 1963).

12. A Dallas Public Library card, undated but with an expiration date 7 December 1965, issued to Lee Harvey Oswald of 602 Elsbeth, Dallas — the assassin's correct address in December 1962 — and with his business address stated correctly to be Jaggars-Chiles-Stovall, and followed by the name 'Jack L. Bowen' of 1916 Stevens Forest Drive, WH 8-8997. ('Jack Leslie Bowen' was the alias of 38 years old John Caesar Grossi, the sometime inmate of penitentiaries who had obtained employment in that alias at Jaggars-Chiles-Stovall shortly before 6 April 1963, the date on which the spy/assassin left the firm. This library card must have been issued to the spy/assassin on 7 December 1962, because he was not in the United States in December 1960 and 1961, and he was dead by 7 December 1963. He had therefore been acquainted with 'Jack L. Bowen' from 7 December 1962 or before, and until 6 April 1963 and possibly thereafter. The library card thus not only established the relationship between the spy/assassin and Grossi alias 'Jack Leslie Bowen' but disclosed that Jaggars-Chiles-Stovall, employing only some 20/30 persons, had in its employ at the same time the spy/assassin working in the

name of 'Lee Harvey Oswald' and Grossi working in the name of 'Jack Leslie Bowen'. Stevens Forest Drive is in Oak Cliff, in which Dallas suburb resided both the assassin and Jack Ruby).

13. A cheque stub dated 1960 from American Bakeries, Dallas. (As the assassin was alleged to have defected to Russia in October 1959 and not to have returned to the United States until June 1962, the mystery of the stub was resolved only when it was discovered that the previous tenant of an apartment on Neely Street, Dallas, occupied by the assassin and Marina in the spring of 1963, had been employed by American Bakeries in 1960. How the assassin obtained the stub and deemed its preservation to be necessary remains obscure).

14. A snapshot of Lee Harvey Oswald in Marine uniform.

15. A snapshot of a woman (presumably Marina) and a snapshot of an infant.

16. A Marine Marksman's medal.

17. $13.00 in currency, consisting of one $5.00 bill and eight $1.00 bills.

It is desirable briefly to discuss the method of counterfeiting and, although the possession of counterfeit documents containing information differing from the originals from which they had been constructed is prima facie evidence of conspiracy, it will be seen that the counterfeiting also supports the evidence provided by the differing heights and other discrepancies that the arrested man was not Lee Harvey Oswald.

The counterfeit 'Hidell' cards (1a and 2a) had been produced by a lengthy process involving photography of the original Oswald cards, obliteration by opaquing, rephotography, forgery and reduction in size of part of the legend at the bottom of one of the original cards. All this work could have been carried out secretly and piecemeal on the premises of Jaggars-Chiles-Stovall, probably over a period of some two months. False information had to be typed on the two 'Hidell' cards and for this purpose towards the end of his employment with Jaggars-Chiles-Stovall, the assassin had attended spasmodically a typing course at a Dallas school. The typewritten matter on the 'Hidell' cards shows that more than one typewriter was used and that sometimes a typewriter had been set at stencil to create a just visible imprint for the purpose of judging the correct spacing and alignment of subsequently typed words and figures. (The assassin had left behind at his residence the negatives and other materials necessary for the purpose of counterfeiting, apparently to indicate that he was a loner or counterfeiting on behalf of those who did not – unlike the Russians – have the means and the ability to counterfeit. From these negatives and the positive counterfeits the FBI and the Secret Service were able to reconstruct the counterfeiting methods employed by the assassin. The testimony of Cadigan (VII.418-438), and the evidence of Cole (IV.380-394. XV. 703-709) describes the counterfeiting methods used by the assassin, and the Report (R.571-577) records the testimony of the experts.)

The counterfeit 'Hidell' card (1a) was created by glueing together the photographically counterfeited front of the Oswald Selective Service System notice of classification and the photographic counterfeit of the reverse side of an Oswald Selective Service System registration certificate. The result was that (1a) showed on its face the typed name Alek James Hidell in place of the typed name Lee Harvey Oswald. The perpendicular handwritten signature of Lee H. Oswald on the Left side of the card had been replaced by the handwritten signature, Alek J. Hidell. Oswald's correct selective service number had been changed. The signature of the official issuing the Oswald card had been changed from something that reads like Schiffen to something that reads like Goodhoffer, and the name Goodhoffer had been written with a different pen and different coloured ink to the signature Alek J. Hidell. The Oswald card contained a printed legend of nine lines running along the bottom of the card, and this legend had been photographically reduced in size so as to create a space at the bottom of the Left side of the 'Hidell' card (1a) for the adhesion of a photograph – the original Oswald card having no such space and therefore no photograph affixed. A photograph perhaps of the assassin had been affixed to the face of the card in the created space.

The reverse of the 'Hidell' card (1a) was a photographic reproduction of the Oswald registration certificate and glued to the reverse of the 'Hidell' card. On the thus affixed reverse side reproduction, the physical description of Oswald had been changed. The colour of eyes had been changed from blue to grey, the complexion had been changed from medium to fair, the height of 5' 11" had been changed to 5' 9", and the weight of 155 lbs. had been substituted for 150 lbs. The name and address of the local board on the Oswald registration certificate had been opaqued out, but substantially the same name and address had been typed back on to the 'Hidell' card (1a). As with the signature of the local board official on the face of the 'Hidell' card (1a), a possible reason for deleting the original draft board name and the address, and substituting substantially similar material in its place, is that if the original material had not been deleted it would have appeared as a photographic reproduction which would not look authentic.

The face and reverse of the 'Hidell' card (2a) were produced from the face and reverse of the Oswald certificate of service. This 'Hidell' card now showed the name Alek James Hidell on the face and Oswald's service number had been opaqued out. On the reverse of the 'Hidell' certificate of service (2a) the signature, Lee Harvey Oswald, and the dates 24 October 1956 and 11 September 1959, showing the beginning and the end of Oswald's period of service in the Marines, had been opaqued out. No signature for 'Hidell' had been inserted into the resulting blank signature space, but the period of service had been changed to 'Oct. 13 1958 and Oct. 12 1961'.

The genuine Department of Defence identification card (4) in the name of Lee Harvey Oswald had been changed in a significant manner, and the significance is emphasized by the fact that Cadigan, Cole and the Report do not mention its existence; it is photographically reproduced in this book. The printed and typed words on this Oswald card had not been altered, but the photograph of Marine Lee Harvey Oswald at the top Left hand corner of the card had been *removed* and replaced with a photograph, perhaps of the assassin, this photograph being a duplicate of the photograph affixed to the face of the 'Hidell' card (1a). Over the Right hand portion of the newly affixed photograph had been implanted a counterfeit stamp showing the year '1963'. Oswald had left the Marines in September 1959, and the counterfeiter had found it necessary to remove the photograph of Marine Oswald and replace it with another dated 1963. The substitution of the 1959 photograph of Marine Oswald by another photograph reinforces conspiracy based *inter alia* on the evidence of the differing heights and the existence of multifarious counterfeiting, because substitution of photographs indicates substitution of individuals.

On page 396 of the Report, the lower Left hand photograph is a copy of the two affixed photographs – one placed upon the 'Hidell' card (1a), and the other upon the genuine Department of Defence identification card of Oswald (4), the latter in place of the photograph of Oswald at the time of his separation from the Marines in September 1959. The Commission was informed by the FBI that the implanted photographs were photographs of Lee Harvey Oswald taken in Minsk, Russia, but no explanation has been provided about when and where these photographs were taken nor how the FBI or the Commission could be sure that it was a photograph of the 5' 11" Lee Harvey Oswald and not that of the 5'9" assassin, the two men – if there were two – being facially almost identical. When Lee Harvey Oswald left the Marines, however, his hair was considerably shorter than the hair in the photographs, and it may be that the photograph was of Oswald after he had allegedly been in Russia for some months. The hair in the photograph, however, is unlike that of the arrested man, whose hair was shorter, considerably thinner and somewhat kinky.

All the above facts must have been apparent to Fritz and the other investigating agents in Dallas police station within a short time of the arrival of the assassin at 2.0 p.m. Three cartridge cases and a rifle had been found on the 6th floor of the Depository where the arrested man had been employed and it was known that shots had been fired from a window on that floor. There must have been instant radio communication between the Dallas FBI and the Secret Service with their superiors in Washington, and between their superiors and President Johnson in the plane flying to Washington from Dallas apprising him of all discovered facts, and certainly on his arrival at the White House at about 6.20 p.m.

The Oswald card (4) carrying the substituted photograph, and the library card (12) carrying the name 'Jack L. Bowen' are not mentioned in the Report, and the Exhibits omit both these telling cards. The Report, therefore, does not mention the name on the library card, 'Jack L. Bowen'.

The name 'Jack L. Bowen' should now be discussed. The FBI knew from the library card the name 'Jack L. Bowen', and from a list of employees at Jaggars-Chiles-Stovall they knew that a 'Jack Leslie Bowen' had been employed at that firm in 1963. Earlier FBI files disclosed that on 6 July 1956, the FBI had had occasion to obtain descriptive data from John Caesar Grossi, and the result of their interview is set out below (**XXV.**65-66):

Name	JOHN CAESAR GROSSI, also known as *Jack Leslie Bowen* (Author's italics)
Age	30
Born	8/5/25, Paterson, New Jersey
Height	6'
Weight	168-170 (normally over 200)
Build	Medium
Hair	Dark brown, wavy, thick
Teeth	Good
Complexion	Tan (normally medium), clean shaven
Eyes	Blue, no glasses
Military Service	None
Education	1 year high school, Paterson, New Jersey, high school diploma obtained while serving time at El Reno, and equivalent 2 years college at other penitentiaries
Peculiarities	Accomplished artist, caricaturist
Father	JOHN GROSSI, whereabouts unknown
Mother	ROSE GROSSI, believed to reside at Paterson, New Jersey
Sister	JEAN GROSSI, (married name unknown)
Brother	ALBERT GROSSI, believed to reside in Paterson, New Jersey
Wife	LUCILLE RYDER BOWEN (now pregnant).

Shortly after the assassination, the FBI were to discover that when the assassin had travelled to Mexico City from the United States there had been seated beside him on the bus an old man, 'John Howard Bowen'. The FBI then commenced an inter-state, inter-country and inter-continental investigation (many American states, Canada, Mexico, Britain, France and Spain) to discover who and what was 'John Howard Bowen'.

On 7 January 1964, the FBI visited a native mud-walled hut at Texmelucan, Mexico, expecting to find 'John Howard Bowen'. Instead they found Albert Osborne, who stated that he knew Bowen but did not know where he was at that time although he believed him to be in the United States. From two old newspaper photographs of a 'John Howard Bowen' that they had discovered on 30 December 1963 at the offices of the *Knoxville Journal* in the United States, the FBI were reasonably certain that Osborne and Bowen were the same person.

On 21 January 1964, they attempted to re-interview Albert Osborne in Mexico, but he had left the hut, the teenage Mexican caretaker of the hut saying that Osborne was on a trip to an unknown part of the United States. The caretaker and a local minister identified the two photographs of 'Bowen' as being identical with Osborne.

On 8 February 1964, 'John Howard Bowen' was located and interviewed by the FBI at Florence, Alabama. 'Bowen' said, *inter alia*, that he knew Osborne, and he agreed that he and Osborne were about the same size and age. When shown the two photographs, he identified one as being of himself, and the other as being of Albert Osborne, explaining how it was possible that he might be confused with Osborne because, not only were they of the same general appearance, but they were both itinerant Baptist preachers and had both travelled extensively in Mexico. The FBI now knew beyond reasonable doubt that Osborne and 'Bowen' were the same person, and that the man's real name was probably Albert Osborne, 'John Howard Bowen' being his alias.

The FBI knew that the assassin had travelled on the bus to

Mexico City in the company of Albert Osborne travelling in the name of 'John Howard Bowen', but they also knew that the assassin had a friend, 'Jack L. Bowen', and from a list of employees that a 'Jack Leslie Bowen' had worked at Jaggars-Chiles-Stovall. They decided that it was an appropriate time to find out if the 'Jack Leslie Bowen' employed at Jaggars-Chiles-Stovall was the same man as 'Jack L. Bowen' on the assassin's library card and was, in fact, John Caesar Grossi and perhaps connected with 'John Howard Bowen'.

On 15 February, 1964, they approached an ex-employee of Jaggars-Chiles-Stovall, Gary Lawler, and the FBI report of the interview is as follows (**XXV.66-67**).

GARY EUGENE LAWLER advised he resides at 3235 Seevers, Dallas, Texas, and is employed by the Prior Products, Inc., at 4828 Recell in Dallas. He said his residence telephone number is FR 4-5305 and his business telephone number is HA 8-7411. He observed a photograph of JOHN CAESAR GROSSI, FBI No. 3 967 794, and advised he is identical' with a person whom he knew as JACK BOWEN who formerly lived in the Oak Cliff area of Dallas at an apartment on Stevens Forest Drive. He said he last saw BOWEN about three weeks prior to February 15, 1964 (Author's note: about 26 January) when BOWEN was residing at the Executive Inn and told him he was leaving the following day on a trip to Mexico and New York. BOWEN told him on that occasion he could be reached through MAX CHERRY c/o Mrs. M.M. CHERRY, at 3542 Purdue, Dallas, telephone EM 3-1246. He said that BOWEN told him he and CHERRY planned to go into the import-export business at El Paso, Texas, and Chihuahua, Mexico. BOWEN told him about a deal he had with a Mr. McCOLLOM who was in the insurance business in Dallas which had fallen through so he was going into business with MAX CHERRY.

He said BOWEN married a Canadian whose name is PATRICIA GERVAN BOWEN about three or four years ago and she lives with her mother, MABLE GERVAN, at 50 Ragland North, Renfrew, Ontario, Canada, and BOWEN is occasionally in contact with his wife's sister EDNA ELIOTT, who resides at 39 Lorne Street South in Renfrew, Ontario, Canada. LAWLER said he was employed at Jaggars-Chiles-Stovall until about November, 1963, and BOWEN was there for some time leaving about August. He said he recalled that LEE HARVEY OSWALD, the accused assassin of President JOHN FITZGERALD KENNEDY, was employed at this same firm for a very short time while BOWEN was there.

He said BOWEN had never discussed anything about the import-export business until after August of 1963, LAWLER said he was barely acquainted with LEE HARVEY OSWALD and only saw him when he went into the department where OSWALD was employed at Jaggars-Chiles-Stovall. He said he, LAWLER, was in the production office and BOWEN and OSWALD were in the camera department. He said that BOWEN set up a form of type called 'Headliner' and produced miscellaneous art work, cartoons, etc.

LAWLER said he never discussed any political beliefs or anything except the production work with LEE HARVEY OSWALD while OSWALD was employed at the Jaggars-Chiles-Stovall plant in Dallas.

LAWLER said he did not know JACK RUBY, however, he had visited the Carousel and Vegas Clubs when they were operated by RUBY at Dallas. He said he had no personal knowledge of any association between LEE HARVEY OSWALD and RUBY and he felt certain that BOWEN had not discussed any import-export business with OSWALD because LEE OSWALD left his job with Jaggars-Chiles-Stovall long before JACK BOWEN first began to talk about the import-export business.

He said he never heard JACK BOWEN mention Texas Import-Export Company and never heard of or knew a person whose name is ALEXANDER KLEINLERER. (Author's note: Polish-born but American citizen Kleinlerer of Fort Worth was an acquaintance of the assassin and his wife. He executed an affidavit for the Commission on 16 June 1964).

He advised he knew of no other associates of JACK L. BOWEN and he would immediately notify the FBI if he determined BOWEN's current location and/or address.

on 2/15/64   at Dallas, Texas   File No. DL 100-10461
by Special Agent   ARTHUR E. CARTER: vm Date dictated 2/19/64

Astonished perhaps that two of Oswald's few known acquaintances used a similar alias and were connected with Mexico, and that on one of them they had an 'Internal Security' file and on the other a 'Criminal' file, on 16 February 1964, being *the day after* Gary Lawler in Dallas had satisfied the FBI that 'Jack Leslie Bowen' was Grossi and a friend of the assassin, the FBI re-interviewed 'John Howard Bowen' at Laredo, Texas. He repeated that he and Osborne looked very much alike and were often mistaken for each other in Mexico; he denied his double-identity and said that he never used the name Albert Osborne although he knew him as a preacher and missionary in Mexico. He said that the young man seated beside him on the bus was probably a Mexican, and that they did not converse. The FBI now knew that the elder 'Bowen' was lying, and that the assassin had had two friends using similar aliases: (a) Albert Osborne (75) in his alias of 'John Howard Bowen' had travelled to Mexico City seated beside the assassin also travelling in a false name, and (b) Grossi (38) in his alias of 'Jack Leslie Bowen' had worked with the assassin in the camera department at Jaggars-Chiles-Stovall, and had stated to Lawler that he was leaving for Mexico on about 27 January 1964.

Apart from an FBI re-interview with Albert Osborne in March 1964 at the YMCA, Nashville, Tennessee, where he had registered in the name of 'John H. Bowen' of 'The Old Folks Home', Grimsby, England, and when he finally admitted his double-identity and that he had used the alias 'John Howard Bowen' for many years, but denied conversing with the young man seated beside him, according to the Exhibits *no further enquiries* were made of Albert Osborne or John Caesar Grossi. Apparently none of the staff of Jaggars-Chiles-Stovall were questioned about 'Jack Leslie Bowen', and it is possible that they were all unaware of his real name; it is unlikely that the FBI would have told Gary Lawler of the double-identity. So far as the Commission and their Report are concerned, the activities and the alias of Osborne became 'non-events', and Grossi became a 'non-person'.

Immediately after the assassination, Hoover in Washington would have called for the master file on Oswald held at the Bureau of the FBI, this file being a duplicate of the Oswald file then in the possession of the field office of the FBI in Dallas. It would seem unlikely that the file on the apparently unimportant Oswald would have been brought earlier to his notice. He would have been told by his agents in Dallas of the physical description of the arrested man and of the contents of his wallet. Reading through the file from front to back he would have found:
(a) The FBI had opened a file on Lee Harvey Oswald in October 1959 when they had been informed that ex-Marine Oswald had gone to Russia and had there attempted to renounce his United States citizenship, but that two years and eight months later he had returned to the United States with his Russian wife.

He would also have seen his warning of 3 June 1960 against imposture, which will be discussed later.

(b) Twelve days after the arrival of Oswald in the United States, on 26 June 1962 he had been interviewed by two FBI agents in Fort Worth but had refused to tell them why he had gone to Russia in the first place as he did not wish to 're-live the past', although saying that he had become disillusioned with the Russian way of life. The written report of the agents stated that from 'observation and interrogation' the height of the man they interviewed was 5' 11". Two months later the FBI had re-interviewed the man who again refused to tell them why he had gone to Russia, saying, 'I went and I came back. It was something that I did'. Satisfied that the man did not present a threat to the security of the United States, the agents had recommended that the file on Oswald be given a 'closed status'; the recommendation was accepted at the Bureau in Washington. (On the next day, 23 November, Hoover was to realise that it was during the 'closed status' period that Oswald had obtained employment at Jaggars-Chiles-Stovall.)

(c) At various times during and after the assassin's employment at Jaggars-Chiles-Stovall, FBI informants in the United States had notified the Bureau that Oswald had been in contact with the Socialist Workers Party (SWP), the Communist Party of the United States (CPUS) and the Fair Play for Cuba Committee (FPCC), all three New York bodies being 'connected'. After Oswald's contact with the Socialist Workers Party was discovered, his file was re-opened on 31 March 1963.

(d) On 10 August 1963, the FBI in New Orleans had interviewed Lee Harvey Oswald and from 'observation and interrogation' had recorded his height as 5' 9". The contents of the written report of this interview showed that Oswald had lied to this agent for he had omitted to tell him about his long residence in Russia, stating that after leaving the Marines in 1959 he had gone to live with his mother in Fort Worth where he had met and married his wife, and that he and his wife had come directly from Fort Worth to New Orleans where they were now living. (Hoover would have noted the discrepancy in height and that the man interviewed in New Orleans had lied to the FBI agent about his background, omitting his nearly three years in

Russia and his nearly seven months in Dallas when he was employed at Jaggars-Chiles-Stovall. Hoover would also have noted that the discrepancies in the height and the background had not either been perceived or acted upon by the field office of the FBI in New Orleans or by the 'domestic intelligence' division of the FBI Bureau in Washington. Some days later, Hoover was to find that Oswald, while in the United States in 1962/3, had written his height as 5' 9" on many forms of application for employment etc.)

(e) On 10 October 1963, the FBI had received the following teletype message from the CIA, who had sent the same message to the Departments of State and the Navy:

Subject: Lee Henry (sic) OSWALD

1. On 1 October 1963 a reliable and sensitive source in Mexico reported that an American male, who identified himself as Lee OSWALD, contacted the Soviet Embassy in Mexico City inquiring whether the Embassy had received any news concerning a telegram which had been sent to Washington. The American was described as approximately 35 years old, with an athletic build, about six feet tall, with a receding hairline.

2. It is believed that OSWALD may be identical to Lee Henry OSWALD, born on 18 October 1939 in New Orleans, Louisiana. A former U.S. Marine who defected to the Soviet Union in October 1959 and later made arrangements through the United States Embassy in Moscow to return to the United States with his Russian-born wife, Marina Nikolaevna Pusakova, and their child.

3. This information in paragraph one is being disseminated to your representatives in Mexico City. Any further information received on this subject will be furnished you. This information is being made available to the Immigration and Naturalization Service.

(It was clear to Hoover that the above description of the American male in no way tallied with that of Marine Oswald or of the arrested man then incarcerated at Dallas police station. During the afternoon or evening of 22 November, the CIA delivered to Hoover one daylight photograph of this man, hatless and wearing a dark jacket, the photograph having been covertly obtained by a surveillance camera positioned somewhere in Mexico City. The man in the photograph in no way resembled the arrested man but tallied, of course, with the description of the American male supplied by the CIA informant stationed inside the Russian Embassy in Mexico City. Hoover would realise that the visit of this 'Lee Oswald' to the Russian Embassy was powerful evidence of conspiracy. The photograph had been taken on 4 October 1963, which was two days after the assassin had left Mexico City for Dallas. On 23 November, Hoover was to learn from the Mexican authorities that the assassin calling himself Lee Harvey Oswald had openly visited the Çuban Consulate in Mexico City on 27 September 1963 allegedly to obtain a visa to enter Cuba en route to Russia; the assassin's visit to Mexico City was corroborated by the discovery at his residence of dated written material obtained in that city. Hoover could see that nothing had been done about the CIA teletype message of 10 October, except that in late October 1963 an FBI agent in Dallas had been asked to locate and interrogate (5' 9" and future assassin) Lee Harvey Oswald, about what at the time was inexplicably believed to have been *his* visit to the Russian Embassy. Later in the file Hoover was to read a letter of 9 November 1963 written by Lee H. Oswald from Irving near Dallas, and addressed to Consul Reznichenko at the Russian Embassy in Washington referring to 'meetings with comrade Kostin' at the Russian Embassy in Mexico City. Hoover would realise that the 'meetings' must have been held after dark or with the assassin using a different entrance to the compound in which the Russian Embassy was situated, because the assassin had not been observed by the CIA informant inside that Embassy nor photographed outside by the CIA's surveillance cameras. He would realise that if the assassin's meetings with Kostin at the Russian Embassy had been innocent they would not have had to be conducted in secret, and that there could have been no reason for a stand-in, the approximately 35 years old American male, to make enquiries about a reply to the telegram 'sent to Washington'. If the American male calling himself 'Lee Oswald' had not been photographed, after the assassination both the CIA and the FBI might have believed that the informant must have been mistaken as to the age and description of the American male. The photograph delivered by the CIA to Hoover on 22 November confirmed, however, the age and description, and that it was neither ex-Marine Lee Harvey Oswald nor the assassin.

(f) On 18 October 1963, the FBI had received another message from the CIA stating that on 28 September 1963 (being the day after the assassin arrived by bus with Albert Osborne in Mexico City) the same American male, 'Lee Oswald', had been observed by the CIA informant inside the Russian Embassy to be in contact with Soviet Vice Consul Valeriy V. Kostikov at the Russian Embassy in Mexico City. (It was known to the CIA that Kostikov was a clandestine KGB officer with a cover consular position. It might not have been known to them that Kostikov may have been a member of the KGB sabotage and assassination squad, Department 13. Hoover must have called the CIA to enquire about Kostikov and would have learnt, at the least, that he was a clandestine KGB officer. Hoover would now realise that if the assassin's visit to Mexico City had been innocent, (1) he would not have required a stand-in to contact clandestine KGB officer Kostikov in the Russian Embassy on 28 September and again to visit the Russian Embassy on 1 October to enquire about a reply to the telegram 'sent to Washington', and (2) that the assassin's own meetings with Kostin at the Russian Embassy in Mexico City had been effected in secret.)

It has recently been disclosed that the CIA had 'bugged' telephones in the Russian Embassy and that they monitored on 27 and 28 September two calls to the Embassy by 'Oswald' – whether it was the assassin or the American male is not known because these monitored calls are not mentioned in the Report and do not appear in the Volumes of Testimony or Exhibits. The calls had been reported to the FBI.

Before proceeding to discuss Hoover's next discovery in the file, the letter of 9 November, which will be (g), it is necessary to consider at length the allegedly 'unidentified' American male, and the reactions of the CIA, the FBI, the Secret Service and the Commission both to this man and to the CIA discoveries on 28 September and 1 October 1963 at the Russian Embassy in Mexico City.

First, on 23 October 1963, apparently puzzled by the

approximate age of 35 years given by their informant, the CIA asked the Department of the Navy to forward to them as soon as possible two copies of the most recent photographs they had of Lee 'Henry' Oswald, saying that they would be forwarded by the CIA to their own representatives in Mexico who would attempt to ascertain if the 'Lee Oswald' at the Russian Embassy in Mexico City and ex-Marine Lee 'Henry' Oswald were the same individual.

Secondly, in a memorandum to the Commission, the CIA stated that they had never received from the Navy the photographs of Oswald, and concluded only after the assassination that two different people had been involved. The CIA did not disclose what reply, if any, they received from the Navy.

Thirdly, the Commission's Report mentions the photograph of the 'unidentified' man wearing a dark jacket and it is included in the Exhibits, apparently because Marguerite Oswald, the mother of Marine Lee Harvey Oswald, testified that she had been shown such a photograph by an FBI agent in Dallas on 23 November 1963. (The agent had endeavoured to show the photograph to Marina Oswald, then secreted in an hotel with Marguerite, to ask her if she knew the man, but had been prevented by Marguerite from so doing on the ground that Marina was too exhausted to speak to anyone). It would seem that this photograph appears in the Exhibits only to show that it was not of Jack Ruby, Marguerite in testimony having said that after seeing Ruby's photograph in newspapers on 24 November 1963, she thought that he was the subject of the photograph she had been shown.

Fourthly, the Report says that according to a CIA affidavit of 7 August 1963 supplied to the Commission, the photograph 'was taken outside of the Continental United States during the period July 1, 1963 to November 23, 1963'. The Report does not disclose that 16 days earlier, 22 July 1963, the Commission had received from the same representative of the CIA (Helms) an affidavit that the photograph 'was taken in Mexico City on October 4, 1963'. (This was two days after the assassin had left Mexico City for Dallas). The second affidavit giving the blanket period of five months – on any day of which the photograph might have been taken anywhere in the world – was supplied to the Commission and reported by them, thus obliterating from the record the first affidavit stating the precise place and date of the photograph, Mexico City and 4 October, 1963. The Volumes of Testimony contain the second affidavit (XI.470), but *exclude* the first affidavit which gave place and date for the photograph, and this affidavit does not, of course, appear in the Exhibits but was placed in the National Archives and only recently released.

Fifthly, the Commission had in its possession the CIA report that the described American male using the name 'Lee Oswald' had visited the Russian Embassy in Mexico City on 28 September 1963 and had been in contact with Kostikov (28 September being the day after the arrival of the assassin and Albert Osborne in Mexico City). They had in their possession the CIA report that the American male had again visited the Russian Embassy on 1 October 1963 to enquire about a reply to a telegram 'sent to Washington'.

Sixthly, they had in their possession a photograph of the American male taken in Mexico City on 4 October 1963. The Commission, the FBI and the CIA knew from the photograph and the physical description of the American male that he was neither ex-Marine Lee Harvey Oswald nor the arrested assassin; conspiracy should have been apparent. The Report states untruthfully that it was the young 5' 9" assassin, ex-Marine Oswald, who had visited the Russian Embassy and had made contact with Kostikov, and who had called three days later to enquire about a reply to a telegram 'sent to Washington'.

Seventhly, on 24 March 1964, the CIA reported in a memorandum to the Commission: 'On 22 and 23 November, immediately following the assassination of President Kennedy, three cabled reports were received from (deleted) in Mexico City relative to photographs of an unidentified man who visited the Cuban and Soviet Embassies in Mexico City during October and November 1963 . . . '. Based on these cables, the CIA sent several reports to the *Secret Service* one of which, delivered by hand on 23 November 1963, said: 'Through sources available to it, the CIA (deleted) had come into possession of a photograph of an unidentified person thought to have visited the Cuban Embassy in mid-October. This individual, it was believed at the time, might be identical with Lee Harvey Oswald.' A second message to the

Secret Service was delivered by hand again on 23 November and said: 'The CIA headquarters was informed (deleted) on 23 November that several photographs of a person known to frequent the Soviet Embassy in Mexico City and who might be identical with Lee Harvey Oswald, had been forwarded to Washington by the hand of a United States Official returning to this country.'

Eightly, shortly after 23 November, the CIA supplied to the *Secret Service*, who should have supplied them to the FBI, two further photographs (at least) of the American male. These two photographs now released from the National Archives are larger and clearer than the photograph of the same man in the dark jacket that is reproduced in the Exhibits. They show a man of between 35 and 45 years of age with curly and apparently darkish hair, of powerful build, no glasses, clean-shaven but this time attired in a white short-sleeved shirt. Under his Left forearm and clasped to his side is a small bag or pouch, in his Left hand he is holding what appears to be a wallet and in his Right hand he is holding what appears to be a passport-size booklet. The first of the two photographs shows him studying intently the 'wallet' and the 'passport', and the second shows him replacing either the 'wallet' or the 'passport' in the pouch. It was known to the Commission that on the bus journey to Mexico City the assassin had 'an overnight bag or pouch' on the rack above his head and from which he extracted Oswald's 1959 passport in order to show the Russian visas stamped thereon to the Misses Mumford and Winston, two Australian girls who were travelling south on the bus as part of their world tour (Testimony of Mumford. XI.221). Neither the Commission's Report nor the CIA have disclosed on what date these two 'white-shirt' photographs were taken; this failure to give a date encourages a surmise that the 'unidentified' American male might have been inspecting the contents of the assassin's pouch on or shortly after the latter's arrival in Mexico City on 27 September 1963. No such pouch was found among the assassin's possessions after the assassination, and neither of the two 'white-shirt' photographs is referred to in the Report or shown in the Exhibits, but were placed in the National Archives and recently released.

While the assassin was secretly in Mexico City from 27

September through 2 October 1963, the American male calling himself 'Lee Oswald' paid two visits to the Russian Embassy. He was photographed in the city wearing a dark jacket on 4 October and again when wearing a white shirt on an undisclosed date when possibly examining the contents of the assassin's pouch. He remained in Mexico City after the assassin had departed for Dallas on 2 October, and was known 'to frequent the Soviet Embassy' and to have 'visited the Cuban and Soviet Embassies in Mexico City during October and November 1963'. It would seem beyond reasonable doubt that the 'unidentified' American male was a confederate of the assassin, and that he and the assassin were plotting with KGB officers, Kostikov, Yatskov and Kostin, the assassination of the President and the escape of the assassin. It may be that the American male met the assassin on his arrival in Mexico City on 27 September 1963, examined his credentials from his pouch on arrival, remained in Mexico during October and November 1963 to identify and receive the assassin fleeing from Dallas, and perhaps to supervise the next stage of his flight to Russia.

It has now been demonstrated (a) that the activities and character of Albert Osborne *alias* 'John Howard Bowen' and the existence of John Caesar Grossi *alias* 'Jack Leslie Bowen' are expunged from the Report of the Commission, (b) that the CIA messages to the FBI of 10 and 18 October 1963 describing the American male and his activities are not referred to in the Report nor in the Exhibits, but placed in The National Archives, (c) that the affidavit of Helms dated 22 July 1964 giving the place and date (Mexico City on 4 October 1963) of the 'dark-jacket' photograph of the American male is omitted from the Volumes of Testimony, and also placed in The National Archives, (d) that the subsequent affidavit from Helms dated 7 August 1964 obscuring the place and date of the photograph is contained in the Volumes of Testimony and quoted in the Report, (e) that the CIA memorandum to the Commission of 24 March 1964 referring to three cabled reports received by the CIA from their agents in Mexico City disclosing further information on the activities of the American male and the existance of additional photographs, was placed in The National Archives, and (f) that the two 'white-shirt' photographs of the American male holding a pouch and apparently inspecting its contents are not shown in the Exhibits nor referred to in Testimony, and were placed in The National Archives.

It would appear that the United States authorities did not wish any evidence of conspiracy in Mexico City to be disclosed, and that the placing in the archives of CIA messages, a memorandum, an affidavit and photographs all relating to the American male indicates that the conspiratorial significance of this man was recognised, possibly because his identity was known.

The successful identification of 'John Howard Bowen' as Albert Osborne through the apparently almost limitless resources of the FBI, make it surprising that they – according to the Report – made no effort to identify the American male of whom they had not only a definitive description corroborated by clear photographs, but also the dates of his presence in Mexico City. According to the Report and the Volumes of Exhibits, neither the Mexican authorities nor the Cuban Embassy and Consulate were asked to help, although both the Mexicans and the Cubans were helpful in other matters. The failure of the Commission, the FBI, the CIA and the Secret Service to make *any* attempt to identify the American male indicates that at some time after Hoover received the 'dark-jacket' photograph of this man on the evening of 22 November, he was able to discover but never revealed the identity of the American male.

In the nearly 10,000 pages in the Volumes of Exhibits, there are hundreds of FBI reports relating to interviews concerning a wide variety of matters but which interviews were not productive. If the FBI had conducted unproductive interviews to determine the identity of the assassin, their reports of these interviews would have appeared as Exhibits; no such interviews are recorded and from 22 November 1963 the American male became a 'non-person'.

The result of the suppression of the truth about the American male, and the suppression of the height of the Marine and other physical differences between him and the assassin, enabled the authors of the Report to state that it was only ex-Marine Lee Harvey Oswald who paid visits to the Russian Embassy in Mexico City and that the visits were for the purpose of obtaining a visa to visit Russia by way of Cuba. *Ergo*, there was no Russian conspiracy in Mexico City.

It is now possible to continue with Hoover's perusal of the file and to discuss the next and final document that he would read,. the letter of 9 November 1963.

(g) On 18 November 1963, an informant working for the FBI inside the Russian Embassy in Washington had copied a letter written in English on 9 November and posted on 12 November by Lee H. Oswald from Irving to Consul Reznichenko at the Russian Embassy in Washington. A copy of the letter had been delivered to the field office of the FBI in Washington and by them to the Bureau in Washington, the field office or the Bureau sending a copy of the letter to the field office in Dallas. This letter was the last entry in the FBI file on Oswald and it will be reproduced in full and discussed later in this book. In short, the significant parts of the letter said, 'This is to inform you of recent events since my meetings with comrade Kostin in the Embassy of the Soviet Union, Mexico City, Mexico ... I was unable to remain in Mexico indefinitely because of my Mexican Visa restrictions ... I could not take a chance on requesting a new visa unless I used my real name, so I returned to the United States. I had not planned to contact the Soviet Embassy in Mexico ... had I been able to reach the Soviet Embassy in Havana as planned, the Embassy there would have had time to complete our business ... The FBI is not now interested in my activities ... '. (Hoover would have discovered that the field office in Dallas received their copy on the morning of 22 November 1963 but that it had not come to the attention of the FBI agent in charge of the Dallas file on Oswald until just after the assassination. Hoover must have enquired of the CIA if they knew of Kostin, the Report is silent on the matter, but there did exist a clandestine KGB officer by the name of Valerie Dimitrevich Kostin and, whether or not the CIA knew of his existence, it would appear likely that this was the man to whom Oswald was referring. Hoover now knew that both the American male and the assassin had visited the Russian Embassy in Mexico City, that there appeared to be a conspiracy and that in some way the Russian Embassies in Mexico City and Washington were involved.)

On 17 September 1964, being one week before the Report of the Commission was presented to President Johnson on 24 September 1964, the CIA wrote to the General Counsel to the Commission (XXVI.149):

CENTRAL INTELLIGENCE AGENCY
WASHINGTON 25 D.C.

17 September 1964

MEMORANDUM FOR: Mr. J. Lee Rankin
General Counsel
President's Commission on the
Assassination of President Kennedy

SUBJECT: Valeriy Vladimirovich KOSTIKOV

1. In reply to your request, I am forwarding information on Valeriy Vladimirovich KOSTIKOV, one of the Soviet officials with whom Lee Harvey Oswald is believed to have dealt during his visit to Mexico City on 28 September/3 October 1963.

2. In his letter of 9 November to the Soviet Consulate in Washington, OSWALD wrote about his ' ... meetings with comrade Kostin in the Embassy of the Soviet Union, Mexico City, Mexico.' There was no officer with that name listed as being a member of the Soviet representation in Mexico City during September and October 1963. 'KOSTIN' is probably identical with Attache KOSTIKOV, who was serving in the Consular Section of the Soviet Embassy in Mexico City at that time. KOSTIKOV is one of several Consular representatives who deal with visas and related matters. Paval Antonovich YATSKOV, Second Secretary of Embassy, was in charge of the Consular Section at the time of Oswald's visit. Oswald may also have discussed his visa problems with YATSKOV and other members of the Consular Section.

3. KOSTIKOV and YATSKOV are known officers of the Soviet State Security Service (KGB). The State Security Service is the principal Soviet intelligence service, and is charged with espionage, counterintelligence and related matters.

4. It should be noted that Soviet intelligence and security officers such as KOSTIKOV and YATSKOV, when placed under official cover, are required to perform the routine and legitimate functions demanded by their cover positions in an embassy or consulate.

5. I hope that the information given above is responsive to the Commission's needs.

Richard Helms
Deputy Director for Plans

In paragraph 1, the letter states that Kostikov was one of the Soviet officials 'with whom Lee Harvey Oswald is believed to have dealt during his visit to Mexico City on 28 September–3 October 1963.' From 22 November 1963, the CIA knew that the man who had dealt with Kostikov was not Lee Harvey Oswald but an approximately 35 years old American male using the name 'Lee Oswald'. This paragraph, therefore, eliminated from the record the existence of the American male. Paragraph 2 said: 'There was no officer with that name (Kostin) listed as being a member of the Soviet representation in Mexico City during September and October 1963. 'KOSTIN' is probably identical with Attache KOSTIKOV ... ' Accepting this view, the Commission in their Report say that when Oswald said in his letter of 9 November 1963 that he had had meetings with Kostin he was 'undoubtedly' referring to Kostikov (R.734); Kostin thus became a 'non-person'.

It would seem strange that the CIA, despite their immense resources, had been unable to discover between 22 November 1963 and 17 September 1964 that there existed a clandestine KGB officer of the name of Kostin. It might be that Kostin was stationed in the Russian Embassy in Havana and travelled to Mexico City after Oswald had failed to get to the Russian Embassy in Havana 'as planned', in order to brief Oswald about the assassination and subsequent escape.

On the afternoon of 22 November, Hoover might have realised that his 'domestic intelligence' division of the Bureau and his field agents had failed (a) to pick up the discrepancies in Oswald's stated height and biography in the two FBI reports – in Fort Worth in June 1962 and in New Orleans in August 1963, (b) to act upon the information covertly obtained by the CIA in the Russian Embassy in Mexico City about the two telephone calls to the Embassy made by someone calling himself 'Oswald' and the two visits of the approximately 35 years old American male calling himself 'Lee Oswald' – reported to the FBI on 10 and 18 October 1963, and (c) to react correctly to the contents of the letter of 9 November 1963 written by the assassin. Hoover would realise that if any one of these premonitory incidents had been followed up, the assassin thereafter would have been kept under surveillance and probably would not have been able to assassinate the President. He could see that although the assassin had been available he had not been interviewed or watched by FBI agents from 10 August 1963 – when he gave his height as 5' 9" and lied about his background to the FBI agent in New Orleans – until about $1\frac{1}{2}$ hours after the assassination in Dallas. Probably about a week after the assassination, Hoover was to learn that the assassin had indeed travelled from New Orleans to Mexico in the false name of 'Lee', had registered in an hotel in Mexico City in that name and had returned from Mexico City to Dallas in that name, these activities occupying the assassin from 25 September 1963 (New Orleans), from 27 September through 2 October (Mexico City) and to 3 October 1963 (Dallas). By February 1964, Hoover would have discovered all there was to be known of Albert Osborne *alias* 'John Howard Bowen', the 75 years old Englishman who accompanied the assassin on the bus journey from the United States to Mexico City on 26 and 27 September 1963.

On the afternoon of 22 November, it would have been imperative for Hoover to ascertain why the two Marine cards in the assassin's wallet had recorded the height of Marine Oswald as 5' 11" although the height of the arrested man was 5' 9", which facts must have been transmitted to him from the FBI in Dallas, all 55 FBI field offices having radio intercommunication and with the Bureau over their own system – and what height had been shown on the passport on which Lee Harvey Oswald apparently must have travelled to and returned from Russia. Instant communication with the office where Oswald's Marine records were preserved would have shown that before leaving the Marines on 11 September 1959, Oswald had undergone a full medical examination on 3 September 1959 and that his height had been recorded as 71" (5' 11"), this height perhaps being confirmed by a photograph of Oswald standing against a scale, such photographic recording being customary in the United States military and police to avoid error. Oswald had again been measured as 5' 11" by a Marine officer on 11 September 1959. The passport office would have disclosed that when Oswald applied for a passport on 4 September 1959 he had stated his height to be 5' 11", that the passport showed this height, and that using this document a man calling himself Lee Harvey Oswald – later found to be 5' 9" – had entered the United States from Russia on 13 June 1962. The office also would have disclosed that on 24 June 1963 in New Orleans a man calling himself Lee Harvey Oswald had applied for a new passport and that he had stated on his application form that his height was 5' 11", and that the new passport also showed this height. On 10 February 1964 and as a result of Marguerite Oswald's testimony, Hoover was to learn that six months prior to leaving the Marines in September 1959, in March of that year, Oswald had applied to the Albert Schweitzer College in Switzerland for permission to attend their 1960 Spring course and that on his application form – recovered by Marguerite from the College and handed to the Commission during her testimony – he had stated his height to be 5' 11". He had paid a $25 deposit in June 1959; thus suggesting to Hoover that three months before leaving the Marines in September, Oswald appeared to have had no intention of defecting to Russia.

On the afternoon of 22 November, Hoover might have wondered whether there had been two men of differing heights each calling himself Lee Harvey Oswald and operating in the United States from 13 June 1962 through 22 November 1963, or whether there had been only one man operating during this period whose height was 5' 9" and who apparently could not be the 5' 11" Marine; that problem was to be resolved for Hoover on the afternoon of the next day, 23 November. He would wish to discover the identity of the approximately 35 years old American male; this person was ostensibly to remain for ever unidentified.

By the evening of 22 November – and apparently before 9.00 p.m. at which hour President Johnson left the White House for his own home – the new President should have been told by Hoover of the contents of the FBI file, the height of the arrested man and the contents of his wallet. He should have been apprised of the conflicting heights, that the assassin might not be the real Oswald and that there might have been one or two men using the same name. He should have been told (a) about the two visits of the American male using the name 'Lee Oswald' to the Russian Embassy in Mexico City and his contact with the KGB officers Kostikov and Yatskov, his return to the Embassy three days later to enquire about a reply to the telegram 'to Washington', (b) about the contents of the letter of 9 November 1963 to Reznichenko referring *inter alia* to meetings with comrade Kostin at the Russian Embassy in Mexico City, (c) that at this juncture the evidence indicated an international conspiracy to assassinate the President, apparently operated through the Russian Embassies in Mexico City and Washington, and (d) that in April 1960, Hoover had been alive to the possibility of imposture.

It would appear that the White House did not wish any suggestion of such conspiracy to be made public. Johnson had arrived at the White House from Dallas on 22 November at about 6.20 p.m. and had departed for his own home at 9.00 p.m. In June 1964, the Attorney General of Texas, Waggoner Carr, was to testify in Washington to the Commission *inter alia*: 'As I recall it was around *8 or 9 o'clock at night* on November 22, 1963 when I received a long-distance telephone call from Washington from someone in the White House. I can't for the life of me remember who it was. A rumour had been heard here (Washington) that there was going to be an allegation (in Dallas) in the indictment against Oswald connecting the assassination with an international conspiracy, and the enquiry was made whether I had any knowledge of it, and I told him I had no knowledge of it ... I received the definite impression that the concern of the caller was that because of the emotion or the high tension that existed at the time that someone might thoughtlessly place in the indictment such an allegation without having proof of such a conspiracy ... There was no direct talk or indirect talk or insinuation that the facts, whatever they might be, should be suppressed.' Carr went on to testify that he was asked to contact District Attorney Wade to find out if such an allegation was in the indictment, and that he telephoned the District Attorney who told him, ' ... that he had no knowledge of anyone desiring to have that or planning to have that in the indictment; that it would be surplusage, it was not necessary to allege it, and that it would not be in there, but he would double-check to be sure.' Carr then telephoned the White House with the information he had received from the District Attorney, presumably to speak to the man whose name he was able to recall (V.258-260).

The last thing to occur on the night of Friday 22 November was that the Dallas police arranged for a midnight 'show-up' of the assassin in the assembly room of the police station. This room measured some 50' x 20' and was to be crowded by some 50 newsmen. At the end of the room there was a platform and in front of this was a 'one-way' screen – the platform and the screen being used for identity parades so that the persons asked to identify could see the parade without the persons in the parade being able to see them. The assassin was brought by some 12 policemen on to the platform behind the screen, but the newsmen shouted that they could not photograph properly through the screen, and the assassin was brought off the platform on to the floor on which the newsmen were standing. They immediately crowded in on him to the point of being able to touch him, and shouted questions at him. Calmly, he made non-committal replies, and after a minute or two he was taken upstairs to the jail. Films that chanced to be taken at the time show that Jack Ruby was standing on a table at the back of the room behind about 10 rows of newsmen and about 12' to 15' from the assassin. He was posing as an Israeli press reported armed with pencil and notebook, wearing horn-rimmed spectacles and apparently the only unauthorised person in the room. Whatever virtue the 'show-up' may have had in the pursuit of justice – the arrested man could have been murdered then and there – it gave Ruby an opportunity to listen to and identify perhaps for the first time the man who, as the evidence indicates, he already knew he would have to silence before an all-revealing trial took place.

Saturday 23 November, 1963

In the morning, the Director of Jaggars-Chiles-Stovall telephoned the Secret Service to inform them that a man calling himself Lee Harvey Oswald had been employed by his firm. The Service went immediately to the firm's premises and presumably discovered that the firm had a 'secrets' department, that the assassin had obtained employment there by lying, that he had joined the firm on 12 October 1962 and that on the morning of his first working day, 16 October, he had photographed material for the Army Map Service. (On 14 October the U-2 had brought back to the United States the definitive photographs of missiles in Cuba and on 16 October Kennedy received the 'first hard preliminary information' of the construction of offensive missile sites and bomber bases.)

In the early afternoon, the mother and brother of Lee Harvey Oswald, and the wife of the assassin were allowed to visit and talk to the arrested man. The mother and the brother accepted that the man they visited was the man who had arrived in the United States from Russia on 13 June 1962. The wife, Marina, did not dispute the fact that the man she saw and with whom she spoke was other than the man she had met and married in Russia, the father of a daughter born in Russia, who had left Russia and entered the United States with her on 13 June 1962, and was the father of a second daughter born a month before the assassination. The two FBI agents who had interviewed the man calling himself Lee Harvey Oswald in Fort Worth on 26 June 1962 should have been asked to view the assassin and would have confirmed that he appeared to them to be the same man. The deception of the mother and the brother will be explained later in this book. (The problem of the 'two Oswalds' that the day before had confronted Hoover was now resolved; the man who arrived with Marina from Russia was 5' 9" in height and apparently not Lee Harvey Oswald. This fact when combined with (a) the assassin's activity in Jaggars-Chiles-Stovall, (b) his and the American male's activities at the Russian Embassy in Mexico City, and (c) the letter of 9 November, established beyond reasonable doubt that on 13 June 1963 the Russians had infiltrated a 5' 9" spy/assassin into the United States.

Hoover would then have realised that on 26 June 1962 the two FBI agents in Fort Worth had been deceived by the spy/assassin into believing that he was Lee Harvey Oswald and 5' 11" in height, and Hoover would have understood that this deception had been the *sine qua non* for the espionage three months later and the assassination 17 months later.)

On 22 November, the rifle had been found on the sixth floor of the Depository and traced to the assassin, and by the evening of 23 November Hoover would know that the assassin had also been spying at a critical moment in the history of the United States.

Late that night, Chief of the Dallas Police, Curry, told his officers to be back at the police station by 10.0 a.m. next morning in order to assist in the transfer of the assassin from the police jail to the County jail, and he told the exhausted newsmen that if they were back by that time the next morning they would not miss anything.

Sunday 24 November, 1963

In the early hours of the morning, the threats against the life of the assassin had been received and armoured trucks requested for the transfer, the trucks arriving at the police station at about 11.07 a.m.

At 11.21 a.m. the assassin, who had been exposed to opportunities for murder during the previous 46 hours while at the 'show-up' and some 15 times in the passages of the police station when being brought for interviews from the jail office through throngs of newsmen to the office of Captain Fritz, Chief of Homicide, was shot dead by Jack Ruby in the basement. When Ruby became involved, the significance of the Marsalis bus transfer ticket became apparent. The original ticket issued to the assassin before he left the bus and was given a transfer had been for the 23c. journey which took him to a point half way between the site of the Tippit killing and Ruby's apartment in Oak Cliff, the 23c. stop being two short blocks east of the killing and two short blocks west of the apartment. After the murder of the assassin the investigators must surely have realised that he might have been on his way to the vicinity of Ruby's apartment when on the bus and when later walking in the same direction before meeting and killing Tippit.

According to the Report, Ruby left his apartment by car a few minutes before 11.0 a.m. and parked his car in a lot directly across the street from a Western Union office. Without locking the car doors or taking the ignition key he entered the office where, after waiting in line with one other customer, he filled out forms for sending $25 by telegraph to one of his 'strippers', 'Little Lynn' (Karen Carlin), the time-stamped receipt showing that the transaction was completed at almost exactly 11.17 a.m. FBI agents were to calculate that as the time it would have taken Ruby to walk to the police station would have been about 2 minutes, he would have been in position in the basement at 11.19 a.m. (The sending of the money order was an unlikely action on the part of a murderer acting with premeditation in the killing 4 minutes later, but it had provided him with the excuse to be downtown and near the police station. It also gave considerable colour to his later defence of emotional spontaneity.)

If the Commission's estimate of the time when Ruby left his apartment is correct, and as the murder of the assassin was premeditated, the surmise would be that before leaving his apartment Ruby knew that Captain Fritz would rise from his desk at 11.15 a.m. to terminate the interrogation of the assassin – with sinister implications. This deduction is unavoidable because the Report fails to tender an explanation of 'the greatest coincidence in history'.

It would seem, however, and it can only be speculation, that there was no coincidence and that the explanation of Ruby's perfect timing was that he was responsible for the early morning telephonic threats against the assassin's life, as Fritz himself was later to believe. He might have expected that armoured trucks would be called to the police station and, if so, he knew that the transfer would not take place until the trucks arrived (11.07 a.m.). He saw them take up their positions and estimated that the transfer of the assassin, including finding suitable clothing and other arrangements, would take more than 10 minutes. He then walked to the Western Union office, and after transacting his business walked to the basement of the police station, arriving there at 11.19 a.m. One minute later the assassin stepped from the elevator that had carried him down from the third floor to the basement and at 11.21 a.m. Ruby killed him.

That the persons present at the last interrogation of the assassin could not knowingly have been involved in his murder is supported by the fact that on Saturday afternoon, 23 November, Ruby had been telephoning and otherwise speaking to newsmen to ask if they knew when the prisoner would be transferred but they were unable to help him. It would seem that it was late on Saturday evening that Ruby had devised the plan whereby he would be able to calculate the time of the transfer. He had then alarmed the police by calling the FBI and the Sheriff's office threatening to kill the prisoner, the calls being so worded and calmly spoken that the police could not disregard them; the reference to the large number of men who might attack the assassin necessitated the employment of armoured trucks. Ruby could not call the police station for his voice had a pronounced lisp which might have been recognised.

If what Captain Fritz believes is correct, then Ruby had been premeditating the murder of the prisoner for some time; this is indicative of conspiracy. Once the chronology of the facts is appreciated, and the words of the threats and to whom they were made are understood, Ruby's perfect timing appears to be clear; the Commission in their Report chose to disregard it and by so doing distracted attention from Ruby's premeditation and therefore from conspiracy.

Immediately after the murder in the basement, the FBI in Dallas, Chicago, New York and elsewhere began wide-ranging interviews of members or suspected members of OC. No doubt the FBI had a file on Ruby as a result of his alleged narcotics and other operations, and by the next day, 25 November, they were interviewing John Capone, the brother of Al Capone who had been murdered in prison many years previously.

Initial demands for a public enquiry to be held concerning the assassination had been intensified by the murder of the assassin. Waggoner Carr immediately announced that a court of enquiry would be held in the State of Texas 'to develop fully and disclose openly the facts of the assassination'. This enquiry was postponed at the request of Warren until after the Commission had published its Report, and Carr accepted the offer of the Commission to work with them; an independant enquiry was never held in Texas or elsewhere. At the end of his testimony before the Commission, Carr was complimented by Warren and another Commissioner on the fact that 'from the very beginning of the Commission's investigation his co-operation had been complete, enthusiastic and most helpful to the Commission', and that the Commission appreciated it very much indeed. Carr replied, 'Well, thank you, sir. I will say this, that it has been a very pleasant experience for us, and I think set a good example of how a State Government and a Federal Government can co-operate together where we have common objectives such as this, where we are trying to determine the facts and nothing else'.

During 22/23/24 November, Chief of Dallas Homicide, Fritz, Chief of Dallas Police, Curry, and District Attorney Wade had severally or jointly given interviews to the news media, and these are recorded on television companies' tapes (XXIV.748-847). It might be thought that a better procedure would have been that any statement made before the man in custody was charged should have been limited to the words, 'A man is now helping the police with their enquiries', and that after the man had been charged, 'The matter is now *sub judice* and no comment can be made'. If any statements were to be made to the news media, it would seem that they should have reflected the information already in the hands of the Dallas police, but this was not the case and it is important for a better understanding of the events of the three days to quote at some length from the statements of the three men. It would seem that the police would rather have said nothing but in doing so would have aroused the suspicions of the news media, and it would appear that they were under pressure from 'above' and were in the position that they had to say something to the news media in order to dampen their suspicions. After Ruby had murdered the assassin, the position of the three men and particularly that of District Attorney Wade was intolerable. A full enquiry appeared inevitable at which they would be required to testify about the three days, perhaps without disclosing — if they knew — the source of the pressure.

Quotations from the tapes which were, of course, made after the 5' 9" height of the assassin had been ascertained and the contents of his wallet examined, are as follows:

After the assassin had been charged with the murders of Tippit and the President, a statement was made late on Friday 22 November. After referring to 'evidence gathered by four agencies', in answer to a question whether there was any indication that it was 'an organised plot', or whether there was 'just one man?', the officials replied, 'there's no one else but him'. During Saturday 23 November, in answer to several questions as to the possibility of accomplices, after referring to a joint effort by six agencies, the officials said, 'Not that we know of', 'We don't believe so at this time', and 'There is no one else but him'. The man charged was then stated to be 24 year old Lee Harvey Oswald, but when asked, 'Is he a former Marine?', the reply was, 'I don't know the answer to that'. (The 5' 9" man charged had given his name as Lee Harvey Oswald and in his wallet were five genuine 1959 Marine cards in that name – two of the cards giving his height as 5' 11".) In reply to the question, 'Did he (Oswald) get back to his room over on Beckley and then leave it and then encounter the officer (Tippit)?', the reply was, 'That's right. He changed clothes. He went to his room, changed his clothing, then started to the picture show and encountered the officer on the way to the picture show'. (Reference to any map of Dallas in the police station would have shown that the assassin was walking east, directly *away* from the 'picture show' and towards the 23c. bus stop when he encountered Tippit near the bus stop, and that after Shooting Tippit he ran away west *towards* the 'picture show'. It would seem that the investigators were aware that the assassin had twice been approaching the same point in Dallas – the 23c. bus stop – and that this was indicative of something or somebody in connection with his escape from Dallas, and therefore of conspiracy which was not to be disclosed.)

In reply to a question about a Post Office Box rented by Oswald and to which Box the rifle had been delivered, the reply correctly stated that A. Hidell was the name of the person to whom the rifle had been addressed at the Box, but the officials made no reference to the 'Hidell' counterfeit cards (1a and 2a) nor to card (4). When questioned about the assassin's background, the reply way, 'Well, he has a background of course. It's generally known now he defected to Russia in 1959 and married a Russian girl and last August, I understand, he went to the American Consul (Moscow) and asked to be brought back to the United States'. When asked how the police viewed Oswald as a type, the reply was, 'Well, I think he's a man that planned this murder weeks or months ago and has laid his plans carefully and carried them out, and has planned at that time what he's going to tell the police that are questioning him at present'.

On Sunday morning, 24 November, and shortly *before* Ruby was to shoot the assassin, in reply to the question, 'Is there absolutely no doubt now that nobody else is involved as an accomplice?', the reply was, 'I would not make that statement ... I wouldn't comment on it, because I would certainly hate to say we were convinced that nobody else is involved and then have somebody else involved ... But to say that there was no other person had any knowledge of what this man might do, I wouldn't make that statement, because there is a possibility that there are people who might have known this man's thoughts and what he might do, could do, or what he might do ... I'll only say this again: we're open-minded regarding this issue, and we will continue to exhaust every effort to explore any possibility that there might have been someone that even was friendly with him that might have known that he even had an idea of trying to harm ... (tape ends)'. A few minutes later Ruby murdered the assassin, and in answer to the post-murder question, 'Was anyone else connected with Oswald in the matter?', the reply was, 'Well, now, not that I know of'.

The District Attorney then called a press conference at which representatives of newspapers and five television stations were present. He said that the purpose of the conference was to detail some of the evidence against the accused, he was asked whether Oswald 'was on foot when Tippit saw him?', and he repeated what had been said the day before, 'Yes, he was on foot, and apparently headed to the Texas Theater (the 'picture show'). He then walked across a vacant lot ... '. When questioned about the possibility of Russian Marxism in relation to Oswald's background, he said, 'There's some things found on him like newspapers and things – didn't necessarily connect him with the organisation, like the Communist *Daily Worker* or something. I don't think you can necessarily say he was – the fact he read it doesn't necessarily mean that he's, you couldn't prove that he belonged to it. I've read quite a bit about this subject. I know what you're talking about, but I've read interviews from reporters from over in Russia all on this subject but apparently they know quite a bit more about it than I do'. (No newspapers were found on the assassin.)

When asked by the appointed representative of the media present, 'Mr. Wade, I'd like to ask one more question. Why did you call us tonight and why did you go over this evidence?', he replied, 'Well, there's a lot of reasons. Probably the main one – I received a call from Paris, France and Stockholm, Sweden, and nearly every foreign country asking me about this evidence and I thought from those newsmen in those countries – (apparently interrupted)'. He was then asked whether 'Robert Kennedy or anybody from his office – (apparently interrupted)?', he replied, 'I have heard nothing from any of the – from Washington or any of the officials in this country on this matter. But I decided that I heard, I've had, a number of newsmen call me from all over the world wanting to know why and it wasn't, and I thought in my own mind – decided that it's a good idea. So, – (apparently interrupted)'. When asked, 'Are you aware that the Justice Department before you made this announcement and before you came into the building tonight had said that new evidence, the evidence would all be released and given to newsmen – (apparently interrupted)?'. He replied, 'No, sir, I'm not familiar with that other than as I walk out of the door one of the – one of your men – I think, called me and told me that there was something on that – that they were considering that, but I was already up and coming out to see you. It had nothing to do with me getting this ready'. When asked, 'Do you feel that list (of evidence against Oswald) is complete? anything is withheld by Government agencies, Federal Bureau of – (apparently interrupted)?, he said, 'This is all I know of'.

It would seem that after the call from Waggoner Carr, the Dallas officials were under instructions to make statements but to refer only to such things as would divert the attention of the news media from the possibility that the assassin might not be Lee Harvey Oswald and from the possibility of international conspiracy. Whatever may have occurred, at no time did the officials mention the differing heights of 5′ 9″ and 5′ 11″, the 'Hidell' counterfeit cards (1a and 1b), the genuine Marine card with the substituted photograph stamped 1963 (4), any of the other contents of the wallet, or the assassin's twice attempted approach to the vicinity of Ruby's apartment — all of which was known to one or more of the three officials.

The events of the three days are crucial to the post-assassination story and I (the author) would like to enlarge upon the conclusions I formed. I had read all the Testimony, and from the Exhibits I knew the contents of the wallet before I read the statements. I could not understand why, if statements had to be made, they omitted the startling evidence provided by the contents of the wallet and the known height of the arrested man; I decided to read again the testimony of the three officials and other Dallas police officers; this testimony appeared to confirm that Chief of Police Curry and perhaps District Attorney Wade were under pressure not to disclose the evidence of conspiracy supplied by the height of the assassin, the contents of his wallet, and his twice attempted approach to the vicinity of Ruby's apartment.

Captain King, the press relations officer with the Dallas police, was to testify to the Commission *inter alia*, ' ... Chief Curry was not there, but he had said to the press in my presence and said to me that there were elements of evidence that he was not going to comment on, and he told me that the Federal Bureau of Investigation had requested *that we do not comment on some of the evidence* and that it was not his intention to do so (XV.58)'.

Chief of Police Curry, was to testify *inter alia*, ' ... we felt that this was a murder that had been committed in the City and County of Dallas and that we had prior, I mean we had jurisdiction over this. The FBI actually had no jurisdiction over it, the Secret Service actually had no jurisdiction over it. But in an effort to cooperate with these agencies we went all out to do whatever they wanted us to do that we could do to let them observe what was taking place, but actually we knew that this was a case that happened in Dallas, Tex., and would have to be tried in Dallas, Tex., and it was our responsibility to gather the evidence and present the evidence. We kept getting calls from the FBI. They wanted this evidence up in Washington, in the laboratory, and there was some discussion, Fritz told me, he says, 'Well, I need the evidence here. I need to get some people to try to identify the gun, to try to identify this pistol and these things, and if it is in Washington how can I do it?' But we finally, the night, about midnight of Friday night (22 November), we agreed to let the FBI have all the evidence and they said they would bring it to their laboratory and they would have an agent stand by and when they were finished with it to return it to us'. Curry said that to his knowledge no agent of the Dallas police was sent to Washington with the evidence (thereby destroying the chain of evidence). When asked whether that arrangement worked out alright, Curry replied, 'Well, not exactly, because they were to give us pictures of everything that was brought to Washington, and Fritz tells me that some of these little items that it was very poor reproduction of some of the items on microfilm. Subsequently they photographed these things in Washington and sent us copies, some 400 I think, 400 copies of different items. So far as I know, we have never received any of that evidence back. It is still in Washington, I guess. Perhaps the Commission has it'. Counsel then informed Curry that the Commission was still working with it, and Curry continued, ' ... they were in a tremendous hurry to get all of these items to the laboratory here in Washington, and our only concern was this, that if this case is tried in Dallas, we need the evidence to be presented here in court in Dallas and we were a little bit apprehensive about it if it gets to Washington will it be available to us when we need it. If we need somebody to identify, attempt to identify the gun or other items would it be here for them to see? And that was our only concern. We got several calls insisting we send this, and nobody would tell me exactly who it was that was insisting, "just say I got a call from Washington and they wanted this evidence up there, insinuating it was someone in high authority that was requesting this, and we have finally agreed as a matter of trying to cooperate with them, actually'. When asked whether he recalled a message from Hoover asking that the police should not disclose the results of the FBI investigation with reference to

Oswald, Curry said that he did not recall having received a direct communication from Hoover but that, ' ... I had a lot of communications from the local FBI who inferred that these orders were coming out of Washington, or the questions were coming out of Washington, about various things, insisting that the evidence be shipped up there immediately, and the fact that we shouldn't show anything on television (IV.195)'. (If the contents of the wallet had been shown on television disclosing counterfeiting, forgery, differing heights, a substituted photograph, the name Reznichenko and the Communist newspaper, 'The Worker', powerful evidence of Russian conspiracy would have been apparent and immediately publicised.)

Chief of Homicide Fritz was to testify *inter alia* that although he was the only police officer who interrogated Oswald, officers from the FBI and the Secret Service had also done so. He did not say whether he had been under any pressure. He said that there had been fairly continuous questioning by him, although interrupted by identity parades and other matters. The interrogation had started shortly after 2.00 p.m. on Friday 22 November and covered a period of some twelve hours between that time and 11.15 a.m. on Sunday 24 November. (Allowing for interruptions, this period could perhaps be reduced to 6 hours, but it is impossible to identify more than about 30 questions asked of Oswald at any time. Many more questions must have been asked, and it is not the replies of the assassin that would be interesting – for he could be silent, evasive, truthful or untruthful at will – but the nature of the questions that were asked, for there must have been many that enquired in depth into the making and purpose of the counterfeit cards (1a and 2a), why Marine Oswald's photograph had been removed from card (4) and 1963 stamped on the substituted photograph, how the Marines had come to measure him at 2″ above his height of 5′ 9″, as to his name, as to his and the American male's visits to the Russian Embassy in Mexico City, and as to the identity of 'Jack L. Bowen' on the library card. As Fritz alleged that he made only rough notes and as nobody else took notes, the extent and essence of the questioning cannot now be discovered). Oswald had denied killing Tippit or the President, or wounding the

Governor, and when asked if he thought the country would be better off with the President killed, replied 'Well, I think that the Vice President has about the same views as the President has', adding that Johnson 'would probably do about the same thing' that president Kennedy would have done. When Fritz was asked by Counsel whether he had asked Oswald about 'this card he had in his pocket with the name Alek Hidell?', Fritz replied that he believed that Oswald had three of those cards if he remembered correctly and that 'One of the cards looked like it might have been altered a little bit … ' On being shown the bus transfer ticket on 23 November, Oswald had altered the story that he had told on 22 November in which he had said that he had taken a bus to his rooming house, now admitting that he left the bus because 'the traffic was heavy' and that he then took a taxi to his rooming house.

The police had discovered two photographs of the assassin (dressed in black like a guerilla with a rifle in one hand and a revolver strapped round his waist), and when Fritz showed him the photographs Oswald said that they had been made up in the police station and that his face had been superimposed upon the body of another man. He denied that he had ever lived at Neely Street (presumably because that was where the photographs had been taken by Marina, which the police and the Secret Service later were able to establish from her and from the background). He said that he was a Marxist but that he was not a Marxist-Leninist and repeated – what he had several times told Fritz – that he believed in the Castro revolution. Fritz said that Oswald had acted like a person who was prepared for what he was doing and that he suspected that Oswald had been 'trained in sabotage from the way that he talked and acted', but when asked about this Oswald replied that he had worked only in a radio factory. Fritz said that if he asked him a question that 'meant something', he immediately replied that he would say nothing about it and he seemed to anticipate what Fritz was going to say, 'in fact, he got so good at it one time I asked him if he had had any training, if he hadn't been questioned before'. The reply that Fritz obtained was that the FBI had interviewed Oswald in Fort Worth and that they had 'tried the buddy boy method and thorough method'. Fritz thought that Oswald had shot the President 'because of his feeling about the Castro revolution', and that he did not think that Oswald was 'afraid at all' and 'was a person who had his mind made up what to do ... like a person dedicated to a cause'. Fritz also thought that he was of above average intelligence and 'was not a "nut" which people had been saying'.

With regard to Ruby, Fritz said that Ruby told him he had been 'all torn up about the Presidential killing, that he felt terribly sorry for Mrs. Kennedy. He didn't want to see her to have to come back to Dallas for a trial, and a lot of things like that'. When Fritz had asked him how he had entered the basement, Ruby said that he had walked down a ramp to which Fritz replied that as there had been 'an officer at the top and an officer at the bottom', Ruby could not have entered that way. Ruby had replied, 'I am not going to talk to you any more, I am not going to get into trouble', and Ruby 'never talked any more about it'. When Fritz asked Ruby when he had first decided to kill Oswald, Ruby avoided the question and talked about something else.

Fritz first testified in April 1964 and was asked to testify again in July 1964. It would seem from the line of questioning on the second occasion that between these dates the Commission had concluded (perhaps incorrectly) that Ruby had left his apartment just before 11.00 a.m., and (correctly) that Ruby must have entered the Western Union office, two minutes walk from the police station, at about 11.15 a.m. at which time Fritz had terminated the last interrogation of the assassin. The Commission appear to have failed to grasp the significance of the early Sunday morning threats against the life of the assassin and the consequent ordering of the armoured trucks, with the result that they did not appreciate that the arrival of the trucks would have given Ruby an intimation of the cessation of interrogation. This interpretation of the events is supported by Fritz, because in testimony in July he said that he thought that Ruby had been responsible for the threats and that it had been 'a trick'. (IV.202-249. XV.145-153.)

As with Curry and Fritz, District Attorney Wade was to testify at length and said *inter alia* that Fritz 'ran a kind of a one-man operation where nobody else knew what he was doing', but that 'Fritz was about as good a man at solving a crime as he had ever know'. He said that on the evening of 22 November he had heard on the radio or on television that the police were going to file a charge on Oswald as part of an *international* conspiracy to murder the President, and that he then talked to United States Attorney, Barefoot Sanders, and discussed with him these media statements. As there was no such crime in Texas as being part of an *international* conspiracy, it was just 'murder with malice' and, as anything else alleged had to be proved, he went to the police station and took a charge on the arrested man as a case of simple murder. He said he thought that if somebody was going to take a complaint that the arrested man was part of an international conspiracy 'it had to be a publicity deal, somebody being interested in something other than the law because there was no such charge in Texas'. He said that he also talked to Waggoner Carr on the evening of Friday 22 November and that Carr had mentioned that there was a rumour that the police were getting ready to file a charge on Oswald as being part of an *international* conspiracy, but that he had told Carr that this was not going to be done. Both Sanders and Carr had told him that they were concerned about having received calls 'from Washington and somewhere else', and they had said that if it was not absolutely necessary they thought that it should not be done. When Wade was asked by Counsel whether in his conversations with Carr he could remember anything else that Carr had said to him, Wade replied, 'I don't actually even remember, you know, he said that he had had a call from Washington, I don't actually remember anything about that. I remember he said that about this charge that this is going (*sic*), 'This would be a bad situation, if you allege it as part of a Russian, the Russian conspiracy, and it may affect your international relations, a lot of things, of the country', and I said it was silly because I don't know where the rumour started but I will see even if it was so we could prove it, I wouldn't allege it. Isn't it about it, the way you recall it, Mr. Carr?'. (Carr apparently was sitting near Wade during the latter's testimony and, according to the transcript, did not reply.) After agreeing with a Commissioner that the law in Texas permitted a charge of conspiracy to commit murder, Wade said that no evidence had been brought to him upon which he could have based an indictment or warrant for conspiracy to commit murder, and he had never seen any of the physical evidence in the Oswald case other than one or two statements and the assassination rifle. He said that he thought that Oswald had planned the assassination, had practised shooting and had his inspiration from someone else. Before he called his press conference at about 8.00 p.m. on the night of Sunday 24 November, he and Fritz had listed about seven pieces of evidence that he was going to give to the news media, but Curry told them that they should not do this because he had told the FBI inspector that there would be nothing said about the assassination of the President and the murder of the assassin. However, Wade had considered it to be in the interests of the police that he should dispel rumours that the police had arrested the wrong man and had arranged to have him killed, and he thought that somebody ought to go out on television and state the evidence against Oswald, telling the public everything. He said that immediately after the televised press conference the FBI inspector called him and asked him not to say anything further about the case. (V.213-254).

The next Chapter will demonstrate how it could have come about that (a) the Commission were unaware that the recorded height of Marine Oswald was 5' 11", and that of the assassin was 5' 9", and were therefore oblivious to the possibility of imposture, and (b) were unaware of the activities of the American male and his (and not the assassin's) activities on 28 September and 1 October 1963, and were therefore oblivious to the conspiracy crystallising at the Russian Embassy in Mexico City between 27 September and 2 October 1963, and culminating in the assassination of the President.

5

On 6 April 1964, Hoover wrote to the General Counsel to the Commission:

Dear Mr. Rankin:

Your letter dated March 26, 1964, transmitted specific questions pertaining to the investigation of Lee Harvey Oswald prior to the assassination of President Kennedy and requested a reasoned response to each question.

At the outset, I wish to emphasise that the facts available to the FBI concerning Lee Harvey Oswald prior to the assassination did not indicate in any way that he was, or would be, a threat to President Kennedy; nor were they such as to suggest that the FBI should inform the Secret Service of his presence in Dallas or his employment in the Texas School Book Depository.

The Oswald case was one of many thousand investigative matters handled by the FBI. During the fiscal year ending June 30, 1963, the FBI handled 636,371 investigative matters in the criminal, civil and security fields. The extent, depth and urgency of each investigation necessarily are dependent on the available facts in the case. A file concerning Oswald was opened at the time newspapers reported his defection to Russia in 1959, for the purpose of correlating information inasmuch as he was considered a possible security risk in the event he returned to this country. When we learned in 1960 that his mother was sending him money, we interviewed her and his brother, Robert Oswald, to determine the reason. Again in 1960 investigation was conducted to determine if he was in Switzerland, as we were advised he contemplated enroling in a College there. The investigation was re-instituted at the time of his return to the United States in 1962, and he was interviewed on two occasions in 1962 in an effort to ascertain if he had been recruited by the Soviet intelligence services and to evaluate him as a possible security risk.

The investigation was continued in 1963 when it was reported that Oswald had corresponded with 'The Worker', an east coast community newspaper, and it was also reported he was engaged in activities on behalf of the Fair Play for Cuba Committee. This investigation was in progress when he was reported in October, 1963, to be in contact with the Soviet Embassy in Mexico, and on November 18, 1963, in contact with the Soviet Embassy in Washington, D.C. The purpose of the investigation was to determine the extent of his activities on behalf of the Fair Play for Cuba Committee and the reasons for his contacts with the Soviet Embassy.

In short, Oswald had gone to the Soviet Union at the age of 19 and attempted to renounce his American citizenship. He had recanted; his passport had been returned to him and he had been permitted by the Department of State to return to the United States as an American citizen. After his return, he had subscribed to 'The Worker', had distributed pamphlets for the Fair Play for Cuba Committee and had admitted publicly that he was Marxist. He had been in contact with the Soviet Embassy in Washington, D.C.; and it was reported, but not confirmed, that he had been in contact with the Soviet Embassy in Mexico. The reason indicated for his contacts with the Soviet Embassies was to obtain visas to re-enter the Soviet Union. As previously indicated, his activities as known at the time of the assassination did not suggest in any way that he was a dangerous subversive; that he was violating any Federal law; or that he represented a threat to the personal safety of the President. There was no basis for the FBI to keep him under observation. In the absence of any information showing Oswald to be a possible threat to the President, there was no basis to inform the Secret Service concerning Oswald's presence or employment in Dallas, Texas.

The answers to your specific questions are set forth in the attached memorandum.

Sincerely yours,
Signed J. Edgar Hoover (XVII.787-788.)

When Hoover wrote the above letter, he had known from the afternoon of 22 November that it was not the slender assassin (whether Marine Oswald or a 5' 9" substitute) who twice visited the Russian Embassy in Mexico City, but an approximately 35 years old American male of athletic build. Hoover knew that the assassin would hardly have required a stand-in to assist him 'to obtain visas to re-enter the Soviet Union', and he did not mention the American male. He was also aware of the differing heights of 5' 11" and 5' 9" respectively recorded by his agents in Fort Worth in June 1962 and in New Orleans in August 1963.

Attached to Hoover's letter was a list of the questions asked by Rankin on behalf of the Commission, and the answers supplied by the FBI (XVII.789-803). The list contained thirty questions and the answers thereto, but only five are pertinent:

Question 5:   What was the FBI evaluation of Oswald as a result of the June, 1962 interview?

The answer dealt with the FBI evaluation of Oswald resulting from the first FBI interview with him on 26 June 1962 in Fort Worth, but did not inform Rankin that FBI agents had recorded Oswald's height from 'observation and interrogation' as 5′ 11″.

Question 6:   Why was Oswald interviewed so soon thereafter on August 14, 1962? What was the FBEI evaluation of Oswald as a result of this interview? Where was this interview held, how long did it take, and was there anything remarkaele about Oswald's demeanour during the course of the interview?

The answer dealt in full with the question, but Hoover did not disclose to the Commission that after this interview the file on Oswald was given a 'closed status'. This fact was later to appear during the testimony of FBI agent Fain.

Question 12:   Did SA. Quigley, who interviewed Oswald at the New Orleans jail, or SA Kaack who prepared a report on Oswald, review earlier FBI reports on Oswald? Were they aware that, contrary to his statement, Oswald had not lived with his mother following discharge from the Marine Corps, but rather had gone to Russia. Were they aware that, contrary to his statement, his wife's maiden name was not Prossa and that they had not married in Fort Worth but in Russia.

The answer dealt with Quigley's interview with Oswald on 10 August 1963, and said ' ... SA. Milton R. Kaack, who prepared a report concerning Oswald dated October 31, 1963, did review the results of prior FBI investigation concerning Oswald and he, of course, was aware of the various contradictions in the information furnished by Oswald. In the event the investigation of Oswald warranted a further interview, these discrepancies would have been discussed with him.' Hoover did not inform Rankin that FBI agent Quigley from 'observation and interrogation' had recorded Oswald's height as 5′ 9″; all of Quigley's report was included in Kaack's report. Rankin must have failed to notice the different recorded heights of 5′ 11″ and 5′ 9″.

Question 23:   What was the FBI reaction to the CIA report of October 10, regarding Oswald's visit to the Soviet Embassy in

Mexico City? Why did the FBI not request additional information or follow-up information by the CIA? What was the FBI evaluation of Oswald in view of the CIA report?

The question is impossible to understand. If Rankin had been provided with and had read the full CIA report he would have seen that the approximately 35 years old American male of athletic build in no way resembled the younger, slender now murdered assassin. It would seem that Rankin could not have appreciated that two men were involved, for he would have asked the FBI to identify the American male and to evaluate the American male's presence in the Soviet Embassy on 1 October 1963 in the name 'Lee Oswald'.

The answer to this question was, *verbatim*:

'The investigation of Oswald in 1963 prior to receipt of the Central Intelligence Agency communication dated October 10, was directed toward the primary objective of ascertaining the nature of Oswald's sympathies for, and connection with, the FPCC or other subversive elements. The Central Intelligence Agency communication which reported that a man, tentatively identified as Oswald, had inquired at the Soviet Embassy concerning a telegram which had been sent to Washington did not specify the nature of the telegram. This contact with the Soviet Embassy interjected a new aspect into the investigation and raised the obvious question of why he was in Mexico and exactly what were his relations with the Soviets. However, the information available was not such that any additional conclusions could be drawn as to Oswald's sympathies, intentions or activities at that time. Thus, one of the objectives of the continuing investigation was to ascertain the nature of his relations with the Soviets considering the possibility that he could have been recruited by the Soviet Intelligence services. The Central Intelligence Agency communication dated October 10, 1963, stated that any further information received concerning Oswald would be furnished and that our liaison representatives in Mexico City were being advised. On October 18, 1963, one of our FBI liaison representatives in Mexico City was furnished this information by Central Intelligence Agency and he arranged to follow-up with Central Intelligence Agency in Mexico City for further information and started a check to establish Oswald's entry in Mexico. Subsequent to the assassination, Central Intelligence Agency also advised us of Oswald's contact with the Cuban Embassy in Mexico City at the time of his visit there.'

The first part of the answer dealt with the CIA teletype message of the FBI on 10 October and does not mention that the man 'tentatively identified as Oswald', was so identified by the CIA and not by the FBI who do not appear after 10 October either to have noticed or acted upon the description of the American male, such description fitting neither Marine Oswald nor the assassin. It would seem that this answer should have apprised the Commission that the approximately 35 years old American male who visited the Russian Embassy on 1 October, although using the name 'Lee Oswald', was not the assassin, which Hoover knew from the CIA photographs of the man, one photograph supplied to him on 22 November and (at least) two others on or just after 23 November 1963. The words 'this information' in the second part of the answer dealing with the CIA message to the FBI liaison representative on 18 October 1963 are misleading because this second message from the CIA to the FBI indicated that the American male in the name of 'Lee Oswald' had visited the Russian Embassy on 28 September and there had been in contact with KGB officer Kostikov; Hoover should have mentioned Kostikov and that it was not the assassin who spoke with him. The whole answer is misleading because it makes it appear that the assassin and the American male were the same person. The question referred only to the CIA message of 10 October, and it would appear that Rankin was unaware of the message of 18 October 1963 involving Kostikov, and of the two telephone calls to the Russian Embassy; none of Rankin's other questions refers to these matters.

Question 28: What was the FBI evaluation of confidential information received on November 18, 1963 regarding Oswald's letter to the Soviet Embassy in Washington?

The answer to this question was, *verbatim*:

'The information received on November 18, 1963, concerning Oswald's contact with the Soviet Embassy tended to confirm his contact with the Soviet Embassy in Mexico City as reported by the Central Intelligence Agency and to indicate the reasons for such contact, namely to secure visas to the Soviet Union.'

This answer implies that the assassin, 'Lee H. Oswald', (who wrote the letter of 9 November which was copied by the FBI informant in the Soviet Embassy in Washington) was the American male who had contacted the Soviet Embassy in

Mexico City on 28 September and 1 October 1963; the answer to the question is misleading because it again makes it appear that the assassin and the American male were the same person. Hoover should have told Tankin that the assassin would hardly have required a stand-in to 'secure visas'.

After requests from the Commission for more details from the FBI Bureau master file on Oswald, on 4 May 1964 Hoover wrote to Rankin as follows:

Dear Mr. Rankin:
Reference is made to the discussion between staff members of the Commission and Mr. A.H. Belmont of this Bureau, May 4, 1964.
In accordance with this discussion, there are listed below the contents of the FBI headquarters file concerning Lee Harvey Oswald up to the time of the assassination of the later President John F. Kennedy on November 22, 1963:

(The letter then lists in summary form the 69 items contained in the master file on Lee Harvey Oswald (XVII.804-813), but only 13 of these are pertinent):

Item 5:   A copy of an Office of Naval Intelligence memorandum dated November 2, 1959, containing the results of a check of the U.S. Marine Corps file regarding Oswald.

(This memorandum might have contained the physical data of ex-Marine Oswald, including his height of 71".)

Item 17:   A letter to this Bureau from the Legal Attache in Paris dated October 12 (1960), advising that information from his sources indicated that Oswald was not in attendance at the Albert Schweitzer College in Churchwalden, Switzerland.

Item 18:   A letter to this Bureau from the Legal Attache in Paris dated November 3, 1960, which set forth additional data developed from officials of the Albert Schweitzer College regarding Lee Harvey Oswald.

(This additional data should have disclosed Oswald's application form for enrolment at the College on which he had written his height as 5' 11" and his weight as 160 lbs.)

Item 21:   A letter from the Washington Field Office to this Bureau dated

May 23, 1961, setting forth results of a review of the files in the Passport Office, Department of State, concerning Oswald.

(This should have included Oswald's application for a passport dated 4 September 1959, on which he had stated his height to be 5′ 11″. The Passport Office should also have provided the Bureau with the physical data stated on the face of the passport including his height of 5′ 11″.)

Item 25: A letter from the Washington Field Office to this Bureau dated September 1, 1961, which set forth results of a review of the records of the Passport Office regarding Oswald.

(See comment on Item 21 above.)

Item 31: A copy of a communication classified 'Confidential' from the Director of Naval Intelligence to the Naval Attache in Moscow dated March 3, 1962, which set forth information in Office of Naval Intelligence files regarding Oswald.

(The information in the Navy files should have contained reference to the Marine's recorded height of 71″.)

Item 41: A report of SA John W. Fain dated July 10, 1962, at Dallas, which set forth results of investigation regarding Oswald and his wife, Marina. This report also set forth results of the interview of Oswald on June 26, 1962, by SAs John W. Fain and B. Tom Carter.

(The report dated 10 July 1962 contained the height of 5′ 11″ for Oswald obtained by Fain and Carter from 'observation and interrogation', but Hoover did not advise Rankin of this.)

Item 57: An airtel from Dallas to this Bureau dated October 22, 1963, reporting that INS in Dallas had received a communication classified 'Secret' from the Central Intelligence Agency (CIA) Mexico City, which indicated that an individual, possibly identical with Lee Harvey Oswald, was in contact with the Soviet Embassy in Mexico City.

(The contents of this airtel and the CIA communication are probably the same as Item 58 (or 61) below. At the time this Item was prepared, Hoover knew from information supplied by the CIA informant and from photographs of the American male supplied to him by the CIA that this man was neither ex-Marine Lee Harvey Oswald nor the assassin, but he did not advise Rankin of this.)

Item 58: A CIA Release dated October 10, 1963, which was sent to the

FBI, Department of State and Department of the Navy classified 'Secret' which reported that an American male who identified himself as Lee Oswald had contacted the Soviet Embassy, Mexico City, on October 1 1963. The CIA release indicated Oswald may be identical to Lee Henry Oswald, born October 18, 1939, in New Orelans, Louisiana.

(See comment on Item 57 above.)

Item 61:   A cablegram to this Bureau from our Legal Attache in Mexico dated October 18, 1963, which furnished information from CIA classified 'Secret' – Not To Be Further Disseminated', reporting that Lee Oswald had contacted Soviet Vice Consul Valeriy V. Kostikov of the Soviet Embassy, Mexico City, Mexico on September 28, 1963. Our Legal Attache indicated he was following this matter with CIA and was attempting to establish Oswald's entry into Mexico and his current whereabouts.

(At the time this Item was prepared, Hoover was aware that 'Lee Oswald' was the American male, and was neither ex-Marine Lee Harvey Oswald nor the assassin, but he did not advise Rankin of this.)

Item 63:   The Report of SA Milton R. Kaack dated October 31, 1963, at New Orleans, Louisiana, which set forth results of additional investigation regarding Oswald.

(The Report of Kaack included the Report of an FBI agent Quigley regarding his interview with a man calling himself Lee Harvey Oswald in New Orleans Police Station on 10 August 1963, when Quigley recorded from 'observation and interrogation' that the height of the man was 5' 9". When this Item was prepared, Hoover was aware from his own files of the 5' 11" height for the assassin recorded by his agents, Carter and Fain, in Fort Worth in June 1962, and of the height of 5' 9" recorded by his agent, Quigley, in New Orleans in August 1963, but he did not advise Rankin of this.)

Item 69:   An airtel from the Washington Field Office to this Bureau dated November 19, 1963, reporting that an informant advised on November 18, 1963 that Lee Harvey Oswald had been in contact with the Soviet Embassy, Mexico City, Mexico.

(This airtel was the result of the discovery of the letter of 9 November 1963 written by 'Lee H. Oswald' from Irving to Consul Reznichenko at the Russian Embassy in Washington. The letter referred to Oswald's 'meetings' with comrade Kostin at the Russian Embassy in Mexico City, stated that it was through the 'stupidity' of the Cuban Consul in Mexico City, that he had been unable to reach the Russian Embassy in Havana 'as planned', stated that he had not used his real name in Mexico, and that the FBI were not 'now interested' in his activities. Hoover did not tell Tankin that the FBI informant had obtained *all* the contents of the letter, and had not only reported 'that Lee Harvey Oswald had been in contact with the Soviet Embassy, Mexico City, Mexico'. Although this letter indicated that the assassin had 'meetings' with Kostin, Hoover did not tell Rankin that these meetings were in addition to the meeting of the American male with Kostikov and perhaps Yatskov. (Author's note: It would seem that at diplomatic level the United States authorities informed the Russian Embassy in Washington that they knew of the existence of the letter. The Russians would not know how or when the Americans discovered its existence, nor how much of the contents were already known to the Americans. After the assassination, the Russians supplied their Washington Embassy file on 'Lee Harvey Oswald' and perforce included the letter and its envelope. They were, however, unaware that the Americans knew that the Russian Embassy in Mexico City had sent a telegram 'to Washington' and to which presumably the Russian Embassy in Washington had replied. The Russian Embassy file supplied to the Americans *excludes the telegram and any reply thereto.* If the FBI informant had not discovered the letter of 9 November the Russian Embassy in Washington might have excluded it from their file supplies to the Americans.)

It has been demonstrated above that (a) Hoover's letter of 6 April 1964 enclosing answers to questions and (b) his letter of 4 May 1964 summarising the contents of the Bureau master file on Oswald in no way informed the Commission of what Hoover knew: (1) that Lee Harvey Oswald was 5' 11" in height when he separated from the Marines and that the assassin was 5' 9", (2) that there were two documented heights of 5' 11" and 5' 9" for the assassin recorded by his agents, the second recording of 5' 9" in New Orleans being confirmed on the arrest of the assassin, (3) that the American male who twice visited the Russian Embassy in Mexico City in the name of 'Lee Oswald' could not be the ex-Marine Oswald nor the assassin, and (4) that there had been two telephone calls to that Embassy by an 'Oswald'.

When Hoover was to testify to the Commission on 14 May 1964, he was neither asked about nor did he volunteer these matters.

On 6 May 1964, Alan H. Belmont testified before the Commission (V.1-32). He said that he had joined the FBI in 1936 and that about June 1961 he had been made assistant to the Director in charge of all investigating work of the FBI in Washington, and that that was his present position. As the individual in charge of all investigative operations, the Lee Harvey Oswald investigation was his responsibility, but prior to the assassination the Oswald case was not of such importance or urgency that it was considered necessary to call it to his attention for personal direction. In regard to Oswald, he said ' ... we have no reason to believe that he was an agent of any other country ... and I could support no conclusion that this was other than an act of Oswald'. He said that there was no credible evidence which would support a conclusion or an opinion that the death of the President was the result of a conspiracy. In regard to Ruby, he said that the FBI has found no evidence to the effect that Ruby was a Communist. In regard to Oswald and Ruby, he said, ' ... we did not come up with anything of a solid nature, that is anything that would stand up to indicate that there was any association between Ruby and Oswald. We had numerous allegations which we ran out extensively and carefully, but there is nothing, no information, that would stand up to show there was an association between them.'

Belmont said that he had supervised the preparation of the FBI answers to the 30 questions contained in Hoover's letter to Rankin of 6 April 1964 and the summaries of the 69 documents in the FBI file contained in Hoover's letter to Rankin of 4 May 1964. When testifying, he had brought with him the 'actual file' as it was maintained at the Bureau 'with all information in it' and he said that he was willing to leave the file for a reasonable time in case any of the Commissioners desired to examine it personally.

It is not satisfactory to quote extracts from Belmont's important testimony relating to the proferred file, and that part of his testimony relating to Hoover's two letters to Rankin (Commission Exhibits Nos. 833 and 834) appears as Appendix A to this book. In short, Belmont offered the file for inspection, Warren appears not to have wished to have the file in the possession of the Commissioners, but the other Commissioners present, Dulles and McCloy, appear to have wished to inspect the file. As a result of the discussions during testimony between Belmont, Warren, Dulles, McCloy and Counsel, it would appear that the FBI file was not scrutinised by any Commissioner at any time.

Belmont did not mention the two heights, and as a result of Hoover's two letters and Belmont's testimony, the attention of the Commission was never drawn to the differing heights and therefore to the possibility of imposture. The Commission were not told by Belmont that a man other than the assassin had visited the Russian Embassy in Mexico City on two occasions while the assassin was secretly in that city, of the two 'bugged' telephone calls, or of Hoover's warning on 3 June 1960 of the possibility of imposture, and therefore were unaware of the possibility of conspiracy in Mexico City. This resulted in their belief that the assassin was ex-Marine Lee Harvey Oswald who was 5' 9" and that it was he who had visited the Russian Embassy on 28 September and 1 October 1963. Having 'glanced' during Marina's testimony at a copy of the letter of 9 November 1963 and having no copy in their hands, none of the six Commissioners then present appears to have been in a position to comprehend its significance.

As mentioned earlier, they knew little if anything of the activities of Albert Osborne *alias* 'John Howard Bowen' and nothing of John Caesar Grossi alias 'Jack Leslie Bowen'.

It would seem that, uninformed, the Commission in their report could only state that the assassin was 5' 9" ex-Marine Lee Harvey Oswald who acted alone, that Jack Ruby acted alone and that there was no connection between the two men.

It is now necessary to consider a matter that recently has come to light; it is the key to the plot and to the Report.

In April 1960, Marguerite Oswald called the FBI in Dallas to say that she was worried about her son, then believed by her to be in Russia, because her last letters to him had been returned to her undelivered, and that she feared for his safety. At a subsequent interview with an FBI agent on 28 April 1960, the agent learned that Oswald had taken his birth certificate with him when he left his mother's house in Fort Worth for New Orleans on 16 September 1959. Hoover was already aware that a man identifying himself as ex-Marine Lee Harvey Oswald had visited the American Embassy in Moscow on 31 October 1959 in order to renounce his United States citizenship and had handed in his passport, but that, although being asked to return in a few days to complete the formalities, he had not reappeared. On 3 June 1960, in a memorandum to the Department of State, Hoover therefore warned the Department that an impostor might be using the identification data of ex-Marine Oswald in the Soviet Union or elsewhere. The memorandum ended, 'Since there is a possibility that an impostor is using Oswald's birth certificate, any current information the Department of State may have concerning subject will be appreciated'. In response to the memorandum the Passport Office warned the American Embassy in Moscow not to *post* Oswald's revalidated passport to him but to *hand* it to him before he left Russia for the United States in May 1962 so that the Embassy officials could be satisfied that they were dealing with 'the real Oswald' who had attempted to renounce his citizenship on 31 October 1959.

It will later be demonstrated in this book that it is possible that the real Oswald never reached Russia, but that even if he did it is more probable than not that it was the impostor in the name of Lee Harvey Oswald who went to the American Embassy in Moscow and handed over the real Oswald's passport. The Embassy never doubted that the man who first visited them in October 1959 was the real Oswald. Having wrongly accepted that this was Oswald, they were content to hand back the revalidated passport to the *same* man. Hoover would have been told by the Department of State that no imposture had been effected; neither he nor his agents gave the matter further consideration until the truth emerged when the impostor was arrested by the Dallas police on 22 November 1963. It might be thought that Hoover should not have relied upon the Department of State – for it is not an investigative agency – but should have instructed his or CIA agents to shadow the man when he left Russia and on his arrival in the United States to check his physical data against that recorded by the Marines and already contained in the FBI file on the alleged defector, Lee Harvey Oswald.

The 'genius' of the Russian plot was to send the impostor to the American Embassy in Moscow on 31 October 1959; thereafter the route to Dealey Plaza would be unimpeded.

Hoover's memorandum and two Department of State memoranda relative thereto are not referred to in the Volumes of Testimony or in the Report, are not shown in the Exhibits, and perhaps were removed from both the FBI and State Department files before submission of their contents to the Commission.

The next Chapter will record the testimony of Hoover for the FBI, McCone and Helms for the CIA, Dillon for the Secret Service, and Rusk for the Department of State.

6

The Federal Bureau of Investigation

On 14 May 1964, Hoover testified *inter alia*: 'When President Johnson returned to Washington (from Dallas) he communicated with me within the first twenty four hours, and asked the Bureau to pick up the investigation of the assassination because as you are aware, there is no Federal jurisdiction for such an investigation. It is not a Federal crime to kill or attack the President or the Vice President or any of the continuity of officers who will succeed to the Presidency. However, the President has a right to request the Bureau to make special investigations, and in this instance he asked that this investigation be made. I immediately assigned a special force headed by the special agent in charge at Dallas, Tex. to initiate the investigation, and to get all the details and facts concerning it, which we obtained, and then prepared a report which we submitted to the Attorney General for transmission to the President ... I have read all of the requests that have come to the Bureau from this Commission, and I have read and signed all the replies that have come to the Commission. In addition, I have read many of the reports that our agents have made and I have been unable to find *any scintilla of evidence* showing any foreign conspiracy or any domestic conspiracy that culminated in the assassination of President Kennedy ... I, personally, feel that any finding of the Commission would not be accepted by everybody, because there are bound to be some extremists who have very pronounced views, without any foundation for them, who would disagree violently with whatever any findings the Commission makes. But I think it is essential that the FBI investigate the allegations that are received in the future so it can't be said that we had ignored them or that the case is closed and forgotten. I would estimate ... that there are at present at least 50 or 60 men giving their entire time to various aspects of the investigation, because while Dallas is the office of origin, investigation is required in auxilliary offices such as Los Angeles or San Francisco, and even in some foreign countries like Mexico. We have representatives in Mexico City.'

A Commissioner then said: ' ... the point that I think ought to be made is that despite the magnitude of the effort that has been made by the FBI and by other agencies, and despite the tremendous effort that has been made, I believe, by the Commission, to help and assist and to consolidate all of the evidence that we possibly could, that there is always the possibility at some future date that some evidence might come to the surface ... I want just to be sure that no leads, no evidence regardless of its credibility will be ignored, that it will be pursued by the Bureau or any other agency to make certain that it is good, bad, or of no value.' Hoover replied, 'Well, I can assure you so far as the FBI is concerned, the case will be continued in an open classification for all time ... I think this will be questions asked by individuals, either for publicity purpose or otherwise, that will raise some new angle or some new aspect of it. I think we must, and certainly intend in the FBI to continue to run down any such allegations or reports of that kind'.

A Commissioner then said: 'I read the FBI report (on the assassination: A four-volume summary on 9 December 1963 and one supplement on 13 January 1964) very carefully and the whole implication of the report is that No.1, Oswald shot the President; No.2, that he was not connected with any conspiracy of any kind, nature or description. Do you still subscribe to that?' Hoover replied, 'I subscribe to it even more strongly today than I did at the time the report was written. You see, the original idea was that there would be an investigation by the FBI and a report would be prepared in such form that it could be released to the public ... Then a few days later, after further consideration the President decided to form a Commission, which I think was very wise, because I feel the report of any agency of Government ought to be reviewed by an impartial group such as this Commission. And the more I have read these reports, the more I am convinced that Oswald was the man who fired the gun; and he fired three times; killed the President and wounded Governor Connally. And I also am further convinced that there is absolutely no association between Oswald and Ruby. There was no such evidence ever established ... There was suspicion at first this might be a Castro act'.

Although Hoover said that the FBI knew of Oswald's contact with the Russian Embassy in Washington by letter of 9 November 1963 but that this contact gave no 'indication of any tendency to commit violence', he said nothing about Oswald and the 75 years old Albert Osborne, nothing about Oswald and the 38 years old John Caesar Grossi, nothing about the approximately 35 years old American male's two visits to the Russian Embassy in Mexico City, and did not mention Reznichenko, Yatskov, Kostikov or Kostin. He did not mention that the contents of the letter of 9 November 1963 written by Oswald to Reznichenko in Washington shortly before the assassination had come into the hands of the FBI in Washington on 18 November 1963, although the field office of the FBI in Dallas did not receive information about the letter and its contents until the morning of 22 November 1963, nor that the FBI agent in charge of Oswald's file in Dallas did not read this communication until shortly after the assassination. He did not mention Nosenko's alleged defection to the United States some three months prior to his (Hoover's) testimony and which must have been known to him. He did not mention his own warning of 3 June 1960 against the possibility of imposture.

Hoover testified of Oswald: ' ... We went back into his Marine Corps record. He was a 'loner'. He didn't have many friends. He kept to himself, and when he went abroad he defected to Russia ... and then later, about 22 months later, he returned to the (United States) Embassy there and according to the report at the Embassy we have and which the Commission has furnished, the Embassy gave him a clean bill. He had seen the error of his ways and disliked the Soviet atmosphere, et cetera, and they therefore, cleared him, paid his way and paid his wife's way to come back to this country ... He had been over there long enough but they never gave him citizenship in Russia at all. And I think they probably looked upon him more as a kind of

queer sort of individual and they didn't trust him too strongly ...
In Oswald's case we had no suspicion that any pressure like that
had been brought to bear on him because he had gone
voluntarily and had obviously wanted to live in Russia and had
married a Russian woman.'

Although Hoover discussed Oswald's Marine Corps record, he
did not inform the Commission that Oswald's height had been
recorded as 5' 11'' when he separated from the Marines, nor did
he mention the mastoidectomy and the other scars stated on the
Marine records, and that the post mortem report on the body of
the assassin indicated differences.

Hoover testified of Ruby: ' ... Ruby comes from Chicago, he
was on the fringe of what you might call the elements of the
underworld there. He came to Dallas, opened up a nightclub and
it was a place where, certainly not the better class of people
went, but it wasn't any so-called joint, to use the vernacular. It
was just a nightclub.' Hoover's opinion of Ruby and his
nightclub takes little account of the many interviews conducted
by his own agents in Dallas with people who subscribed
information about Ruby. By socially elevating both him and his
'joint', Hoover apparently was suggesting that Ruby was
unimportant and might have murdered the assassin for the
emotional motives that Ruby had profferred at his trial for this
murder, and not for the apparent purpose of silencing him.

Hoover testified of Marina: 'I think his wife was a far more
reliable person in statements that she made so far as we were able
to ascertain, than his mother. I think the mother had in mind,
naturally, the fact that she wanted to clear her son's name, which
was a natural instinct, and more importantly she was going to see
how much money she could make, and I believe she has made a
substantial sum ... There is no way of knowing whether she
(Marina) belonged to the Russian Communist party in Russia.
She is a rather intelligent woman, and notwithstanding that you
have to talk with her through an interpreter, 'we have no
indication of her association with communists in this country,
nor have any of her close friends or relatives. As to his
(Oswald's) mother, we found no indication she is associated or
closely associated with the communists. She is the only one of the
group that we have come in contact with that I would say is

somewhat emotionally unstable. Our agents have interviewed her. She sometimes gets very angry and she won't answer questions.' Hoover did not mention that from 1959 through 1961 Oswald's mother had made substantial efforts in person and by correspondence to persuade the authorities in Washington to recover her son from Russia, wrongly suspecting that he must have gone there as an agent on behalf of the CIA. She had apparently based her belief upon the fact that he had not mentioned Russia to her before he left her house in Fort Worth for New Orleans on 16 September 1959, and she testified that she was surprised when she heard that he was in Russia. Hoover did not mention the large amounts of money Marina may have received from various sources, (perhaps $200,000), and that they greatly exceeded the amount that Marguerite may have received (perhaps $1000).

Hoover knew, however, (a) that Marina had told the United States Embassy in Moscow that she had not been a member of Komsomol – the Communist Party Youth organisation in Russia to be later described; an admission of membership might have prevented her admittance to the United States; (b) that the uncle with whom she lived in Minsk was a Colonel in the Secret Police (MVD) and was a member of the Communist Party; (c) that after the assassination she had been interviewed on some 46 occasions by FBI agents and had been consistently untruthful when denying any prior knowledge of her husband's secret trip to Mexico seven weeks previously, and (d) when testifying to the Commission in February 1964 through an interpreter, she said, 'I will not be charged with anything', and that she had not been sworn in before but now, inasmuch as she was sworn in, she was going to tell the truth (I.14).

It would seem that Hoover wished to discredit the testimony of the mother who appears to have told and been dangerously near the truth, and by comparison to emphasize Marina's reliability, her veracity being the keystone of the conclusions of the Commission, their Report quoting extensively from her supporting testimony.

Hoover continued: 'But just the day before yesterday (12 May 1964) information came to me indicating that there is an espionage training school outside Minsk – I don't know whether it is true — and that he (Oswald) was trained at that school to come back to this country to become what they call a 'sleeper', that is a man who will remain dormant for three or four years and in case of international hostilities rise up and be used. I don't know of any espionage school at Minsk or near Minsk, and I don't know how you could find out if there ever was one because the Russians won't tell you if you ask them. They do have espionage and sabotage schools in Russia and they do have an assassination squad that is used by them but there is no indication he had any association with anything of that kind.' (Oswald is alleged by the Russians and by himself to have resided in Moscow for some two months before leaving for Minsk where he lived for some two and a half years. In reply to an interim Commission Interrogatory (XXVI.111), the CIA stated that an earlier defector had disclosed that in 1947 there existed a spy school in Minsk.)

Hoover did not mention Jaggars-Chiles-Stovall and therefore did not mention Oswald's employment in the firm, nor that this employment was obtained by a trick, nor that on his first working day he had executed work for the Army Map Service. He did not tell the Commission that the assassin's friend Grossi under the alias of 'Jack Leslie Bowen' had been employed at Jaggars-Chiles-Stovall at the same time as the assassin. Hoover did not call the attention of the Commission to the fact that under the name of the firm in Oswald's notebook, Oswald had written the word 'microdots', nor that Oswald's spying equipment had been found.

Hoover continued: 'There was no question but that the gun and the telescopic lens could pinpoint the President perfectly. The car was moving slowly. It wasn't going at a high rate of speed, so that he had a perfect opportunity to do it.' He was asked by a Commissioner whether it did not seem to him that defectors who returned to the United States should be given some special attention to determine whether they were a risk to become Soviet or Communist espionage agents, or in fact become dangerous. He replied, 'We have taken steps to plug that gap.'

Hoover continued: 'In going back over the record, and I have read each of the reports dealing with that and the reports of Mr.

Hosty (an FBI agent) who had dealt with the Oswald situation largely in Dallas, we have the matter that I have previously referred to, the report of the State Department that indicated that this man was a thoroughly safe risk, he had changed his views, he was a loyal man and had seen the light of day, so to speak. *How intensive or how extensive that interview in Moscow was, I don't know.* But, nevertheless, it was in a State Department document that was furnished to us.' (Testimony of Hoover with author's italics: V.97-120.)

The Central Intelligence Agency

When Hoover had completed his testimony, the Commission took the testimony of John A. McCone and Richard M. Helms, respectively Director and Deputy Director of the CIA. They testfied together *inter alia*: 'We made an investigation of all developments after the assassination which came to our attention which might possibly have indicated a conspiracy, and we determined after these investigations, which were made promptly and immediately, that we had no evidence to support such an assumption.' When asked whether their agency had made a particular investigation in connection with any allegations about a conspiracy involving the Soviet Union or people connected with Cuba, they replied: 'Yes, we did. We made a thorough, a very thorough investigation of information that came to us concerning an alleged trip that Oswald made to Mexico City during which time he made contact with the Cuban Embassy in Mexico City in an attempt to gain transit privilege from Mexico City to the Soviet Union via Havana. We investigated that thoroughly.' When asked, 'Do you also include in your statement that you found no evidence of conspiracy in all of that investigation?', the reply was, 'That is correct' and 'We have no evidence that he was working for or on behalf of the Soviet Union at any time'. When asked whether the CIA investigated any aspects of Oswald's trip to Mexico, they replied: 'Yes; we did ... We were aware that Oswald did make a trip to Mexico City and it was our judgment that he was there in the interest of ensuring transit privileges and that he made contact with the Cuban Embassy while he was there. We do not know the precise results of his efforts, but we assume, because he returned to the United States he was unsuccessful. We have examined to every extent we can, and using all resources available to us, every aspect of his activity, and we could not verify that he was there for any other purpose or that his trip to Mexico was in any way related to his later action in assassinating President Kennedy.'

Although it was a CIA informant who had twice reported the presence of the American male in the Russian Embassy in Mexico City and some of his activities while there – including being photographed, the representatives of the CIA did not refer to his visits to the *Russian* Embassy in Mexico City in the name of 'Lee Oswald' and did not point out that he was not the assassin. They did not mention Reznichenko, Yatskov, Kostikov, Kostin or the American male. They did not mention the alleged defector, Nosenko, who must have been debriefed by the CIA. Helms did not mention his two affidavits. (Testimony of McCone and Helms with author's italics: V. 120-129.)

The Secret Service

On 2 September 1964, C. Douglas Dillon testified before the Commission. He was the Secretary of the Treasury, and as such was responsible for the Secret Service of the United States. His testimony was almost entirely devoted to the past, present and future protection of the President, Vice President and others in line for the Presidency, and during his lengthy testimony there was only a short reference to the assassin. After disposing of the rumour that Oswald might have been an agent of the Secret Service, Dillon was asked, 'Do you know of any area of the investigation of the Commission that you would like to suggest that we do more than we have insofar as you are familiar with it?', Dillon replied, 'No. As far as I know, the investigation has been very thorough'. When asked, 'Do you know of any credible evidence that would lead you or anyone to believe that there was a conspiracy, foreign or domestic, involved in the assassination of the President?", he replied, 'No. From all the evidence that I have seen, this was the work of one deranged individual ... Lee Harvey Oswald'. When asked, 'Is there anything that you would like to call to the attention of the Commission at this time that we should know or that we should cover?', he replied, 'No. I think we have covered my area of competence pretty thoroughly this morning. I can't think of anything else'.

He did not mention that it was Secret Service agents who, on 23 and 24 November, went to the premises of Jaggars-Chiles-Stovall to investigate and presumably to discover the activities of the spy in that 'sensitive' firm. He did not mention that on 23 November 1963 the CIA had informed the Secret Service that they had several photographs of the American male believed by the CIA at the time of photography to be 'identical with Lee Harvey Oswald', although on 22 and 23 November the FBI, the CIA and the Secret Service knew that they were not identical. (Testimony of Dillon: V573-588).

The Department of State

The evidence indicates that if a substitution for the real Oswald was made, it was more probably than not effected in Russia and, if so, may have been at any time after he crossed the border from Finland on 15 October 1959.

The Department's contacts with Oswald had been considerable. Their passport division had issued Oswald with a passport in September 1959, showing his height as 5′ 11″. After he entered Russia, he (or an impostor) visited the United States Embassy in Moscow on five occasions. The first visit was on Saturday 31 October 1959, and he handed over his passport to Embassy officials saying that he renounced his citizenship and had applied for Soviet citizenship. His attitude was arrogant and he said that he would supply the Russians with what he had learned as a radar operator in the Marines. He was advised to think over his renunciation and come back in a couple of days to complete the formalities should his mind be unchanged. He never went back to renounce his United States citizenship, thereby leaving the door open for a return to the United States at a later date. (In making their decision to give Oswald time to think the matter over, the officials had been greatly influenced by the case of Petrulli, a man who only a month earlier had renounced his citizenship, which had been accepted forthwith by the Embassy officials, but the Russians had then refused to allow him to stay in the country. The Embassy had thus been placed in a difficult position for they now had a stateless citizen on their hands. They had managed, however, to return Petrulli to the United States on the basis that he had not been in a fit state of mind when he had attempted to renounce his citizenship.) Fifteen months after Oswald's first visit to the Embassy, the Embassy received a letter from him expressing a wish to return to his own country. In due course his passport was renewed, valid only for a journey direct to the United States, and handed back to him. Oswald, who during the last part of his stay in Russia had re-visited the Embassy on four occasions, finally told the Embassy officials that he had 'learned a hard lesson the hard way', and now appreciated the United States and the meaning of freedom.

In the meantime, Oswald had married Marina and as there had been delay in the Russians giving her permission to leave, the United States Embassy tried to persuade Oswald to return to his own country and to leave Marina behind to join him at a later date. This suggestion was refused, Oswald protesting that he might not see his wife again. After considerable correspondence between Oswald and the Embassy, and between the Embassy and the Department of State in Washington, it was agreed that Oswald had not expatriated himself and that he could return to the United States with Marina and their newly-born daughter, June. In allowing Marina to enter the United States, the Department had persuaded the Immigration and Naturalisation Service to withdraw their objection under Section 243 (g) of the Immigration and Nationality Act of 1952 to the admittance of Marina to the United States, and the Department then loaned Oswald $435.71 to assist him and his family in travelling from Moscow to New York.

On Saturday 23 November 1963, the Department issued a statement to *The Washington Post*, and the newspaper reported, 'Today in Washington State Department officials said they have no evidence indicating involvement of any foreign power in the assassination'. The ordinary reader might have construed these words as the Department's belief based on evidence that there had been no foreign involvement; the proper statement to the press should have been – as the Department should have known – 'A man has been charged, the matter is now *sub judice* and no comment can be made'.

During the testimony of the Secretary of State to be mentioned below, a Commissioner referred to a newspaper report which he had seen shortly after the assassination, and that it had said, '*The Voice of America* beaming its message into Russia immediately blamed the reactionary rightwing movements after Kennedy's death.' During his testimony, the Secretary of State undertook to supply the Commission with copies of all broadcast scripts but, as these do not appear in the Volumes of Exhibits, it is not possible to ascertain the day or the time when this broadcast went out, nor its content.

If the assassin was not Lee Harvey Oswald, then the man who married Marina and who visited the Embassy in Moscow on five occasions was not Lee Harvey Oswald. The Department of State had erred in accepting him at his face value, and then overruling the objections of the Immigration and Naturalisation Service to the admittance of Marina to the United States – thus their apparent anxiety forthwith to blame the rightwing in the United States and to exculpate any foreign power, perhaps having learned from the FBI that the assassin and the man who visited their Embassy were one and the same man, and probably an impostor.

On 10 June 1964, the Hon Dean Rusk, Secretary of State, testified *inter alia*: 'I would like to be just as helpful as possible to the Commission. I am not quite clear of testimony in terms of future publication. There may be certain points that arise where it might be helpful for the Commission for me to comment on certain points but there – it would be a very grave difficulty about publication, so I wonder what the Commission's view is on that.' Chief Justice Warren replied, 'Well, Mr Secretary, our purpose is to have available for the public all the evidence that is given here. If there is any phase of it that you think might jeopardise *the security of the Nation*, have no hesitation in asking us to go off the record for a moment, and you can tell us what you wish'. A Commissioner asked, 'Would it be feasible to have a discussion here of the points that are vital from the point of view of our record, and so forth, and maybe a little informal conversation afterward to cover the other points?'. The

Commission then recessed and, when back on the record, Rusk was asked, 'In your opinion, was there any substantial interest or interests for the Soviet Union which would have been advanced by the assassination of President Kennedy?'. Rusk replied, 'I would first have to say on a question of that sort that it is important to follow the evidence. It is very difficult to look into the mind of someone else and to know what is in someone else's mind. I have seen no evidence that would indicate to me that the Soviet Union considered that it had an interest in the removal of President Kennedy or that it was in any way involved in the removal of President Kennedy ... I was with several colleagues in a plane on the way to Japan at the time the assassination occurred. When we got the news we immediately turned back. After my mind was able to grasp the fact that this event had in fact occurred, which was the first necessity, and not an easy one, I then, on the plane, began to go over the dozens and dozens of implications and ramifications of this event as it affects our foreign relations all over the world ... But one of the great questions in my mind at that time was just that question could some foreign government somehow be involved in such an episode. I realised that were this so this would raise *the gravest issues of war or peace*, but that nevertheless it was important to try to get at the truth – the answer to that question – wherever that truth might lead; and so, when I got back to Washington I put myself immediately in touch with the processes of inquiry on that point and as Secretary of State had the deepest possible interest in what the truthful answer to those questions would be, because it would be hard to think of anything more pregnant for our foreign relations than the correct answer to that question. I have not seen or heard of any scrap of evidence indicating that the Soviet Union had any desire to eliminate President Kennedy nor in any way participated in any such event'. Rusk proceeded to develop this argument and said, 'I think also that it is relevant that people behind the Iron Curtain, including people in the Soviet Union and including officials in the Soviet Union, seemed to be deeply affected by the death of President Kennedy. Their reactions were prompt and, I think genuine, of regret and sorrow. Mr Khrushchev was the first to come to the Embassy to sign the book of condolences. There were tears in the streets of

Moscow. Moscow radio spent a great deal of attention to these matters. Now they did come to premature conclusions, in my judgement, about what this event was and what it meant in terms of who might have been responsible for it and – ideology effect has crept into that. But I have the impression that the regret was genuine and that the ordinary Soviet citizen joined with ordinary people in other parts of the world in feeling the loss of the President in a very genuine sense'.

Rusk was then asked if he could give an opinion to the Commission in regard to Cuba in the same general way, and he replied, 'Well, I would again repeat that the overriding consideration is to make every possible effort to find evidence and follow the evidence to wherever it leads. I think it is, at least for me, more difficult to try to enter into the minds of the present leadership in Cuba than, perhaps, even of the present leadership of the Soviet Union. We have had very few contacts, as the Commission knows, with the present government of Cuba. But again, I have seen no evidence that seems to point in that direction. There were some exchanges, with which the Commission is familiar, that seemed to be – seemed to come to another conclusion. But I would think that objective considerations would be that it would be even greater madness for Castro or his government to be involved in that question. We were under the impression that there was very considerable concern in Cuba as to whether they would be held responsible and what the effect of that might be on their own position and their own safety. But I have seen no evidence that points to involvement by them, and I don't see any objective facts which would seem to make it in their interests to remove Mr Kennedy. You see, this embarks upon, in any event it would embark upon, an unpredictable trail for them to go down this path, but I would think again the Commission would wish to examine the evidence as it had been doing with meticulous care and follow the evidence in these matters'. When asked whether there was any possibility that the Government of Mexico could have been in any way involved, Rusk replied, ' ... we never had the slightest view that Mexico was involved in this, the problem, the question arose because Mr. Oswald had been in Mexico, and was known to have been in touch with some Cubans at the Cuban Embassy in Mexico. But the Mexican authorities gave us complete and most helpful co-operation in full investigation of this matter'. Rusk did not mention the Russian Embassies in Mexico City and Washington (Yatskov, Kostikov, Kostin and Reznichenko), the defector Nosenko or Hoover's memorandum to the Department of State of 3 June 1960 and the two Department memoranda relative thereto. (Testimony of Rusk with author's italics: V. 353-371.)

The Commission did *not* write their Report, it was constructed by others and presented to the members of the Commission for their approval and signatures. The first paragraph of Chapter 1 of the Report (R.1) says: 'The assassination of John Fitzgerald Kennedy on November 22, 1963, was a cruel and shocking act of violence directed against a man, a family, a nation and against all mankind. A young and vigorous leader whose years of public and private life stretched before him was the victim of the fourth Presidential assassination in the history of a country dedicated to the concepts of reasoned argument and peaceful political change. This Commission was created on November 29, 1963, in recognition of the right of people everywhere to full and truthful knowledge concerning these events. This report endeavors to fulfill that right and to appraise this tragedy by the light of reason and the standard of fairness. It has been prepared with a deep awareness of the Commission's responsibility to present to the American people an objective report of the facts relating to the assassination'.

The wording is credible only if the Commissioners were unaware of pertinent material, such as Hoover's 3 June 1960 warning to the State Department of the possibility of substitution. Had the Commission examined the complete FBI file on 'Lee Harvey Oswald' and then questioned the representatives of the federal agencies, the evidence thus obtained would have disclosed the discrepancies between the Marine and the assassin, and the conspiracy in Mexico City. If made public, apart from disclosing the errors of the FBI and possibly others, this might perhaps have raised what President Johnson appears to have feared:

THE GRAVEST ISSUES OF WAR OR PEACE

I make no apology for again mentioning Hoover's memorandum to the State Department of 3 June 1960, and for drawing attention to the fact that on reading through the file Hoover would almost immediately have seen this document. He would then have realised that (a) the Dallas FBI had waited 12 days before interviewing the 'returning defector' after his arrival in the United States, and (b) that their attention had not been drawn by the 'domestic intelligence' department at the Bureau of the FBI to the possibility of imposture. If Hoover knew that no substitution for Oswald had been effected there would have been no reason for his memorandum to be withheld from the Commission by the FBI and the Department of State. A conclusion that can be drawn is that on the late afternoon of 22 November 1963 Hoover became aware that it was through the errors of the Department of State and the FBI that the President had been assassinated, and that there had occurred what he appears to have feared:

IMPERSONATION OF THE MARINE

The next Chapter will recount the apparent discrepancies between Marine Lee Harvey Oswald and the man who assassinated the President.

7

'In view of the intensity of his earlier commitment to the Soviet Union, a great change must have occurred in Oswald's thinking to induce him to return to the United States.' The Report of the Commission (R.394).

Whatever change in Oswald's thinking must have occurred, there was a great change in his physical data when he entered the United States in June 1962. The conflicting heights will first be discussed at length.

Below are the details of Marine Oswald's height from 1956 to 1959 inclusive, as recorded by the Marines or given by Oswald himself:

1. On 24 October 1956, when just 17 years of age, Oswald enlisted in the Marines and his height was recorded as 5' 8" (XIX.615.656).
2. On 28 December 1956, on completion of initial training, Oswald's height was recorded by the Marines as 5' 9" (XIX.717).
3. On 4 March 1959, Oswald applied for admission to the Albert Schweitzer College in Switzerland to attend the Spring term in 1960, and on the application form he gave his height as 5' 11" (XVI.622).
4. On 3 September 1959, at Santa Ana, California, Oswald underwent a full medical examination prior to his release from the Marines and transfer to the inactive reserve. His height was taken and recorded by a Marine doctor (Vincent) as 71" (XIX.584.XXIII.744).
5. On 4 September 1959, Oswald applied for a passport and gave his height as 5' 11" (XXII.77).
6. On 10 September 1959, Oswald was issued a passport recording his height as 5' 11" (XVIII.161).

7. On 11 September 1959, at Santa Ana, Oswald was issued with a Department of Defense Identification card by a Marine officer (Ayers) who took and recorded his height as 71″ (XIX.720.R.616).

8. On 14 September 1959, at the Fort Worth, Texas, Local Board, Oswald was issued with a Marine Selective Service System Registration card on which his height was recorded by a Marine official as 5′ 11″ (XXIII.294.743).

A few days later, Oswald was on his way to Russia and if the story had ended there, commonsense and the records would have indicated that Marine Oswald was 5′ 11″ in height in September 1959.

Shortly after his arrival in Russia in October 1959, Oswald went to the American Embassy in Moscow to renounce his citizenship and handed over his passport which showed his height as 5′ 11″. A few days later, Oswald was interviewed by a journalist at the hotel in which he was staying, and she recorded his height in her notes as 5′ 9″. Some three days later another journalist interviewed Oswald at the same hotel and she recorded his height in her notes as 5′ 11″. They were the only journalists to interview him at length and to record the height given them by the man they interviewed; it is significant that these are the precise heights of the assassin and the Marine, 5′ 9″ and 5′ 11″.

In June 1962, Oswald entered the United States with his Russian born wife, Marina, and infant daughter, June, using Oswald's original passport showing the bearer's height to be 5′ 11″.

After arriving in the United States, Oswald was twice to give his height as 5′ 11″ and many times as 5′ 9″. These different heights were recorded at different times by the FBI, the New Orleans police, the Dallas police, two doctors at Parkland Hospital in Dallas, or given by Oswald himself:–

1. On 26 June 1962, being twelve days after he had entered the United States from Russia, Oswald was interviewed by appointment at the offices of the FBI in Fort Worth, Texas, by Special Agents Carter and Fain who were trained in anti-subversive activities. The interview lasted between 1½ and 2 hours and in a written report on this interview under the heading, 'From observation and interrogation', is a

physical description of 'Lee Harvey Oswald' giving his height as 5' 11" (XVII.730). In reply to their question about the height of his wife, Oswald added two inches to her height, saying that she was 5' 5" (XVII.730). Her height as shown in her Russian passport issued on 11 January 1962 was 5' 3" (XVI.138).

2. On 13 July 1962, Oswald completed an application form for employment at Leslie Welding Company, Fort Worth, stating his height as 5' 9" (XXIV.885).

3. On 14 August 1962, Oswald was reinterviewed at Fort Worth by FBI agent Fain who this time was accompanied by FBI agent Brown. Oswald did not correct the false heights that he had given at the first interview, and his file was then given a 'closed status' (IV.403-430).

4. On 10 October 1962, Oswald, having now moved from Fort Worth to Dallas, registered with the Texas Employment Commission, stating his height as 5' 9" (XIX.399).

5. On 12 October 1962, Oswald completed an employment questionnaire at Jaggars-Chiles-Stovall, Dallas, stating his height as 5' 9" (XVII.156).

6. In April 1963, Oswald, having now moved from Dallas to New Orleans, Louisiana, registered with the local Department of Labour, stating his height as 5' 9" (XXI.282).

7. On 9 May 1963, Oswald completed an application for employment at William B. Reily Company, New Orleans, stating his height as 5' 9".(XXIV.902).

8. On 10 May 1963, Oswald's employee's Withholding Exemption Certificate recorded his height as 5' 9" (XXIV.905).

9. On 24 June 1963, Oswald applied in New Orleans for a new passport and on the application form stated his height as 5' 11" (XVII.666). (The original 1959 passport showed a height of 5' 11" and the 1963 application had to tally to avoid complications and perhaps suspicion at the Passport Office in Washington.)

10. On 25 June 1963, Oswald was issued with a new passport in the name of Lee Harvey Oswald giving his height as 5' 11"

(XXIII.819).

11. On 9 August 1963, Oswald was arrested by the New Orleans police for causing a (minor) disturbance on the street, and the Police Identification Bureau recorded his name as Lee Harvey Oswald, and measured against a scale and recorded his height as 5' 9" (XXII.820.828).

12. On 10 August 1963, Oswald was interviewed by FBI agent Quigley at New Orleans police station. Included in Quigley's report of this interview under the headings, 'Lee Harvey Oswald' ... 'Physical description obtained by obervation and interrogation', the man's height was recorded by Quigley as 5' 9" (XVII.762).

13. On 15 October 1963, having now returned to Dallas, Oswald completed an application for employment at the Texas School Book Depository, Dallas, stating his height as 5' 9" (XVII.210).

14. On 9 November 1963, Oswald partly filled in an application for a driver's licence, stating his height as 5' 9" (XVI.483).

15. On 22 November 1963, Oswald was arrested by the Dallas police and his height was, apparently inaccurately, recorded as 5' 9½" (XVII.285). The police found in his wallet the 1959 Marine Selective Service System Registration card which recorded the height of the Marine as 5' 11" (R.615) together with the Department of Defense Identification card recording his height as 5' 11" (R.616). Also in his wallet they found the counterfeit Selective Service System Registration card in the fictitious name of 'Alek James Hidell' on which the height of Hidell was recorded as 5' 9" (XVII.682-683.R.615).

16. On the evening of 22 November 1963, at Dallas police station FBI agent Clements interviewed Oswald for the purpose of obtaining 'descriptive and biographical' data. Clements' report recorded the height of 'Lee Harvey Oswald' as 5' 9" (R.614). Clements also observed and recorded the contents of the three cards mentioned in No.15 above.

17. On 24 November 1963, an autopsy was performed on the body of Oswald by two doctors at Parkland Hospital,

Dallas. The report of the autopsy recorded the length of the corpse as 5' 9" (XXVI.521).

It would appear from the evidence supplied by the above details that Marine Oswald was 5' 11" when he left the United States for Russia in September 1959, and that in June 1962 an impostor calling himself Lee Harvey Oswald and whose height was 5' 9" entered the United States accompanied by his Russian wife and child. It will be noted that on two occasions when he was not measured – the FBI interview in Fort Worth and the passport application in New Orleans – the man was able to give the false height 5' 11" in order to maintain that he was the real 5' 11" Lee Harvey Oswald. If while in Russia the real Oswald had discovered that his height was only 5' 9" it would have caused him no great harm to disclose the earlier misapprehension about his height to the two FBI agents who interviewed him in Fort Worth after he had arrived in the United States in June 1962, or even to the Passport Office in New Orleans in June 1963. It would appear, therefore, that the man interviewed by the FBI agents in Fort Worth deceived them about his own and his wife's heights; the addition of two inches to Marina's height seemingly was (a) a safeguard in case the FBI were to see them standing or walking together, or (b) to emphasise that he was 'vague' about heights. The Report of the Commission, in addition to disregarding the several recorded heights of 5' 11" for Oswald in 1959 and again in 1962 (FBI, Fort Worth) and 1963 (Passport, New Orleans), does not mention the addition of two inches to Marina's height.

The Commission should have questioned closely the two FBI agents, Carter and Fain, as to how they had obtained the height which they had recorded as 5' 11" when they interviewed the man in Fort Worth, for the Commission were aware that the height of the assassin was 5' 9". But they did not do so and called only Fain to testify, to whom they put no question either about the height of 5' 11" that he had recorded, or about the irreconcilable 5' 9" height of the assassin. The Marine doctor and officials not being asked to testify, the Commission should have demanded that the FBI interview them to obtain statements and any supporting photographic evidence of the taking of Marine Oswald's height in 1959, but there is no record in the Exhibits of FBI interviews with these officials, nor is there any record that either the Commission or the FBI attempted to verify that the correct height of Marina was 5' 3".

As Oswald's Marine medical and other records were obtained from Marine headquarters by the FBI and appear in the Exhibits, the FBI knew that the Marine doctor (Vincent) had recorded Oswald's height as 71" (5' 11") on 3 September 1959, and that the Marine officer (Ayres) had recorded this height on 11 September. Their attention had been specifically drawn to the two heights by the discovery that on arrest the 5' 9" assassin was carrying genuine Marine cards that recorded Marine Oswald's height as 5' 11", and they would have checked the recorded height of 71" in the Marine records against the stated height of 5' 11" shown on the Marine cards. It should have appeared unlikely that on different dates Vincent and Ayres could have read 71" for 69".

The Report quotes extensively from the report of the two agents, Carter and Fain, who interviewed Owwald in Fort Worth in June 1962 (R.434-435), but does not mention the assassin's deception of the agents about his height or that of Marina. The Report states correctly that Oswald was just 17 years old and 5' 8" when he enlisted in the Marines in October 1956 and was 5' 9" when he was arrested (R.681.144) but says nothing about his height of 5' 11" when released from the Marines in September 1959 (R.688-689). The Exhibits do not include a photographic record (if any) of the taking of Oswald's height by Vincent and Ayres in September 1959, although Marine photographs of his height taken on 28 December 1956 with the usual readable scale at the back of his head showing 5' 9", appear prominently twice in the Exhibits (XIX.656.717). The date, however, 28 December 1956, appears only on the bottom of one of the photographs and in what might be described as the 'small print'. The Report does not say that the recording of this 5' 9" height was in 1956 and does not comment upon the fact that after ten weeks training Oswald had grown one inch, nor that, according to the conclusion of the Commission, he had ceased to grow on or just before that date, although just seventeen years of age. A student of the Report and the Exhibits could be misled − by a combination of (a) the omission of any mention of 5' 11" in the Report, (b) the statement in the Report that the assassin was Marine Oswald and 5′ 9″ in height, and (c) the two 5′ 9″ photographs of Marine Oswald in the Exhibits — into assuming that when Oswald was released from the Marines in September 1959 he had grown only one inch since October 1956.

That the Commission were aware that the man interviewed by the two agents in Fort Worth might have been wearing elevated footwear to assist him in deceiving the agents, appears to be shown by the testimony of the assassin's landlady, Mrs Bledsoe, about his arrival at her roominghouse on 7 October 1963 where he was to rent a room for a week. The matter of footwear was raised by *her* in testimony before the Commission:

BLEDSOE: 'Now, I think he said he was going to get some more (luggage). He was going to get some more and he had some boots, too, in his hand. I — maybe he brought those the last time. I don't remember.

COUNSEL: What kind of boots?

BLEDSOE: Well, they looked like they were about up to here (indicating).

COUNSEL: Up to the knees?

BLEDSOE: No: about to there (indicating).

COUNSEL: Oh —

BLEDSOE: There.

COUNSEL: Just a little above the ankle?

BLEDSOE: Uh-huh.

COUNSEL: About three inches above the ankle?

BLEDSOE: I don't know what they used them for.

COUNSEL: Were they cowboy boots?

BLEDSOE: No: it wasn't cowboy boots.

COUNSEL: Were they canvas, leather, or rubber?

BLEDSOE: No: just leather.

COUNSEL: Heavy soled?

BLEDSOE: Heavy soled.

COUNSEL: Heavy soled. Rubber soles?

BLEDSOE: Oh, no; leather.

COUNSEL: Any hobnails in them?

BLEDSOE: No.

COUNSEL: Hard heel or flat heel? I mean, flat sole and heel?

BLEDSOE: Oh, they had a heel, too. I remember them having

that'. (VI.420-421)

The Exhibits contain a photograph of the assassin's possessions including sandals and shoes, but there are no photographs of boots, and presumably none were found. Marina was not asked by the Commission or any law enforcement agency whether her husband possessed a pair of boots and, if so, to describe them.

When Oswald was in Russia he wrote often to his brother, Robert Oswald, 5 years his senior and living in the United States, and in one of his letters he asked Robert if he would like him to send him a pair of Russian boots, and to mark the size of his foot on a piece of paper and send it to him. Robert did not do this but would not have been surprised to see Oswald on his return from Russia wearing high-heeled Russian boots. Oswald did bring back a pair of Russian boots from Russia and these were observed by an acquaintance (Paul Gregory) shortly after the two interviews with the FBI agents in Fort Worth. Furthermore, boots or shoes with slightly higher heels than usual but with a build-up *inside* the back have been on sale for many years in the western world advertised with the words, 'Add two inches to your height'.

Other discrepancies between Lee Harvey Oswald and the man who came from Russia will now be discussed.

When Oswald was six years old he was admitted to a hospital in Fort Worth with acute mastoiditis and a mastoidectomy was performed behind his left ear. The operation leaves a life-long scar of about 1-1½″, and a depression where bone has been removed, the depression sometimes filling up around middle age. The mastoidectomy and the scar were noted on Oswald's Marine health records in 1956 and 1959 (XIX.582-590).

On 24 November 1963, Doctor Earl Forrest Rose, Dallas County Medical Examiner, together with Dr Sidney Stewart, performed an autopsy on the body of the assassin in Parkland Hospital, Dallas. Commencing with the head, the doctors examined the body externally from the crown of the head to the soles of the feet, recording some slight wounds, scratches and bruises on the head that the assassin had sustained in his struggle with the police on arrest, and also other wounds, marks and scars on his body. Incisions were made behind both ears over the mastoid area preparatory to cutting round the back of the head and peeling the scalp to expose the skull, so that the upper part of the skull could be removed for the purpose of extracting the brain and examining the interior of the head. The upper neck was also examined, and this examination would take the doctors up to the mastoid area. The post mortem report on the autopsy (XXIV. 7-11) says under the heading, 'Scalp, Skull, Cranial Cavity and Dura'; Not remarkable. No evidence of injury is noted'. Under the heading 'Neck Organs', the report says 'They are not remarkable. The hyoid is intact. No evidence of injury is noted. The thyroid is not remarkable grossly.'

Neither the mastoidectomy scar nor bone removal was recorded, and it is difficult to accept that two doctors performing an autopsy upon the body of the alleged assassin of the President could have missed the external and internal evidence of mastoidectomy had such an operation been performed. That the autopsy was carried out with special interest is established by the fact that Dr Rose took 27 colour 35mm. Kodachrome slides during the autopsy, later exhibiting them to the FBI but retaining them in his possession.

Although the report of the autopsy appears in the Exhibits, the Commission's Report does not mention it but says that Oswald underwent a mastoidectomy in childhood.

The two doctors who performed the autopsy were not asked to testify, and none of the witnesses who knew the substitute socially or at work were asked if he had a scar or any depression in the flesh. Although Marina was asked about the scar on her husband's wrist, she was not asked whether he had had a mastoidectomy or had a scar and depression behind his left ear. She should have known, for she was married to him for nearly three years.

In addition to this apparent absence of mastoidectomy, there were discrepancies between certain scars on the Left upper arm of the assassin and scars on the left upper arm of Marine Oswald. After considering all the medical records, a British surgeon prepared for me an analysis of the scars accompanied by a drawing showing the Left arm of the Marine and the Left arm of the assassin with the positions and discrepancies in these scars marked on the drawing. The post mortem report had disclosed only two scars on the Left upper arm of the assassin, whereas there had been three scars on the Left upper arm of Marine Oswald. Both the position and description of the two scars recorded in the post mortem report differ dramatically from two of the three scars recorded in the Marine medical reports.

The importance of the number, position and description of the scars lies not so much in the possibility that either the Marine or the autopsy doctors might have been in error, but in the fact that *three months after the autopsy and after Ruby had been tried and convicted of the murder of Lee Harvey Oswald*, the FBI were still interested in the recorded physical discrepancies between the Marine and the assassin.

On 25 February 1964, Dr Rose was interviewed by agents of the field office of the FBI in Dallas, Carter and Clements, regarding the scars mentioned in his post mortem report. Hoover had appointed the Dallas field office as the principal office of investigation, and Carter had been the senior of the two agents who had interrogated Oswald in Fort Worth after his arrival in the United States in June 1962. Clements had been sent especially to Dallas police station on 22 November 1963 to obtain, *inter alia*, a physical description of the assassin. Carter was aware that in June 1962 and in his presence, the assassin had stated that his height was 5′ 11″, and on 22 November 1963 Clements had been told by the assassin that his height was 5′ 9″, and he had inspected and recorded the contents of the two Marine cards found in the assassin's wallet showing the height of the Marine as 5′ 11″ in September 1959. The report of the FBI interview with Dr Rose appears in the Exhibits (XXVI.161-162), but pages 412 through 418 are missing from the report of the interview. Some of the colour slides taken by Dr Rose were of the Left arm but all the slides were over-exposed and the doctor could indicate only that the scars would have been in light portions of the slides and could not be identified. He was asked for his opinion of a long scar on the inside of the assassin's Left wrist, and said that this might 'possibly be associated with a suicide attempt' — thus corroborating an 'attempted suicide' episode in October 1959 described in a 'Historic Diary' allegedly kept by Oswald in Russia and found amongst his possessions after the assassination. Dr. Rose was not asked about the mastoidectomy and, if he had been asked whether his and Dr. Stewart's examination of the head had disclosed a scar and removal of bone, he would have referred the FBI to the post mortem report.

It is clear that the FBI agents who interviewed the doctor had read the Marine medical reports on Oswald and had observed in those reports not only the recording of the scars on the Left upper arm but the recording of the mastoidectomy. They must also have read the post mortem report and in so doing would have noted not only the discrepancies in the descriptions of the scars on the Left upper arm, but also that there was no record of a mastoidectomy, a matter which they could not raise without arousing the suspicions of the doctor and possible subsequent disclosure of the facts by him – particularly as he had been the most vociferous and active of the doctors who three months earlier had tried to prevent the removal of the body of the President from Parkland Hospital in Dallas.

The FBI agents must have read the 'Historic Diary' and, doubting its veracity and possibly wondering if the 'attempted suicide' scar had been implanted to link the assassin to the alleged author of the 'Historic Diary' (the assassin thus made to appear to be the same man as the 'suicidal' Marine in Russia), have asked the doctor if the scar on the wrist was a genuine attempt at suicide.

The medical records of the Marine and the post mortem report on the assassin are precise. The discrepancies in the scars on the Left upper arm and the apparent absence of mastoidectomy suggest that the assassin was not Lee Harvey Oswald, and that the exact positions and descriptions of the scars on the Left upper arm of Marine Oswald were unknown to a person implanting 'false' scars on the Left upper arm of the assassin. If Oswald were alive and available in Russia where the 'false' scars could only have been implanted, it is curious that such mistakes should have been made. It would seem that scars might have been implanted on the arm of the assassin in case Marine Oswald's mother and brother might know of their existence (although probably unaware of their position and appearance) and remark on their absence after his return to the United States. The Russians could have known of the existence but not the exact position and appearance of two scars which were the result of a bullet wound while Oswald was in the Marines, but might not have known of the existence of the earlier, possibly childhood, scar at the top of the Left upper arm. The mastoidectomy scar was behind the Left ear at the point where the ear joins the neck, and such a scar for cosmetic reasons is 'socially' unnoticeable but readily observable at autopsy. It would have been both unnecessary and dangerous to submit a substitute to a mastoidectomy because the finding of a suitable substitute so facially resembling a young military marksman would have been difficult.

When Clements interviewed the assassin in Dallas police station on the evening of 22 November 1963 he recorded in his notes that he had been told by Oswald that he had *no permanent scars* (R.614), but Oswald had been wearing a shirt and Clements did not examine him physically. It would seem that the assassin knew that he had no mastoidectomy scar and knew that the scars on his Left upper arm might have been incorrectly implanted, therefore requiring that he distract the attention of the agent from them in order to avoid inspection and recording. He would know that at his trial the question of substitution possibly might not be raised; he did not know that two days later there would be a revealing autopsy on his body. *Had he escaped, he would have taken with him his true height, the scars on his Left upper arm and the apparently absent mastoidectomy.*

Marina, a well educated young woman, commenced her testimony on 3 February 1964. She was the first witness to appear before the Commission and said, *inter alia*, that she first met her husband at a dance in Minsk in March 1961, eighteen months after his arrival in Russia. He told her that his name was Alek, and at first she accepted him as a fellow countryman and only later that evening learned that he was an American and that his name was Lee Harvey Oswald, Alek being a nickname. She said that at Oswald's place of work in Minsk ' ... everyone there called him Alek ... because Lee is an unusual, cumbersome name.

In Russian it (Alek) was easier ... ' They were married six weeks after meeting and prior to the marriage Oswald had told her 'he had no mother'. When she asked him what had happened to her, he told Marina not to question him about it. After their marriage, Oswald told her that he had not told her the truth. Later in testimony, Marina was to say that when she first met Oswald, she had thought from his accent that he was from one of the Russian-speaking Baltic states.

When Oswald entered Russia, he could barely speak the language. On 21 October 1959, being five days after he had entered Russia, Oswald was admitted to a hospital after the alleged attempt at suicide. The hospital records state that Oswald did not speak Russian and could communicate only by 'gestures and facial expression'. (XVIII.464). A contemporaneous medical report is quoted in the Commission's Report as saying that Oswald understood some Russian (R.692). It is to be noted, however, that an interpreter was present on this occasion and that the wording in the contemporaneous medical report under the heading 'Psychiatric Examination' is: 'The patient apparently understands the questions asked in Russian. Sometimes he answers correctly, but immediately states he does not understand what he was asked' (XVIII.470). It would seem to be unlikely that at their first meeting only eighteen months after his hospitalization the real Oswald would have been able to pass as a native Russian when conversing with Marina in her own tongue.

After the assassin arrived in the United States in June 1962, he met several Russian-born people in Fort Worth and Dallas, and they were surprised that after 2 years and 8 months in Russia he was able to speak the Russian language so well. He was able to obtain a recommendation as an interpreter and translator from a Russian teacher of the language in Fort Worth, and the teacher thought that the man spoke with what appeared to be a Polish accent. The teacher asked him if he was of Polish (a Baltic State) origin, but Oswald told him that he was not Polish and that he had learned Russian in the Soviet Union (II.338). It would seem to be clear that when Oswald arrived in Russia in October 1959 he could barely speak or understand Russian, although he had studied the language but was rated 'poor' after a test while in the Marines.

Certain physical differences between Marine Oswald and the man who returned from Russia which were noticed by Oswald's mother, Marguerite Oswald, and Oswald's brother, Robert, 5 years older than Lee Oswald, will now be set out. It will also be shown how the impostor deceived Marguerite and Robert into believing that he was the ex-Marine.

When the impostor 'Oswald' entered the United States from Russia in June 1962, Robert saw him frequently because on arrival in the United States Oswald, Marina and their child stayed in Robert's house for about a month. Oswald and his family then moved to Marguerite's house, remaining there for about another month.

Marguerite was the second witness to appear before the Commission, commencing her testimony on 10 February 1964. She said, *inter alia*, that she had noticed that Lee had lost some hair and that he had told her that it had been caused by the cold weather; she had searched her medical dictionary to find a prescription against baldness. She said that Lee had become 'very, very thin'. She also produced for the Commission a surprise document, Lee's March 1959 application for enrolment in the college in Switzerland and on which in his own handwriting he had stated that his height was 5' 11" and his weight 160 lbs. The burden of her understandably somewhat confused testimony was that she could not believe that her normal and happy son who 'loved the Marines' could have changed into a double-murderer unless he had been a United States agent or had been 'framed'.

Robert was the third witness to appear before the Commission, commencing his testimony on 20 February 1964 and finishing on *22 February 1964*; the date of the cessation of Robert's testimony is important as will be shown later. He said, *inter alia*, that Lee's complexion ' ... had changed somewhat to the extent that he had always been very fair complected – his complexion was rather ruddy at this time (1962) – you might say it appeared like an artificial suntan that you get out of a bottle, but very slight – in other words, a tint of brown to a tint of yellow'. It appeared to him that Lee had picked up something of an accent, but Robert put it down to being in Russia for over $2\frac{1}{2}$ years and speaking only the Russian language. He said that Lee's hair ' ... used to be brown and curly, a full set of hair'. Robert testified that he had pointed out to Lee the difference in his hair and ' ... actually had him bend his head down to where I could look at the top of it, and it was very thin on top – you could see just right down to the scalp'. Lee had ' ... commented that he thought the cold weather (in Russia) had affected it'. Robert had formed the opinion after his brother's death, ' ... due to the nature of the change in his hair and in the baldness that appeared, that he had been given something in the nature of shock treatments or something along that line had been given to him in Russia'. Robert also said that he was unaware of any tendency towards baldness on either his father's or mother's side of the family; he himself, his father and half brother had all full heads of hair. Robert said that Lee to some extent had appeared 'drawn' as compared with his appearance in 1959 and that he had lost weight.

Neither Robert nor Marguerite had been in a position fully to observe Oswald maturing between the ages of 17 and 22 years. Oswald was 12 years old when Robert enlisted in the Marines and from that time onwards they were not to live together until June 1962, when Oswald, Marina and their infant daughter stayed in Robert's house. Prior to June 1962, except for brief and infrequent periods, Lee Harvey Oswald and Robert Oswald had not met for 11 years. For $5\frac{1}{2}$ years before June 1962, Robert had not seen Lee at all except for part of one day in 1959 when they went hunting (XVI.758). Robert told District Attorney Wade at Dallas police station on 22 November 1963 that the family was 'not too close' and 'didn't have much in common'. In testimony, Marguerite said, ' ... we are not close as a family'.

Before June 1962, Marguerite had seen little of Oswald for $5\frac{1}{2}$ years for he had been in the Marines and in Russia, and during his Marine service she may have seen him on two or three occasions, and then only as a growing and changing young man. After his discharge from the Marines in September 1959, Oswald had spent three days with Marguerite and it was on one of these days that he went hunting with Robert. After September 1959, Robert and

Marguerite were not to see him again for 2 years and 8 months. In a book published in 1965, 'A Mother in History', on pp.32 and 33, Marguerite is recorded as telling the authoress, 'From what I know of my boy, and of course you have to understand that actually the last time I was very close to Lee was before he joined the service in 1956 (Lee was just 17 years old). After that, it was just through correspondence and his leaves home from the Marines that I knew him'.

When Oswald arrived in Russia in October 1959, of his own volition or under pressure he wrote a few letters to Robert signed 'Lee', coldly and cruelly renouncing his family and denigrating the United States. This was followed by a period of some 16 months of silence, Robert and Marguerite receiving no news of him. In May 1961, they began to receive from him a stream of affectionate letters and cards, those to his mother ending with 'love' or kisses, and some to his brother ending with 'Your brother, Lee'. This correspondence told of his marriage to Marina, the birth of a daughter, and of his wish and efforts to return to the United States. Robert and Marguerite were affected by this change of attitude, and they wrote frequently to the man they believed to be Oswald and to Marina, and presents were exchanged. The correspondence continued regularly up to the time when Oswald, Marina and infant daughter departed from Russia for the United States, arriving in June 1962.

Enclosed in some of the letters from Oswald were snapshots and other photographs of himself and Marina photographed together or separately or standing side by side, with the result that when Oswald was seen by Robert and Marguerite in June 1962 he was accepted by them because not only did he resemble the Oswald that they remembered, but they had been *conditioned* by the photographs to a slightly altered appearance; when he arrived in the United States they expected him to look as in the photographs. Recognising that the wife, Marina, whom they were meeting for the first time, was the same young and pretty person appearing in the photographs, they could not have imagined that the husband accompanying her was not the real Oswald whom they had last seen 2 years and 8 months previously. In addition, when Oswald began his affectionate correspondence from Russia with Robert, he had asked Robert to visit him and Marina in Russia sometime, a suggestion that would help to dispel any doubts that Robert might have about the identity of the man accompanied by wife and child that he was to welcome off an aeroplane from New York to Dallas on 14 June 1963; Robert had been in no financial position to accept such an invitation and already had heard from Oswald that he might be returning to the United States. It would be reasonable to think that Robert and Marguerite would have expected to see changes in the young man they last saw when he was only 19 years of age.

The deception of Robert and Marguerite would require only that the man should evade or parry awkward questions about his childhood or Marine days, profess loss of memory, change the subject, talk in Russian with his wife who could not speak English, etc., the focus of attention on the man *being reduced by the presence of his wife and daughter.* To Robert, and perhaps to Marguerite, he intimated that he did not wish to talk about his alleged defection and, as with the FBI agents in Fort Worth, what had prompted it. According to Marina in testimony, her husband frequently refused to talk and quarrelled with Marguerite while they were living in her house.

There was always the possibility that any deception of Robert, Marguerite and the FBI agents might not have succeeded unless Oswald, unknowingly, willingly or under pressure, had tutored a substitute – possibly selected and being trained prior to Oswald leaving the Marines. This would mean that an impostor would have had at least the 2 years and 8 months in Russia to absorb from Oswald names, places, and boyhood activities, while all the time observing, copying and practising Oswald's manner, gait, tone of voice and accent. Any gaps in the biography of the young Oswald could have been filled through the resources of KGB agents in the United States.

The importance of the date, *26 February 1964*, when FBI agents Carter and Clements interviewed Dr. Rose must now be discussed.

Prior to the murder of the assassin on the morning of 24 November 1963, the FBI knew (a) that Marine Oswald's height had been recorded by two Marines as 71″ (5′ 11″) immediately prior to Oswald's separation from the Marines, (b) that on the date after the Marine medical examination (Vincent), Oswald had applied for a passport and had given his height on the application form as 5′ 11″, that height being recorded on the passport, (c) that the assassin in June 1962 had told FBI agents Carter and Fain that his height was 5′ 11″, and (d) that the assassin had applied for a new passport in New Orleans in 1963 and had stated on his application form that his height was 5′ 11″, that height being recorded on the new passport.

They also knew (a) that in New Orleans in August 1963 FBI agent Quigley had been told by the assassin that his height was 5′ 9″ and that the New Orleans police had measured and recorded his height as 5′ 9″, (b) that the assassin had stated his height as 5′ 9″ when applying for employment at the Depository, (c) that on the evening of 22 November the assassin had informed FBI agent Clements that his height was 5′ 9″, and (d) that the autopsy on the body of the assassin on 24 November had disclosed its length to be 5′ 9″.

On this confusing evidence the FBI would, at first, have been uncertain whether there had been one or two men using the name Lee Harvey Oswald and operating in the United States from June 1962 through 22 November 1963, but on 23 November they knew from his identification by Marguerite, Robert and Marina that he was 5′ 9″ when he entered the United States in June 1962. The FBI would have realised that if the assassin had escaped they would not have been sure what height he was; they could not have given the Dallas police a description of the wanted man.

Reference to the fingerprint files at the Bureau of the FBI disclosed that Marine Oswald had been fingerprinted when he enlisted in the Marines in October 1956, and that these prints matched the prints taken from the 5′ 9″ assassin after his arrests both in New Orleans in August 1963 and in Dallas on 22 and 24 November 1963. Fingerprint proof is regarded as infallible, and the FBI must have wondered why Vincent and Ayres on separate occasions (3 and 11 September 1959), and the two FBI agents in

Fort Worth in June 1962 had made the *identical error* when recording the height of Lee Harvey Oswald as 5' 11". In addition, the FBI knew that Oswald had applied for a passport in September 1959 giving his height as 5' 11", and that his passport showed this height. Early in February 1964, they were to learn that in March 1959 Oswald had given his height as 5' 11" when applying for enrolment in the college in Switzerland.

As the FBI knew that a 5' 9" man had entered the United States from Russia in June 1962, they would know that if 5' 11" was the correct height of the Marine, the prints of the assassin could only match those of the Marine if a forged fingerprint card had at some time been substituted in the FBI fingerprint files for the original October 1956 fingerprint card of Marine Oswald.

On the day of the murder of the assassin, 24 November, the autopsy was performed on his body and on 25 November he was buried. On reading the report of the autopsy which they could not have received until the evening of 26 November or the morning of 27 November because certain post-autopsy tests had to be made, the FBI would have seen that there was a discrepancy between the scars on the Left upper arm of the assassin and those on the Left upper arm of Marine Oswald as disclosed in his Marine medical reports. They would have seen that the assassin might not have been the Marine, which would possibly explain why the assassin had told Clements in Dallas police station on 22 November that he had 'no permanent scars'. The evidence in the hands of the FBI now powerfully suggested that another man had at some time been substituted·for Marine Oswald and sent from Russia to the United States accompanied by Marina and their infant daughter, that a fingerprint card had been substituted for the 1956 Marine card, that the assassin had untruthfully told the FBI agents in Fort Worth that his height was 5' 11", and that he had untruthfully stated his height to be 5' 11" when applying in New Orleans for a new passport in June 1963.

The FBI, nevertheless, were still faced with the fact that the fingerprint card of the Marine showed prints matching those of the assassin, but they could not establish that the original card had been substituted by what would have been a perfect forgery. In June 1962, furthermore, the Marine's brother and mother had accepted the 5' 9" man as the 5' 11" ex-Marine they had last but briefly seen in September 1959.

There had been one way only by which the FBI could have been satisfied about the identity of the assassin, and that would have been for his body to be inspected before burial on 25 November, but apparently this had not been done because at that time the FBI must have believed that the Marine fingerprint card was genuine, concluding that the several recorded heights of 5' 11" had been inexplicable errors; they were yet to receive the autopsy report and to hear from Marguerite that in March 1959 her son had believed his height to be 5' 11".

If it was the intention of the United States authorities that all evidence of international conspiracy should be kept secret, after 26/27 November they could not without arousing suspicion order an exhumation of the body to ascertain (a) whether the record of the two scars on the Left upper arm of the assassin had been correctly described and placed by Drs. Rose and Stewart, (b) whether the third scar on the Left upper arm was present and overlooked by the doctors, and (c) whether the head of the corpse disclosed a mastoidectomy scar and removal of bone, also overlooked by the doctors.

At some point in time and probably two days after the burial of the assassin on 25 November, the FBI must have come to suspect that the assassin was not the Marine; they must have awaited with interest the testimony of Marina, Marguerite and Robert commencing on 3 February 1964 and terminating on *22 February 1964.*

This testimony disclosed further evidence indicating that the assassin was not Marine Oswald, and that consequently the Marine and his fingerprint card had both been substituted. First, the testimony of Marina indicated that the man she had met at the dance in Minsk was a Russian named Alek, and that he told her that he had no mother and forbade her to question him about this. Secondly, Marguerite testified that she had noticed a considerable change in her son's hair and that he had become 'very, very thin'. On 11 February 1964, she had produced her son's application in March 1959 for enrolment at the college in Switzerland and on which he had stated his height to be 5' 11". This documentary evidence indicated that Vincent and Ayres, who in September 1959 had recorded Oswald's height as 5' 11", had made no error, and that the FBI agents in Fort Worth had been deceived by the assassin into believing he was Lee Harvey Oswald and 5′ 11″ in height. Thirdly, Robert's testimony disclosed that he had detected a number of differences between the man who arrived at his house in June 1962 and the man who had left the United States in September 1959. Like Marguerite, he had testified that the Lee he knew would never have killed anybody.

The testimony of Marina, Marguerite and Robert ended with the last day of Robert's testimony, *22 February 1964*. The FBI would have required a few days to study the testimony of those closest to Oswald and the assassin, and to realise that it corroborated the evidence provided by the differing and documented heights, and the medically recorded physical data of the Marine and the assassin.

The testimony of the three persons must therefore have reversed the early view of the FBI that the assassin might be ex-Marine Oswald, replacing this view with a strong suspicion that a Russian had been substituted for Marine Oswald and that a forged fingerprint card showing the prints of the assassin had at some time been substituted for the 1956 Marine prints of Lee Harvey Oswald.

On *26 February 1964*, Carter and Clements were to interview Dr. Rose, apparently in the hope that this might help to decide the identity of the assassin; the interview appears to have been unproductive with the result that today the FBI – like this author – do not know if the man buried in Fort Worth was the Marine or an impostor.

Prior to the testimony of the three persons, the 5-Volume FBI report on the assassination (four initial Volumes on 9 December 1963 and one supplementary Volume on 13 January 1964) had been submitted to the Commission and therein had stated that the ex-Marine was the assassin; no further supplementary Volume was submitted to the Commission detailing all the evidence pointing to substitution of the Marine and his fingerprints, nor indeed a dissertation upon Albert Osborne, John Caesar Grossi and the American male. Although aware that the testimony of Marina, Marguerite and Robert disclosed puzzling discrepancies between the Marine and the assassin, the Commission were never informed of the differing heights, the differing medical records, the possible substitution of a forged fingerprint card in the FBI fingerprint files, Hoover's memorandum of 3 June 1960, the activities of Osborne, Grossi and the American male, and the evidence of conspiracy at the Russian Embassy in Mexico City. Had the Commission known of all this, the testimony of the three persons closest to the assassin and to Oswald would have gathered weight, and instead of relying upon the 5-Volume FBI report the Commissioners would, no doubt, have ordered an exhumation of the body of the assassin.

Marguerite was described by Robert in testimony as 'normal and stable until 24 November 1963', and by others in testimony as a truthful person. Her lengthy testimony suggests that from the time of the murder of the assassin – this killing being indicative of conspiracy – the Secret Service, who had taken immediate charge of Marina, Marguerite and Robert, endeavoured successfully to separate Marguerite from Marina although, according to Marguerite, Marina had wished to take her two children to live with Marguerite despite the fact that it would have been a financial struggle for the two women to make ends meet.

On the morning of 24 November the Secret Service, who knew all that there was to be known at that point, including the espionage at Jaggars-Chiles-Stovall which they had investigated on 23 and 24 November, were conscious that there might have been a conspiracy and that the assassin might have been an impostor. When later that morning an ex-Chicago and Dallas Russian-Jewish hoodlam killed the assassin, the Secret Service must have guessed that the killling had been to avoid a trial of the assassin.

It was at this point, according to the testimony of Marguerite, that the Secret Service tried to persuade her to move from the hotel where she and Marina had been secreted to the home of Robert's father and mother-in-law, some 45 miles from Dallas. She refused, saying that she wanted to be near her imprisoned son; she and Marina were then moved to another hotel outside Dallas which Marguerite testified she thought was a 'hideout' of the Secret Service.

By the late afternoon of 24 November the autopsy on the body of the assassin had been completed and it disclosed the discrepancies between the corpse and the body of the Marine in September 1959. After the autopsy, on 25 and 26 November various tests were made at the hospital by analysts et al, and it would not have been until the morning of 27 November that the complete post mortem report and appendages could have been digested by the Secret Service and compared with the Marine medical reports.

On the night of 27 November, with the aid of Robert who had been influenced in his desire to separate his mother from Marina by information that a wealthy woman (Mrs. Pultz) had offered to take Marina and the two children into her home, and to pay for the education of the children (Marina did not join this lady who faded from the picture after Marguerite and Marina were to be finally separated) the Secret Service, according to Marguerite (I.164-186), alienated Marguerite and Marina by removing the latter from the twin-bed bedroom into the sitting room of the two-room hotel suite where the two women were then secreted. After the morning of 28 November 1963 when she was prevented from seeing or speaking to Marina, Marguerite was never again to see or speak to her. Whatever the purpose of the separation, it divided for ever Marguerite, who knew that her son was 5' 11" and had suffered a mastoidectomy, from Marine who knew that her husband was 5' 9" and – if the post mortem report is accurate – had not suffered a mastoidectomy. If Marguerite's and Marina's original wishes had been observed and had they lived together, in due course Marguerite would have learned from Marina and disclosed the apparent discrepancies between her son and the assassin; she would have started an avalanche of public enquiry. A newspaper article of 27 November 1963 reporting an interview with Mrs. Pultz appears as Appendix B to this book.

According to the testimony of Marguerite, as from the evening of 27 November 1963, the Secret Service had treated her with disdain, and Marina with respect, despite the fact that their own agent (as shown later in this book) had given an unsatisfactory report of Marina during an interview with her on 25 November 1963 which included his opinion that she had not been telling the truth to him.

Marina was also separated from Mrs. Ruth Paine, a woman who had befriended her, with whom she had lived for $2\frac{1}{2}$ months prior to the assassination, and who had seen and talked to the assassin on many overnight and other occassions. Ruth and her husband were intelligent and were tall, over-shadowing the slight and shorter assassin; in due course they might well have come to realise that the assassin was not the ex-Marine. In March 1964, Ruth was to testify that she could not understand why Marina had apparently turned against her shortly after 23 November 1963 and believed that for some reason unknown others had been responsible for Marina's sudden and unexplained withdrawal of loving friendship.

It would seem that the Secret Service, unlike the FBI who would be averse to admitting that a Russian agent had penetrated their fingerprint department in order to substitute a forgery for the 1956 Marine fingerprint card, were not so averse to believe that this probably had occurred. By the evening of 27 November 1963 the weight of the evidence in the possession of the Service indicated a Russian conspiracy in which Marine Oswald and his fingerprints must have been replaced by an impostor and his fingerprints.

Whether or not the Secret Service delivered to the Commission any volumes of reports upon the assassination based upon their own investigations, it would seem that the Commission were bereft of all the information that the Service must have obtained; the Service were with the assassin from the time of his arrival in Dallas police station at about 2.00 p.m. on 22 November until he was murdered on 24 November, and after 24 November with Marina, Marguerite, and Robert Oswald, and on 23 and 24 November had investigated the activities of the assassin in Jaggars-Chiles-Stovall, and, no doubt, the work of John Caesar Grossi *alias* 'Jack Leslie Bowen'.

It might appear that when President Johnson on 22 November overtly appointed the FBI as the agency entrusted with the post-assassination investigation, he covertly instructed the Secret Service to suppress the evidence that might point to a Russian conspiracy to spy and to assassinate. Whether or not the Service were so instructed, the Report of the Commission makes no reference whatever to the 'sensitive' nature of Jaggars-Chiles-Stovall or of the assassin's espionage in that firm. The Report does not mention the difference in height and the other physical differences between the Marine and the assassin, and, therefore, discloses neither the apparent espionage nor the apparent substitution of the individual and his fingerprints.

If the Commission were unaware of evidence pointing to imposture, it is therefore not incredible that during the testimony of Marina, in which she was asked thousands of questions by Counsel and the Commissioners, she was not asked whether her husband had suffered a mastoidectomy, the results of which should have been apparent to the wife with whom he had lived for nearly three years.

The next Chapter will discuss the fingerprints of Marine Oswald and those of the assassin.

8

Fingerprints are considered, in appropriate circumstances, to be proof of identity, for as yet no two people have been found to possess identical prints. Oswald had been fingerprinted when he enlisted in the Marines in october 1956 (XVII.289). He had been fingerprinted when he was arrested on the disturbance charge in August 1963 in New Orleans (XXII.828), and again in Dallas on his arrest on 22 November 1963 (XVII.282). On 25 November 1963, the assassin was again fingerprinted after death and before burial on that day (XVII.285). If the recorded heights of Marine Oswald and the assassin were known to the Commission and to the FBI to differ, it would seem that a comparison of the 1956 prints with the 1963 prints would have been their *first* objective.

If the Commission had found that the 1956 prints differed from the 1963 prints or that a forgery had been substituted it would have established once and for all that the assassin was not the real Oswald.

Sebastian Latona LL.B. LL.M. M.P.L. Supervisor of the Latent Fingerprint Department of the Identification Division of the FBI, was called on 2 April 1964 principally to testify about finger and palm prints found on cardboard boxes, etc. in the 'sniper's nest' at the Depository and to compare them for the Commission with the fingerprints taken from the assassin on 22 November by the Dallas police (IV. 1-47). In view of the disparity in the heights of Oswald and the assassin, and other apparent differences, it would seem that a comparison of the 1956 Marine prints and the 1963 Dallas prints would be of greater importance to the Commission and the FBI than a comparison of prints found in the 'sniper's nest' with the Dallas police prints of the arrested man – necessary though the latter comparison would be.

Latona was asked by the Commission to describe the FBI Latent Fingerprint department and extracts from his replies are as follows: ' ... We have two main files; we have a criminal file and we have what are referred to as civil files ... In that file (criminal) we have approximately 15 million sets of fingerprints ... In our civil files, in which are filed fingerprints of various types of applicants, service personnel and the like, we have fingerprints of approximately $62\frac{1}{2}$ million people'. In describing the receipt of fingerprints by the FBI from various agencies, he testified, ' ... then they are checked through our files to see if the person has or has not a prior criminal record ... '

When he was asked if the FBI had in its files fingerprints of Oswald received prior to 22 November 1963, he replied, 'Yes, sir; I believe there is a Marine Corps print'. When asked if he had compared the 1963 prints received by the FBI from the Dallas police with the 1956 Marine prints and if they were identical he replied, 'They were the same'. This testimony is curious in view of his prior words, 'I *believe* there is a Marine Corps print'. When asked if he recalled whether Oswald had signed the Marine card he said, '*Offhand, I do not*'.

When asked whether he knew if any fingerprints were taken from Lee Harvey Oswald after he returned to the United States in June 1962, apart from the fingerprints obtained after the assassination, Latona, apparently unaware of the August 1963 New Orleans police prints sent to and acknowledged by the FBI, replied, '*I do not*'.

After the assassination, the FBI file on Oswald should have contained three sets of fingerprints taken from him, being (a) his prints on enlistment in the Marines in 1956, (b) his prints taken by the New Orleans police in August 1963 and (c) his prints taken by the Dallas police on 22 and after death on 24 November 1963.

It would not be unreasonable for Latona to believe that there was a Marine Corps print, because he knew that all servicemen were fingerprinted on enlistment and the prints forwarded to the FBI to ascertain if the enlisting man had a prior criminal record. If Latona was unsure if there were Marine Corps prints and if Oswald had signed the card, his testimony that he had compared them with the Dallas prints and found them to be 'the same' is surprising. That he did not know of the existence of the New Orleans prints is incomprehensible, particularly as his testimony was required in connection with an official investigation into the assassination of a President of the United States.

Although he produced to the Commission the 22 November 1963 prints of the assassin taken by the Dallas police and the fingerprint specimens taken from the objects found at the Depository — demonstrating with prepared drawings and a blackboard the manner in which identification was effected — *he did not take Oswald's 1956 Marine prints to the Commission hearing.* Remarkable though this may seem, the Marine prints were nevertheless given an Exhibit number, *although they had not been produced in testimony.* Latona was asked to supply the Commission with a copy of the Marine prints, and this must have been done at a later date as they were filed under the given Exhibit number (XVII.289), but were never compared with the Dallas prints before the Commission.

In the absence of Latona, if the Commission — not being fingerprint experts — happened to look at these prints they would have been unable to compare them with the 1963 Dallas police prints. Unfortunately the photograph of the 1956 prints shown in the Exhibits is in about half size and the prints are heavily inked and smudged, thus making comparison difficult.

I (the author) took the advice of the senior fingerprint expert in Britain upon the Marine prints and the Dallas prints, and he identified for me a few points of similarity between the two sets of prints. His view was that they were 'the same', but that the points of similarity were insufficient for evidence to be given in a British court that the two sets of prints came from the same man. He pointed out that blank fingerprint cards are easy to obtain, and that prints can also be forged. He said that sixteen points of similarity on one finger is the minimum number upon which a fingerprint expert in Britain is prepared to base evidence of proof of identity.

Latona, however, said that he had testified in court to as few as seven points of similarity and might possibly testify to six, five or perhaps four points on an individual case before he could render a conclusion. The FBI had been approached by foreign experts in an attempt to set a worldwide standard of sixteen characteristics

but the FBI would not subscribe to that at all ... 'and I feel this
way, it is purely a matter of experience. They simply do not have
the experience that we have in the FBI. The FBI has the world's
largest practical fingerprint file'. Latona said, 'In my opinion,
there are no number of points (of similarity) which are a
requirement. Now, there is a general belief among lots of
fingerprint people that a certain number of points are required. It
is my opinion that this is an erroneous assumption that they have
taken, because of the fact that here in the United States a person
that qualifies in court as an expert has the right merely to voice
an opinion as to whether two prints were made by the same
finger or not made. There are no requirements, there is no
standard by which a person can say that a certain number of
points are required – primarily because of the fact that there is
such a wide variance in the experience of men who qualify as
fingerprints experts ... In the United States, to my knowledge, I
know of no group or body that subscribe to a particular number
(of points). Now, quite frequently some of these departments
will maintain a standard for themselves, by virtue of the fact that
they will say, "Before we will make an identification, we must
find a minimum of twelve points of similarity" ... We simply
say this: We have confidence in our experts to the extent that
regardless of the number of points, if the expert who has been
assigned to the case for purposes of making the examination gives
an opinion, we will not question the number of points.'

The Commission took proper care when examining the points
of similarity between the prints taken by the Dallas police on 22
November 1963 and the prints found in the 'sniper's nest' and on
the rifle on that day. This was necessary to establish that the man
arrested on 22 November was the man who had been in the
'sniper's nest' with a rifle, but it was imperative that the 1956
Marine prints should have been produced to the Commission
during Latona's testimony; the points of similarity between them
and the 1963 New Orleans and Dallas prints could then have
been demonstrated by Latona with drawings and his blackboard.

In addition to having omitted to have compared for them the
Marine prints with the New Orleans and Dallas prints, the
Commission should have followed up Latona's testimony *with a
proper chain of evidence* by calling the Marine official to testify that
the fingerprints alleged to be those of Oswald and later placed in

the Exhibits were in fact those taken by him when Oswald joined the Marines in October 1956. The official who took these prints signed his name, Melam?, in the appropriate space on the fingerprint card; he should have been called to identify his signature and that the prints had been routinely forwarded to the FBI at that time for checking against a possible criminal record. Witnesses should have been called to continue the chain of evidence by establishing the continued existence of the card in the FBI files – October 1956 to the date of Latona's testimony. The Commission had even been reminded by Latona of the necessity for a proper chain of evidence for, when he testified that he could not certify the 1963 Dallas police prints as being those of Oswald and asked to explain this, he said, 'As I am not the one who fingerprinted Oswald I cannot tell from my own personal knowledge that those are actually the fingerprints of Lee Harvey Oswald'. Counsel then said, 'We will get other evidence on the record at a subsequent time to show those (Dallas 1963) prints were of Oswald.' The Commission did call the man who took the assassin's prints in Dallas police station to establish the chain of evidence regarding the Dallas prints but, in addition to their failure to compare them with the 1959 Marine prints, they neglected to call 'Melam' and others to establish the chain regarding the Marine prints.

Latona testified that every day the FBI received an average of 23,000-25,000 sets of prints for processing. He was asked, 'What is your card system like? If this is too confidential I don't want to get anything in the record that is too secret. We can take it off the record.' Latona replied, 'Nothing is secret about our files'.

Had the conspirators wished to substitute the assassin's prints for Oswald's prints in the FBI fingerprint card system, it would have been a simple task compared with the extraction of secret files from closely guarded filing systems over periods of years that has been accomplished from time to time by filing clerks or others.

It would seem that if a fingerprint card was substituted for the original Oswald card, the forgers had implanted the impostor's prints on the substitute card in such a way that the prints could possibly be those of the impostor but equally those of the Marine whose fingerprints had been taken only once – when he joined the Marines. (The inconclusiveness of the Marine prints could have been one of the reasons why the FBI agents, Carter and Clements, talked to Dr. Rose about scars on the Left arm of the assassin and about the suicide attempt.)

After the assassination, the Dallas police collected the belongings of the assassin from his roominghouse and elsewhere, and Latona testified that he had identified the assassin's prints on these 'Personal effects, wallet, pictures, papers and things of that sort ... which they should because they belong to him'. On a page of the assassin's notebook is written the word 'Fingerprints' (XVI.67).

On the basis of Latona's testimony, it would appear that on arrest in New Orleans the future assassin had not been worried about the taking of his prints by the New Orleans police.

When Latona gave his evidence on 2 April 1964, the Commission should have been aware of all the physical differences between Oswald and the assassin. The differing heights and the contents of the post mortem report on the corpse of the assassin were available by the end of November 1963, and in February 1964 they had listened to the testimony of Marina, Marguerite and Robert Oswald disclosing considerable physical discrepancies between the Marine and the assassin, and Marguerite had handed to the Commission the Albert Schweitzer application form completed by her son giving his height as 5' 11". The evidence of Latona traversed all these physical differences between Oswald and the assassin, and although it would seem that the Commission should have been mystified, it appears that they did not envisage the possible substitution of Oswald and his fingerprints. (Testimony of Latona with author's italics: IV. 1-47.)

Following the testimony of Latona, Arthur Mandella of the New York Police Department, Bureau of Criminal Identification, testified to the Commission but his testimony was limited to the comparison of the prints found in the 'sniper's nest' and those taken by the Dallas police. He was not asked to compare the 1956 Marine prints with the 1963 New Orleans and Dallas prints.

If the assassin had not encountered Mrs. Bledsoe on the bus, it would seem that he would soon have disappeared with the aid of Jack Ruby; Tippit would not have been murdered and the assassin would not have been arrested.

As it was to transpire, the secrecy of the conspiracy had foundered on three mishaps. First, seven weeks prior to the assassination the informant working for the CIA in the Russian Embassy in Mexico City had discovered that on 28 September 1963 the American male calling himself 'Lee Oswald' had been in contact with Kostikov and Yatskov, on 1 October 1963 had again visited the Russian Embassy to enquire about a reply to a telegram, and on more than one occasion had been photographed. Secondly, four days before the assassination the informant working for the FBI in the Russian Embassy in Washington had discovered the letter, signed Oswald and posted ten days before the assassination to Consul Reznichenko at the Russian Embassy in Washington referring to meetings with comrade Kostin at the Russian Embassy in Mexico City. Thirdly, the assassin failed to escape, his height of 5' 9" was recorded, it was discerned that he was the man who had entered the United States from Russia on 13 June 1962, the contents of his wallet were examined and an autopsy on his body was performed.

The subsequent murder of the assassin by Ruby, together with an examination of Oswald's movements after the assassination and of Ruby's activities before and after the assassination establishes beyond reasonable doubt that the two men were conspiring together in the United States. The combination of the three mishaps and Ruby's activities indicate beyond reasonable doubt that the KGB organised the killing and Jack Ruby took charge of the escape.

From this point in the story little can be added to what has already been said, but it is desirable to show chronologically what occurred from the birth of Lee Harvey Oswald in 1939 to the date of the Report, 24 September 1964; to assist the reader to keep abreast of the involved KGB plot, considerable repetition will be unavoidable.

The next Chapter will discuss Oswald's childhood, his service in the Marines and his alleged departure for Russia in September 1959.

9

Lee Harvey Oswald was born in New Orleans on 18 October 1939. His father, Robert Edward Lee Oswald, had died of a heart attack two months before he was born and his mother, Marguerite, was then left to provide for her three small sons – John Pic, seven years old and born of a previous marriage, Robert Oswald, five years old, and the infant Lee. In this chapter Lee Harvey Oswald will be called by his first name.

For a time the family lived on the deceased father's life insurance but when this was exhausted, Marguerite found it increasingly difficult to support the family. There were several changes of address and she had to find someone to look after her children while she went out to work.

When Lee was three years old, he was sent to join his brothers at an orphanage and was to remain there for 13 months.

During this period Marguerite married Edwin Ekdahl and, taking her three boys from the orphanage, she moved to Dallas with her new husband. Ekdahl treated the three boys well, accepting them as his own children, and Lee appears to have been happy in the family life and found in Ekdahl – according to Robert – 'the father he never had'. When six years old, Lee underwent a mastoidectomy behind his Left ear.

When Lee was 8 years old, Marguerite and Ekdahl were divorced. Marguerite had paid for Lee's two brothers to go to Chamberlain-Hunt Military Academy, and Lee was left alone with his mother who again was working all day. After school he would return to an empty house and prepare his own evening meals, sometimes preferring to stay at home to read rather than mixing with other children, although John Pic was to testify that as a child Lee did play with other children.

At the age of 13, Lee moved with his mother to New York in August 1952, where they stayed with John Pic who by this time had left the Marines and was married. John Pic said that he 'was glad to see Lee and Lee was glad to see him', and that he took Lee to the zoo, Natural History Museums and other places, and that Lee seemed normal and happy. Lee used to enjoy riding the subway all day by himself, one ticket enabling him to do this. Robert was serving in the Marines but on one occasion visited his mother and Lee for several days in New York, taking Lee on outings to the zoo, Natural History museums and elsewhere. He testified that he found him a happy boy.

Lee attended school during this period but, perhaps taunted by his school-fellows for his southern accent and dress, constantly absented himself from school so that he could go to the zoo or elsewhere – frequently being picked up by the authorities at the zoo – and finally refusing to register at the school. Several court hearings for truancy were held and at one stage Lee was sent to a Youth House, similar to a detention centre. There he received psychiatric treatment and tests, which showed that he was a withdrawn and socially maladjusted boy, but of above average intelligence. To Lee it may have seemed a continual fight against the climate and the people, whilst having to submit to interviews by psychiatrists, probation officers, welfare officers and school attendance officers. John Pic testified that Lee did not like his school, and that he did not blame him for not liking it. There is no evidence that Lee exhibited any form of delinquency other than truancy, or displayed any criminal tendencies.

Fearing that her son might again be taken from her, after some 17 months in New York Marguerite returned with Lee to New Orleans, where the New York truant went back to school and caused no further trouble.

In New Orleans, at 15 years of age Lee joined the Civil Air Patrol for a brief period and it was in the Patrol that it is alleged he came in contact with 'Captain' David Ferrie, an experienced private pilot who was in charge of the patrol. (After the assassination, Ferrie was arrested by the New Orleans police and 'booked' at the First District Station in New Orleans, but apparently was never charged with anything; the arrest was later suspected to have been in connection with the assassination. After the assassination the FBI were certainly interested in the activities of Ferrie, asking a boyhood friend of Oswald who was also in the CAP whether he knew if Ferrie ever undertook 'long flights'; the friend said that he did not know anything about this. There is no record of any interview with Ferrie nor was he called to testify before the Commission. In 1967, the District Attorney of New Orleans, James Garrison, endeavoured to bring certain charges of conspiracy to assassinate the President, but the day before he was about to arrest Ferrie the latter was found dead in his apartment.)

At about this time and according to Marguerite in testimony, Lee began to read communist literature possibly obtained from the public library and, with his character largely formed by his mother's poverty and his own insecurity, found much to appeal to him. The evidence on this aspect of Lee's reading is both contradictory and sketchy, his brother Robert and Lee's best schoolboy friend never having heard Lee mention either Communism or Marxism, the friend also saying that Lee read only comics and magazines.

When Lee was 16 years old, he endeavoured to enlist in the Marines, using a false affidavit from his mother which stated that he was 17 years old – it had been successful in the case of John Pic many years earlier. The attempt failed and according to his mother Lee spent the next year reading and memorising the Marine Manual which he had obtained from Robert, while 'living for the time when he would be old enough to join the Marines'. At this point in his life, Lee appears to have been a thoughtful boy, interested in astronomy, wild life, fishing, stamp collecting and other normal activities.

Anticipating that her son would soon enlist in the Marines, in July 1956 Marguerite moved from New Orleans to Fort Worth where she took an apartment for herself, Lee and Robert, the latter having completed his Marine Service.

On 3 October 1956, Lee is alleged to have written to the Socialist Party of America in New York, saying that he was a Marxist and had been studying Socialist principles for well over 15 months, and asking for further information. At that time the Socialist Party of America was believed to have Communist connections and it appears that in due course it was 'designated' as such and finally disbanded. Its records were placed in the archives of Duke University, Durham, North Carolina, and Oswald's letter was discovered on a 'routine check' after the assassination. It cannot be proved that he wrote the letter, which is the only written evidence of young Lee's interest in Marxism.

On 15 October 1956, Lee completed the necessary formalities preparatory to joining the Marines, and he was enlisted on 24 October 1956. After completing the basic training course he was selected to work in a section covering radar; for most of his service he was to be employed as a radar operator in Japan, the Philippines and Taiwan, and finally in the United States.

While in the Marines he tried to learn the Russian language, obtaining Russian language newspapers and appearing to be interested in what was happening in Russia. None of this was done in secret and he was sometimes called 'comrade' by his fellow Marines, although he never expressed Communist sympathies.

As a rifleman, he was just able to qualify as a 'sharp-shooter', which designation represents someone who is not 'expert' but is above 'marksman'.

Off duty, he played chess and sometimes chose the red pieces intimating that they represented the Red Army. He possessed records of classical music and was an inveterate reader of books, including *Leaves of Grass* (Walt Whitman), *Das Kapital* (Karl Marx), *Mein Kampf* (Adolf Hitler), his favourite books being the anti-Communist *Animal Farm* and *1984* (George Orwell). He enjoyed engaging his officers in political argument and, being better informed than they, was more than able to hold his own. He was regarded as having a sense of humour, being witty, and at his best in company. He never displayed disloyalty to his country.

After he had been in the Marines for about a year, he acquired an automatic .22 pistol which he kept in his locker but one day allowed to fall to the ground, where it went off and wounded him above the Left elbow. The slug did not exit and was later removed, creating a second scar. He was court-martialled for illegal possession of the pistol and punished. Later, in Japan, he was court-martialled for insulting a non-commissioned officer over an incident involving a spilt drink, and he was again found guilty and punished accordingly. Apart from these two incidents, he appeared to have been an average First-Class Private, performing his duties reasonably satisfactorily. Donovan, the officer in command of the crew that included Oswald, found him competent in all functions during his last year of service, whether radar surveillance of aircraft or sweeping the floor. 'He waited for you to tell him what to do, and he did it, no matter what you told him ... *I know that Cuba interested him more than most other situations ... But I never heard him in any way, shape or form confess that he was a Communist, or that he ever thought about being a Communist ...* I believe he drank, sometimes to excess.' (Author's italics.)

In March 1959, while still in the Marines but back from the Far East and now in the United States, Lee, giving his height as 5' 11" and his weight as 160 lbs., filled in an application form for entrance to the Albert Schweitzer College in Switzerland, a small college specialising in religion, ethics, science, literature and projects for peace. On the application form he said that after a period at the College he intended to take a summer course at the University of Turku in Finland, and would then return to America to pursue his chosen vocation of a short story writer on contemporary American life. His application to attend the College was accepted for the Spring term of 1960 and he was told that a deposit of $25 was required, which he sent to the college in June 1959 enclosed in a letter expressing his pleasure at being accepted and looking forward to 'a fine stay'. He added that any information on the school or even the students who would attend the course would be appreciated and he wrote to tell his mother that he was happy to have been accepted.

He was committed to serve on active duty until 7 December 1959 but on 17 August he submitted a request for a dependency discharge on the ground that his mother needed his support, having heard from her in July 1959 that she had been injured in an accident at work some months previously. He had made a voluntary allotment of part of his salary to her, under which arrangement she received $40 in August, and he had submitted an application for a 'Q' allotment (dependency allowance) in her behalf of $91.30; one payment of the 'Q' allotment for the month of August was made in September.

His request for discharge was accompanied by an affidavit from his mother and corroborative affidavits from an attorney, a doctor and two friends, attesting that she had been injured and was unable financially to support herself. Lee's dependency discharge was approved and on 3 September he underwent a full medical examination by Marine doctor Vincent, when he was measured and his height recorded as 71".

On 4 September, he applied for a passport and stated on the application form that he intended to leave the United States by Grace Lines on about 21 September and would be away for some four months. On the form he gave his height as 5' 11" and his weight as 150 lbs., and stated that his purpose in applying for a passport was to attend the Albert Schweitzer College and the University of Turku and to visit other countries as a tourist. He named the countries that he would visit in the following order; Cuba, Dominican Republic, England, France, Switzerland, Germany, Finland and Russia. He was routinely issued with a passport which gave his height as 5' 11".

On 11 September, his physical and other details were taken by a Marine officer for the purpose of issuing identification cards and other material in connection with his release from the Marines and transfer to the inactive reserves. His height was taken and recorded as 71".

Nelson Delgado, Lee's best friend in the Marines during Lee's last year of service in 1959 was to testify (VIII.228-265) that Lee had been corresponding with a Cuban Consulate – apparently in Los Angeles – and one night had an unidentified civilian visitor with whom he talked for 1½ to 2 hours outside the camp gates. At one time Lee told Delgado that he was in touch with Cuban diplomatic officials. Lee and Delgado, both 19 years of age, often talked about joining the Cuban Army and perhaps leading expeditions to free Caribbean countries, Castro's revolution being at that time popular amongst young Marines. Delgado was once 'scared' because Lee had actually started to make plans to go to Cuba, how they would go there, where to apply to go and the people to contact for that purpose; Delgado had not realised that Lee had been serious when they were having discussions about taking over, for example, the Dominican Republic. Delgado, who used to be in the practice firing line with Lee, said that Lee was a poor rifleman, getting a lot of 'Maggies drawers' (missing the target completely), was not interested in rifle practice whereas the others 'loved going to the range', and did not keep his rifle in proper order. Lee bought a Spanish-English dictionary and Delgado taught him to speak simple Spanish to the point where Lee could converse to a limited extent in that language. Delgado was surprised when he heard that Lee had gone to Russia because he had expected him to go to the college in Switzerland, but if Lee was to go elsewhere abroad he would have expected him to go to Cuba. Lee had never said anything about going to Russia, and Delgado did not think he would have had sufficient money to get there.

After leaving the Marines on 11 September 1959, Lee went to Marguerite's home in Forth Worth, arriving there on 14 September. On this day, he registered his dependency discharge and entry into the Marine Reserve at the Fort Worth Selective Service Board, and his height was noted as 5' 11". He told Marguerite that he intended to get a job on a ship or possibly in the export-import business, saying that he would be able to earn more money than if he stayed in Fort Worth, and that on a ship he could earn 'big money' and be able to send home 'substantial' amounts.

After giving Marguerite $100, he left for New Orleans on 16 September and there booked a passage on a Lykes Lines freighter to Le Havre, France, sailing on 20 September 1959. His mother received the following undated letter from New Orleans:

Dear Mother:

Well, I have booked passage on a ship to Europe, I would of had to sooner or later and I think it's best I go now. Just remember above all else that my values are very different from Robert's and your's. It is difficult to tell you how I feel, just remember this is what I must do. I did not tell you about my plans because you could harly (sic) be expected to understand.

I did not see Aunt Lilian while I was here. I will write again as soon as I land.

(Signed) Lee.

Lee, who had helped to support his mother and apparently wished to continue to do so, appears to have had an unexpected change of heart in New Orleans, for this was the last she was to hear of her son — if he was the author of the letter — until about a month later when she read in the Fort Worth newspapers that he had defected to Russia. When she read the news, she was 'shocked' for, if Lee was to leave the country, she would have expected him to go to Cuba or a South American country. When testifying as to this, she could not have known of the testimony of Delgado two months later; the testimony of the mother and Delgado are thus independently corroborative.

The freighter carried only four passengers, a married couple and a young man with whom Lee shared a cabin. Lee told the other passengers that he intended to travel in Europe and possibly attend a college in Switzerland if he had sufficient funds. On arrival at Le Havre on 8 October, he left the ship and crossed by boat to England, arriving the following day at Southampton. There he told the immigration officials that he had $700 and that he intended to stay in England for a week before going to school in Switzerland, but on the same day he travelled, presumably by train, to London and flew from there to Helsinki, Finland, where he applied at the Russian Consulate for a visa to visit Russia. After two days, a six-day tourist visa was granted and Lee, travelling by train, arrived in Russia on 15 October 1959 – perhaps to disappear for ever behind the Iron Curtain.

If a 5' 11" Lee entered Russia, it is remarkable that less than a month later a woman journalist who interviewed him at length in Moscow should have recorded in her notes that Lee Harvey Oswald was 5' 9" in height. (When I telephoned the journalist in Paris to ask if she could have made a mistake, she said that she had not made a mistake and that the man was 5' 9" but possibly might have been 5' 8½". When told that the Marines had measured Oswald on discharge as 5' 11", she said that they must have made a mistake.) Lee also told her that he had saved $1500 while in the Marines in order to make the trip to Russia. Another woman journalist recorded the height of the man she interviewed about three days later as 5' 11". They were the only journalists permitted by Oswald to interview him at any length – a woman could be less aware of a man's height than another man might be.

It is surprising that the KGB, who inspect every foreigner entering Russia and especially a Marine apparently wishing to defect, should – according to the Commission – have allowed a 5' 9" man who was carrying a passport showing his height as 5' 11" to enter and remain in their country, later entrusting him with espionage and political sabotage despite the possibility of United States citizen Lee Harvey Oswald having a change of heart after returning to the United States and being reunited with his family.

Neither before enlisting in the Marines nor during his service is Lee known to have been violent or to have committed offences or crimes other than the illegal possession of the pistol. All the photographs of Lee shown in the Exhibits from childhood to the age of 19 years show a happy person and he appears in no way to have been the withdrawn child, boy and young man as suggested by the Report of the Commission.

In addition to the testimony of Marguerite, Robert and John Pic, the Commission took the testimony of many people who knew Oswald from childhood until he left the Marines in September 1959. The testimony of Marguerite and Robert Oswald will be found in Volume I and the testimony of John Pic in Volume XI. The testimony of those who had contact with Lee from childhood until he left the Marines will be found in Volume VIII. The man who came from Russia and who was in the United States from June 1962 to 24 November 1963 behaved in a manner that appears to be inconsistent with the known character and behaviour of Lee Harvey Oswald.

At this point in the story, there are several indications that the assassin was not Lee Harvey Oswald: height, mastoidectomy, scars, hair, skin colour, American accent, fluent Russian, inability to speak *any* Spanish on the bus to and in Mexico City, and change in character. (Before the assassin left for Mexico and for his use while there or in Cuba, Marina made a long list of simple Russian words and their Spanish equivalents including the numbers 1-17.) Against the evidence of imposture there appears to be but one matter; the acceptance of the assassin as the real Lee Harvey Oswald by the mother and brother. The fingerprints of Oswald taken when he enlisted in the Marines in 1956 may or may not be those on the Marine fingerprint card as shown in the Exhibits.

It is interesting to recount the first appearance of Jack Ruby in the story and to record his activities in August and September 1959 in which two months Oswald was negotiating and completing his release from the Marines.

In these months Ruby was working in Dallas and living at 4727 Homer in that city. He was known to have been in New York during the first week in August, but during the latter part of August (while Oswald was obtaining his discharge from the Marines), Ruby paid an eight-day visit to Havana to see a friend Lewis McWillie. Ruby was to testify that this was a pleasure visit and made at the invitation of McWillie who bought and mailed a ticket to him from Havana because, according to Ruby in testimony, it was cheaper than buying it in the United States. After eight days Ruby returned to Dallas.

Oswald had been discharged from the Marines on *11 September 1959* and was on his way to his mother's home in Fort Worth on 12 September, arriving on 14 September and leaving for New Orleans on the evening of 16 September. It is possible that it was on *11 September* that Ruby left Dallas for Miami because on 12 September he flew from Miami by American Airlines again to visit Havana. He bought the ticket in his correct name and address, and arrived in Havana that day. The next day, 13 September, Ruby, in his correct name and address flew by Delta Airlines, not back to Miami or Dallas, but to New Orleans, arriving there on the same day. The FBI obtained the information about Ruby's one-day trip to Havana from the airlines on 4 and 5 December 1963, and in a statement to the FBI, McWillie did not mention this one-day visit and may not have seen Ruby.

Ruby was to testify before the Commission on 7 June 1964 and admitted the eight-day visit to McWillie in August because it could not be denied, others having provided information that he had been in Havana at that time. In his testimony, however, Ruby four times denied his later one-day trip to Havana in September, saying in reply to a question whether he had made a trip to Cuba other than the eight-day one in August, 'Never; that is the only one that I made (R.205)'. When asked about the step-by-step process by which he had arrived in Havana in August to visit McWillie, he replied, ' ... I only went to Cuba once, so naturally ... I only made one trip to Havana (R.207)'. In reply to the question ' ... this trip to Cuba (August) was the only time you left the country other than military service (during World War II)?' Ruby replied, 'Actually I didn't leave in the military. I was stationed $3\frac{1}{2}$ years here in the States. Let's see, never out of the United States except at one time to Havana, Cuba (R. 208)'.

Although in December 1963 the FBI had obtained from the airlines confirmation of Ruby's one-day September 1959 trip to Havana, in June 1964 the Commission did not confront Ruby with the evidence of this trip nor ask him to explain why he made the trip and how he had forgotten it. They did not ask him on what day he left Dallas for Miami, what he did in Havana on 12 September or in New Orleans on and perhaps after 13 September, nor on what day he returned from New Orleans to Dallas.

The corresponding chronology of Oswald's and Ruby's movements in September 1959, together with Ruby's lies and the failure of the Commission to question him about the one-day trip, raises interesting questions for it would seem that neither Ruby nor the Commission wished to disclose the trip. The Commission must have had in their possession the evidence that the FBI had obtained from the airlines in December 1963, for in their Report (R.802) they say: 'There is no reliable evidence that Ruby went to Havana subsequently to *September* 1959'. Although Oswald's two passports appear in the Exhibits, Ruby's passport is *not* shown.

It would seem that there are three possibilities: (a) the trip had no connection with Oswald, (b) Ruby gave Oswald $1,500 and/or instructions in New Orleans or (c) Ruby killed Oswald, an impostor taking Oswald's identity, documents and clothes, and making the zig-zag journey to Russia in place of the deceased Oswald; this possibility perhaps illuminating all that was to follow and the reluctance of the Commission to press Ruby about his one-day trip to Havana on 12 and 13 September 1959.

The Commission calculated how much Oswald had received

while in the Marines, $3,452.20, and in their Report they speculated that Oswald could have saved this amount, although they were unable to discover where he had deposited it nor, if not deposited, how Oswald had managed to carry his steadily increasing savings on his person or elsewhere while on active service. As the armed forces had facilities for servicemen to deposit savings with them for safety and financial benefit, it is remarkable that no evidence could be found that Oswald had saved this large sum; he did not even tell his best friend, Delgado.

It would seem that it is more probable than not that Marine Oswald *did* make the journey to Russia however it was financed, and this book will continue on the basis that the real Oswald entered Russia from New Orleans in October 1959, but on the balance of evidence it is more probable than not that another returned, and this book must therefore proceed on the assumption of imposture in Russia rather than in New Orleans.*

After Ruby returned to Dallas from New Orleans, on a date unknown but 'late' in 1959, he was to acquire a club situated in the 1300 block of Dallas, then known as 'The Sovereign Club' and later to become 'The Carousel' at the same address, 1312½ Commerce Street. It will be shown later that the number 1300 is the 'catalyst' number used by the assassin for encoding purposes, including the encoding in Oswald's notebook of the unlisted telephone number of the apartment occupied by Ruby in November 1963. As the story progresses, it will be seen that in addition to being in New Orleans on 13 September 1959 and in addition to killing the assassin on 24 November 1963, Ruby appears on the scene at moments of importance.

The next Chapter will describe Oswald's alleged activities while in Russia from October 1959 and until his 'return' to the United States in June 1962.

*See page 351 for important additional information

10

The Chapter will proceed upon the basis of the information contained in the Commission Report under the head 'Soviet Union' (R.689-713), which information was drawn by the Commission from (a) the testimony of Marina, (b) a 'Historic Diary' left behind by Oswald purporting to recount his activities while in Russia, (c) documents and medical records of Lee Harvey Oswald and Marina supplied by the Russian authorities to the American authorities after the death of the assassin, (d) testimony and documents obtained by the Commission from officials at the United States Embassy in Moscow and from the State Department in Washington, and (e) the testimony and evidence of the two American women journalists who interviewed Oswald shortly after his arrival in Moscow. These women had been informed by the United States Embassy that a defector had arrived in Moscow and that. they might be interested in interviewing him.

It would seem that reliability can be placed only upon information emanating from American sources, so that much of what is recounted in this Chapter may well be the result of disinformation.

Based on the evidence of imposture, it is probable that if it was Oswald who arrived in Russia on 15 October 1959 he was in some way trapped and unknowingly, willingly or unwillingly, assisted in the preparation of an impostor for infiltration into the United States. Although the name Oswald will be used, it must be borne in mind that the truth may never be known and that *all* the events set out in this Chapter can be attributed either to Oswald or to an impostor. The Report says (R.691) that the Commission was aware 'that many of the Soviet officials with whom Oswald came into contact were employees of the KGB, the agency which had primary jurisdiction for the treatment of defectors'. According to the February 1964 alleged defector, Nosenko, it was he who took charge of Oswald upon the arrival of the latter in Russia; the Report does not mention him.

The 'Historic Diary' purports to be Oswald's account of his stay in Russia (Appendix C), and it may be thought that it is all disinformation. According to the Diary, after travelling by train from Helsinki he was met at Moscow railway station on 16 October by an Intourist representative and taken by car to the Hotel Berlin where he was met by an Intourist guide, Rimma Sherikova. He told her that he intended to apply for Russian citizenship; she agreed to assist. She then communicated with her superiors and helped Oswald to prepare a letter to the Supreme Soviet asking for citizenship. The next day, 17 October, Rimma took him for a sight-seeing tour in Moscow and asked him questions about himself and his reasons for wanting to become a Russian citizen. The next day, 18 October, Rimma and Oswald were again together in the morning and the afternoon. There is no mention of Oswald meeting Rimma on 19 October but a man named Lev Setayev probably interviewed him in his hotel room. Setayev said he was from Moscow Radio and seeking statements from American tourists about their impressions of Moscow; he was probably also acting for the KGB. On 20 October, Rimma told him during the afternoon that Intourist had been told by the Passport and Visa Department that they wanted to see him.

On 21 October, being the day on which his visa expired, according to the Diary he was told that his application for citizenship had been refused and that he must leave Russia by 8.00 p.m. Having planned his defection for two years Oswald was 'shocked' and returned to his hotel where, at 7.00 p.m., he decided to 'end it'. He soaked his left wrist in cold water to numb the pain and then slashed it. He plunged it into a bath of hot water and watched his 'life whirl away'. He was found unconscious at 8.00 p.m. by Rimma who took him to a hospital where he was treated. He remained in the hospital until the wound had healed and was discharged on 28 October. On this day, *instead* of returning to the Hotel Berlin he checked into the Hotel Metropole, both hotels being under the same management.

Included in the Commission's Exhibits are the Russian medical records of Oswald covering the period of his stay in Russia and supplied by the Russians to the State Department after the death of the assassin. The first of these records is a report from the Botkin Hospital, Moscow, dealing with the treatment of 'Oswald, Lee Harvey' after his alleged suicide attempt (XVIII.461-473). The report records that the ambulance called for Oswald at 3.14 p.m. on 21 October, and that he was admitted to the hospital at 4.00 p.m. Under the heading 'Place of Employment', is recorded K-4-19-80 Service Bureau, Radio Technician. The report also records that he was visited in the hospital by the Head of the Service Bureau and an interpreter (XVIII.472). The Diary records that an Intourist guide stayed by his side as an interpreter, but it does not mention that he was visited by the Head of the Service Bureau. The hospital record also says that Oswald had inflicted the injury upon himself in order to delay his departure from the Soviet Union. The Diary makes no reference to his employment at K-4-19-80. It is apparent that there are significant differences between the Diary and the records supplied by the hospital authorities, and that either the Diary or the medical records (or both) are false. The Commission's Report, although quoting from the hospital report, does not mention Oswald's alleged employment in the Service Bureau immediately upon his arrival in Moscow, or being visited in hospital by the Head of the Bureau, and there is no way of knowing what K-4-19-80 Service Bureau represents.

On *Saturday* 31 October, being three days after his discharge from hospital, Oswald went from the Hotel Metropole to the American Embassy in Moscow and handed in his passport stating that he wished to renounce his American citizenship, and that he had applied for Russian citizenship. He did not mention his attempt to kill himself. In testimony to the Commission, the Embassy officials later confirmed his statements, and added that he was 'arrogant and showed bravado', telling the officials that he had already offered to give the Russians information that he had learned as a radar operator in the Marines. Oswald's offensive attitude could not have endeared him to the officials who would, it might seem, have been disinclined to accede to his immediate demands, especially on a Saturday morning, but his threats to disclose information obtained in the Marines would have convinced the officials — if conviction was necessary — that it was the ex-Marine, Lee Harvey Oswald, who had appeared at the Embassy.

With the recent case of the defector from the United States to Russia, Petrulli, in mind, the Embassy told Oswald that it would take some time for the necessary papers for a formal renunciation of his citizenship to be prepared and that he should return to the Embassy in a few days if he still wished to proceed. The officials testified that Oswald never returned to complete the formalities and that Oswald's American citizenship therefore remained intact.

The threat to give information to the Russians was taken seriously. Aircraft call signs and codes were changed which, as a Marine officer testified, involved much time and effort. Other matters, such as the positioning of radar sites and the details of equipment and various systems could not be changed; the Americans believing and having to accept that the Russians now knew them.

On the day after Oswald's appearance at the Embassy, his family read in the newspapers of his defection and tried to contact him. Marguerite placed a telephone call to him but he cut her off very quickly, and on 2 November he rejected the Embassy's efforts to deliver or read over the telephone a telegram from Robert. A telephone call from Robert was refused and Robert's telegram, along with a message asking Oswald to contact him immediately which Robert had asked the State Department to deliver, was finally sent by the Embassy to Oswald at the Hotel Metropole by registered mail. John Pic also tried unsuccessfully to contact him. Sometime in January 1960, Marguerite sent Oswald $25. She was to testify that she respected his motives for defecting but later came to suspect that he had been forcibly removed to Russia.

On 3 November, Oswald wrote to the Embassy requesting that his citizenship be revoked. The letter said that he had appeared at the Embassy 'for the purpose of signing the formal papers to this effect' and protested against the 'conduct of the official' who had refused him 'this legal right'. Oswald said that his application for Soviet citizenship was pending and that if it were granted he would ask the Soviet Government 'to lodge a formal protest' on his behalf.

Between 8 November and 17 December 1959, Oswald wrote three letters from Moscow to Robert. In the first letter he said that Robert did not know anything about him and would not understand his reasons for wishing to remain in the Soviet Union and applying for Soviet citizenship, and that he had waited to do this for well over a year and had been studying Russian for many months. He would not leave Russia under any conditions and he would never return to the United States which was a country he hated. He would not speak to anyone from the United States over the telephone because he thought it might be 'taped' by the Americans. In the second letter he said that 'in the event of war I will kill any American who put on a uniform in defence of the American Government – any American'. He went on to say that he wanted to live a normal, happy and peaceful life in Russia for the rest of his life, and that his mother and Robert were not 'objects of affection' but only 'examples of workers' in the United States. In the third letter Oswald said that he would not write again and did not wish Robert to write to him, because he was starting a new life and did not want to have anything to do with the old life. He signed the three letters with the one word, 'Lee'.

On 9 November, the American Embassy replied to Oswald's letter of 3 November telling him that he could renounce his citizenship by coming to the Embassy and executing the necessary papers; he did not appear.

Early in November, Mr Goldberg, an American journalist in Moscow, having heard that a defector had arrived from the United States, endeavoured to interview Oswald. On Goldberg's arrival outside the door of Oswald's room in the Hotel Metropole a young man wearing a white shirt and black slacks opened the door slightly. In response to Goldberg's question, he said that his name was Lee Harvey Oswald. Goldberg then told Oswald that he would like to interview him but Oswald said that he did not wish to furnish any statement. Goldberg succeeded, however, in speaking to Oswald through the slightly opened door. Goldberg asked Oswald why he was going to remain in Russia and Oswald replied only, 'I've got my reasons' and would say nothing further. Goldberg endeavoured to discourage Oswald from remaining in Russia and when he asked Oswald if he knew the Russian language, Oswald replied that he did not know the language but that he could learn and that he would 'make out'. Goldberg wanted to take a photograph of Oswald, but the young man refused. In a statement to the FBI after the assassination of the President, Goldberg stated that another journalist, Aline Mosby, contacted Oswald a few days after he had spoken with the young man, but Oswald refused to be interviewed by her, although apparently agreeing to an interview some days later. Goldberg told the FBI that he could not understand why Oswald subsequently consented to an interview with Miss Mosby instead of himself, but was of the opinion that Oswald may have thought himself to be a 'ladies man' and preferred to furnish his story to a female instead of a male reporter.

On 13 November, Oswald was interviewed at the Hotel Metropole in Moscow by Miss Mosby. She was not asked to testify but in an article (XXII.701-710) she later wrote about Oswald she said *inter alia* that he was neatly dressed in a suit, white shirt and tie. The interview lasted two hours with Oswald carrying on a monologue. He said that the Russians would let him stay even if they did not grant him citizenship, and that they had told him they were investigating the possibilities of finding him an occupation, thinking it would be best if he were to continue his higher education. He told her he had lived for two years in New York and that his widowed mother then took him and his two brothers to Fort Worth, Texas, then to New Orleans and again to Fort Worth. He said that his mother 'works in shops mostly, in Fort Worth and around'. He said he was a Marxist and had become interested at about the age of 15 when an old lady gave him a pamphlet about saving the Rosenbergs. He said, 'I looked at that paper and I still remember it for some reason, I don't know why'. In New Orleans he had discovered a book in the library, *Das Kapital*, and that it was what he had been looking for as it was like a religious man opening the Bible for the first time. He had also read the *Manifesto* (Marx) and started to study Marxist economic theories, but did not mention his favourite books, *Animal Farm* and *1984*. For the Marine Corps and United

States policy Oswald showed deep hatred and said that life as he saw it in the Marine Corps had convinced him that he should move to the other side of the Iron Curtain. While in the Marines, he had continued to read Marxist books and had laid careful plans to go to Russia, as it would give him a chance to observe what he had read. He told her that he had saved $1,500, and for two years he had had it in mind to divest himself of anything to do with the United States. None of his fellow Marines knew of his plans to give up his country, and his superiors thought that he was just interested in the Russian language. He said of his mother, 'She's rather old I couldn't expect her to understand. I guess it wasn't quite fair of me not to say anything, but it's better that way. I don't want to involve my family in this. I think it would be best if they would forget about me. My brother might lose his job because of this'. Miss Mosby noticed the secretive smirk that he wore when he related his self-imposed mission. After two hours she was tired of listening to what sounded like recitations out of *Pravda* and she decided to leave. Oswald had appeared totally disinterested in anything but himself, never asking her what she was doing in Moscow or how foreigners lived there. He did not tell her of a suicide attempt, hospitalization or K-4-19-80 Service Bureau. He appeared to be 'a one-man third category ... But instead of defecting for economic or love reasons, he apparently had made the plunge for the glory he might receive in Moscow that he had not received in his own country". She recorded his complexion as sallow, that his hair and eyes were brown, and that his height was 5' 9". She was later to say that the same little smile which she had noticed in Moscow was on Oswald's face just before he was shot by Ruby, and that he looked just the same in the newspaper photograph that she saw on the morning after his murder.

On 16 November, the other woman journalist, Miss Johnson, had a five-hour interview with Oswald at the same hotel (XI.442-460). She was to testify that Oswald had told her that he had lived in New York for two years and that he 'struck me as noticeably reticent about his finances, about his financial situation. He told me ... that he had been for ten days on Intourist. He said he was paying the standard room and food rate, and said 'I want to make it clear they are not sponsoring me.' ...

His use of (English) words struck me very much in conversation; he sometimes pronounced a particular word correctly and later pronounced it incorrectly, and that simple words he sometimes mispronounced and hard ones he got right'.

Oswald complained to her about the treatment he had received at the Embassy and said that he was not going back there 'merely to get the run-around again, and that they should have allowed him to renounce his American citizenship there and then'. Although he emphasised to her his determination to renounce his American citizenship and to remain in Russia, she felt that Oswald was leaving a loophole for himself to return to the United States, and that his attempts to blame the Embassy were an excuse for not going back to renounce formally his citizenship. Oswald talked about himself the whole time, and whatever he was talking about 'was really Lee Oswald'. His reticence and secretiveness aroused her suspicions because he seemed to have something to hide; he would not say what books he had read and would not talk about his life in the Marine Corps. He told her that he had started learning Russian a year ago along with his other preparations, and had been able to teach himself to read and write from Berlitz. When she asked him whether he just got a text book or went to some city nearby for lessons at a school, he would not answer, and that struck her as being a strange thing about which to be evasive. She asked him again whether he practised by himself or had a teacher, and again he would not say anything. It kept coming up again and again that he had recently heard from the Russians that he would not have to leave the Soviet Union, saying more than once that, even if the Russians refused him citizenship, he would not have to leave, using the words 'until some solution is found what to do with me'. She received the impression that he was avoiding hearing from his family, and he told her that they were asking him to come back, but that he would not answer the telephone. She wondered how he knew that they were asking him to come back if he did not answer the telephone, and that he was 'full of those kinds of contradictions'. She said that 'from what appeared to be a boyish pique (refusing to return to the Embassy) lay something else. He was leaving himself a way out and I was fully aware of it at the time ... He left a loophole and the scapegoat was the Embassy'. When she asked him about his political reading during the previous 5 years, he could remember only the writers Marx and Engels, and only the book *Das Kapital*. As with Miss Mosby, Oswald did not tell her about his suicide attempt, hospitalisation or K-4-19-80 Service Brueau. In her notes she had recorded his hair as brown, his eyes as blue and his height as 5' 11"; in her testimony the physical data was not mentioned.

Also in testimony, Miss Johnson discussed Oswald's case. She said that he was unique because defectors to Russia went because they had some powerful emotional reason to do so – such as a broken marriage – but he was the exception that proved the rule because he purported to be acting for ideological reasons. She went on, ' ... whenever I thought about him I thought: what is behind these professed reasons? They are really emotional reasons in his case, too, and I don't understand, although it is not obvious like a wife he is leaving, nor still emotional responses, and I don't know what is behind his professed ideological reasons. And I can't guess. So he was the pin really for the piece and I couldn't guess them. If I had known he was back in the States – I had thought about him, it seems to me as recently as three weeks before the assassination, and wondered, and the way that the thought used to come to me was, 'I wonder whatever happened to that little Lee Oswald?' and had I known he was back – I thought he would have been disenchanted, trapped in Russia, unable to get out – if I had known he was back I probably would have tried to see him, write him, go to see him. And if I had been able to figure out his reasons and what had happened to him, maybe I could have written that piece (a newspaper article)'. She said that at the time she interviewed Oswald in Moscow she had had plenty of indication that people could not leave the Soviet Union once they had entered the country. She said, ' ... and I didn't assume for a second that he had ever left or gotten out and I wanted, if I could, to help him, warn him subtly that he was going to be trapped. That is why I spent so long talking to him. But I assumed that my room was wired, and I couldn't be obvious about it and I tried to do it by talking to him about economics.'

On 4 January 1960, Oswald was issued with a Soviet Identity

Document for stateless persons. P.311479, but was not granted the citizenship that he said he desired. Thus, having failed to return to the American Embassy to complete the formalities for a renunciation of his American citizenship and not having been granted Russian citizenship, the door was left open for infiltration of an impostor into the United States.

On 7 January 1960, according to the Diary and Russian records, Oswald was sent to Minsk – some 450 miles southwest of Moscow and with a population of about 500,000. According to the Diary and Russian records, he was there employed as an unskilled labourer at a factory manufacturing radios and where he was to continue to work until shortly before leaving Russia for the United States in May 1962. During much of the time he was in Minsk, again according to the Diary and Russian records, Oswald received a supplementary allowance from a Government agency called the 'Red Cross' of an amount almost equal to his wage. He was also alloted an attractive apartment with a balcony overlooking a river; such an apartment was not immediately available to Russians who might have to wait for several years to obtain one, and then only if they had a family. Oswald's Diary records that he enjoyed his first months in Minsk and went to a theatre, a movie or an opera almost every night.

Oswald's union card described him as a 'middle worker' in the factory which employed about 5,000 people. At one time, Oswald recorded that the shop in the factory in which he worked was called the 'experimental shop' and employed 58 workers and 5 foremen.

A gift of additional money and a good apartment are standard treatment for defectors. It is almost certain that there was a spy-school in or near Minsk and at which Oswald was trained, and it would seem that Oswald's factory employment may have been the 'cover' for his espionage and political sabotage training.

Sometime in June 1960, he met Ella German, a worker at the factory, of whom he later said that he 'perhaps fell in love with her the first minute' he saw her. On New Year's day 1961, he was at the home of Ella and her family, and during a walk back to his apartment, he decided to ask Ella to marry him. On the following night, after he had brought her home from the 'movies', he proposed on her doorstep but she rejected him, saying that she did not love him and that she was afraid to marry *an American*. His affection for Ella apparently continued for some time, and he had his last formal date with her in February 1962 but remained on friendly terms until he was to leave Russia in May 1962.

On 4 January 1961, being one year after he had been issued his 'stateless' residence permit, Oswald was summoned to the passport office in Minsk and asked if he still wanted to become a Soviet citizen. He replied that he did not but asked that his residence permit be extended for another year. The entry in his Diary for January 4-31 reads: 'I am starting to reconsider my desire about staying. The work is drab. The money I get has nowhere to be spent. No nightclubs or bowling allys, no places of recreation accept the trade union dances. I have had enough." (Before leaving the United States Lee Harvey Oswald is not know to have been interested in nightclubs or bowling alleys. He did not mention theatres, operas or movies, and this entry in the Diary suggests that he was saving money. It would seem that when the State Department were to lend Oswald a substantial sum to assist in paying the fares of himself, Marina and infant child, they lent only about half of what it would cost Oswald and family to return to the United States; the suggestion of saving money may have been to remove from the KGB the suspicion that they provided the necessary travel money over and above the State Department loan).

The American Embassy had not heard from Oswald after receiving his letter of 3 November 1959, but on 13 February 1961 it received a letter from him which had been mailed from Minsk. He asked for the return of his passport, saying that he wanted to return to the United States if he could 'come to some agreement concerning the dropping of any legal proceedings' against him, that he had not become a Soviet citizen and was living in Russia with 'non permanent type papers for a foreigner', and that he did not appear personally because he could not leave Minsk without permission. The letter ended: 'I hope that in recalling the responsibility I have to America that you will remember yours in doing everything you can to help me, since I am an American citizen.' Marguerite, who in January 1961 had enquired at the Department of State about his whereabouts, was notified of his letter.

On 28 February 1961, the Embassy wrote to Oswald telling him that he would have to appear at the Embassy personally to discuss his return to the United States. On 20 March, the Embassy received a second letter from Oswald reiterating that he was unable to leave Minsk without permission and asking that 'preliminary enquiries be put in the form of a questionnaire' and sent to him. Soon after the correspondence with the Embassy began, Oswald's monthly payments from the 'Red Cross' were cut off.

On 17 March 1961, Oswald attended a train union dance at the Palace of Culture in Minsk. Marina Nikolayevna Prusakova was also at the dance and they were introduced. Oswald asked her to dance and according to the Diary they liked each other immediately and he obtained her telephone number before she left. She was to testify that she did not intend to go to the dance and was only persuaded to do so by her uncle Prusakov in whose house she was living and who was a member of the Communist Party and a Colonel in the Secret Police – the MVD. It was at this first meeting that Marina thought that 'Alek' was a fellow-countryman until he later told her that he was an American, Lee Harvey Oswald. Marina was to testify that she told Oswald that she might see him at another dance and did not give him her telephone number.

The Commission Report says of Marina: 'Marina Prusakova was 19 years old when she met Oswald. She was born on July 17, 1941, at Severodvinsk (formerly Molotvsk), Arkhangel Oblast', Russia. A few years later, her mother Klavdiya Vasilievna Prusakova, married Aleksandr Ivanovich Medvedev, who became the only father Marina knew. While she was still a young girl, Marina went to Arkhangel'sk, Arkhangel Oblast', to live with her maternal grandparents, Tatyana Yakovlevna Prusakova and Vasiliy Prusakov. Her grandfather died when Marina was about 4 years old; she continued to live with her grandmother for some time. When she was not more than 7, she moved to Zguritva, Moldavian SSR (formerly called Bessarabia) to live with her mother and stepfather, who was an electrical worker. In 1952, the family moved to Leningrad, where the stepfather obtained a job in a power station. Marina testified that neither he nor her mother was a member of the Communist Party.

In Leningrad, Marina attended the Three Hundred and Seventy-Fourth Women's School. After she had completed the seventh grade at the school in 1955, she entered the Pharmacy Teknikum, she joined the Trade Union for Medical Workers and, in her last year there, worked part time in the Central Pharmacy in Leningrad. She graduated from the Teknikum with a diploma in pharmacy on 29 June 1959.

Marina's mother had died in 1957 during Marina's second year at the Teknikum; she continued to live with her stepfather but had little contact with him. She testified that she did not get along with her stepfather whom she displeased by her fresh conduct; saying that she was not easily disciplined and was a source of concern to him. Because of the friction between them, Marina regarded her childhood as an unhappy one.

After her graduation, Marina was assigned to a job preparing and packing orders in a pharmaceutical warehouse in Leningrad; as a new employee she had the right to leave this job within 3 days after the assignment, and she did so after the first day'. (Author's note: This would be in *July 1959*.) 'She took no job for the next 2 months, at the end of which she went to live in Minsk with an aunt and uncle, the Prusakovs, who had no children. She had known them since she was a child and there was a mutual affection between her and them. Her uncle, a member of the Communist Party, was assigned to the Ministry of Internal Affairs and headed the local bureau concerned with lumber. The Prusakovs had one of the best apartments in a building reserved for MVD employees.

Marina was 18 when she arrived in Minsk. She had had boyfriends in Leningrad but was not interested in marriage. In October 1960 she started work in the drug section of the Third Clinical Hospital where she earned about 450 rubles per month; at about the same time she became a member of the local Komsomol, the Communist youth organisation. Her friends were mostly students, whose social life consisted of meeting in cafes to sip coffee, read newspapers, gossip, and carry on discussions. The group of friends 'ran together', and Marina did not attach herself to a particular boyfriend. She enjoyed this life, which she had been living for about 7 months when she met Oswald at the dance at the Palace of Culture in March 1961.

When Marina met Oswald she thought he was from one of the Russian-speaking Baltic countries because he spoke with an accent; later that same evening she learned that he was an American. She met him again at another dance a week later. They danced together most of the evening, at the end of which he walked home with her. They arranged to meet again the following week. Before the scheduled time, Oswald called to say that he was in the hospital and that Marina should visit him there. Medical records furnished to the Commission by the Russian Government show that Oswald was admitted to the Clinical Hospital – Ear, Nose, and Throat Division – on Thursday, March 30, 1961. Marina visited him often, 'taking advantage of her uniform' to visit him outside regular visiting hours, which were only on Sunday. On Easter Sunday, the first Sunday after his admission to the hospital, she brought him an Easter egg. On a subsequent visit, he asked her to be his fiancée, and she agreed to consider it. He left the hospital on April 11.' (Author's note: The hospital recorded the mastoidectomy and scar. The length of the scar was not noted and the record says that, 'At the age of 10-12 an antrotomy' – mastoidectomy – 'of the Left ear was performed'. The patient was named on the record as 'Oswald Harvey Alik'. XVIII.450-460). The Commission's Report continues: 'During these visits, Marina apparently discussed with Oswald his reasons for coming to Russia and his current status. According to her later account, he told her that he had surrendered his American documents to the Embassy in Moscow and had told American officials that he did not intend to return to the United States. He did not say definitely that he was no longer an American citizen, but said in answer to a question about his citizenship that he could not return to the United States.

Oswald visited Marina regularly at her aunt and uncle's apartment; they were apparently not disturbed by the fact that he was an American and did not disapprove of her seeing him. He continued to ask her to marry him and, according to her recollection, she accepted his proposal on April 20; Oswald's diary puts the date 5 days earlier. Marina testified that she believed that Oswald could not return to the United States when she agreed to marry him, and that she had not married him in hope of going to the United States. (R.703-704)'.

A part of the Commission's Report quoted above says that it was *in October 1960* that Marina started work in the drug section ... at about the same time she became a member of the local Komsomol ... She enjoyed this life, which she had been leading for about 7 months when she met Oswald . . . in March 1961.

These words are misleading and the Commission should have known this to be so for it was in October *1959* that Marina started work in the drug section of the hospital in Minsk, and therefore she would have been in the local Komsomol for *19* months rather than 7 months before she met Oswald at the dance in March 1961. In testimony, Marina said that when it was known that she was marrying an American and preparing to leave Russia for the United States, she was dismissed from Komsomol. After the assassination, the Russians and Marina supplied a number of records in relation to her occupations, but neither supplied anything that related to her membership of Komsomol and, as a result, no documents have been produced to indicate when, why and where Marina joined Komsomol, and when she left the organisation. In testimony, she said, 'I was persuaded or talked into joining the Komsomol organisation'; she did not say when or where this was or who persuaded her, and the Commission did not ask her to supply details.

The records in relation to her employment obtained from her or supplied by the Russians are contradictory. If this book were fictional, these records could be taken to suggest that the woman who entered the United States with Oswald had been supplied with a 'legend', i.e. a false background, but this story is not fictional and no thought should be entertained that the fatherless and motherless Marina was other than the person she said she was. The records are without doubt susceptible to explanation but it is unfortunate that the Commission did not provide the answers.

Marina's Trade Union card issued in Leningrad had on its cover the usual legend, 'Proletariat of all countries unite!', and each page of the booklet contains a watermark with the legend, 'Trade Unions are a School of Communism'. The first page of the booklet states that Marina was born in *1940* and joined the Union in 1956, although the pages for stamps are headed in ink 1959, 1960 and 1961, and stamps are affixed only for June/July *1959* and for the first eight months of 1960 (XVI.73-77). When shown the booklet on the first page of which there is a photograph of a young woman, Marina in testimony said, 'I never have a good photograph.' She also said that she had 'forgotten to paste the stamps in' the booklet. Marina's Work Book gives the date of her birth as *1941* and her profession as pharmacist, and her work record shows it was on 29 October 1959 that she was taken on the staff of United 3rd Clinical Hospital of the city of Minsk as an analytical chemist, this appointment being confirmed on 31 October 1959. In testimony, Marina said, 'the girl who prepared the booklet thought I was older and put down 1940 instead of 1941.' Marina was unable to produce her birth certificate which she said had been mislaid, but produced a 19.7.61 certified copy showing her to have been born in 1941. On - August 1960, she was transferred to the position of Assistant of Pharmacy, and on 20 March 1962 (shortly before departing from Russia) she was released from work, 'according to application filed' (XVI.78-80). On 28 October 1959, Marina had been issued with a Draft Registration Certificate by the District Military Commander in Minsk and, inter alia, her height was recorded as 160 cm (5' 3"), but the certificate was not signed in the appropriate space by Marina. There is a stamp in the booklet reading, 'Mobilization Order issued on 28 July 1961', followed by a stamp, 'Mobilization Order Withdrawn 4 August 1961' (XVI.81-93). Oswald's Diary does not record Marina's 7-day call-up by the Military, which was at the time of the 'Berlin Crisis'. On the first page of the Draft Military Certificate there is another photograph of a young woman, and it, too, is not 'a good photograph' of Marina. In a Russian language questionnaire filled out by Marina when she was requesting permission to go to the United States, she stated that she had been a student at the Leningrad Pharmaceutical School from 1 September 1955 to 1 December 1959 – where she was awarded the qualification of a pharmacist on 29 June 1959 having 'in 1959 completed the full course' at the Leningrad Pharmaceutical School (XVI.72), and she also stated that she became assistant of the pharmacy of the 3rd Clinical Hospital of Minsk on 29 October 1959 (XVI.125-132). In testimony, Marina was not asked to enlarge upon the one year's discrepancy in the year of birth and overlapping dates in the Union Card and Work Book, but she was asked: 'Did you have to ask anyone in Leningrad in order to be able to leave there to go to Minsk, or you just go to Minsk and ask the people there to register you?'. She replied: 'I simply bought a ticket and went to Minsk, to my uncle.' She was not asked what arrangement or correspondence, if any, she had had with the authorities or with her uncle, the MVD Colonel Prusakov, before making the 600-miles journey to join him in his house in Minsk (I.88).

A study of the dates on which initial steps were taken by Oswald, Marina and Ruby shows that each made their first moves in July and September 1959, and that from then until the assassination they were to move contemporaneously, for example (a) as mentioned in this book Oswald and Ruby respectively arrived in New Orleans on 13 and 16 September 1959, and (b) when Oswald left the hospital in Moscow on 28 October 1959 after his alleged attempt at suicide, and went to the Hotel Metropole instead of returning to the Hotel Berlin, on the same day in far away Minsk Marina was enlisted in the Military, and when Oswald made his first visit on 31 October 1959 to the American Embassy in Moscow to achieve his deliberately unsuccessful renunciation of his American citizenship, on the same day in Minsk Marina's appointment as pharmacist to the local hospital staff was confirmed. The assassin having failed to escape, Oswald, Marina and Ruby were all to be in Dallas police station on 22 November 1963, the alleged Marine incarcerated, the pharmacist taken there by the police and the gangster haunting the passageways in the guise of an Israeli press reporter.

On 24 March 1961, the Embassy again wrote to Oswald telling him that he would have to come to Moscow. Later, the Department of State decided that Oswald's passport should be returned to him only if he appeared at the Embassy and if the Embassy, after exploring the matter with him, was satisfied that he had not renounced his citizenship. At this time, apart from any propaganda value in the return of a defector, the Americans were trying to reduce east-west tension.

After marrying Marina on 30 April 1961, the next day Oswald wrote in his diary 'in spite of fact I married Marina to hurt Ella I found myself in love with Marina'. The next entry reads: 'the transition of changing full love from Ella to Marina was very painful esp. as I saw Ella almost every day at the factory but as the days and weeks went I adjusted more and more my wife mentally . . . she is madly in love with me from the very start'.

Shortly after they had married, Oswald told Marina that he wished to go back to the United States and she testified that she had encouraged him to do as he wished.

On 5 May 1961, after 16 months of silence Oswald began to correspond with Marguerite and Robert in the United States. He first sent a friendly letter to Robert in which he said nothing about his approaches to the American Embassy, but advised him that he had married and was living well. He asked Robert for Marguerite's address and told him 'You should try to visit us sometime'. Robert answered the letter immediately and on 31 May Oswald again wrote to express his pleasure at receiving Robert's letter. He suggested that Robert might send Marina a small wedding present, saying that he did not know if he would ever return to the United States but that before he could return he would have to obtain the permission of the Soviet Union for him and Marina to leave, and he would have to be satisfied that no charges would be lodged against him in the United States. In this letter he said that he had been in touch with the American Embassy in Moscow.

On 25 May, the American Embassy received a letter from Oswald asking for assurances that he would not be prosecuted if he returned to the United States and informing the Embassy that he had married a Russian woman who would want to accompany him. The Embassy sent this information to the State Department in Washington and took their time in answering Oswald's letter.

Oswald and Marina now began to make enquiries from the Russians about obtaining exit visas. The man with whom they were in touch was another MVD officer, Colonel Aksenov, who was to grant their exit visas and who worked in the same office as Marina's MVD officer, Colonel Aksenov, who was to grant their exit visas and who worked in the same office as Marina's MVD uncle, Colonel Prusakov. There has been some suggestion that Aksenov's wife might have been another aunt of Marina.

On *Saturday* 8 July and again without warning, Oswald appeared at the Embassy and found the offices closed. He was able to reach one of the officials on the house telephone and the official came to the office to talk with him briefly and suggest that he return on the following Monday. Oswald telephoned Marina in Minsk and asked her to come to Moscow, to which she responded rapidly, arriving on Sunday 9 July when they booked into Hotel Ostakimo and then Hotel Berlin. Oswald returned to the Embassy on Monday 10 July, and Marina waited outside during his interview with the official, who asked to see Oswald's Soviet papers, and examined him closely about his life in Russia and any possible expatriating acts. Oswald told him that he was not a citizen of the Soviet Union and had never formally applied for citizenship, that he had never taken an oath of allegiance to the Soviet Union, and that he was not a member of the factory trade union organisation. He added that he had never given Soviet officials any confidential information that he had learned in the Marines, had never been asked to give such information and doubted that he would have done if he had been asked. Oswald was worried that he might be prosecuted and imprisoned if he returned to the United States, but was told by the official informally that he did not know of any grounds on which he would be prosecuted although he could give no assurance on this point. The official testified that Oswald seemed to have matured while in Russia and did not show the 'arrogance, contemptuousness and all-round offensiveness' of his first visit to the Embassy, Oswald saying that he had 'learned a hard lesson the hard way', acquiring a new appreciation of the United States and the meaning of freedom. Oswald's 1959 passport was to expire on 10 September 1961 before he would be able to obtain Russian exit papers. He therefore filled out an application for a renewal of his passport and, on a questionnaire attached to the application, he repeated his oral statements that he had obtained only a residence permit in the Soviet Union and was still an American national. On the basis of his oral and written statements the official concluded that Oswald had not expatriated himself, and returned his passport.

The next day Oswald and Marina came to the Embassy to commence procedures for her admittance to the United States as an immigrant, and this time they had an interview with another official. On the same day, Oswald wrote to Robert telling him that he had recovered his passport, and that he and Marina were doing all they could to hasten to the United States. He wrote, 'I can write a book about how many feelings have come and gone since that day', apparently referring to the day on which he had attempted to renounce his United States citizenship some 16 months previously. Ten days later, Oswald and Marina returned to Minsk.

On their return, Oswald and Marina began their efforts to obtain exit visas from Colonel Aksenov; they were to wait for about 11 months for these. Although under Soviet practice this was not an especially long period of waiting, it appears to have been designed to fit Oswald's time schedule after arriving in the United States – four months for him to set the scene with Robert, Marguerite and the FBI before moving, if required, into Jaggars-Chiles-Stovall.

On 15 July, Oswald informed the Embassy of his and Marina's efforts and said that he would keep them informed 'as to the overall picture'. The letter said that Marina was having great difficulities because of her decision to leave the country. Marina was to testify that when news of her visit to the American Embassy reached Minsk, meetings were arranged in Komsomol at which members of various organisations attempted to dissuade her from leaving the Soviet Union. She testified that her uncle and aunt, the Prusakovs, did not speak to her for a long time.

On 4 October, Oswald wrote to the American Embassy to ask them to intervene to assist him in obtaining his and Marina's exit visas, saying that there had been a systematic and concerted attempt to intimidate Marina into withdrawing her application for a visa which had resulted in her being hospitalized in September for nervous exhaustion. On 12 October, the Embassy replied that they had no way of influencing Russian conduct and that action on applications for exit visas was seldom taken rapidly. Marina was to testify that she was never in hospital, and the matter is not mentioned either in the Diary or in letters to his family.

In October 1961, Marina went on holiday for about three weeks to visit an aunt in Kharkov. She was pregnant at this time and Oswald noted in the Diary that he was lonely while she was away, but that he and a friend went to some dances and other public amusements; on his 22nd birthday he had gone by himself to see his favourite opera, *The Queen of Spades*. For a birthday present Marina sent him a gold and silver cup, inscribed 'To my dear husband on his birthday ...' and other presents, for which he wrote to thank her. She returned to Minsk on 12 November 'radiant, with several jars of preserves for me from her aunt'.

The Diary and Marina's testimony draw a picture of domestic bliss that is difficult to reconcile with their relationship early in the United States to be described in the next Chapter. Marina was to testify ' ... immediately after coming to the United States Lee changed. I did not know him as much a man in Russia ... He helped me as before, but he became a little more of a recluse ... He was very irritable, sometimes for a trifle ...' (R.718)

After Marina returned from holiday, Oswald went to see Colonel Aksenov in order to expedite their application for exit visas. Marina also visited the Colonel, but both she and Oswald were told that they would have to wait their turn.

On 1 November, Oswald wrote to the Embassy to tell them that if his Russian residence permit was to be renewed in January 1962 for another year, he would object. On 13 November the American Embassy wrote to Oswald telling him that this would not prejudice his claim to United States citizenship, the letter adding that he could discuss the renewal of his American passport – the original passport handed back to him had expired in September – *if he appeared in person at the Embassy for that purpose.*

On 25 December, Marina was called to the Soviet Passport

Office and told that exit visas would be granted to her and her husband. Oswald wrote to the Embassy on 27 December saying that they would be given exit visas and asking that his old passport be extended without his having to make another trip to Moscow, but adding that he would come to Moscow if this would assist the processing of his application.

On 2 January 1962, Oswald wrote to Marguerite telling her that he and Marina expected to arrive in the United States some time around March. He asked her to contact the local Red Cross for them to put his case before the International Rescue Committee or some other group which aids immigrants to the United States. He said that he would need about $800, and that she should insist on a gift rather than taking a loan, and he told her not to send any of her own money. This financial assistance was refused to Marguerite, although she did try to obtain a loan from the Red Cross. on 13 January, Oswald himself wrote to the International Rescue Committee asking for $800 to pay for two tickets from Moscow to Texas, and on 26 January he again wrote to the Committee, but this time asking for $1,000; no rescue was forthcoming.

On 5 January, the Embassy wrote to Oswald suggesting that if there were difficulties in Marina obtaining an immigration visa, he should consider returning alone and bringing her over later. On 16 January, Oswald replied, *inter alia*, 'Since I signed and paid for an immigration petition for my wife in July 1961, I think its about time to get it approved or refused ... I certainly will not consider going to the US alone for any reason ...' On 15 January, the Embassy wrote to Oswald saying that because Marina had not yet obtained an American visa and no evidence had yet been submitted that she would not become a public charge in the United States, Marguerite or some other close relative should file an affidavit of support on Marina's behalf. Apparently before receiving this letter Oswald wrote out such a document himself and mailed it to the Embassy, and on 23 January he wrote to the Embassy saying that his own affidavit should be sufficient since he had been away from the United States for more than two years and could not be expected to obtain an affidavit from someone else. On the same day, he wrote to Marguerite asking for her to file an affidavit of support with the Immigration and Naturalisation Service. On 24 January, the Embassy acknowledged receipt of his own affidavit in support but again suggested that he should obtain one from someone else.

Later in January, Oswald received a letter from Marguerite telling him that he had been given a dishonourable discharge from the Marines and on 30 January 1962 he wrote to his brother for more information. On the same day he wrote to John B. Connally who had been Secretary of Navy but had resigned to run for Governor of Texas:

'I wish to call your attention to a case about which you may have personal knowledge since you are a resident of Ft. Worth as I am. In November 1959 an event was well publicated in the Ft. Worth newspapers concerning a person who had gone to the Soviet Union to reside for a short time – much in the same way E. Hemingway resided in Paris.

This person in answers to questions put to him by reporters in Moscow criticized certain facets of american life. The story was blown up into another 'turncoat' sensation, with the result that the Navy department gave this person a belated dishonourable discharge, although he had received an honourable discharge after three years service on Sept. 11, 1959 at El Toro, Marine corps base in California.

These are the basic facts of my case.

I have and always had the full sanction of the U.S. Embassy, Moscow USSR, and hence the U.S. government. In as much as I am returning to the U.S.A. in this year with the aid of the U.S. Embassy, bringing with me my family (since I married in the USSR) I shall employ all means to right this gross mistake or injustice to a bona-fide U.S. citizen and ex-service man. The U.S. government has no charges or complaints against me. I ask you to look into this case and take the necessary steps to repair the damage done to me and my family. For information I would direct you to consult the American Embassy, Chikovski St. 19/21, Moscow, USSR.'

Connally referred the letter to the Department of the Navy, which sent Oswald a letter stating that the Department contemplated no change in the undesirable discharge, and on 27 March Oswald wrote to the Department asking for his discharge to be given a further full review. The Department replied that it had no authority to hear and review petitions of this sort and referred Oswald to the Navy Discharge Review Board, enclosing an Application for Review. Oswald filled out the enclosed Application but did not mail it until he returned to the

United States. No doubt the undesirable discharge had been the result of his statement at the American Embassy in Moscow that he would divulge radar and other information to the Russians.

The Department of State had written to Marguerite telling her that it would need $900 to make the travel arrangements for her son and daughter-in-law. On 1 February, Oswald wrote to Marguerite rejecting her suggestion that she try to raise the money by telling the newspapers about his financial plight. Five days later, the Embassy wrote to Oswald and asked him to make formal application for a loan. On 9 February, Oswald wrote to Marguerite reminding her once more to file an affidavit of support and asking that she send him clippings from the local newspapers about his defection to Russia; the request for clippings was later repeated to Robert. He told Marguerite that he wanted to know what had been written about him, so that he could be 'forewarned'; the clippings were sent.

On 15 February, Marina gave birth to a baby girl who was named June Lee. After the birth, Oswald wrote to Marguerite and Robert telling them that he would probably not arrive for several months, and advising them of the birth.

On 3 March, the Embassy received a letter from Oswald in which he applied for a loan of $800, but the Embassy replied that it was authorised to loan him only $500. In the meantime, the Embassy had decided that Oswald's own affidavit of support for Marina was sufficient in the circumstances. On 15 March, in a letter dated 28 February Oswald received notification from the District Director in San Antonio, Texas, of the Immigration and Naturalisation Service that Marina's petition for a visa had been approved (XXII.55). In requesting that INS permit the grant of a visa the State Department had over-ridden objections raised by INS to Marina's petition for, although INS did not know that Marina had been a member of Komsomol, they did not wish her to enter the United States with the alleged defector, as is shown in INS final letter to the Department of State (XXIII.383):

Oswald, Marina - 4

May 9, 1962   CO 243.1-P

Mr. Michel Cieplinski
Acting Administrator
Bureau of Security and Consular Affairs
Department of State
Washington, D.C.

Dear Mr. Cieplinski,
    The Service file relating to the case of Mrs. Marina N.P. Oswald, subject
of your letter of March 27, 1962, has been carefully reviewed in this office.
    On February 28, 1962, the District Director at San Antonio wrote the
Assistant Director of the Visa Office that he declined to waive in Mrs.
Oswald's case the sanctions against the issuance of immigrant visas in the
Soviet Union imposed pursuant to Section 342(g) of the Immigration and
Nationality Act. Your letter states that preventing Mrs. Oswald from
accompanying her husband and child to the United States would weaken
the attempts of the Embassy in Moscow to encourage positive action by the
Soviet authorities in other cases involving Soviet relatives of United States
citizens. Your letter also states that waiving of sanctions on behalf of Mrs.
Oswald would be in the best interests of the United States.
    In view of the strong representations made in your letter of March 27,
1962, you are hereby advised that sanctions imposed pursuant to Section
243(g) of the Immigration and Nationality Act are hereby waived in
behalf of Mrs. Oswald. (Author's note: 243(g) is correct).

Sincerely yours,
Robert H. Robinson
Deputy Associate Commissioner
Travel Control

REGIONAL COMMISSIONER, SAN PEDRO, CALIFORNIA
For your information.
DISTRICT DIRECTOR, SAN ANTONIO, TEXAS
For your information.

    This matter of waiving sanctions is confusion because the
District Director in San Antonio appears to have told Oswald by
letter of 28 February that Marina's position was approved, the
same day writing to the Department of State in apparently
contrary terms. A study of other communications shows
however, that there was nothing malign in this matter.
    On 12 April, Oswald wrote to Robert telling him that the
American Embassy was holding up their departure, but on 10

May the Embassy wrote to Oswald telling him that everything was in order and suggesting that he should come to the Embassy with his family to sign the final papers.

On 22 May, Oswald received his Soviet Exit visa but it is unclear on what date Marina received hers. On this day he wrote to Robert that he and his family would leave Minsk for Moscow on the following day and depart for England in ten to fourteen days time, expecting to cross the Atlantic by ship and probably arriving in New Orleans. He said that he knew from the newspaper clippings what Robert had said about him when he had left for Russia and he thought that Robert had talked too much at that time; he now emphatically requested Robert to say nothing to the newspapers, and wrote to Marguerite in similar vein.

On 24 May, Oswald and Marina with their infant daughter arrived in Moscow and after filling out various documents at the American Embassy, Marina was given her American Immigrant M.I. visa; the pregnancy and birth had perhaps helped to soften the heart of the Department of State.

On 1 June, Oswald signed a promissory note at the Embassy for a repatriation loan of $435.71, but it is not known who provided the balance of about $370. His passport was marked valid only for his return to the United States, and he and his family then boarded a train for Holland which, passing through Minsk that night, crossed the Soviet frontier on 2 June. Two days later, they departed from Holland by ship and while on board the Oswalds kept to themselves; Marina was to testify that she did not go on deck because she was poorly dressed and Oswald was ashamed of her.

On 13 June, the ship docked at Hoboken, New Jersey, and the Oswalds were met by a representative of the Traveller's Aid Society which had been contacted by the Department of State. The representative obtained the impression that Oswald was trying to avoid meeting anyone and that he passed through the Immigration Office without any trouble, the representative having helped them through customs.

The Traveller's Aid Society had referred the Oswalds to the New York City Department of Welfare which assisted in finding a room in the Times Square Hotel. Oswald told both the

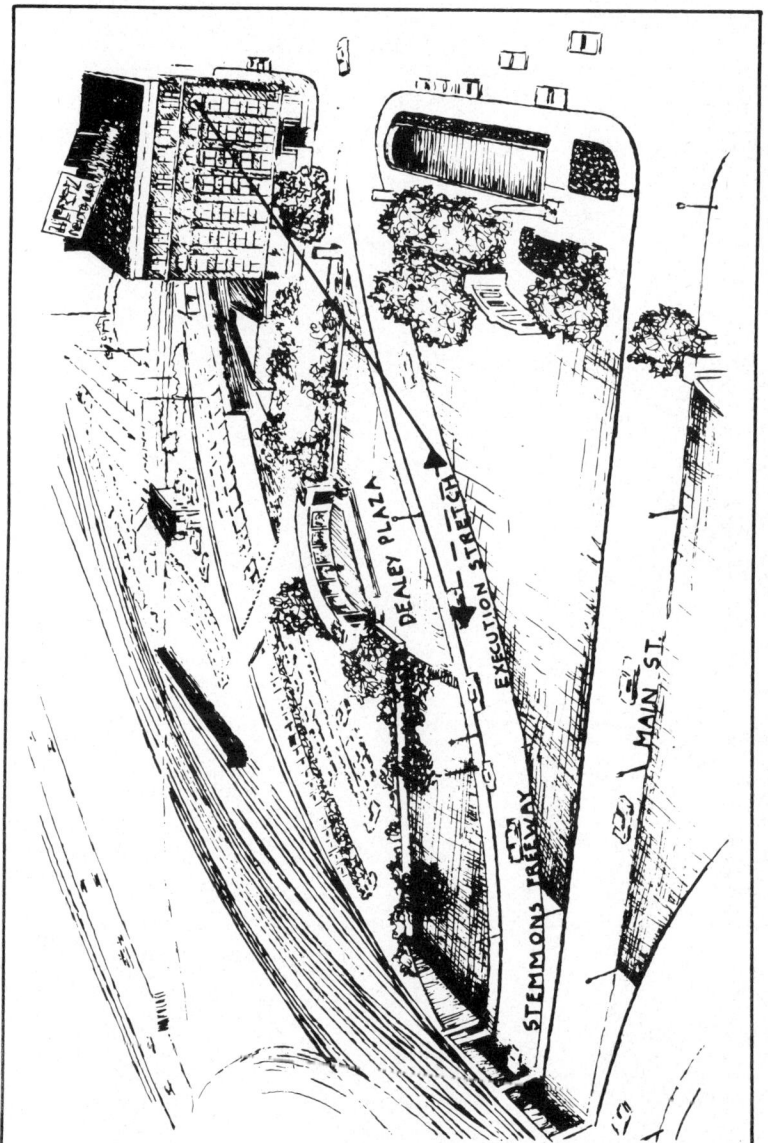

1. Dealy Plaza, Dallas, showing Depository and Execution Stretch. The tree in front of the Depository prevented the assassin from firing sooner

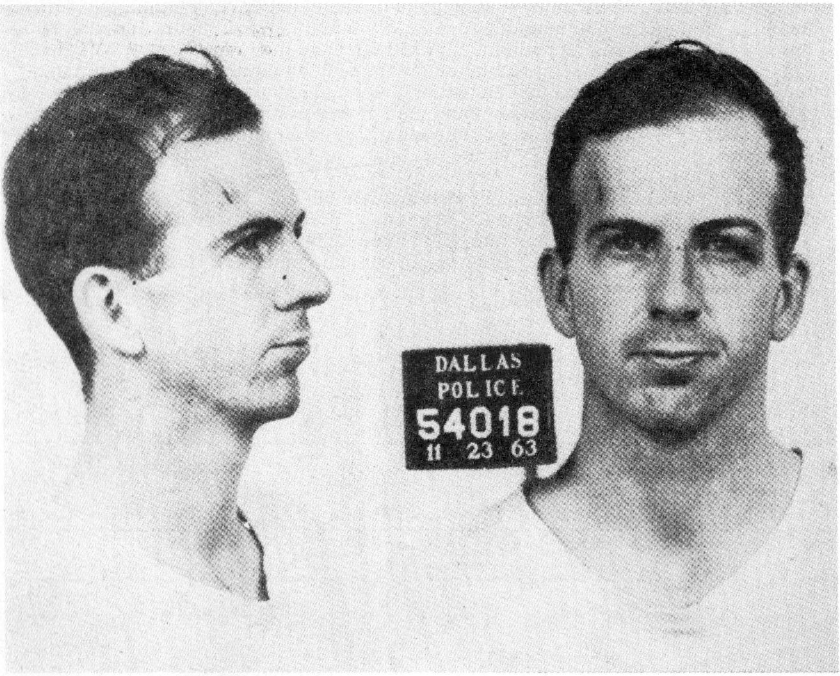

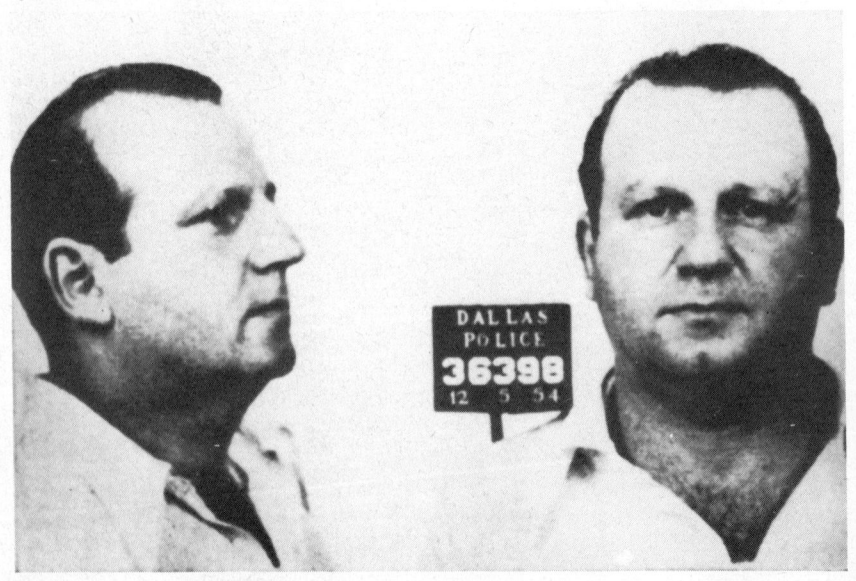

2. Police shot of the assassin under arrest in 1963

3. Police shot of Jack Ruby under arrest in 1954 (offence unknown)

4. Lee Harvey Oswald at about the time of his defection in October 1959

5. The assassin after his return from Russia in June 1962

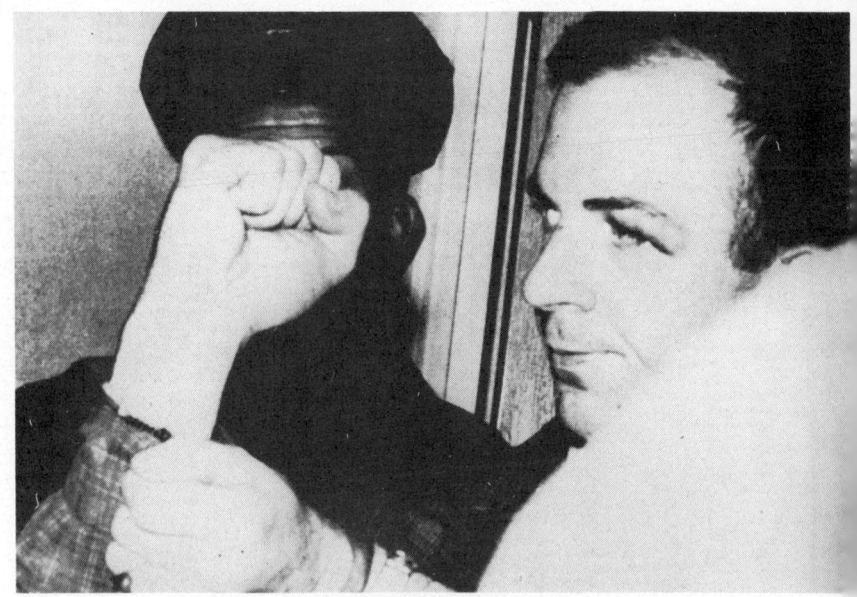

6. The assassin after arrest

7. The assassin and wife leaving Russia

8. Photograph of a man received by Oswald's mother from Minsk in 1961/2. Copies of this photograph appear on the real and counterfeit Marine cards found in Oswald's wallet at the time of his arrest (9a–f)

9a Forged Marine Identification Card found in the assassin's wallet at the time of his arrest. The name "Alek" is the nickname used by the man calling himself Oswald, in Russia. The assassin used the name Hidell in his activities with the Fair Play for Cuba Committee

CERTIFICATE OF SERVICE
ARMED FORCES OF THE UNITED STATES

THIS IS TO CERTIFY THAT
ALEK JAMES HIDELL
HONORABLY SERVED ON ACTIVE DUTY IN THE

United States Marine Corps

DD FORM 217 MC   1 JAN 51

9b Forged Marine Classification card. The name has been changed and the service number partially altered; an attempt has also been made to obliterate the signature and date. The information in the lower half had been photographically reduced to allow space for the insertion of a copy of the photograph sent from Minsk to Oswald's mother

**SELECTIVE SERVICE SYSTEM
NOTICE OF CLASSIFICATION**   Approval not required

ALEK   JAMES   HIDELL
(First name)   (Middle name)   (Last name)

Selective Service No. 42 224 39 532 1 has
been classified in Class ____ I-V ____ (Until ____
19____) by   ☐ Local Board   ☐ Appeal Board,
by vote of ____ to ____   ☐ President
(Show vote on appeal board cases only)
____, 19____
(Date of mailing)   (Member or clerk of local board)

The law requires you, subject to heavy penalty for violation, to carry this notice, in addition to your Registration Certificate on your person at all times—to exhibit it upon request to authorized officials—to surrender it to your commanding officer upon entering the armed forces,
The law requires you to notify your local board in writing (1) of every change in your address, physical condition, and occupational, marital, family, dependency, and military status, and (2) of any other fact which might change your classification.
FOR ADVICE, SEE YOUR GOVERNMENT APPEAL AGENT

9c Dallas Public Library card found in the assassin's wallet. His referee is Jack L. Bowen, his fellow employee at Jaggers-Chiles-Stovall

Name Oswald, Mr. Lee Harvey
M. Address 602 Elsbeth
City Dallas   Zone   Phone

Signature
Address Same
City   Zone   Phone
School or Business Jaggers-Chiles-Stoval
Name Jack L. Bowen
Home Address 1916 Stevens Forest Dr
Phone WH8-8997   Expires 12-7-65
DALLAS PUBLIC LIBRARY   cr
(See Reverse Side)

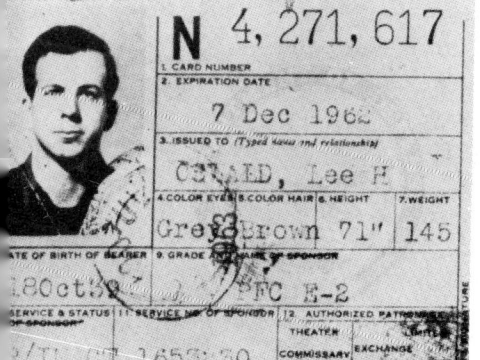

9d (*top*) and 9e (*centre*) Genuine Marine Classification cards, found in the assassin's wallet

9f Genuine Marine card in the name of Oswald, found in the assassin's wallet. The original photograph has been replaced by a copy of the one sent to Oswald's mother from Minsk and the stamped date altered to July 1963

10. Photograph of Marina taken in Minsk

11. Marina visits the assassin in
Dallas jail after his arrest

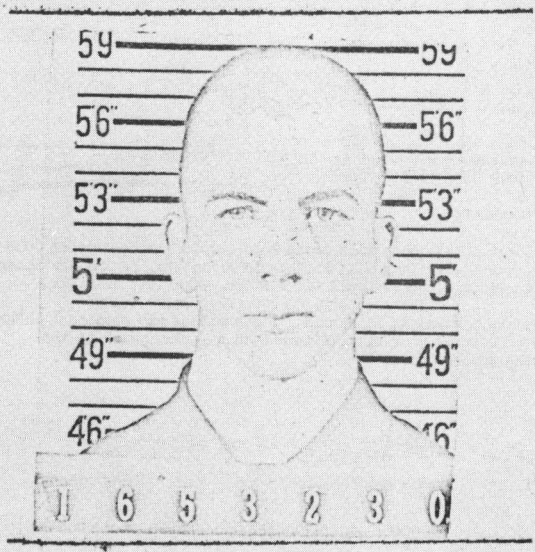

2nd Recruit Training Battalion
Marine Corps Recruit Depot
San Diego 40, California

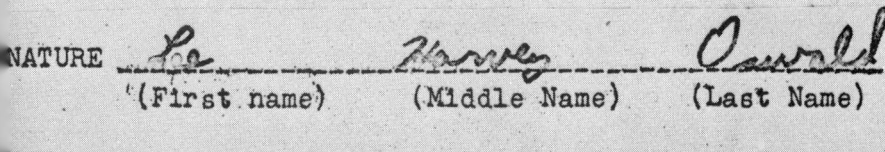

NATURE _____Lee_____ _____Harvey_____ _____Oswald_____
'(First name)   (Middle Name)   (Last Name)

E HARVEY OSWALD   PVT   1653230   28Dec56

12. Oswald's height of 5′ 9″ recorded by the Marines on 28
December 1956. This photograph appears to be that on which the
Warren Commission bases its conclusion that the assassin was Lee
Harvey Oswald, height 5′ 9″

Standard Form 88
(Rev. Aug. 1360)
PROMULGATED BY
BUREAU OF THE BUDGET
CIRCULAR A-24

REPORT OF MEDICAL EXAMINATION

1. LAST NAME—FIRST NAME—MIDDLE NAME	2. GRADE AND COMPONENT OR POSITION	3. IDENTIFICATION NO.
OSWALD, Lee Harvey	Pfc	165 30

4. HOME ADDRESS (Number, street or RFD, city or town, zone and State)	5. PURPOSE OF EXAMINATION	6. DATE OF EXAMINATION
3124 West 5th St. Fort Worth, Texas	Seperation	3 Sept 1959

7. SEX	8. RACE	9. TOTAL YRS. GOVT. SERVICE		10. DEPARTMENT, AGENCY, OR SERVICE	11. ORGANIZATION UNIT
M	C	MILITARY 03	CIVILIAN	USMC	H&HS SEP SEC

12. DATE OF BIRTH	13. PLACE OF BIRTH	14. NAME, RELATIONSHIP, AND ADDRESS OF NEXT OF KIN
18 Oct 39	Louisiana	Mrs. M. OSWALD, Same as 11no #4 (M)

15. EXAMINING FACILITY OR EXAMINER, AND ADDRESS	16. OTHER INFORMATION
U. S. MARINE CORPS AIR STATION EL TORO (SANTA ANA). CALIF.	Rel: Luthern

17. RATING OR SPECIALTY	TIME IN THIS CAPACITY: TOTAL	LAST SIX MONTHS

CLINICAL EVALUATION

NOTES.—Describe every abnormality in detail. (Enter pertinent item number before each comment; continue in item 73 and use additional sheets if necessary.)

	NORMAL	ABNORMAL	(Check each item in appropriate column: enter "N E" if not evaluated)
18. HEAD, FACE, NECK, AND SCALP		X	
19. NOSE			
20. SINUSES			
21. MOUTH AND THROAT			
22. EARS—GENERAL (Int. & ext. canals) (Auditory acuity under items 70 and 71)			
23. DRUMS (Perforation)			
24. EYES—GENERAL (Visual acuity and refraction under items 58, 60, and 61)			
25. OPHTHALMOSCOPIC			
26. PUPILS (Equality and reaction)			
27. OCULAR MOTILITY (Associated parallel movements, nystagmus)			
28. LUNGS AND CHEST (Include breasts)			
29. HEART (Thrust, size, rhythm, sounds)			
30. VASCULAR SYSTEM (Varicosities, etc.)			
31. ABDOMEN AND VISCERA (Include hernia)			
32. ANUS AND RECTUM (Hemorrhoids, fistulae) (Prostate if indicated)			
33. ENDOCRINE SYSTEM			
34. G–U SYSTEM			
35. UPPER EXTREMITIES (Strength, range of motion)			
36. FEET			
37. LOWER EXTREMITIES (Except feet) (Strength range of motion)			
38. SPINE, OTHER MUSCULOSKELETAL			
39. IDENTIFYING BODY MARKS, SCARS, TATTOOS	As Noted		
40. SKIN, LYMPHATICS			
41. NEUROLOGIC (Equilibrium tests under item 72)			
42. PSYCHIATRIC (Specify any personality deviation)			

Females only (Check how done)

43. PELVIC	☐ VAGINAL	☐ RECTAL

(Continue in item 75)

(39) S operation, 1" left mastoid
S operation, 1" ULA
S gunshot, left elbow
S ½" left hand
VSULA

(18) Mastoid operation 1945 NCD

44. DENTAL (Place appropriate symbols above or below number of upper and lower teeth, respectively)		REMARKS AND ADDITIONAL DENTAL DEFECTS AND DISEASES

O.—Restorable teeth   X.—Missing teeth   (8 X 8).—Fixed bridge, brackets to
I.—Nonrestorable teeth   XXX.—Replaced by dentures   include abutments

RIGHT | X 1 | 2 | 3 | 4 | 5 | 6 | 7 | 8 | 9 | 10 | 11 | 12 | 13 | 14 | 15 | X 16 | LEFT
| | 32 | 31 | X 30 | 29 | 28 | 27 | 26 | 25 | 24 | 23 | 22 | 21 | 20 | 19 | 18 | X 17 | |

TYPE 111
CLASS 1
QUALIFIED

LABORATORY FINDINGS

45. URINALYSIS: SP. GR. 1.022	46. CHEST X-RAY (Place, date, film number, result)	47. SEROLOGY (Specify test used and result)
	70mm #6318 - 3Sep1959	

ALBUMIN	SUGAR	MICROSCOPIC		
NEG	NEG	ND	NEGATIVE	VDRL - NEGATIVE

48. EKG	49. BLOOD TYPE AND RH FACTOR	50. OTHER TESTS

13. *Above and opposite* A page of Oswald's Marine medical examination, 3 September 1959, showing evidence of mastoid operation, gunshot scars and height of 71″. (VSULA = Vertical Scar Upper Left Arm)

MEASUREMENTS AND OTHER FINDINGS

HEIGHT	52. WEIGHT	53. COLOR HAIR	54. COLOR EYES	55. BUILD:	56. TEMP.
71 "	150	Brown	Grey	SLENDER ☐ MEDIUM ☒ HEAVY ☐ OBESE ☐	N

BLOOD PRESSURE (Arm at heart level)					58. PULSE (Arm at heart level)				
TING	SYS. 110	RECUM-BENT	SYS.	STANDING (3 min.)	SYS.	SITTING	AFTER EXERCISE	2 MIN. AFTER	RECUMBENT	AFTER STANDING 3 MIN.
	DIAS. 58		DIAS.		DIAS.	62				

DISTANT VISION		60.	REFRACTION		61.	NEAR VISION	
T 20/ 20	CORR. TO 20/	BY	S.	CX		CORR. TO	BY
20/ 20	CORR. TO 20/	BY	S.	CX		CORR. TO	BY

| ETEROPHORIA (specify distance) | ES° | EX° | R. H. | L. H. | PRISM DIV. | PRISM CONV. | PC | PD |

CCOMMODATION		64. COLOR VISION (Test used and result)	65. DEPTH PERCEPTION (Test used and score)	UNCORRECTED	
	LEFT	18/18 AOC 1940		CORRECTED	

| ELD OF VISION | 67. NIGHT VISION (Test used and score) | 68. RED LENS | | 69. INTRAOCULAR TENSION |

HEARING	71.	AUDIOMETER								72. PSYCHOLOGICAL AND PSYCHOMOTOR (Tests used and score)
			250 500	500 510	1000 1024	2000 2048	3000 3200	4000 4096	8000 8100	
WV 15 /15 SV	RIGHT						▨			
WV 15 /15 SV 15 /15	LEFT						▨			

TES (Continued) AND SIGNIFICANT OR INTERVAL HISTORY

(Use additional sheets of plain paper if necessary)

MARY OF DEFECTS AND DIAGNOSES (List diagnoses with item numbers)

D

MMENDATIONS—FURTHER SPECIALIST EXAMINATIONS INDICATED (Specify)

NE

76.	PHYSICAL PROFILE					
	P	U	L	H	E	S

UNEE (Check)   RELEASE FROM ACTIVE DUTY IN THE USMC

NOT QUALIFIED FOR   PHYSICAL CATEGORY

QUALIFIED, LIST DISQUALIFYING DEFECTS BY ITEM NUMBER

| A | | C | E |

OR PRINTED NAME OF PHYSICIAN | SIGNATURE
.T. VINCENT, LT. MC, USNR

OR PRINTED NAME OF PHYSICIAN | SIGNATURE

OR PRINTED NAME OF DENTIST OR PHYSICIAN (Indicate which) | SIGNATURE
.W. STEVENS, CDR. DC, USNR

OR PRINTED NAME OF REVIEWING OFFICER OR APPROVING AUTHORITY | SIGNATURE | UMBER OF AT-CHED SHEETS

Photograph of bearer

Lee H. Oswald

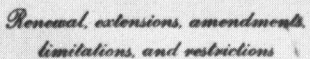

DE_____ OF STATE
LOS ANGELS, CALIF.

Renewal, extensions, amendments, limitations, and restrictions

This passport, properly visaed, is valid for travel in all countries unless OTHERWISE RESTRICTED. It is not valid for travel to or in any foreign state for the purpose of entering or serving in the armed forces of such a state.

This passport is not valid for travel to the following areas under control of authorities with which the United States does not have diplomatic relations: Albania, Bulgaria, and those portions of China, Korea and Viet-Nam under Communist control.

> THIS PASSPORT IS NOT VALID FOR TRAVEL IN HUNGARY.

Renewal, extensions, amendments, limitations, and restrictions

Embassy of the United States of America at Moscow, U.S.S.R. JULY 10, 1961.

THIS PASSPORT IS VALID ONLY FOR DIRECT TRAVEL TO THE UNITED STATES.

RICHARD E. SNYDER
AMERICAN CONSUL

SEE PAGE-15

Visas

SURETE NATIONALE
R.G. LE HAVRE
-3 OCT 1959
9. ENTREE. P.

S.N.
R.G. LE HAVRE
-8 OCT 1959
SORTIE

VISIT UP TO THREE MONTHS
IMMIGRATION OFFICER
(26)
-9 OCT 1959
SOUTHAMPTON

IMMIGRATION OFFICER
(144)
EMBARKED
10 OCT 1959
LONDON AIRPORT

4

5

6

7

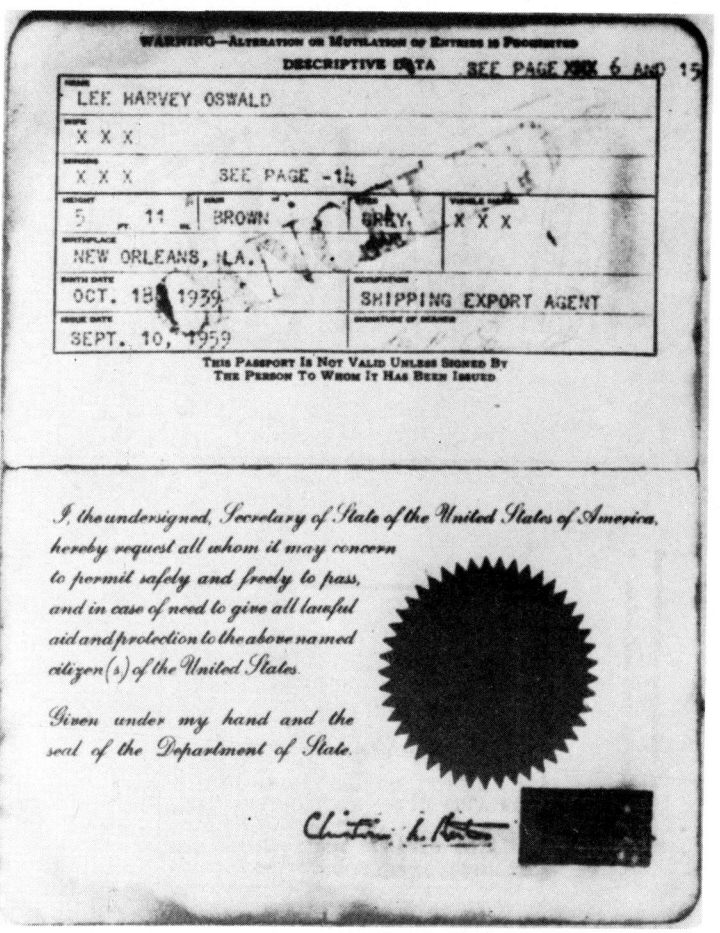

14a and b (*opposite*); c (*above*) Passport on which
Oswald is alleged to have travelled to and returned
from Russia in October 1959 and June 1962
respectively

15a and b. Oswald's fingerprints on Marine card,
15 October 1956 (front and back)

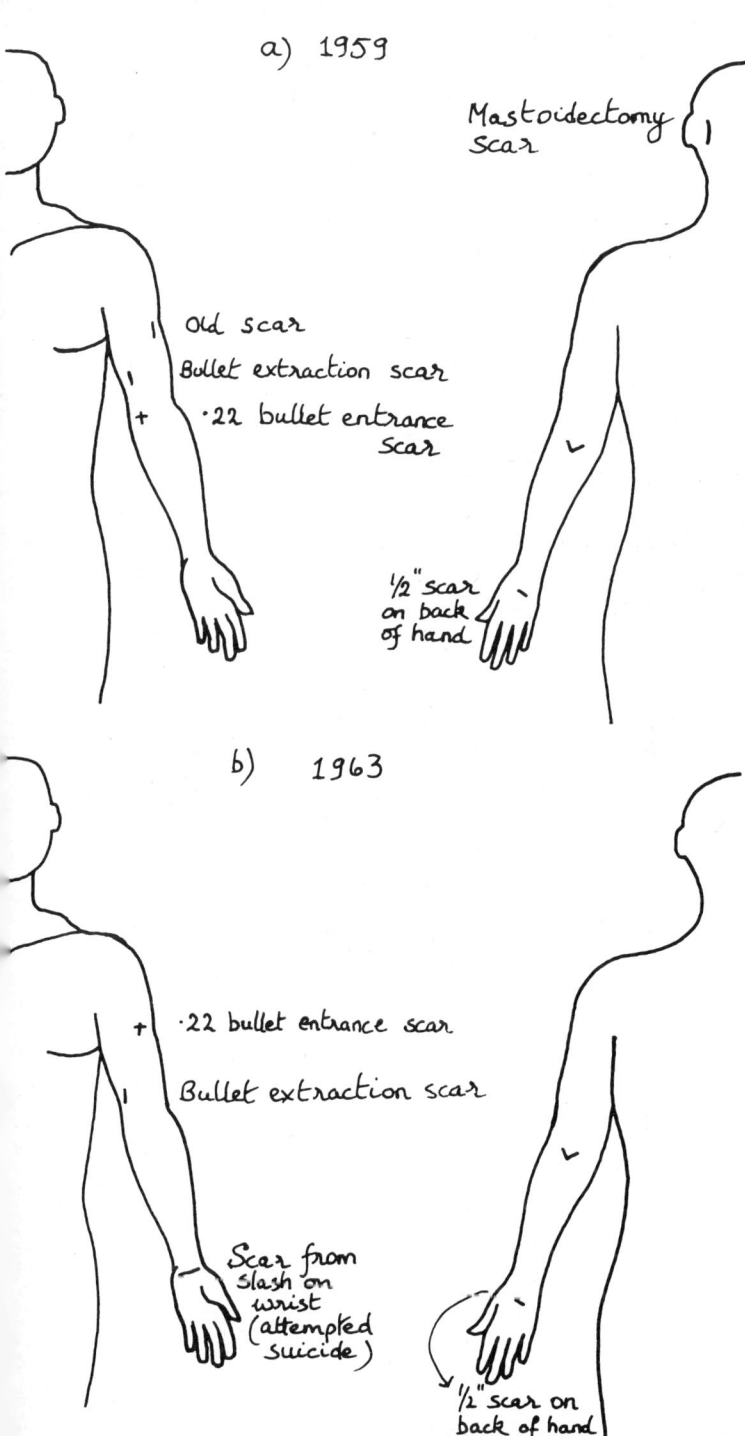

16a. Scars on body of Oswald in 1959
16b. Scars on corpse of assassin in 1963

17. Birth certificate of assassin's second daughter, born 20 October 1963, on which name *Rachel* has been inserted by assassin

18a. The assassin's work sheet, October 12, 1962

18b. The assassin's work sheet, October 15, 1962

18c. The assassin's work sheet, October 16, 1962

19. Members of the Warren Commission

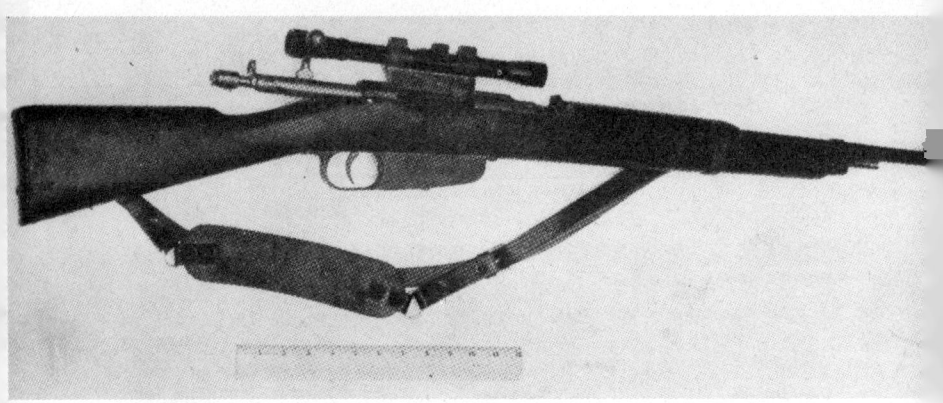

20. The assassination rifle and sling

21. The "sniper's nest" in the Depository

Comm. Exh. 237

22a. The "American Male" in Mexico City

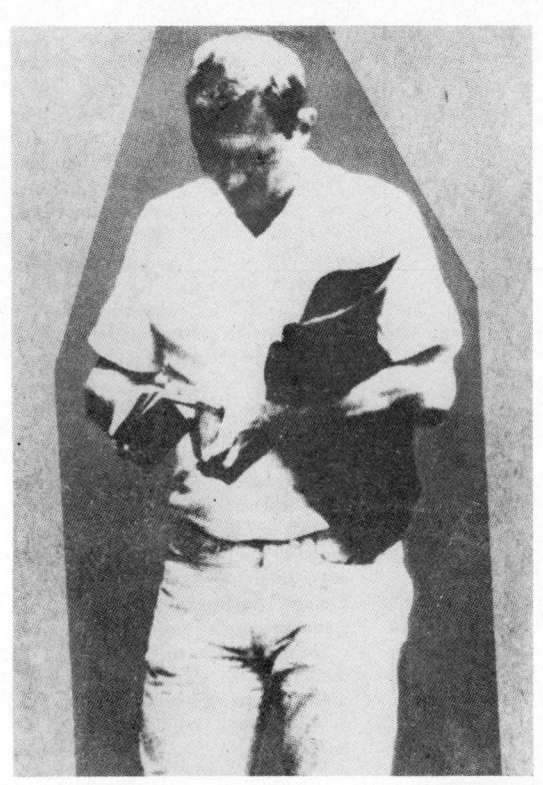

22b. The "American Male" in Mexico City

22c. The "American Male" in Mexico City

representatives of the Traveller's Aid Society and of the Department of Welfare that he had been a Marine stationed at the American Embassy in Moscow, had married a Russian girl, had renounced his citizenship, and had worked in Minsk. He said that he had soon found out that Russian propaganda was inaccurate but he had not been able to obtain an exit visa for his wife and child for more than two years, adding that he had paid the travel expenses himself. Oswald told the representative of the Traveller's Aid Society that he had only $63. The Department of Welfare called Robert's home in Fort Worth; his wife, Vada, took the call and said that they would help Oswald with money to enable him to travel to Robert's home. Robert sent the Department $200 which Oswald then refused to accept and insisted that the Department itself should pay the fare to Texas, threatening that he would go as far as he could on $63 and then rely on local authorities to get them the rest of the way to Fort Worth. He finally accepted the $200.

On the afternoon of 14 June 1962, the Oswalds and infant daughter June left New York by plane en route for Fort Worth, Texas, where they were to be met by Robert and his wife.

When Marina had applied to the American Embassy in Moscow for admittance to the United States as a non-quota immigrant, she denied that she was or ever had been a member of the voluntary organisation, Komsomol (R.761). Had she told the truth to the Embassy, it would seem that INS would have refused her admittance to the United States. Her eligibility to enter the country had depended on the favourable resolution of three questions: 1. It had to be determined whether she was the wife of an American citizen, which depended on whether her husband had ex-patriated himself. 2. It was necessary to determine that she was not and had not been affiliated with a Communist organisation *on other than an involuntary basis*. 3. It had to be determined that she was not likely to become a public charge after she was admitted to the United States.

Marina's untruthfulness about her membership of Komsomol

can only have been to facilitate her entrance into the United States. In testimony, she admitted her deception at the American Embassy in Moscow but maintained that she had been expelled from Komsomol when it was learned that she intended to accompany an American to the United States.

The official Soviet description of Komsomol in the days of Stalin's terror was: 'The very first task of all Komsomol education work was the necessity to seek out and recognise the enemy, who had then to be removed, purely forcibly, by methods of economic pressure, organisational-political isolation, and methods of physical destruction.'

There is a Komsomol centre in every town, and Komsomol attracts dedicated young Communists into its voluntary membership. From its ranks the more intelligent and dedicated become members of the official Communist Party, and from the Party are drawn those who will occupy positions in the Russian hierarchy, Intelligence services etc.

The tutelage of Komsomol and Komsomol training are best symbolised in the book *KGB*. In short, Komsomol students are expected to follow the example of 14 year old Pavlik Morozov who in 1932 betrayed his peasant father for sheltering kulaks, the independent peasant farmers who were fleeing their villages to avoid murder or deportation. The father was executed, the other villagers lynched the boy, but the father's house is still enshrined to the memory of Pavlik. The Communist youth newspaper, *Komsomolskaya Pravda*, has referred to Pavlik as a Hero of the Revolution, and statues to his memory have been erected in Komsomol precincts.

Seeking out, betraying and destroying in the service of the State is Komsomol dogma; it would seem that Marina and probably the assassin were so indoctrinated along with all other Komsomol students.

It would seem that the authors of the Commission's Report were not aware of the nature of Komsomol when limiting the membership of Marina to 7 months, and that they accepted the words of the 'Historic Diary' and her testimony that her persecution and expulsion from Komsomol was other than contrived by the KGB.

The Report says: 'Oswald's marriage to Marina Prusakova on April 30, 1961, is itself a fact meriting consideration. A foreigner living in Russia cannot marry without the permission of the Soviet government. It seems unlikely that the Soviet authorities would have permitted Oswald to marry and take his wife with him to the United States if they were contemplating using him alone as an agent. The fact that he had a Russian wife would be likely, in their view, to increase any surveillance under which he would be kept by American security agencies, would make him even more conspicuous to his neighbours as 'an ex-Russian', and would decrease his mobility. A wife's presence in the United States would also constitute a continuing risk of disclosure. On the other hand, Marina Oswald's lack of English training and her complete ignorance of the United States and its customs would scarcely recommend her to the Soviet authorities as one member of an 'agent team' to be sent to the United States on a difficult and dangerous foreign enterprise (r.274).'

An opposing view could be that the personable Russian-speaking wife and two children were of use to Oswald – the birth of a second child a month before the assassination being the reason for Mrs. Ruth Paine to harbour Marina in her house for the time of Oswald's secret visit to Mexico until just after the assassination, and thereby causing herself to become a prime suspect not only in the attempt to murder a certain General Walker – to be discussed later – but also in the assassination of the President. While making no suggestion that Marina could have been a member of an 'agent team', the fact remains that she was helpful to Oswald; through Marina's friend, Mrs. Anna Meller, Oswald was assisted in obtaining employment in Jaggars-Chiles-Stovall in October 1962, and through Mrs. Ruth Paine Oswald was assisted in obtaining employment at the Depository in October 1963. It cannot therefore be argued that the presence of Marina was a handicap for it would seem that the enterprise would have been successful had it not been for the presence of Mrs. Bledsoe on the Marsalis bus; the information obtained by CIA and FBI informants in the Russian Embassies in Mexico City and Washington would have had rather less value if the assassin had escaped taking with him the major physical discrepancies between him and the Marine.

The view of Marina entertained by the United States Secret Service would appear to differ from the view expressed by Hoover in testimony when he described her as 'reliable'. On 25 November 1963, William H. Paterson, Special Agent, interviewed Marina: ' ... The wife also advised that she had seen the rifle that was used in the shooting at her home about three weeks before the shooting. She advised that she was a Castro supporter and from the interview it was felt that she is still a hard-core Communist. She stated that he had never mentioned killing the President and would not mention anything about shooting Governor Connally. She stated that she did not know the man that killed her husband. It was felt by the interviewer that she was not telling the truth and still believes in Communism (XXIII.390)'.

The doubts held by the Secret Service about the reliability of Marina were to be confirmed by the later discovery of her untruthfulness about Komsomol to the American Embassy in Moscow, her untruthfulness during interviews with the FBI after the assassination, and her failure of memory when testifying before the Commission. Despite the Secret Service record of their 25 November interview with Marina, after 26 November the Service, according to Marguerite, developed an overly solicitous attitude towards Marina and hostility towards Marguerite before successfully separating them on 27 and 28 November 1964; the separation was to be total and permanent.

When Marina was to testify on 6 September 1964 about Oswald and herself in Russia, in answer to the question, 'And none of the (Russian) officials or police examined you at all about your reason for wishing to leave?', she replied 'It's very surprising, but nobody did (V.592)'.

Apparently as a result of this testimony, the Commission asked the CIA for information on the practice in Russia regarding 'Emigration and Travel of Soviet Nationals'. On 10 September 1964, the CIA sent a Memorandum to Rankin:

1. Soviet nationals seeking to emigrate from the Soviet Union or even to

travel abroad are subjected to a thorough screening before receiving permission to go abroad. They are not permitted to emigrate if they are in a position to endanger the national security of the USSR.2. In order to go abroad, a Soviet citizen must withstand a detailed investigation of his overall record and background. He must submit numerous applications, references and other supporting documents and he must undergo personal interviews conducted by government officials.

3. The KGB has the major responsibility for approving or denying requests for emigration or foreign travel. It investigates all applicants and its recommendation is given great weight by the Exit Department of the Central Committee of the Communist Party of the Soviet Union – the agency which makes the final decision.

Thomas H. Karamessines
Acting, Deputy Director for Plans

Marina testified that after arriving in the United States she wrote several letters to her family and friends in Russia but 'I never received any answer'. She said that after the assassination she wrote to her uncle and aunt (the Prusakovs) but received no reply (V.592-593). She said that after the assassination no official of the Russian Government had communicated with her, 'They didn't approach me even as a show of interest in my well-being'. (It might be that if Oswald escaped the plan was for Marina to be at once removed to the Russian Embassy in Washington 'for her own protection' before being returned to Russia; she had retained her Soviet citizenship and had applied for return to Russia as early as 17 February 1963, an application repeated in July 1963 and forwarded by Reznichenko to Moscow for approval in August 1963. This speculation is somewhat supported by the fact, as witnesses testified, that Oswald forbade her to learn English.)

She testified that while in Russia she had understood from Oswald that he was interested in 'Cuba and Cuban affairs', that there were some 300 Cuban students in Minsk, but that she never met any Cuban (V.406-407.590). It can now be seen how, from the time that Oswald was in contact with a Cuban Consulate while in the Marines in 1959 and allegedly became interested in Cuban affairs later in Russia, the implication of Castro in the assassination was pursued until after the event; on arrest in Dallas Oswald told the Dallas police of his support for Castro, and Marina told the Secret Service of her own support for Castro.

Perhaps the most interesting aspect of Marina's lengthy

testimony is that given on 6 September 1964 (V.588-620). She was the last person to testify and this was only 18 days before the 888 page Report with its thousands of references and cross-references to the thousands of pages of Testimony and Exhibits was presented to President Johnson. Her testimony shows that on this date three Commissioners were present (Russell, Cooper and Boggs), that from their searching questions they appear to have been sceptical of the Report of the assassination already drafted, and that these Commissioners perhaps suspected a conspiracy. During this late testimony and apparently at the request of the three Commissioners, two interpreters were present, and for the first time Marina declined the assistance of an attorney because she would 'just tell the truth'. Whereas Marina had always testified in Washington, this last testimony was taken on a Sunday at the U.S. Naval Air Station, Dallas, apparently to avoid publicity.

A student of the assassination might never know of this interesting testimony nor of the apparent scepticism of the three Commissioners, for, although the names of the 552 witnesses and the first pages of their testimony are listed without error or omission under the heading 'Contents' in each of the 15 Volumes of Testimony, the last testimony of Marina is omitted from 'Contents' of Volume V.

The next Chapter will record the activities of the assassin and Marina after entering the United States from Russia on 13 June 1962.

11

The activities of the assassin and Marina from the time of their arrival in New York on 13 June 1962 to the day of the assassination, 22 November 1963, fell into four phases, corresponding in chronological order to his assignments while residing in Fort Worth, Dallas, New Orleans and again in Dallas. They will be set out and explained under the name of the city.

Phase One. Fort Worth. 14 June 1962 to 8/9 October 1962

Oswald's assignments were:
(A) to deceive Robert and Marguerite into believing that he was Lee Harvey Oswald;
(B) to intimate that he had entered Russia as an American agent and to establish that both he and Marina disliked the Russian way of life to the point of her treachery, thereby suggesting that in no way could he be considered a 'sleeper' or agent for the Russians and removing from her any suspicion of collaboration in his assignments;
(C) to infiltrate the Russian emigré and Russian-speaking American groups in the adjacent cities of Fort Worth and Dallas who were to assist him in obtaining employment at Jaggars-Chiles-Stovall at the time of the 'Cuba Crisis' in October 1962 and at the Texas School Book Depository in October 1963;
(D) to deceive the FBI into believing that the man who had arrived in the United States with Marina and infant daughter was 5′ 11″ Lee Harvey Oswald.
(E) to appear to be on bad terms with his wife, thereby allaying

suspicion amongst Russian emigre groups in Fort Worth and Dallas that he and his wife might be an 'agent team'.

Assignment (A). This has been explained earlier in this book.

Assignment (B). Four days after he had arrived at his brother's home in Fort Worth, on 18 June Oswald went to see Pauline Bates, a legal public stenographer. She testified that Oswald apparently had obtained her name from the telephone directory, her name being at the top of the list of stenographers. She said that he was dressed in dark trousers, a white T-shirt and a blazer-type jacket, and he had brought with him a large envelope in which he said he had some notes that he had smuggled out of Russia under his clothes and next to his skin. He said that some of the notes had been typed on a little portable typewriter, some of them had been handwritten in ink or pencil, some of them were in Russian and some in English. Bates was surprised to hear all this because he looked like 'a highschool kid' when he first came in. She asked him a number of questions including the reason for his going to Russia, and 'some questions he would answer and some he would not'. She typed for eight hours a day for him over a period of three days, making an original and one carbon copy. When he left her each day he would not only take the originals, the carbon copies and his notes, but also the carbon paper so that Bates should not retain anything. He told her that he had taken a course in elementary Russian while in the Marine Corps, and that he had wanted to travel and had applied to the State Department for a visa. He said he did not go as an exchange student but that the State Department finally agreed to let him go, saying that they would not be responsible for him. He was 'granted a visa to go over there but the State Department refused to stand behind him in case he got in trouble or anything'. The notes that she copied or were dictated to her by Oswald were written on various kinds of paper, some large and some very small, and they concerned living and working conditions in Russia, all being 'very bitter' against that country. He told her that when he smuggled the notes out of Russia 'the whole time until they got over the border he was scared to death in case they would be found, and then they would not have been allowed to leave Russia'. He did not tell Bates that Marina was aware that he was carrying these notes out of Russia, but said that he had made them 'surreptitiously when Marina would cover for him while he was doing this, in order to muffle the tone of the typewriter ... so people would not know what he was doing'. Bates said that Marina must have known that he was making these notes because he said 'she would cover or watch for him so that nobody would know that he was making them – tried to steer anybody away while he was doing this because he could have got in trouble'. He mentioned Robert to her but did not mention Marguerite and, when he spoke of Marina, he said that she liked being in America but that 'she got very ill from the food because it was too rich, as they had not had enough food in a long time'. He said, 'Anything you hear about vacations and those big May Day celebrations, that's all propaganda ... You don't get vacations ... These May Day celebrations – yes; they have them, but you're forced to go. It's not a voluntary thing. And if you have a radio or a television and don't listen to it, you'd better have a good explanation because all you hear is party politics and you've got to listen to it. You don't have coffee breaks and you go to work before dawn and you get off after dark.' He never once mentioned the word Communist and just referred to 'the Party' and that ' ... you couldn't talk, you couldn't express anything because there was always a Party person around and he'd report you'. He told her nothing about any effort on his part to become a Russian citizen, but said that he was very bitter about his treatment because he went over there on a 2-year visa and, of course, he married Marina. At the end of two years when he wanted to leave, they (the Russians) wouldn't let him bring her back. They had said to him, 'You go ahead and we'll send her to you'. He told Bates that he would never have seen her again if he had left without her. He had had to stay eleven months longer until he could get her out and that 'he raised so much "Cain" with the Russians until they finally let him go'. He did not express any views or opinions in respect of the Government of the United States. Bates said that the notes were coherent, and that they were well written and all in sequence according to city and dates 'and things like that', and that the English and spelling were fairly accurate. He mis-spelled occasionally, although she did not know whether it was mis-

194

spelling words or just that he had been in a hurry and had left letters out. On the final day he was quite nervous, walking up and down and looking over her shoulder and wanting to know how far she had got until she finally finished the 10th page. He told Bates that he had talked to an engineer about these notes and had shown them to him, and the engineer was interested in getting them published. He said that he had actual Russian names of people he had talked to and in order to protect people he would have to change the names and 'things like that. But the man was willing to go ahead'. Bates thought that the notes were not 'anything that could have been got together in just a few months. It was too detailed'. She described Oswald as cool, cold and with 'the deadest eyes I ever saw'. (VIII.330-343).

After the assassination, the authorities discovered the notes and the typed copy, but no 'engineer' was traced who might have been interested. Marina was not questioned by the FBI, the Secret Service or the Commission about her husband's allegations to Bates.

The Report (R.326.660.714) refers briefly to the 'Bates incident' and does not discuss its purposes: the insinuation (a) that the Department of State had connived in the assassin-to-be's departure for Russia in 1959, (b) that he was anti-Russian, and (c) that Marina was a traitor of Russia. The apparent reason for Oswald's involvement of the Department of State is made clear when it is remembered that the Department had overruled the powerful objections of INS to allow Marina to enter the United States, and then had paid part of the Oswalds' fares.

Assignment (C). The day *after* Oswald contacted Bates, he visited Peter Gregory, a consulting petroleum engineer and part-time Russian language instructor at the Fort Worth Public Library whose name Oswald had obtained from the Fort Worth branch of the Texas Employment Commission. His stated object in visiting Gregory was to obtain a letter certifying his proficiency in Russian, and he was able to obtain from Gregory a recommendation as interpreter and translator, but his request for a recommendation was a ruse for he was never to attempt to be either; thus Oswald involved Gregory. It was through the people to whom Gregory was to introduce the Oswalds that they were able to meet other members of the Russian and Russian-speaking community, for he was to introduce them *inter alia* to Mrs. Anna Meller who lived in Dallas and who, in common with other members of the Russian emigré community, became sorry for Marina and concerned in her welfare because she was believed to be maltreated by Oswald. Four months later, in October 1962, Anna, who had by then become friendly with Marina, was to persuade her husband to telephone a counsellor at the Dallas branch of the Texas Employment Commission to ask the counsellor to help Oswald get work; with the aid of this call Oswald was to obtain employment in Jaggars-Chiles-Stovall.

A member of the Russian emigré group in Dallas was the 52 years old (Baron) George De Mohrenschildt, and according to his testimony and that of Marina, he became friendly with the Oswalds soon after they arrived in Fort Worth, being the only member of the Russian emigré community who liked Oswald and continued to see him and Marina until the Spring of 1963, when he left Dallas to work in Haiti and Oswald was to leave Dallas for New Orleans. It was through the Baron introducing Oswald and Marina to Everett Glover (who later gave a party to which the Oswalds were invited), that Marina was to meet Mrs. Ruth Paine, a Russian-speaking American who later at the request of Marina was to assist Oswald by making a telephone call in October 1963 to the personnel manager of the Texas School Book-Depository asking if he could employ Oswald at the Depository.

Assignment (D). Oswald and his family had arrived in New York on 13 June 1962 and the next day they had travelled by plane to Love Field Airport, Dallas, where they were met by Robert and his family. There had been no press reporters, either in New York or at Love Field, because Robert and Marguerite had respected Oswald's wishes that his return should not be announced to the press. The FBI did not meet the Oswald family off the boat in New York and they waited for twelve days before interviewing him in Fort Worth, on the ground that they wanted the family to have time to settle down.

On 26 June, Oswald, then living with Robert, was interviewed by appointment at the office of the FBI in Fort Worth, Texas, by Special Agents Tom Carter and John W. Fain LL.B. (XVII.728-731). Carter was the senior agent, but Fain had

had charge of the FBI file on Oswald from the time that the latter went to Russia. Fain, who had been in the FBI for twenty years, was a law-trained agent and had specialised mostly in security matters for the previous eleven years. The interview lasted between $1\frac{1}{2}$ and 2 hours, with the man seated at a desk facing Fain, and Carter seated on Fain's Left. While Carter watched and listened, Fain took notes from which he prepared a written report of the interview.

Under the heading ' … from Observation and Interrogation', the report contained a physical description of 'Lee Harvey Oswald' that stated his height to be 5' 11" and his weight to be 150 lbs. – on arrest in Dallas 17 months later the man they had interviewed was 5' 9" in height and weighed 131 lbs. It would seem that they did not pause to consider by 'Observation' whether what the man told them about his height was correct, but accepted his word or the details in his passport; it is possible that to aid the deception he was wearing some kind of elevated footwear. Furthermore, at the time of the interview, the agents knew that the man and his family were staying at Robert's house; perhaps they did not realise that the Oswald family was disunited and its history was such that Lee Oswald and Robert Oswald had seen little of each other since Lee's birth, that they were almost strangers and that Robert, five years Lee's senior, had seen Lee for only one day in the previous $5\frac{1}{2}$ years; years in which Lee was changing and growing from youth to man.

In testimony in May 1964, Fain said of the man, 'He was tense, kind of drawn up, and rigid. He is a wiry little fellow, kind of waspy … He was a little insolent in his answers. He was the type of individual who apparently does not want to give out information about himself, and we asked him why he made this trip to Russia, and he looked like it got under his skin, and I noticed that he got white around the lips and tensed up, and I understood it to be a show of temper, and in a show of temper he stated that he did not care to relive the past. He didn't want to go into that at all … I asked him, in various ways, three or four times, trying to ascertain just what the situation was, and he finally stated that Soviet officials had asked him upon his arrival why he had come to Russia, and he told us, 'I came because I wanted to'. That is what he said he told the Soviet people … He told them 'I came over here to see the country'. That is the kind of answers he gave ... He exhibited an arrogant attitude, arrogant, cold ... He was evasive about why he went to Russia ... Fain did not comment on the 2″ difference between the height he had recorded and the height of the assassin, nor did the Commission invite him to do so.

When asked why two agents were present at the interview, Fain testified:

Fain: 'In internal security cases, in a case of this magnitude and this importance we would always have two agents present.'

Counsel: 'When you say a case of this magnitude and a case of this importance, what do you have in mind?'

Fain: 'Well, this man has been in Russia and we want to try to find out whether he had been recruited by the Russians to do a job against the United States.'

This testimony shows that the agents were concerned about Oswald's intentions and that when they interviewed the man it was not in their minds that he might have been an impostor. (IV.403-430.)

The successful infiltration of the impostor into the United States depended upon deception. Once the American Embassy in Moscow had been deceived and Robert in Fort Worth had been deceived, the deception of Marguerite, who saw 'Lee' a few days after his acceptance by Robert, and finally of the FBI would follow automatically. The imposture having succeeded, the man became a 'United States citizen' and a 'sleeper'.

If the FBI agents were *correct* in recording that the man they had interviewed was 5′ 11″, this would prove that the real Oswald had returned from Russia with Marina and child, and that in the United States, at some time after 26 June, a 5′ 9″ substitute had replaced the real Oswald, with Marina's knowledge had posed as her husband, and had then assassinated the President. If the agents were *incorrect* and the man they had interviewed was 5′ 9″, this would prove that a 5′ 9″ man had entered the United States in June 1962 carrying a passport that gave his height as 5′ 11″, and that he had lied to them about his own and Marina's heights; *either way conspiracy would seem to be established.*

On 13 July 1962, which was 17 days after telling Carter and Fain that his height was 5' 11", Oswald correctly stated his height as 5' 9" on an application form at Leslie Welding Company, Fort Worth, with head office in Chicago; a deception might arouse suspicion. The FBI would not think of looking at this or any subsequent forms, although thereafter — except on the one occasion in June 1963 when he was to give his height as 5' 11" when applying for a new passport in New Orleans — Oswald was always to give his height as 5' 9".

On 14 August 1962, Oswald was re-interviewed at Fort Worth by Fain and another FBI agent, Brown (XVII.736-739). The two agents had waited in a car out of sight of the house where the Oswalds were living and when Oswald came home from work they drew up beside him, inviting him to sit in the back of the car. The interview lasted for $1\frac{1}{2}$ to 2 hours. Fain testified *inter alia* that Oswald again refused to answer questions about the purpose of his visit to Russia and again displayed anger. 'When we asked him again why he went to the Soviet Union in the first place, and I didn't like his answer there ... he still declined to answer questions as to why he went to the Soviet Union in the first instance. He said he considered it nobody's business why he wanted to go to the Soviet Union. Finally he stated he went over to Russia for his own personal reasons. He said it was a personal matter for him. He said "I went and I came back". He said, "It was something that I did". So he just bowed his neck and apparently wasn't going to do anything further at all on that point.' Oswald agreed to advise the FBI if he was approached in suspicious circumstances by foreign agents, but he deprecated the possibility of this happening because his employment at that time did not involve any sensitive information or manufacturing, and as the company did not have any government contracts he could see no reason why the Soviets would desire to contact him. Fain said that the man ' ... had actually settled down. He had got a job with Leslie Machine Shop and he wasn't so tense. He seemed to talk more freely with us ... He appeared a lot more relaxed than he was the first time.' The agents thought that Oswald was not co-operative about his reasons for going to Russia but they decided that he was not a security risk, potentially dangerous or violent. His application for a review of his 'undesirable' discharge from the Marines, prepared in Russia but not posted until 18 June 1962, might have impressed the agents with his desire to obliterate his 'defection', thus affirming his loyalty to the United States. On Fain's recommendation and approved by the Bureau of the FBI in Washington, *Oswald's file was given a 'closed status'*.

The agents had again failed to notice that the man's height was not 5' 11" and the man did not choose to correct the false heights that he had given at the first interview. No longer under FBI surveillance, shortly thereafter Oswald was able to obtain employment at Jaggars-Chiles-Stovall.

Assignment (E). After leaving his mother's house in Fort Worth and shortly before 14 August, Oswald had taken his wife and child to live in a one-bedroom furnished apartment at 2703 Mercedes Street. It was here that many of the Russian emigré group and their friends visited them, and from here that the Oswalds visited the houses of other people. Many of the Russian emigré group testified that the Oswalds were quarrelling and that Marina had been seen with a black eye which she said had been given her by Oswald. Marguerite, unexpectedly calling on Marina, also happened to see the black eye, and Oswald arriving home later admitted to her that he was responsible. Nobody, however, actually saw them fighting except Kleinlerer who saw Oswald slap Marina's face, and on a few occasions they seemed to be happy together. Marina told Anna Meller that her black eye was caused by running into a door when getting up in the middle of the night to attend to the child. Although Anna did not like Oswald, she was to try to help him by persuading her husband to call the Dallas branch of the Texas Employment Commission to ask the counsellor to assist Oswald to get work, as this would directly benefit Marina and the child. If Marina had told her that Oswald had given her a black eye it might have prejudiced the chance of Anna instigating the telephone call that ultimately led to Oswald's employment in Jaggars-Chiles-Stovall. Although the emigré group were suspicious of Oswald and Marina in the sense that they could not understand his change of heart in Russia nor how Marina had been able to leave Russia so easily, the fact that they were apparently fighting and quarrelling would allay suspicion that he was a Russian agent and, after the assassination, would allay suspicion in the minds of the authorities that Marina could have been half of an 'agent team', i.e. a team that by its nature indicated conspiracy, but of which it must again be emphasised Marina knew nothing and played no part other than perhaps doing as she was told by her husband. After the assassination she would be left in the United States in a position so vulnerable that it is unlikely that she would have been allowed to know the truth about her husband. Alone with Oswald in the United States and barely able to speak English, Marina may have come to suspect that her husband was a Russian agent but, perhaps frightened both of him and of the KGB, could do no more than carry out her husband's instructions. In testimony she reiterated that her actions had been dictated by Oswald; on one occasion when she signed a name that she knew to be false, she said that she had done so only under a threat of physical violence from him.

The emigré group had been particularly anxious to help the young wife who had little furniture, clothes or food in the apartment – the child slept in an open suitcase. As a result of what they saw and heard, the group gave Marina presents of clothes, food, help for the child, and payment for some dental treatment for herself. According to the testimony of some of the witnesses, Marina sometimes complained to them in Oswald's presence of his inadequacy and inability to satisfy her sexually, thus underlining their incompatibility.

The wife of the Baron was a Russian who had been born in China and had arrived in the United States with her previous husband in 1938. They had been professional dancers in China but when she arrived in the United States she gave birth to a daughter and was unable to continue her career. She then became a fashion model in New York and later a successful dress designer, travelling extensively in the United States and abroad before finally arriving in Dallas where she divorced her husband. Here she met the thrice married Baron and married him; at the time that she met Marina in the summer of 1962 she was a woman of some experience.

She was to testify of Marina: ' ... in fact Marina doesn't fit at all my ideal, not ideal but how to say it, my feeling about Soviet Youth. I pictured them all sportsmen, very tough, you know, just thinking of their work, sportsmen or something, you know. Some field that they are interested in and that is it. She seems to be exactly opposite to everything. She wasn't a sports girl at all. She didn't have any particular desire for anything, you know. She didn't have determination and goal or anything like that in her life. She was just loving, you know, absolutely opposite, and when she told us how they behaved in Russia, that was absolutely too – I never thought that. I thought they were very, very proper and very–'. She was asked, 'What did she say about how they behaved?'. She replied, 'Well, these sort of orgies, you know, wild parties, and things like that that I would never think that youth would be busy with that because we saw some youngsters in Yugoslavian companies in the camps, maybe we saw the healthier ones and the bad ones stayed in the city probably, but they were just like scouts, you know, just like we were brought up, all interested in sports or in collections of something, you know. They had wonderful healthy interests. And Marina was exactly opposite of all these things. In fact, in spite of that, she was a pharmacologist, that means she had a good head. But somehow she was not at all what I would picture of a Soviet girl. It was entirely opposite, and maybe she is an exception, or maybe they all are, I don't know.' She was asked, 'And she related to you these wild parties and orgies in Minsk? Was that in the presence of Lee?' She replied, 'No, I don't think so. Lee was there very, very little because he was always working or something. One evening I talked to her very long when she came over to me to go to the dentist, and the baby was asleep and she wanted to talk, and we sat down and had some wine and she could smoke all she wanted and she had wine that she wanted. So she told me quite a lot of things. I was really sorry for her'. The Baroness was asked what she meant about 'these wild orgies', and she replied: 'Sexual orgies. I mean things that would never occur to us. In this country. I would say China, too. I was brought up in China and never heard of such things, you know. You never acted like that at all. So it definitely looks like a degeneration, you know, definitely, degeneration.' When asked to give her impression of Marina, she said, 'She impressed me as an honest girl. She really impressed me as an honest girl, and not malicious, not malicious, promiscous, you know'. Counsel asked, 'What?' and she replied, 'Promiscous'. She was asked, 'She was promiscuous, but not malicious?' and she replied, 'Not malicious. That is how I would put it, you know. She wanted to have it all, you know what I mean? She wanted a car and she wanted to have a little apartment and have all these little gadgets that fascinated her, like they fascinated me when I came to the United States. She was living in that poor, poor apartment. Of course, it was depressing for her'.

The Report, which appears to be based primarily upon the testimony of Marina, does not record this part of the testimony of the Baroness, nor does it record the following testimony. The Baroness also testified that she had found it strange that the pharmacist Marina appeared to her to be ignorant and to know nothing of hygiene in her treatment of the infant daughter. She said, 'That is what didn't make sense. Didn't make sense at all. After all, a pharmacist – it didn't make any sense to me how could she, came from a country where all the medical help is supposed to be absolutely free'. (IX.322324).

On Monday 8 October, Oswald was still employed at Leslie Welding Co. in Fort Worth, but without warning he did not arrive at work on Tuesday, leaving Fort Worth for Dallas that evening or early next morning. His employer was to testify that Oswald, ' ... was a good employee. I imagine if he had pursued that trade he might have come out to be a pretty good sheet metal man ... He kept totally to himself ... ' He was not argumentative or quick tempered with the other employees.

When Oswald departed for Dallas, Marina remained in Fort Worth with her child, staying at the houses of various Russian speaking women friends while Oswald, supported by Mr. Meller's telephone call to the counsellor at the Texas Employment Commission in Dallas, sought employment through that Commission and, according to Marina, looked for an apartment for them in Dallas.

Phase Two. Dallas. 8/9 October 1962–24 April 1963

Oswald's assignments were:

(A) To obtain employment by deceit in Jaggars-Chiles-Stovall;
(B) To manufacture counterfeit Marine cards in the fictitious name of Alek James Hidell, this work probably being executed at or with materials obtained from the 'secrets' firm;
(C) To acquire the assassination rifle and a revolver, and immediately upon acquisition of the rifle to appear to make an abortive attempt at assassination of a leading rightwing figure in Dallas, General Walker, thereby indicating that the rifle had been acquired for that purpose and not for the assassination of the President some six months later;
(D) To throw suspicion of conspiracy upon the young American married couple, Ruth Paine and her husband, Michael, who were members of ACLU.

Assignment (A). On 9 October, Oswald took a room at the YMCA in Dallas and on this day opened Post Office Box No. 2915. He also visited the Texas Employment Commission where, on expressing reluctance to accept industrial work, he was placed in the clerical category and referred to Mrs. Cunningham, the counsellor asked by Mr. Meller to help Oswald. Anna Meller was to testify that her husband had made a point of telling the counsellor that Oswald had been in Russia, but the counsellor did not enter this fact on Oswald's application form (XIX.399-400). The counsellor testified that she had been told that Oswald had been in Russia but that she did not enter it on the form as she considered it to be a handicap for an applicant in trying to obtain employment.

Oswald, after untruthfully telling the counsellor that he had been 'laid off' by Leslie Welding, was given three special aptitude tests – for general clerical work, as an insurance claims examiner and for drafting. He scored high on all three tests and the counsellor noted on the application form that he was 'well groomed and spoken, business suit, alert replies, expresses himself extremely well.' The counsellor decided that, although Oswald could be classified for clerical work, in view of his urgent need for money she would try to get him any available work as quickly as possible.

On 11 October, Oswald was referred by the counsellor to the placement office, Mrs. Latham, and by that officer to Jaggars-Chiles-Stovall who required a photoprint trainee. After an interview with John Graef, head of the photographic commercial department of the firm which also did 'highly secret' work for the armed forces, Oswald was accepted and started training on Friday 12 October 1962, earning $1.35 an hour as opposed to the $1.25 an hour he had been earning at Leslie Welding in Fort Worth. The increase in wages being so small, it would appear unlikely that any man would abandon steady work for possible unemployment in another city unless he knew that he would at once be employed; the employment could not have been happenstance.

On 30 March 1964, Graef was to testify and his testimony was taken by one of the assistant Counsel to the Commission. No Commissioner was present to hear the testimony, nor was any Commissioner present when the testimony of the principal of the firm, Robert Stovall, and an employee, Dennis Ofstein, was also taken on the same day by the same assistant Counsel.

Graef testified *inter alia* as follows: He had worked for Jaggars-Chiles-Stovall for about 11 years and on about 1 October 1962, as director of the firm's photographic department, finding himself in need of another man he called the Texas Employment Commission and asked them to send someone along to him having as close as possible the abilities that might work out in their photographic department. He knew Mrs. Latham as the placement officer at the Employment Commission as it was through her that he had obtained other men, and it was to her that he applied on this occasion. He said that it was difficult for the firm to find experienced personnel readily, because their work was quite different in various ways from ordinary photography. Two or three men were sent to Graef who could not remember whether Oswald was first or last but all of them were average young men and Oswald was average. However, Oswald seemed to be the most serious and a shade more determined than the others, and he had a slight edge of them. Oswald was 'modestly dressed in a dark grey suit, and was very business-like and likeable, presenting a nice appearance'. He had understood from Mrs. Latham that Oswald was recently discharged from the Marines and that he had some photographic experience, both factors operating in Oswald's favour. Oswald told Graef that his last position had been in the Marines, that he had served in Korea and obtained an honourable discharge. Looking for someone dependable, a family man such as Oswald – who had told him about his wife and child – offered perhaps 'a little more dependability' than a single man, the necessity to find and hold a job being more important to a married man. Graef did not think of checking on his Marine service or the quality of his discharge because he assumed that as the Employment Commission was a State agency they had a file on him, so that asking Oswald questions would be 'going over the same ground'. From Mrs. Latham and from Oswald he had received the impression that Oswald's discharge from the Marines had been 'a very recent thing', because 'I recall that that's what she told me, and that's what he told me when he came in'. As a neatly dressed man who had been in the Marines and had photographic experience in that service, Oswald 'seemed the applicant with the best chance of success that had been sent over'. Oswald told him that he had no telephone and it was arranged that Oswald should call the next day to hear Graef's decision. Graef thought that Oswald exhibited enough knowledge about photography, but no curiosity was raised in his mind as to his photographic experience, although he was almost certain that he must have asked him one or two things about photography that Oswald had answered satisfactorily. Oswald did not give him an address at their first meeting (presumably because at that time Oswald was living at an apparently secret address that the Commission were never able to trace), but a week or two afterwards when asked to sign his employment card, Oswald wrote in the appropriate space the address and telephone number of the Baron's daughter and son-in-law who lived in Dallas. (Other testimony shows that Oswald did not stay with them at any time but that Marina had stayed there for one or two nights while Oswald was living at the undiscovered address). For the best part of three or four months Oswald worked directly under Graef's supervision, but for the last two months of his employment he worked without direct supervision. He was punctual and he appeared to try to do his best but towards the end of his employment he began to make a considerable number of mistakes in the work that he produced and it had to be done again. (Oswald could have retained the spoiled copies.) During the first two or three months of Oswald's employment, Graef did not hear of any friction between Oswald and the other employees but then he began to hear rumours of friction between Oswald and others while working in the darkroom. There had to be a 'certain amount of give and take in the darkroom' particularly because some of the passageways through the darkroom were narrow. The employees could pass each other but 'not without squeezing by a little bit' when moving from one place to another. Oswald was very difficult to get along with and the other employees would not speak kindly about him. One day Graef saw him reading an unusual newspaper; Oswald said it was a Russian paper and Graef asked him to bring it over. Oswald told him that he had studied Russian in Korea and that he liked to keep in practice reading Russian. Graef said to him, 'Well, Lee, I wouldn't bring anything like that down here again, because some people might not take kindly to your reading anything like that'. Graef thought that Oswald 'might be making trouble for himself by causing suspicion in having that newspaper or at least flaunting it'. The newspaper appeared to Graef to be *The Crocodile*, and it must have been about the 4th or 5th month (January/February) of Oswald's employment that this incident occurred. When Graef was asked, 'Does Jaggars-Chiles-Stovall do any *highly secret work* of any character or any highly confidential work', Graef replied, 'Yes, yes; we do some work for, I think, *the Army Map Service.* We do a certain amount of work for the engineers, I believe, but I couldn't be sure about that'. Graef's 'commercial' department worked quite close to the 'secrets' department which also did photographic work and 'we have a sink on our side for camera work and then there is a developing sink back to back at which this other department develops their work', but Graef said that Oswald would not have had any contact with the 'secrets' department. Counsel did not show Graef Oswald's work sheet for 16 October which showed that while working directly under Graef's supervision, Oswald had executed work for the Army Map Service on the morning of his first working day. There were some twenty employees in Graef's department, but Graef was not asked how many there were in the 'secrets' department. Graef thought that it was in April that there was a downward movement in the firm's business and he thought that it was the time to dismiss Oswald. He called him into the darkroom so that they could not be observed and told him that it was a good time to cut his employment short because business was 'pretty slow' at this time, that Oswald had not been turning out the work that he should have done and that there had also been friction with other employees. Graef offered to give Oswald a good recommendation because he thought he had tried to do his best, but he testified that he would have had to say something about his relations with other employees. When receiving his notice, Oswald only looked at the ground and said, 'Well, thank you', and walked away – allegedly to shoot at the General.

During his testimony, Counsel showed Graef five FBI photographs of a man called Curtis (Larry) Crafard and asked Graef to examine them and say if the man depicted in those photographs bore any similarity or likeness to the man he knew as Lee Harvey Oswald. Graef said that the likeness was 'very slight; but to anyone who knew Lee, they would immediately say "No" '. Counsel knew that Crafard had been employed by Jack Ruby as a sort of living-in handyman at 'The Carousel' on 1 November 1963 and that on the morning or in the early afternoon of the day after the assassination Crafard had fled the club to hide in a cabin in a remote part of far away Michigan.

It was on 15 February 1964, being six weeks *before* Graef testified, that the FBI had discovered from Gary Lawler that 'some short while' before Oswald left the firm on 6 April 1963 it had employed Grossi in the name of 'Jack Leslie Browen' and who had remained with the firm until August 1963 when, for a reason undisclosed, he had left. Counsel should have been told by the FBI of this but Graef was not asked about 'Jack Leslie Bowen', how it had come about that the man was employed and through whom, whether it was apparent that he had known Oswald prior to his employment, whether he worked in the camera department with Oswald, and when and why he left.

Robert Stovall testified on the same day as Graef and was examined by the same Counsel but no Commissioner was present. He said *inter alia*: Jaggars-Chiles-Stovall was a corporation and he was the principal shareholder, the original founders of the firm having disposed of their holdings in 1961 to him, his family, and several of the employees. At the time that he testified he had been with the company for 25 years and it had been his entire business career. When asked whether the firm did secret or confidential work or classified work of any kind he replied, 'On occasion we do. Most of it is not, but we do on occasion. We are cleared through the Navy Bureau Material here and although I believe it now has been incorporated under the Department of Defence as a single unit ... Generally speaking, the nature of the work is charting and mapping, and actually all we do is set words, letters and figures. We have no correlation of what they refer to.' He said that the charting and mapping which they received concerned the charting of coastal areas, sea bottoms and some land areas in the continental United States and some foreign areas. Whatever secret work they did was done only with staff who had been cleared by the appropriate Federal agencies and these members of the staff were the only people who saw the work. So far as Lee Harvey Oswald was concerned 'he had no part in it nor access to any of this work', and the company was at pains to see that none other than those who had been cleared 'by an appropriate Federal Agency' had access to it. Stovall was asked if he knew the term 'microdot printing', and he said that he knew nothing about this kind of work and that the firm did not have any appropriate equipment. He had never spoken to Oswald but he had heard from other employees that he was an 'oddball', had been a constant source of irritation because of his lack of productive ability, and had bumped into other employees in the darkroom causing dissension. During Oswald's employment, Stovall had heard a rumour that Oswald had been reading a Russian newspaper but Stovall had been unable to confirm it. As with Graef he did not mention nor was he asked about Oswald's work for the Army Map Service, nor about 'Jack Leslie Bowen'. Stovall said that he had contacted the Secret Service on Saturday 23 November 1963,

and that a 'Mr. De Prato and another gentleman' came to see him
in his office on that day and on Sunday 24 November. He did
not volunteer nor was he asked by Counsel what had transpired
at these meetings. There is no record in the Exhibits of these
interviews or what the Secret Service discovered; the Secret
Service agents were not called to testify and the Report does not
mention these visits.

After the assassination, Oswald's notebook was discovered and it
contained the entry 'Jaggars-Chiles-Stovall. microdots'
(XVI.53). It is not known whether the firm was carrying out
work in connection with the U-2 photographs or other material
relating to the 'Cuba Crisis' on and after 16 October 1962 for,
although the Commission should have known of the sensitive
nature of the firm's work and knew of the word 'microdots' in
Oswald's notebook, neither Graef nor Stovall were asked during
their testimony whether the firm had executed work for the
Department of Defence – which included the Army Map Service
– during the early period of Oswald's employment. There is no
record in the Exhibits that the FBI interviewed either of them or
others in connection with this matter, although from the
importance thereof it would seem that the FBI must have asked
them about the work they did at the time of the 'Cuba Crisis'. It
is a fact, however, that the FBI did investigate Oswald's activities
during his employment with the firm, but were not asked to
testify and the Report does not mention the matter.

The Report refers to Jaggars-Chiles-Stovall only as a
'commercial, advertising and photography firm' (R.403), and in
another place as a 'graphic arts company' (R.719). No mention is
made of the secret work that was carried out on the premises, nor
that Oswald had written 'microdots' in his notebook under the
name of Jaggars-Chiles-Stovall, nor of the work carried out by
him for the Army Map Service. The Report makes no reference
to the fact that Graef testified he had understood from Mrs.
Latham that Oswald had recently been discharged from the
Marines, and Oswald had told him his last employment had been

with the Marines in Korea and that he had had photographic experience while in the Marines. The Report, not having mentioned Oswald's employment in the 'secrets' firm at the time of the 'Cuba Crisis', does not connect Oswald's sudden departure from Leslie Welding Co. in Fort Worth on 8/9 October with his immediate employment and opportunity for espionage at Jaggars-Chiles-Stovall at the moment when the Russians and the Cubans would have wished to discover the extent of American knowledge of their missile build-up. The Commission did not call Mrs. Latham to testify and there is no record of any FBI or Secret Service interview with her. The Report does not mention the discovery of Oswald's espionage equipment.

On the same day that Graef and Stovall testified, a fellow-employee of Oswald, Dennis Ofstein, testified *inter alia* to the same Counsel; again no Commissioner was present. He was aged 24 and he had worked for the past two years with the firm as a cameraman. When Oswald came to the firm as a cameraman trainee he was in the same 'commercial' department as Ofstein, and due to the fact that Ofstein knew a certain amount about the work he was expected to help Oswald and to keep an eye on him. As with Oswald, he had obtained employment at the firm by registering with the Texas Employment Commission, and he thought it was through Mrs. Latham. Ofstein said that he knew that the firm did work for the Government and that he had sometimes participated in that work, but that Oswald had not done so to his knowledge. He said that most of the staff were unfriendly to Oswald because he was difficult to get along with. Ofstein had been told by Oswald that he had been in Russia and had there married a White Russian and, as Ofstein had studied Russian while in the Army, he had formed an acquaintanceship with Oswald. Although Ofstein had asked Oswald where he had acquired his knowledge of and facility with the Russian language, Oswald would not tell him whether he had learned it in the Soviet Union or before, or 'just how he had picked it up'. Ofstein said that he worked more or less side-by-side with

Oswald when Oswald was training and that Oswald seemed to take a great interest in the work so far as skill went but, although Oswald was fast and his work improved, he never was able to turn out high quality work such as was required by the firm. He said that Oswald's trouble in getting along with people began in about January 1963, and that it was Oswald's personality and bad workmanship that had caused the termination of his employment. It was the custom of the firm to allow their employees to do a little private photography for themselves such as the copying of personal photographs and so on, and on one occasion Oswald had asked Ofstein to help him make an enlargement of a picture showing 'a river and a nice building in the background'. Oswald had told him that the building in the photograph 'was some military headquarters and the guards stationed there were armed with weapons and ammunition and had orders to shoot any trespassers or anybody trying to enter the building without permission'. At other times during his employment Oswald had made enlargements of pictures that he said were taken while he was in the Marines in Japan, showing 'snow on the ground, and bivouac areas and so on with Oswald in several of them'. When Oswald told him that he had been in Russia, Ofstein had assumed that he had been there at first *working as an agent for the United States*, because Oswald was particularly interested in talking to Ofstein about the military disposition of troops, tanks and aircraft in Russia, and appeared to have considerable information as to the methods the Russians used in placing the various branches of the military in different locations. Oswald said that while he was in Russia he had complete freedom of movement except that the MVD had enquired of his neighbours about him and had talked to him on one or two occasions, 'but that they didn't put any holds on him or restrict him from any areas or anything like that'. When discussing the Russian military dispositions, Ofstein said that Oswald, although he never directly said so, gave the impression that he had seen all these dispositions. Oswald had said that he didn't think that life in Russia was the type of life that he wanted to lead because the people were poor, they worked hard and made just enough money to buy their clothes and their food, and that the only people who had enough money left to buy any of the luxuries left in life were those who were Communist Party officials or high ranking members in the Party. Ofstein asked Oswald if he were a Communist and Oswald replied in the negative. On the last day that Oswald was in Jaggars-Chiles-Stovall, Ofstein asked him what he was going to do and where he would work. Oswald had replied that he didn't know, that he liked the type of work and he would like to continue doing that work after looking around to find some, but if he did not find anything he could always go back to the Soviet Union, and 'sort of laughed about it'. Ofstein gave him the names of two other places which did photographic work in Dallas where Oswald might find employment. (Oswald was not to apply to any other firm.) Ofstein confirmed Graef's words about Oswald's psychology and thoughtlessness in the darkroom, with his habit of 'just bursting through there head-on with no regard to who was in the room', and mentioned that the firm had a Bruning copying machine which they had to share with the other department. Oswald did not wish to talk to anybody except Ofstein, and always ate his lunch alone. Oswald seemed to arrive on time and expressed a desire to work overtime if he was needed, except at times during the week when he said he had to go to the Crozier Technical College (which held typing courses) at night. Ofstein saw Oswald with what he believed were typing books from the library but he thought that Oswald's attendance at the typing school was not more than one or two nights a week at the most. When Ofstein was asked by Counsel if he knew what a microdot was, he replied that this had been explained to him by Oswald who had asked him if he knew about microdots. When Ofstein told him that he knew nothing about it, Oswald then told him that was the method of taking a large area of type or a picture and reducing it down to an extremely small size, adding that it was the way spies sometimes sent messages and pictures of diagrams and other material, 'placing it under a postage stamp'. Ofstein had no idea where Oswald had learnt about microdots, but imagined that Oswald must have picked it up from books. Ofstein had seen Oswald on two occasions bringing to the firm newspapers and magazines entitled *Soviet White Russian, The Crocodile*, and *The Agitator*. It seemed to Ofstein that Oswald had obtained this material from a firm in Washington whose name and address he gave to Ofstein who said that after the assassination the FBI had collected some of the Russian papers that Oswald had lent him (confirming that the FBI did investigate the firm). He had asked Oswald to introduce him to Russian immigrants whom Oswald said he knew so that Ofstein could converse in Russian, but Oswald kept putting him off so that Ofstein was never able to meet any of them. Oswald asked Ofstein not to mention anything about his having been in Russia, and Ofstein assumed that he was the only one who knew that Oswald had a White Russian wife, but later was to discover that Oswald must have told others in the firm that he had such a wife. Oswald told Ofstein that he had qualified in the Marines as a marksman. A week after Oswald left the firm, Ofstein wrote to him inviting him and his wife to come and visit them on some Saturday evening. The letter was addressed to P.O. Box 2915, which was the only address that Oswald had given him, although at that time Oswald and Marina were living at Neeley Street in Dallas; no reply was received. Both he and Graef had on occasions offered to give Oswald a lift home from work but Oswald had always refused saying that he would prefer to walk and that he was going to pick up mail at his Box, the result of all this being that Ofstein was never allowed by Oswald to know where the latter lived. (Testimony of Graef, Stovall and Ofstein with author's italics. X.197-213.) It is notable that Gary Lawler was not asked by the Commission to testify although he had been interviewed six weeks before by the FBI and had then identified from a photograph that 'Jack Leslie Bowen' (Grossi) had been employed in the camera department for a short time with the assassin.

Assignment B. The matter of counterfeiting has already been discussed and it would seem that the counterfeits must have been prepared during the last half of Oswald's employment at Jaggers-Chiles-Stovall, although it is impossible to speculate how the assassin proposed to use the counterfeits and other material found in his wallet on arrest, other than to suggest that (a) one of them could have been used to identify himself on the Marsalis bus as 'Alek James Hidell' or (b) they could have provided evidence satisfactorily to identify him to a series of persons assisting him on his escape from Dallas and the United States, perhaps a kind of prearranged 'passport'.

The use of the name 'Alek James Hidell' appears to have been ingenious. Marina had retained in her possession letters to her from Oswald written by him in Minsk and signed 'Alek' and also letters from friends in Russia referring to 'Alek'; after the assassination she handed these to the FBI. Expecting to escape, the assassin had left the negatives of the 'Alek James Hidell' counterfeits at his residence; the use of the name 'Alek' thus connected the assassin with the man she had met in Russia calling himself 'Alek', whose real name she shortly discovered to be Lee Harvey Oswald. 'James' appears to be a name selected at random, but 'Hidell' was the nickname of one of Oswald's fellow Marines, Heindel, thus implying that the 'Alek' who met and married Marina in Russia had served in the Marines. Marina was to testify that she knew that Oswald had used the name 'Hidell' having herself once signed 'A.J. Hidell' on a card that had been found in the assassin's wallet on arrest, and that she was aware that 'Hidell' was but an altered 'Fidel' (Castro); she had been displeased with her husband's foolishness. Ex-Marine Heindel swore an affidavit for the Commission that while in the Marines and serving with Oswald his nickname had been 'Hidell'.

Assignment (C). While working at Jaggars-Chiles-Stovall, in the name 'Hidell' Oswald mail-ordered the revolver and the assassination rifle fitted with telescopic sights respectively from dealers in Los Angeles and Chicago. He obtained the revolver with a mail-order form dated 27 January and the rifle with a mail-order form dated 12 March 1963, both weapons being shipped by the dealers on 20 March to 'Hidell' at Oswald's Dallas P.O. Box 2915. On the mail-order form for the revolver Oswald had given his age as 28 and the false name, D.F. Drittal, as the person certifying that A.J. Hidell was a U.S. citizen. Not only had Oswald purchased the weapons in a false name but he had obtained them from suppliers far distant from Dallas; Los Angeles and Chicago were strongholds of organised crime and in both cities Ruby had many contacts.

When Oswald was discharged from Jaggars-Chiles-Stovall on 6 April 1963, it would appear that he had been inviting dismissal so that he could carry out his next assignment (D), his involvement in the attempted murder of the General, probably the most active and controversial rightwing figure on the American political scene and disliked by extremists in ACLU and other civil liberties movements.

According to Marina's testimony, Oswald had told her that on the evening of 6 or 7 April 1963 he had taken his recently acquired rifle to shoot the General whose home was on the other side of Dallas from where the Oswalds lived. Marina said that Oswald had told her that he had decided not to kill the General on that night because the conditions were unfavourable – the truth was that the General was not at home and it seems probable that Oswald was not near the General's residence on 6 or 7 April.

On 10 April, at about 9.00 p.m. a rifle-shot was fired at the General from outside his house and at a distance of some 35 yards. The bullet passed through a narrow horizontal window frame invisible from outside, just missed the head of the General who was seated at his desk in the lighted room, and then passed through a wall behind his head. The mutilated bullet was found that night; after the assassination of the President it could be identified only as a bullet from a rifle of the same calibre as the rifle of Oswald.

Found among Oswald's possessions after his arrest were several photographs of the General's house, and it was established that they had been taken with Oswald's old camera. Certain construction work in progress appearing in the background of one of the photographs reveals that they had been taken between 9 and 12 March 1963 and, as the rifle had been ordered on 12 March, the conspirators intended it to appear that the crime was planned and photographs taken just before the rifle was ordered, thus indicating that the rifle had been obtained primarily for the purpose of assassinating the General, and that Oswald was the rifleman.

Marina was to testify that on the night of the shooting, 10 April, Oswald had gone out but she did not know what he was going to do and she had not seen him carrying a rifle. It was on his return later that night that he told her about his two visits to shoot the General on 6 or 7 April and 10 April. She said that she had seen Oswald studying bus routes before the shooting and making notes in a notebook; he had tried to prevent her seeing what he was doing. She said that on his return to their apartment on 10 April he told her that after firing the shot at the General he had run away from the scene and hidden the rifle near a railway line, and that he had travelled to and from the General's house by bus. (Photographs of the area of the railway line were found amongst Oswald's possessions.) She added that Oswald had said that the General was a Fascist and that someone should have shot Hitler.

Marina said that before going out on the evening of 10 April he had left in their apartment a note for her written in Russian telling her what to do in the event of his being killed or arrested that night, and that she had read the note and became alarmed because she did not know what her husband might be doing. (This note was found between the leaves of one of her books some little time after the assassination of the President.) She said that on Oswald's return that night she had told him that she would tell the police should he again attempt to murder anyone and that she would keep the note as a 'hold' over him.

It would seem unlikely that the KGB would have allowed the potential assassin of the President to be near the General's house at any time; the killing or arrest of Oswald in the attempted murder of a comparatively minor political figure would have been fatal to the plot to kill the President. It would appear (a) that the note was written and retained in order to suggest that Oswald had fired the shot and that the rifle had been obtained for the sole purpose of killing the 'Fascist' General, and (b) that after the assassination of Kennedy, Oswald would appear to have been a 'loner' who would shoot at anyone, Fascist or 'Liberal', with whose views he disagreed.

There is, however, powerful evidence that Oswald's story as recounted by Marina is untrue. On 8 April, being two nights before the shooting, a friend of the General, Robert Surrey, saw two men 'peeking through the windows' of the General's house. He kept out of their sight but followed them when they drove away in a car, losing them after some distance because they doubled back, appearing to him to have noticed his car and wishing to escape from him. He said that there was no licence number on the car. The next day he had told the General about the two men, and the Police were informed. On the night of the shooting, 10 April, and within a few seconds of the shot –

according to the timing in an FBI report after the assassination of the President – 14 year old Walter Coleman who was on the porch of an adjacent house and thought he had heard a gun shot, raised himself on a fence and saw two men 'about 30 years old' getting into separate cars; one of them had pushed the front seat forward, had leaned into the back of the car and was placing something under the floorboards. After seeing the car nearest to him drive away – not being the car into which the man was leaning – the boy re-entered his house now believing from the lack of interest displayed by the two men that the sound of a gun shot must have been only a car back-firing. At about the same time the General, running upstairs to get his revolver, saw the tail-lights of a car being driven away, and estimated that the time when he saw the tail-lights would have corresponded to the departure of an assassin by car after the shooting. On the evening of the shooting the boy made a statement to the Dallas police in which he said that he had heard a gun shot and he recounted what he had seen. The place where the boy said that the two cars were positioned was part of a parking area reserved for a nearby church and happened to be floodlit that night for the benefit of the congregation and had not been seen previously or later in that area. After the assassination of the President eight months later, Coleman made a statement to the FBI in which he indicated where the two cars had been parked, one of them being about 10 feet from him when he had looked over the fence. With the boy's aid the FBI parked cars in the positions indicated by him and photographed the situation. Apart from minor details, Coleman repeated to the FBI the statement that he had made to the Dallas police just after the shooting on 10 April.

Marina was to testify that Oswald had told her he had chosen a night when there was a church gathering as there would be more people in the area. (This would be helpful so far as get-away cars were concerned but a hindrance so far as sight of the gunman, the flash and the blast of his rifle were concerned.) When Coleman was shown photographs of the assassin of the President, he said that he had been able to see the faces of the two men fairly well due to the flood-lighting, and that neither of them resembled the man in the photographs. Surrey had never been near enough to the two men 'peeking through the windows' to be able to identify them, but when he was shown the photographs he said that he did not believe that either of the two men he had seen resembled the assassin (XXIII.757-775).

It would seem inexplicable that at night in an extremely quiet residential area, immediately after the explosion from the rifle, the flash and the sound of the bullet passing through the window frame and a wall, two men who were seen only some 35 yards away from the point where it was established that the shot had been fired, should have driven off without pausing to find out what had happened. Although the next day's local and national newspapers and radio narrated the attack, neither of the two men seen by Coleman came forward to the police to report what they must have seen and heard.

Oswald's possession of the photographs of the General's house, the note he left for Marina telling her what to do in the event of his being killed or arrested, and his alleged words to her indicate that he had knowledge of the shooting. It would seem it was intended that after the assassination of the President, the authorities should be led to believe that there was no conspiracy and that he was the only person involved in the attempted murder of the General. To reinforce this deception, Oswald had written in his notebook the General's name and telephone number (XVI.39). (This author's inspection of the site and re-enactment of the shooting revealed that Oswald's story about running away with the rifle after firing, if not impossible, is not credible for he could have been seen and apprehended; it was apparent that get-away cars, one for a look-out man, were necessary, and that the two men seen by Coleman must have been aware of the shot.)

After the assassination of the President, Marina was interviewed by the FBI on 4 June 1964 and was asked about the shooting. She told the FBI that ' ... she was sure in her own mind he had planned and attempted the assassination (Walker) completely alone ... it was not like Oswald to be associated with anybody else in such an endeavour.'

When Marina testified about the shooting (XI.292-294) it would appear that Counsel to the Commission were sceptical of Oswald's account as retold by her:

COUNSEL: You previously told the Commission that Lee Oswald prepared a notebook in which he kept plans and notes about his attack on General Walker; is that right?

INTERPRETER: I saw this book only after the attempt on Walker's life. He burned it or disposed of it.

COUNSEL: Tell me when you first saw the notebook?

MARINA: Three days after this happened.

COUNSEL: You saw the notebook three days after it had happened?

MARINA: I think so.

COUNSEL: How did you come to see it then?

INTERPRETER: When he was destroying it.

COUNSEL: Is that the only time you ever saw it?

INTERPRETER: I saw on several occasions that he was writing something in the book, but he was hiding it from me and he was locking it in his room.

COUNSEL: Did he actually lock the door to his room when he left the apartment?

INTERPRETER: The door to his room could be locked only from the inside and he was locking the door when he was writing in the book, otherwise, he was hiding it in some secret place and he warned me not to mess around and look around his things. He asked me not to go into his room and look around.

COUNSEL: You saw him writing in this book before the night that he shot at General Walker?

MARINA: Not before the night.

COUNSEL: After?

MARINA: No; not before – 1 month before, but not every day, you know, sometimes. I saw him writing on several occasions in that book prior to the attempt on Walker's life, only I did not know what he was writing.

COUNSEL: Even though you could have gone into this room to look at the book, you did not do so, because Lee had told you not to; is that correct?

INTERPRETER: Yes; he forbade me looking around in his room, and so I did not see the book or look at it.

COUNSEL: But three days after he shot at General Walker, you saw him destroy the book; is that correct?

INTERPRETER: Yes.

COUNSEL: How did he destroy it?

INTERPRETER: He burned it.

COUNSEL: Where?

INTERPRETER: In the apartment house on Neely.

COUNSEL: Where in the apartment?

INTERPRETER: He burned it with matches over a wash bowl in the bathroom.

COUNSEL: And you first became aware of this when you smelled it burning; is that correct?

INTERPRETER: I did not see the book but I saw him writing in this book and he showed me several photographs. Before he burned the book, he showed me several photographs that were in the book. I asked him what the pictures were and he said, 'Well, this one is the picture of the house of General Walker's — his residence.'

COUNSEL: And that picture was pasted in the notebook; is that right?

INTERPRETER: No; it was loose in the book — I really don't remember ...

COUNSEL: Did you say anything to Lee when you saw him destroying this book about why he prepared it and why he left it there in the apartment when he went to shoot General Walker?

INTERPRETER: No; I did not. No; I never asked him why he left it in the apartment, why he left his book in the apartment. While he went to shoot General Walker. I did not ask him why he left it in the apartment. I asked him what for was he making all these entries in the book and he answered that he wanted to leave a complete record so that all the details would be in it. He told me that these entries consisted of the description of the house of General Walker, the distances, the location, and the distribution of windows in it.

COUNSEL: What did he want to leave this record for?

INTERPRETER: All these details — all these records, that he was writing it either for his own use so that he would know what to do when the time came to shoot General Walker. I am guessing that perhaps he did it to appear to be a brave man in case he were arrested, but that is my supposition. I was so afraid after this attempt on Walker's life that the police might come to the house. I was afraid that there would be evidence in the house such as this book.

COUNSEL: Did you talk to Lee about that?

INTERPRETER: Oh, yes ... I told him that it is best not to have this kind of stuff in the house — this book.

COUNSEL: When did you tell him that?

INTERPRETER: All the time he was destroying it — he showed me this book after this attempt on Walker's life, and I suggested to him that it would be awfully bad to keep a thing like that in the house.

COUNSEL: When did he first show it to you?

INTERPRETER: Three days after the attempt — 3 days after this attempt, he took the rifle from the house, took it somewhere and buried it.

COUNSEL: Three days after the attempt?

INTERPRETER: Yes, yes.

COUNSEL: So that he actually took the rifle out of the house and took it away and hid it somewhere?

MARINA: Yes.

INTERPRETER: No; the day Lee shot at Walker, he buried the rifle because when he came home and told me that he shot at General Walker and I asked him where the rifle was and he said he buried it.

COUNSEL: He shot at General Walker on April 10, which was on Wednesday.

MARINA: Wednesday?

COUNSEL: Yes; it was on Wednesday.

INTERPRETER: As I remember, it was the weekend — Saturday or Sunday when Lee brought the rifle back home.

COUNSEL: What weekend following the time he shot at

	General Walker?
MARINA:	The same weekend of the same week.
COUNSEL:	Had he destroyed the notebook before he brought the rifle back?
INTERPRETER:	No.
COUNSEL:	How long after he brought the rifle back did he destroy the book?
INTERPRETER:	He destroyed the book approximately an hour after he brought the rifle home.
COUNSEL:	After he brought the rifle home, then, he showed you the book?
MARINA:	Yes.
COUNSEL:	And you said it was not a good idea to keep this book?
MARINA:	Yes.
COUNSEL:	And then he burned the book?
MARINA:	Yes.
COUNSEL:	Did you ask him why he had not destroyed the book before he actually went to shoot General Walker?
INTERPRETER:	It never came to me, myself, to ask him that question.
COUNSEL:	Did you see him take the pictures, the photographs, out of the book when he destroyed it?
INTERPRETER:	When I saw him burning the book – I'm not positive that he burned the photographs or not with the book. He retained the negatives and he preserved either the photographs themselves or the negatives. I know that they have the photographs and I don't know whether they got the originals or whether they made them from the negatives.
COUNSEL:	Now, when you say 'they', Marina, who do you mean by 'they'?
INTERPRETER:	FBI, Secret Service, and the President's Commission ...
COUNSEL:	Did it seem strange to you at the time, Marina, that Lee did make these careful plans, take

pictures, and write it up in a notebook, and then when he went out to shoot at General Walker he left all that incriminating evidence right in the house so that if he had ever been stopped and questioned and if that notebook had been found, it would have clearly indicated that he was the one that shot at General Walker?

INTERPRETER: He was such a person that nothing seems peculiar to me for what he did. I had so many surprises from him that nothing surprised me. He may have wished to appear such a brave man or something.

COUNSEL: Did you ever have the feeling that he really wanted to be caught in connection with the Walker affair?

INTERPRETER: I don't know how to answer that — maybe yes and maybe no. I couldn't read his mind.

COUNSEL: Do you think that the picture that he asked you to take when he was holding the rifle and the newspapers, and that he then autographed for June, do you think that was connected with the Walker thing at all? (Author's note: This picture was one of those recovered from the residence of the assassin and shown to him by the Dallas police.)

INTERPRETER: I think so, because it happened just before he went to shoot General Walker. Then, I asked him why he was taking this silly picture and he answered that he simply wanted to send it to the newspaper.

COUNSEL: *The Militant?*

MARINA: *The Militant.*

INTERPRETER: I didn't attach any significance to what he said at the time, but he added, 'That maybe some day June will remember me.' He must have had something in his mind — some grandiose plans.

It would seem from the evidence of Surrey, Coleman and the General, the behaviour of Oswald and the words of Marina, that the truth of the attempted murder of the General may have been as follows: Someone with Oswald's camera took the photographs of the General's house and gave them to Oswald. Oswald prepared a notebook with instructions for the proposed murderers and lent them his rifle: the notebook and rifle being returned to him about three days after the shooting. The notebook containing directions for third parties had to be destroyed, but the photographs of the General's house taken with Oswald's camera, the photographs of himself holding the rifle and the autographing of one of the photographs, together with the General's name and telephone number in his notebook, were kept for Oswald's later self-incrimination.

The Commission did not ask Coleman to testify. Had they done so and had he repeated in testimony what he told the Dallas police in April 1963 and what he told the FBI in June 1964, powerful evidence of conspiracy would have been disclosed. Surrey was to testify but, as he was approaching the end of his testimony and was about to describe the incident involving the two men 'peeking through the windows', Warren interrupted Counsel and it would seem from the wording that (a) the Chief Justice did not want to hear evidence about the two men, and (b) Counsel had it in mind to 'dissipate any possibility' that there had been two men involved in the shooting. Surrey was determined, however, to mention the two men he had seen and said, 'Well, the gist of the matter is that two nights before the assassination attempt, I saw two men around the house peeking in windows and so forth, and reported this to the General the following morning, and he in turn reported it to the police on Tuesday, and it was on Wednesday night that he was shot at. So that is really the gist of the whole thing'. Surrey was not questioned further about the matter. (V.446.) The Report says that Oswald shot at General Walker and dismisses the evidence about the two men.

Oswald was out of work at the time of the Walker shooting, having left Jaggars-Chiles-Stovall on the afternoon of 6 April, and it would seem that the acquisition of the rifle and the preparation of the double-identity cards as aids in escape indicate that he already knew that he was to assassinate the President at a later date. He left Dallas for New Orleans on 24 April whence he was to travel to Mexico City to obtain final instructions for the assassination of the President and his own escape before returning to Dallas to complete the KGB operation.

To avoid distraction from the story of Oswald's assignments during his first stay in Dallas, certain matters have been omitted, and it is necessary to back-track and describe these additional events that occurred during and after his Dallas assignments (A), (B) and (C) before moving on to describe his last assignment (D), the involvement of the Paines.

Oswald had moved from Fort Worth to Dallas on 8/9 October 1962 and began his employment with Jaggars-Chiles-Stovall on 12 October. The Commission was unable to establish where he had lived after arriving in Dallas until he moved into the YMCA on 15 October, remaining there until 19 October, and they were again unable to discover where he had lived between 19 October and 3 November. Marina testified that she too did not know where Oswald had been living during these periods. It is worth noting that Jack Ruby for many years had frequented the YMCA for physical exercising, but it is not known whether he visited the YMCA when Oswald was there.

The Commission and Marina were not the only people who did not know where Oswald was living for these two periods totalling 18 days. After Oswald and Marina had lived in Marguerite's house in Fort Worth for about 4 weeks during July/August 1962, Marguerite had been a frequent visitor to 2703 Mercedes Street, Fort Worth, the house then rented by Oswald and Marina, but Marina testified that he did not get on well with his mother and that he had tried to prevent Marina from welcoming her to their house. When he had departed Fort Worth for Dallas, Oswald did not tell Marguerite where he was going, and it would seem that this earlier alienation of the mother provided Oswald with the excuse for her total exclusion from his activities from that time on. Oswald did not tell Robert where he was living in Dallas, giving him only his P.O. Box No. 2915. Thus his activities while at Jaggars-Chiles-Stovall, the purchase of the rifle and revolver, the attempt to murder the

General, and his later activities in New Orleans, Mexico City and again in Dallas prior to the assassination would not be interrupted or discovered by an unexpected visit from either of them.

After the assassination of the President, the name, description and photographs of the assassin were for weeks constantly before the Dallas, Fort Worth and American public, but nobody volunteered (according to the Report and the Exhibits) where he had been living during the 18 days of his disappearance; somebody *must* have known and it would seem that he had a confederate to accommodate him.

Marina had joined Oswald in an apartment at 604 Elsbeth Street, Dallas, on 3 or 4 November 1962, and this was the first day on which she was to be living with Oswald in Dallas after he had left her in Fort Worth. According to Marina, within a day or so they were quarrelling violently and a few of their acquaintances felt that she would be better off alone, one man offering to help her if she promised to leave Oswald permanently. Finally on 5 or 6 November, Marina moved into Anna Meller's house with the intention – according to Marina – of not returning to Oswald. Marina was to testify that she was uncomfortable at the Meller house where there was little accommodation, and that she moved to the house of another Russian emigré, Mrs. Ford, where she stayed apparently from 11 to 17 November. She told Mrs. Ford that she had decided never to return to her husband, that he was very cold to her and seldom had sexual relations. Mrs. Ford had the impression that Marina was going to stay at other people's houses until a permanent place could be found for her. When Mrs. Ford's husband returned from a business trip on 17 November, Marina and her child moved to the house of another Russian emigre family, but they did not spend the night, returning to the Fords on the evening of 17 November and going to another house for the night of 18 November.

On 17 November, Robert had written to Oswald at the latter's P.O. Box in Dallas inviting him and Marina to join Robert and his wife and the half-brother John Pic and his wife for Thanksgiving dinner later in November; Marguerite was not invited. Oswald received this letter on 18 November and telephoned the house where Marina was staying the night to ask if he could visit Marina. This he was allowed to do and he was reunited with her despite the fact that she had complained to Mrs. Ford that Oswald had been treating her so badly that she had contemplated suicide, feeling that she had 'no way out'. Marina testified that at this meeting with Oswald on 18 November, he had professed his love for her. She said: 'I saw him cry ... begged me to come back'. Of another occasion she testified: ' ... He cried and you know a woman's heart – I went back to him. He said he didn't care to live if I did not return.'

On 18 November, Oswald returned with Marina to Elsbeth Street and in due course they attended the Thanksgiving dinner with Robert, John Pic and their wives; John Pic had not seen Oswald for 10 years.

Both Robert and John Pic testified that Lee and Marina appeared to be happy on what was a pleasant occasion. John Pic was to testify in May 1964 that 'I wouldn't have recognised him, Sir', because (a) he was 'not the Lee I knew', (b) he had noticed that his 'bull-neck' was not apparent, (c) it had struck Pic 'profusely' that Lee's body and hair were thinner, and (d) when Lee had introduced Pic to a visitor after the dinner as his 'half-brother', Pic was 'mad' because Lee always referred to Pic as his 'brother'. The Report does not refer to Pic's apparently significant testimony, and says only that Pic 'observed, as many others have also attested, that Lee seemed to be a good father and to take an active interest in June'. (R.721.)

When Marguerite, Robert and John Pic testified, they knew nothing of the conflicting heights and physical discrepancies other than those they had themselves observed and to which they would testify; the question of imposture did not enter their minds.

It would appear that during the Oswalds stay in Fort Worth and Dallas, Oswald intended to give Marguerite and Robert the impression that he and Marina were happy, but he so organised matters that Marina would indicate to the suspicious Russian emigré group that they were quarrelling and fighting. The apparent discord between himself and Marina also provided Oswald with an excuse for Marina to be staying with friends while he carried out his assignment at Jaggars-Chiles-Stovall during the 'Cuba Crisis', an assignment which was intended to be discovered after the assassination and thought to have been inspired by Castro.

In May 1962, the State Department had lent Oswald $435.71 to help him and his family travel from Russia to the United States and which he had been repaying by small instalments of $10 at a time. In December 1962 and in January 1963, Oswald repaid the balance of the loan in two large amounts totalling $390. When the State Department loaned money it was their practice for the Passport Office to be informed, the latter placing a 'look-out' card in their file on that person in order to prevent him obtaining a passport and leaving the country whilst still in debt to the State Department. When Oswald repaid his loan, the 'look-out' card was removed from his file, and it would seem that by the end of 1962 Oswald knew that in due course he would be obtaining a new passport to enable him to travel to Cuba via Mexico during the late summer of 1963. In addition, he had prepared his counterfeit 'escape' cards during the first three months of 1963 for use later that year.

Assignment (D). About the end of January 1963, Marina again became pregnant and it was about a month later that 31 year old Mrs. Ruth Paine was to enter the story in connection with the pregnancy, and to her own undoing.

From the fall of 1959 Michael and Ruth Paine had been living together at 2515 West Fifth Street, Irving, near Dallas, until about a year before the events now to be recounted. Michael Paine was a research engineer with a security clearance at Bell Helicopter, Grand Prairie, and he had moved to a separate apartment near his work but continued frequently to visit his wife in Irving, she having the custody of their two small children who remained with her at the Irving address. She was an exceptionally well-educated woman and had indulged, as can be seen from her testimony, in a number of good works. Apart from her academic qualifications, she appears to have been athletic and to have led a rigorous mental and physical life from the age of about 15. In 1956, which happened to be the year when the young Oswald wrote to the Socialist Workers Party and joined the Marines, Ruth began to study the Russian language and was to maintain her interest in that subject until she came to meet

Marina in early 1963. She had been connected in a responsible position with groups endeavouring to encourage East-West friendships and she had carried on 'pen-pal' correspondence with two women in Russia while Oswald was in Russia and before she was to meet Oswald and Marina in Dallas, one of the 'pen-pal' women being called Ella. In testimony, Ruth could remember the full name of one of the 'pen-pals' but could not recollect the surname of Ella. In the 'Historic Diary' Oswald referred at length to his 'love', Ella, and in his notebook he had written her name, Ella German, and her address, drawing attention to the entry by partly encircling it with a black line (XVI.49). Neither from Ruth nor from other sources did the Commission endeavour to establish the surname of Ruth's 'pen-pal', Ella, nor did they ask Ruth where Ella lived. If Oswald's 'love' and Ruth's 'pen-pal' were the same person, the involvement of Ruth would have been complete.

Ruth was a Quaker, and both she and her husband were members of the ACLU and interested in progressive movements. As disclosed in testimony and in the Exhibits, the parentage of the Paines indicates that there had been a Marxist or Communist influence in both their families and it would seem that the Paines would have appeared to the conspirators to be ideal persons upon whom suspicion could be thrown, not only in a conspiracy to murder General Walker but in a conspiracy to murder the President.

On a day in January or February 1963 the Baron and the Baroness had invited Oswald and Marina to a small dinner party in their home, and to this party came Everett Glover. On 22 February, Glover had a gathering at his house, one of the purposes being to invite friends, many of whom were studying Russian, to meet the Oswalds. Oswald mixed with the other guests but Marina spent much of the time alone attending to the child she had taken with her. Ruth Paine was present and talked at length with Marina, making arrangements for them to meet later, and Marina giving Ruth her Elsbeth Street address.

Shortly after the party, Ruth wrote to Marina asking if she could see her to which Marina replied by inviting her to visit, explaining that she and Oswald had just moved from Elsbeth to Neely Street.

On 3 March 1963, the Oswalds had been asked to leave the Elsbeth Street apartment because neighbours had complained that there had been drinking and violent fighting in the apartment. (All other witnesses said that Oswald neither 'drank' nor smoked. Apparently he went to bed early and kept himself in good mental and physical condition.) When Oswald had rented the apartment in early November 1962 he had paid particular attention to the back entrance, insisting on being shown where he could get out, and it seems that he used this entrance almost exclusively.

On being forced to leave the Elsbeth apartment the Oswalds moved to the upper apartment of a small two-storey house, 214 West Neely Street; Oswald told the owner of the house that he had met Marina while he was serving in the United States Marines as a guard at the United States Embassy in Moscow. In answer to a direct question from the owner, Oswald said that he had had no difficulty in getting out of Russia with his wife. At a later date, the occupier of the lower floor told the owner that Oswald was beating Marina. (The check-stub found in the assassin's wallet on arrest on 22 November – and mentioned earlier – had been the property of the previous tenant of the apartment now occupied by the Oswalds.)

The rifle and the revolver had been despatched on 20 March to 'A. Hidell' and 'A.J. Hidell' respectively at Oswald's P.O. Box in Dallas, and shortly before the attempt to murder the General on 10 April, Marina, using one of Oswald's cameras, had taken two posed photographs of her husband standing in the yard of the Neely Street apartment. He was dressed to look like a guerilla in a dark shirt and trousers, and with his revolver strapped round his waist. In one photograph he carried the rifle upright in his Left hand with a copy of *The Worker* in his Right hand. In the other photograph he carried the rifle upright in his Right hand with a copy of *The Militant* in his Left hand, both newspapers being extreme leftwing and carrying articles favourable to Castro.

These photographs were intended to be found after the escape of the assassin from Dallas and would indicate that it was Oswald who had attempted to assassinate the General. Marguerite believed Lee Oswald to be Left-handed, and Robert believed him to be Right-handed, and it may be that the interchange of hands for holding the rifle in the photographs was purposeful to obscure the identity of the assassin still further.

(The photographs of himself with the rifle and pro-Castro newspapers, the photographs of the General's house, the General's name and telephone number in his notebook, the discovery of the same calibre rifle bullet and the note left for Marina would have satisfied the authorities that Oswald had been responsible for the attempted murder of the anti-Castro General, thus suggesting that the guerilla-like assassin was acting for Castro. When the assassin later failed to escape from Dallas and this material was found, he then could have been faced with a charge of the attempted murder of the General – hence his omission to the Dallas police of his Neely Street address and his allegation that the photographs had been 'faked' by the police.)

On 2 April, Ruth Paine had invited the Oswalds for dinner, and her husband picked them up in Dallas and drove them out to Irving. According to Marina, Oswald had told her he had set out to murder the General on 6 or 7 April but had desisted because conditions were not favourable. On 8 April, Surrey saw two men 'peeking through the windows', and on 10 April somebody attempted to murder the General; seconds later the boy Coleman saw two men getting into separate cars and saw one of them driving off. After the assassination of the President, the police took possession of Ruth Paine's diary (XVII.51-83). In the space for 8 April, Ruth had entered the name Marina and in the space for 10 April had entered the name Marina, but with an arrow pointing to the space for 11 April. In testimony, Ruth was to say that these appointments with Marina could only have been made previously because Marina did not have a telephone, and it was some 35-40 minutes drive from Irving to Marina's apartment. She was unable to recall whether she saw Marina on 8 April nor why the appointment on 10 April appeared to have been transferred to 11 April. She was unable to recall whether she had actually seen Marina on 10 or 11 April but if she had seen her on either of these dates then in no fashion had Marina appeared to her to have been upset or disturbed (XVII.452-454). In testimony, Marina was to say Oswald had told her that Michael Paine knew he had shot at the General (V.396), thereby involving Michael Paine – at the least — as an accessory after the fact. As a result of this incriminating testimony, Ruth was to be questioned at length as to whether she or her husband had discussed the General or the attempt upon his life with either Oswald or Marina, or both, in either of their homes or elsewhere. She testified that his name had never been mentioned. Such was the suspected involvement of Ruth and her husband in the story, that she was required to testify at greater length than any other witness, her testimony running to 332 pages and that of her husband to 89 pages. Marina was the first and most important witness to testify before the Commission and, although she was to be recalled on a further four occasions to testify, the sum of her testimony amounted to 315 pages.

On 24 April 1963, the Dallas newspapers carried an announcement by Vice President Johnson that President Kennedy would be visiting Dallas in the autumn, and in Ruth's diary the names Lee and Marina appear in the space for 24 April. Ruth was to testify that on this day she arrived by car at the Neely Street apartment and was surprised to find that Oswald was already packed and preparing to depart by bus for New Orleans. He told her that it was at Marina's suggestion that he should go to New Orleans, and Marina was to testify that it was at her instigation that he did so, she having suggested that as it was the place of his birth he might be happier there and find work. She added, however, that her real reason for suggesting that her husband should go to New Orleans was in order to remove him from Dallas and from the temptation to make another attempt on the life of the General.

Ruth then drove Oswald and Marina to the bus station where Oswald bought tickets to New Orleans for himself and Marina, June apparently travelling without charge. After some discussion, Ruth offered to accommodate Marina in Irving until such time as Oswald could find work and an apartment for himself and his family in New Orleans, when Ruth would drive Marina and June to join him in that city. He then cashed in one of the tickets he had purchased and returned to Neely Street with Ruth and Marina to help pack Marina's clothes. Marina's and June's possessions were loaded on to Ruth's car and taken to her house some 15 miles distant in Irving, while Oswald remained at Neely

Street and returned to the bus station later that evening to leave for New Orleans. The result of this day's activities was (a) that on the day it was first announced that the President would be visiting Dallas in the fall, Ruth appeared at Neely Street and removed Marina to her own house, and (b) that Marina again would be separated from her husband during the early days of his residence in another city, as had been the case when Oswald had left Marina in Fort Worth while he went to Dallas on 8/9 October 1962 and where he was not to be joined by Marina until the beginning of November 1962; Ruth was now further compromised.

Phase Three. New Orleans. 25 April 1963–24/25 September 1963

Oswald's assignments were:

(A) To establish that the man in New Orleans was the real Oswald and was the man who later shot the President;
(B) To throw suspicion upon Castro for the assassination of the President;
(C) To further implicate Ruth;
(D) To visit Mexico City with Albert Osborne, to meet the American male and Kostin for final arrangements for the assassination and escape.

Assignment (A). On 25 April 1963, Oswald arrived in New Orleans and telephoned his aunt, Mrs. Murret, to ask if he could stay at her home while he looked for employment. She was Marguerite's sister and lived at 757 French Street with her husband and two of her four grown-up children. As a small child Oswald had lived with the Murrets for a while and they had known him on and off until he was fifteen years of age and, although they knew that he had gone to Russia, they were unaware that he had returned or that he was married and had a child. The Murret family had always been fond of the young Oswald and Mrs. Murret was pleased to welcome him into their home, where the family found him not only agreeable but polite to Marina when later she arrived in New Orleans with Ruth; on an occasion when Oswald and Marina were to dine with the Murrets, Oswald 'drew back her chair' for her at table. The Murrets had every reason to think that they were a happy couple.

On arrival at the Murret home, Oswald immediately evinced interest in finding out what had happened to the other members of his father's family. He called all the Oswalds in the telephone book and visited the cemetery where his father was buried. He was able to locate one relative, the widow of his father's brother, who gave him a photograph of his father and told him that, so far as she knew, the rest of the family were dead. After the assassination, no photograph was found; Oswald must have lost or destroyed it. It would seem that Oswald's manoeuvre was not only to convince the Murret family but to satisfy post-assassination investigators that it was the real Oswald that had come from Dallas to New Orleans to visit his aunt, and to seek for family history and relatives.

A week later, Oswald wrote to Marina and Ruth: 'Girls, I still have not found work, but I receive money from the Unemployment Office in the amount of $15 to $20. They were mistaken in the Dallas office when they refused, but I straightened everything out. Uncle 'Dyuz' offered me a loan of $200 if needed. Great, eh?'.

On 9 May, Oswald found employment as a greaser of coffee machines with Wm. B. Reily Co., giving his height as 5' 9", and on the same day he rented an apartment at 4905 Magazine Street.

(Oswald was not above implicating Robert Oswald or anyone else, and at Jaggars-Chiles-Stovall he had told Graef that he had served in Korea; Marine Sergeant Robert Oswald had, in fact, done so but Oswald had not. On the application form for employment at the coffee company Oswald gave as fictitious referees, 'Sgt. Robert Hidell' and 'Lt. J. Evans'. Oswald thus hinted that his brother might be involved, and also the Evans family who years before had been very friendly with his mother and one of whom had helped him find the apartment at 4905 Magazine Street.)

On 10 May, he telephoned his news to Marina at Ruth's house in Irving, and — according to Ruth — Marina was elated and repeated in Russian over and over again, 'Daddy loves us.' Later this day Ruth, taking her own two children with her, drove Marina and June to New Orleans to join Oswald, staying in the apartment for three days before returning to Irving with her children on 14 May. She was to testify that she had felt uncomfortable and that there had been friction between Oswald and Marina while she was in the apartment with them, but she thought this might have been due to her presence; Oswald's abrasive attitude appears to have been adopted to intensify Ruth's sympathy for Marina and to stimulate Ruth to further and disastrous action.

Assignment (B). A few days prior to 19 April 1963 and while still in Dallas, Oswald had written an undated letter to the Fair Play for Cuba Committee in New York saying that he was unemployed, but that he had been passing out FPCC pamphlets in Dallas and had carried a home-made placard which said 'Hands Off Cuba! Viva Fidel!'. He asked the FPCC for some more pamphlets to be sent to his P.O. Box in Dallas. The contents of this letter concerning his FPCC activities in Dallas were untrue but on 19 April 1963 the FPCC sent him some pamphlets. It is therefore to be noted that at least a week before leaving Dallas for New Orleans on 24 April 1963, Oswald had it in mind to involve Castro in his later activities in New Orleans.

On 26 May, Oswald, now in New Orleans, wrote to the FPCC requesting formal membership, stating that in the past he had received or bought FPCC pamphlets, suggesting renting a small office 'at our own expense' for the purpose of forming the FPCC branch in New Orleans, asking if the FPCC would give him a charter and requesting information on buying pamphlets etc., in large lots as well as blank FPCC application forms. He asked for advice and recommendations, saying that his project 'might not be a roaring success but that he was willing to try', and ending, 'an office, literature, and getting people to know you are the fundamentals of the FPCC as far as I can see so here's hoping to hear from you'. He also requested 'a picture of Fidel suitable for framing' which would be 'a welcome touch'. On 29 May, the FPCC wrote to Oswald giving him a number of instructions as to the setting up of a local chapter and saying that the opening of a P.O. Box was a 'must'. Oswald was also advised to have access to a mimeo machine to prepare public material if he was going to operate an FPCC chapter.

(After the assassination it was discovered that Oswald had kept a framed photograph of Fidel Castro on the mantelpiece in the apartment in New Orleans, and that he had cut out and retained

New Orleans newspaper reports of inflammatory speeches by Castro which threatened 'American leaders' with violence if they again attempted to interfere in Cuban affairs – thus implementing Oswald's ante-assassination fabrication of Castro involvement in the assassination. It would seem, however, that Castro would not have uttered inflammatory words had he been involved in a conspiracy to assassinate the President in a few weeks time.)

Between 31 May and 5/6 June, Oswald ordered certain FPCC literature and membership application forms of his own design from two different printing firms in New Orleans. To one firm he gave his name as 'Osborne', and to the other, 'Lee Osborne'. The use of false names was not to hide his identity, for the printed matter contained the information that 'L.H. Oswald' was the secretary of the FPCC chapter in New Orleans. The reason for the use of the name Osborne becomes clear when it is related to Oswald's secret journey to Mexico City in Havana – when he was accompanied on a long distance bus by 75 years old Albert Osborne *alias* 'John Howard Bowen'. To post-assassination investigators it would appear that when Oswald ordered his FPCC printed material, he had not acted alone but as agent for Osborne, and that both of them were acting and travelling to Mexico City on behalf of Castro.

During the week surrounding the dates 5, 6 and 7 June, Jack Ruby came from Dallas to New Orleans, ostensibly to look for a striptease act for his Dallas club. It is not known on what date Ruby returned to Dallas, nor is there any evidence that he was in contact with Oswald or Osborne. Ruby did, in fact, employ at 'The Carousel' a striptease dancer from New Orleans called 'Jada' but was to dispense with her services after a quarrel which he started.

On 11 June, Oswald opened P.O. Box 30061 in New Orleans in the name L.H. Oswald, Inserted in the space for names of persons entitled to receive mail through the Box were written 'A.J. Hidell' and 'Marina Oswald'. Heindel, nicknamed 'Hidell', had served with Oswald in the Marines and lived in New Orleans; in no way was he involved but apparently Oswald chose New Orleans as an operational base so that the authorities would later suspect that Oswald and Heindel – two Americans –

might have been conspiring together and with Castro.

About this time, Oswald, apparently thinking it unwise to visit a regular doctor, somehow obtained a blank form of 'International Certificate of Vaccination or Revaccination against Smallpox' which he filled up in the name of Lee Oswald, signing it Lee H. Oswald and inserting the name Dr. A.J. Hideel, P.O. Box 30016, New Orleans, LA. Oswald had dated the certificate 8 June 1963 and impressed a counterfeit stamp'. A vaccination certificate would be required by Oswald to enable him to travel to and from Cuba; after the assassination it was found amongst his possessions, and so further involved Cuba and ex-Marine Heindel. ('Hideel' was poorly written and could be Hidell.)

On 24 June, Oswald applied for a new passport which, having paid off his loan from the State Department some six months earlier, he received the following day. On the application form he gave his height as 5' 11" and this height was recorded in the new passport. On the form he stated that he would be leaving the country by Lykes Line during November or December 1963, and that he planned to visit England, France, Holland, Russia, Findland (*sic*), Italy and Poland; on the application for his 1959 passport Oswald had spelt Finland correctly. Oswald required the passport for the journey to Cuba via Mexico that he intended shortly to make for, although at that time American citizens were banned by United States law from travelling directly to Cuba, it was possible to enter that country by way of Mexico.

On 6 July, one of Mrs. Murret's sons, Gene, who was studying to be a Jesuit priest in Mobile, Alabama, wrote to Oswald asking if he would come to Mobile and speak at the Jesuit House of Studies about contemporary Russia and the practice of Communism in that country. Oswald accepted and on 27 July he, Marina and some of the Murret family travelled from New Orleans to Mobile in Mr. Murret's car, Mr. Murret paying all the expenses. Oswald addressed a meeting attended by some twenty scholastic students and two Jesuit priests for about half an hour, and then answered questions for a further half hour. He indicated that he had become disillusioned during his stay in Russia and that in his opinion the best political system would be one which combined the best points of Capitalism and Communism. He did not mention Cuba, for at this time he had not yet commenced his intended FPCC street campaign in New Orleans although he had obtained the necessary printed material a month previously. According to Gene and the two Jesuit priests who attended the meeting, all of whom were interviewed by the FBI after the assassination, Oswald was 'neatly dressed ... handled himself well' and gave an address of average quality (XXV.920-928).

The Murrets and the Oswalds spent the night in Mobile and returned to New Orleans the next day. In a subsequent letter to Ruth, Marina told her that they had been to visit Oswald's brother and had also visited his cousin in Mobile, staying there three or four days which was 'a pleasant change' for her, for she was seeing 'some different country'.

The Oswalds had not visited Robert or John Pic and they had remained in Mobile only for one night before returning to New Orleans. Marina did not tell Ruth about Oswald's discourse at the Jesuit House of Studies, nor in correspondence some two months later was she to mention that Oswald had twice participated effectively in New Orleans radio broadcasts. In the apparently colourless life of Oswald and herself, these three events must have illuminated their five-month stay in New Orleans; the omission permitted Ruth to retain her poor opinion of Oswald's abilities.

On 19 July, Oswald was dismissed by the coffee company because of inefficiency and inattention to his work, and obtained no further employment in New Orleans. His supervisor in the firm had often found him sitting in the office of the owner of the garage next door. Alba, the proprietor of the garage, was a member of the National Rifle Association and owned many rifles which he collected and sometimes sold or sportorised. He was to testify that during Oswald's working hours he studied the rifle magazines that were in Alba's office and they had long discussions about the merits and killing power of various rifles. Although Alba understood that Oswald owned two rifles and was interested in the acquisition of a third, no business transaction was concluded between them. It would appear that Oswald, an apparent supporter of Castro, wished to identify himself as a person owning rifles and interested in their killing power. It may be thought that Oswald obtained work at the coffee company on account of its location which would give him apparently uncontrived opportunities to talk to Alba. To further demonstrate his murderous nature, when Oswald was going about his work at the coffee company he would frequently meet his supervisor, at whom he would point his hand like a pistol and go 'Pow' without another word or a smile; he sent his supervisor 'half-crazy'.

(As from 17 February 1963 through August 1963, Marina had been writing to Reznichenko, the Senior Consul at the Russian Embassy in Washington, asking for permission to return to Russia. She also wrote several other letters to him reporting change of address as required of her as a Soviet citizen. On 5 August 1963, Reznichenko wrote to her in New Orleans to tell her that her application for permanent residence in the USSR had been forwarded to Moscow for processing. She testified that she had never wished to return to Russia but that her husband desired her to take this course. It would seem that if Oswald were to escape after the assassination, Moscow would rapidly have processed her application and Reznichenko would have issued the necessary re-entry papers into Russia without delay; it would then appear to the American authorities that her departure for Russia soon after the assassination had not been other than the result of her earlier requests and in the normal tardy course of Russian business of this nature. (XVI.7.9. XVIII.480-539.)

On 5 August, Oswald visited a store managed by a Cuban refugee, an opponent of Castro and the New Orleans delegate of the anti-Castro Cuban Student Directorate. Oswald displayed a strong interest in joining the struggle against Castro and he suggested methods of guerilla warfare, including blowing up bridges, derailing trains, making gunpowder and so on. The next day Oswald returned to the store and left his 'Guidebook for Marines' for the delegate, and indicated that he had visited the headquarters of the Directorate in Miami. After the assassination it would be thought that it had been on Castro's instructions that he had infiltrated the opposition; the Marine Guidebook confirmed that the assassin was ex-Marine Oswald.

On 9 August, the delegate and other Cuban exiles happened to hear that Oswald was passing out FPCC leaflets in the street. They succeeded in finding him, and tried to tear up the leaflets and strike him, but Oswald lowered his hands and pushed out his chin inviting a blow. The police arrived, and Oswald and three Cubans were arrested for disturbing the peace. Oswald told the police that he had been born in Cuba, had been in Russia and had married a Russian woman in Fort Worth. He was evasive about his previous places of employment, mentioning Leslie Welding Co. but omitting Jaggars-Chiles-Stovall. The police recorded his height taken against a scale as 5′ 9″ and fingerprinted him, the prints being routinely sent to the FBI fingerprint department at the Bureau. Inspection of the contents of Oswald's wallet disclosed no 'double-identity' counterfeit cards but one genuine Marine card recording Oswald's height as 5′ 11″. On 10 August, Oswald and the Cubans were tried for creating a disturbance; the charges against the Cubans were dismissed but Oswald was convicted and fined $10. Oswald's arrest may or may not have been anticipated by him but from it he was to profit.

While in police custody Oswald succeeded in turning the affair to his advantage by directing the attention of the FBI towards the subversive FPCC. He asked the police to telephone the New Orleans FBI and request them to call to see him at the police station. Special Agent Quigley, who had not previously heard of Oswald nor of his FPCC campaign in New Orleans, arrived at the police station on 9 August and interviewed Oswald for some two hours, recording 'From interrogation and observation' Oswald's height as 5′ 9″. Oswald talked at length to him about the FPCC and mentioned A.J. Hidell as the moving spirit in the New Orleans chapter of the FPCC, hinting that there were other members and several meeting places including his own apartment, but refusing to disclose other names or places – of which there were none. The attention of the FBI agent was thus drawn to Oswald's involvement with the FPCC, and he submitted a five page report of this interview dealing exclusively with Oswald's FPCC activities (XVII.758-762). Quigley was to testify that Oswald told him his wife's maiden name was 'Prossa', that he had met and married her in Fort Worth some five months previously, and that they had come directly from Fort Worth to New Orleans. Oswald did not tell him that he had been in Russia for nearly three years after leaving the Marines, nor that 'Prossa' was a Russian woman whom he had married in Russia some $2\frac{1}{2}$

years previously, but told him that after an honourable discharge from the Marines he had gone straight to Fort Worth – which was actually true, as he had visited his mother in Fort Worth for three days in September 1959. By saying that he had come to New Orleans from Fort Worth, Oswald omitted his visit to Russia, his first stay in Dallas and his employment at Jaggars-Chiles-Stovall. Quigley testified that Oswald had been reticent, evasive, and somewhat antagonistic about specific details of his FPCC chapter, and would not say why he had asked for the interview. He thought that Oswald's request for this had been for the purpose of making a self-serving statement to explain why he had distributed FPCC literature, and Quigley thought Oswald had lied to him about other matters.

Although Oswald's FPCC chapter was a one-man concern, it would seem that he had decided to supply false information to Quigley so that the FBI would believe that there existed an extensive and secret FPCC chapter in New Orleans, and would therefore concentrate their enquiries about Oswald only in that field. He knew that there was limited liaison between the FBI and local police forces, and he knew therefore that Quigley would not check what he had been told against what Oswald had told the police immediately after being arrested.

A week later, Oswald was to make another street appearance, observed by the FBI, distributing pamphlets but after that, according to Marina, he lost interest in the FPCC. On this occasion Oswald was televised and it would seem that he must have arranged for this to be done. The FBI continued to watch him but, according to Marina, he remained indoors in the evenings reading. After some weeks the FBI probably abandoned any night surveillance, thus enabling Oswald six weeks later to slip away from his apartment at midnight to embark upon his secret trip to Mexico City and thence to try to reach the Russian Embassy in Havana.

Oswald's manoeuvre in drawing the FBI to him succeeded for the FBI agent, Kaack, in charge of his file at their office in New Orleans appears not to have been concerned about Oswald's lies and *the recorded height of 5' 9"*, although in Oswald's file there were full details in the June 1962 Fort Worth FBI report of Oswald's visit to Russia, his marriage in Russia to Marina

Prusakova, and the recording of his height as 5' 11"; Kaack was not asked to testify before the Commission.

On 17 August, William Stuckey, a radio broadcaster who had long been looking for a member of the FPCC to appear on his programme, heard through an anti-Castroite that Oswald was interested in the FPCC. He visited Oswald by appointment at 4905 Magazine Street and after noticing that Oswald was wearing a pair of Marine fatigue trousers, he recorded an interview with him in which Oswald talked about his Marine Corps service and the FPCC, giving him a number of pro-Castro pamphlets and telling him some lies. A shortened version of the interview was playing back on the radio show that evening, and the content of the playback was almost entirely about the FPCC and Oswald's activities in that connection. Two days later, the broadcaster asked the amusement director of the station if he could run the entire tape, but the director felt that a debate with local opponents of Castro would be of greater public interest. Consequently it was arranged that there should be a debate between Oswald, Stuckey and two other men who were experienced in Cuban and world affairs generally. In testimony, Stuckey was to say that Oswald was 'Confident, self-assured, logical, articulate, very well able to handle the questions and very well disciplined. He seemed like somebody that took very good care of himself, very prudent, temperate, that sort of person'. It was Stuckey's impression that Oswald regarded himself as living in a world of intellectual inferiors. To an awkward question Oswald would say, 'That is a good question' or 'I am glad you asked that question, it is very good', and then would obliquely avoid answering it or else distort it for his own purposes, saying what he wanted to say while making one think he was answering the question. He was 'expert at dialectics' and 'his manner was sort of quasi-legal, it was almost as if he was a young attorney. He seemed very well acquainted with the legal terminology dealing with constitutional rights'. It was Stuckey's impression that Oswald had done a great deal of reading (XI.156-179). As customary, a copy of the radio transcripts was sent to the FBI a few days after the broadcasts (XXI.621-641), the transcripts showing that Oswald admitted being in Russia.

Through his street appearances and being televised, and the

two radio broadcasts, Oswald had demonstrated publicly and to the FBI that he was a fervid supporter of Castro.

Assignment (C). On 20 April 1963 when still in Dallas and before going to New Orleans, Marina had confided to Ruth that she was pregnant and expecting a second child in October. She asked Ruth to keep it a secret, presumably because the disclosure of this fact would not correspond with her earlier complaints to the emigre group of her husband's lack of warmth. Then, or a little later but before Ruth was to drive Marina from Irving to New Orleans on 10 May 1963, there had been some discussion between them as to the possibility of Marina returning to Irving to stay with Ruth during the latter part of her pregnancy and the birth of the child, but nothing had been decided. The two women had also discussed their relative marital problems and had established a point of mutual sympathy.

After leaving Marina and June with Oswald in New Orleans on 14 May, Ruth had driven back to Irving and departed on 27 July 1963 for a two months holiday to visit relatives in the North. While on holiday she had written several advisory and affectionate letters to Marina in New Orleans offering to take her into her house in Irving for her confinement in October 1963, and Marina had replied to Ruth equally affectionately. Ruth wrote that she would call at the Oswald's apartment in New Orleans on about 18 September and would take Marina back to Irving if she so wished. Oswald made no objection to this arrangement and later appeared to welcome the prospect of Marina having Ruth to assist her in Irving during the pregnancy and birth (XVI.251-254. 263-264. 278-283. XVII.81-149).

(Ruth's feeling for Marina may perhaps be judged from her words in a letter (XVII.108), 'I love you Marina, and want to live with you. I hope that you and Lee will agree. If it is easier for you I can come for you and June in September. I would want to talk with Lee about everything. How is it possible to telephone you … I think you don't have to return to the Soviet Union if you don't want to.' After the assassination Ruth was to try unsuccessfully to continue her friendship with Marina and in her last letter (XXI.18) to Marina, undated but written early in 1964 from Irving abandoning her efforts to remain friendly, the final words were, 'I love you'.)

The day before Ruth was expected to arrive in New Orleans, on 17 September 1963 Oswald called at the office of the Mexican Consulate in New Orleans and applied for permission to travel through Mexico as an intransit tourist, completing the application form for an intransit tourist card in a curious way. He wrote his full name, Lee Harvey Oswald, but left a gap between Lee and Harvey with the result that either the clerk who issued the card wrote 'Lee, Harvey Oswald' or Oswald himself inserted the comma. The issuance of the card thus inscribed enabled him (a) to travel to Mexico City and back to Dallas under the assumed name of 'Lee', (b) while in Mexico City to register at an hotel in the name of 'Lee' and (c) to prevent the FBI 'tailing' him. The visit to Mexico City and the use of an assumed name was intended to be discovered by the FBI after the assassination, but in the absence of the discovery of the letter of 9 November 1963 to Reznichenko referring to the use of an alias, the comma would have appeared to be the result of a clerical error. (The Report says it was either a clerical error or an insertion by Oswald.)

On 20 September, Ruth arrived in New Orleans and again stayed in the Oswald's apartment until 23 September; she was to testify that this time Oswald was 'very outgoing, warm and friendly'. On 23 September, Oswald packed his own and Marina's belongings, and loaded them on to Ruth's station wagon, retaining a few clothes for himself until such time as he would return to Dallas. Ruth was to testify that the parting of Oswald and Marina was affectionate, and that Oswald appeared to be sorry to see his family leave. Marina was to testify that she had seen and heard Oswald practising at night with the bolt of his rifle on the porch of 4905 Magazine Street and that now, wrapped in a blanket, the rifle was transported amongst the luggage on Ruth's station wagon back to Irving. Although Ruth testified that she did not see it, she was further compromised. After an overnight stop at a motel, on 24 September Ruth, Marina and June arrived in Irving, where Marina and June settled into Ruth's small one-storey house, there to remain until after the assassination.

Early on 25 September, Oswald left New Orleans by bus for Houston, the first step on the route to Mexico City and to the assassination. Marina was to testify that the purpose of Oswald's journey was for him to get to Cuba where he intended to stay, but she also testified that he had asked her what she would like him to bring her from Mexico, and that she had told him she would like a Mexican silver bracelet and some Mexican records; the two statements are irreconcilable but the Commission did not ask her to elucidate the contradiction. Whatever her explanation might have been, it is clear that Oswald intended soon to return to Dallas for he had not sold his possessions before he left for Mexico City nor did he take them with him on the bus, taking only a suitcase that was placed in the luggage compartment and a 'small overnight bag or pouch' that he placed on the rail over his head. He possessed expensive spy equipment in addition to his clothes and other belongings, all useless to Marina.

Ruth was to testify that as she and Marina were leaving New Orleans for Irving, Oswald told Ruth that he was going to seek work in Houston or Philadelphia; Philadelphia had been Michael and Ruth Paine's home town. After the assassination Marina was to be questioned by the FBI on about 46 occasions and asked if she had prior knowledge of her husband's visit to Mexico. She denied all pre-knowledge of the visit and it was not until she appeared before the Commission that she admitted that she had lied to the FBI. She then testified that Oswald had told her before he left for Mexico that the trip must remain secret, and that she had told her husband on his return from Mexico that she had not told Ruth about it.

It would appear that she had made a 'deal' with the authorities for she testified (I.14):

COUNSEL: Did you ever see him clean the rifle?
MARINA: Yes. I said before I had never seen it before. But I think you understand. I want to help you, and that is why there is no reason for concealing anything. I will not be charged with anything.
INTERPRETER: She says she was not sworn in before. But now inasmuch as she is sworn in, she is going to tell the truth.
COUNSEL: Did you see him clean the rifle a number of times?
MARINA: Yes.

Marina's word 'anything' would include alleged perjury at the American Embassy in Moscow concerning Komsomol, and admitted accessory after the fact to the attempted murder of General Walker.

Assignment (D). In late September, a decision had been taken by the White House confirming that the President's visit to Texas would now be for two days, 21 and 22 November, with Dallas as one of the stops. Both Dallas morning newspapers, quoting White House sources, gave this information in their issues of 26 September.

On the night of 25 September, Oswald had arrived in Houston from New Orleans. He telephoned the house of a man he had heard of but had not met and spoke to the wife, telling her that he was a member of the FPCC and that he had hoped to see her husband for a few hours that evening before flying to Mexico. Neither the man nor his wife had had contact with Oswald before this and they had no further contact with him afterwards, but the telephone call substantiated the fact that Oswald had gone to Houston where Albert Osborne was falsely alleging that he was resident and employed when he applied for a six-month tourist card to Mexico in the name of 'John Howard Bowen', and that Oswald was flying to Mexico as a member of FPCC. He thus emphasized his connection with Osborne and Castro, and indicated a plane instead of a bus in case the man or his wife told the FBI.

At 2.35 a.m. on 26 September, Oswald boarded a bus in Houston and left for Laredo, Texas. Also on this day Albert Osborne obtained his six-month tourist card for Mexico in the name of 'John Howard Bowen' and from Nuevo Laredo was to travel beside 'Harvey Oswald Lee' on the bus to Mexico City.

On this bus were two British tourists, Dr. and Mrs. McFarland, and Oswald told them that he was going to Cuba via Mexico City, that he hoped to see Fidel Castro in Cuba and that he was the secretary of the New Orleans branch of the FPCC. At between 1.30 and 2.00 p.m., Oswald crossed the international bridge from Laredo to Nuevo Laredo, Mexico, and from there he travelled to Mexico City on a Mexican busline. During the whole of the journey from Nuevo Laredo to Mexico City Oswald and Osborne, travelling in their assumed names of 'Lee' and 'Bowen', occupied a seat for two persons and conversed. Oswald also talked with the Australian girls on the bus telling them that he was from Fort Worth, Texas, but not giving them his name, and advising them to stay at the Hotel Cuba in Mexico City because it was cheap and clean, and untruthfully telling them that he had stayed there previously. During this conversation with the girls, Oswald took his old 1959 passport out of his pouch in order to show the girls that he had been in Russia.

In its only reference to Osborne, the Report (R.733) says: 'The man next to Oswald was probably Albert Osborne, a native of the British Isles who has worked as an itinerant preacher in the southern United States and Mexico for many years. Osborne denied that he sat beside Oswald; but in view of his inconsistent and untrue responses to federal investigators concerning matters not directly related to Oswald the Commission believed that his denial cannot be credited. It appeared to the other passengers on the bus that Osborne and Oswald had not previously met; extensive investigation has revealed no other contact between them'.

The use of the word 'probably' indicates that the Commission were aware of Osborne's alias but made no reference to this alias and under which he was travelling, nor to the other matters disclosed in the extensive FBI investigation into Albert Osborne and 'John Howard Bowen', thus obliterating from their Report the espionage quality of one of the most interesting figures in the conspiracy to assassinate the President.

Set out below are *the facts* about the two men travelling on the bus from Nuevo Laredo to Mexico City:

1. Oswald used the name Osborne on separate occasions when ordering FPCC literature, and visited Houston, Osborne's falsely alleged place of residence and employment;
2. Both of their application forms for tourist cards contained lies;
4. On the bus they travelled on a seat for two persons and conversed;
5. The FBI had an 'Internal Security' file on each man – Osborne's in the name of 'John Howard Bowen' and 'Lee's' in the name of Lee Harvey Oswald;

6. Both men were to change their plans shortly after arrival in Mexico City, only 24 hours separating their departure from Mexico City for the United States on 1 and 2 October 1963;

7. Both men during 1963 both contemporaneously and at different times were carrying counterfeit documents;

8. Both men obtained passports in 1963 at different times by supplying the Passport Office in New Orleans with false information.

It is not known what Albert Osborne did or where he went after arriving in Mexico City with Oswald on 27 September but, although his tourist card was for six months and he took three suitcases to Mexico City, on 1 October he left Mexico for the United States. He then travelled to New Orleans where he called at the Canadian Consulate and obtained a Canadian passport in his real name, falsely stating *inter alia* that he was a Canadian citizen on holiday. He then purchased another Mexican tourist card in this name and returned to Mexico but it is not known where he went or what he did. About a week before the assassination he went to New York whence he flew via Scotland to England for a holiday with relatives in Grimsby before allegedly going to London and Spain and certainly back to the United States on 5 December 1963. This was only the second visit he had made to England in 48 years but it provided him with an alibi should he ever be asked to account for his movements on and around 22 November 1963. On 14 November 1963, the *Knoxville Journal* had published a news article reporting that John Howard Bowen had gone on holiday to Europe. In the long FBI report on Osborne contained in the Exhibits (XXV.25-75), pages 7 and 8 are missing; these pages immediately precede the page which refers to the newspaper article. The extraction of these pages was effected after the FBI report was prepared because in a names index to the Report the pages are mentioned with 'Knoxville Journal' typed beside these page numbers. What the FBI discovered about Albert Osborne is Appendix D to this book, and it includes this author's enquiries in Grimsby.

On his arrival in Mexico City, Oswald booked into an hotel and after signing the register, H.O. Lee, he went to the Cuban Consulate — which shared the building with the Embassy — where he requested a visa to visit Cuba. When he was asked the reason for his intended visit, Oswald said that he was actually going on to Russia but he would like to stay in Cuba for about two weeks before proceeding, adding that he wanted to be in Cuba by 30 September.

In order to facilitate the granting of a visa for Cuba while allegedly in transit to Russia, Oswald supported his application by presenting his old 1959 passport. On this was recorded that he had lived in Russia for over $2\frac{1}{2}$ years. He also presented his work permit for that country written in the Russian language and letters in the same language, proof of his being married to a Russian woman, being the secretary in New Orleans of the FPCC, newspaper cuttings relating to his arrest in New Orleans in connection with his FPCC street campaign, his Marine history and the desire that he should be accepted as a 'friend' of the Cuban Revolution.

A heated argument developed between Oswald and members of the Consulate when they refused to give him a visa and, slamming the door behind him, he left the building and possibly proceeded to the Russian Embassy which he may, of course, have visited before going to the Cuban Consulate. It appears that Oswald intended to go to Cuba for a meeting at the Russian Embassy in Havana on or just after 30 September, but the Russians could not give him overt assistance in this matter as it would have incriminated them. It had been left to Oswald to enter Cuba and if he failed, the meetings with Kostin would have to be held at the Russian Embassy in Mexico City. It would seem that Kostin, on learning that Oswald had been unable to enter Cuba, then travelled from Havana (or directly from Moscow or Minsk) to the Russian Embassy in Mexico City. (It was on *28 September and 1 October* that the American male went to the Russian Embassy in the name of 'Lee Oswald', and it was between *27 September and 2 October* that Oswald had 'meetings' with Kostin at the Russian Embassy.)

On 30 September, Oswald visited a tourist agency in Mexico City to purchase international exchange orders for travel back on 2 October to Nuevo Laredo from Mexico City by Mexican bus in the name of 'Lee' and by Greyhound bus directly from Laredo, Texas, to Dallas still in the name of 'Lee'.

On 2 October, 'John Howard Bowen' crossed the

international bridge from Nuevo Laredo into Texas and proceeded possibly directly to New Orleans.

On 3 October, 'Harvey Oswald Lee' crossed the international bridge from Nuevo Laredo into Texas and arrived in Dallas that afternoon. He or another had reserved a seat – entered in the bus manifest as 'Oswald' – on a bus that left Mexico City several hours after the bus on which he actually travelled back to the United States. It is not known when, why or for whom this reservation was made.

When the bus carrying 'Lee' reached the border between Mexico and the United States, Mexican customs officials boarded it. Oswald was observed hurriedly 'gulping down' a banana before being pulled off the bus presumably to explain why, having an intransit tourist card, he had not moved out of Mexico; mumbling complaints about the officials, Oswald was allowed to continue his journey on the bus. The Report quotes Marina's testimony when she said that her husband liked bananas and frequently ate them, and the Report speculated that Oswald had hurriedly gulped down a banana 'perhaps because he believed that he could not take fruit into the United States'. The customs officials had told Oswald that he could take bananas into the United States, and the intelligence world might consider the Commission's speculation to be naive and that it was more likely that something had been concealed in the fruit.

Had Oswald travelled to Cuba he would have given up his intransit tourist card in Mexico and would have obtained another from the Mexican Consulate in Cuba in order to return to Mexico en route to Dallas, presumably again in the name of 'Lee'; failure to enter Cuba must have been not only the cause of his being pulled off the bus, but the cause of the change in the plans of Oswald and Osborne.

From 27 September through 2 October 1963, Oswald had been in Mexico City and, at the same time in Dallas, Ruby had made what appears to be a significant contact.

In order to comprehend the significance, a student of the

assassination must endeavour to place himself in the position of Oswald in the 'sniper's nest' on the sixth floor of the Depository. The President might be travelling in the second, third or fourth car that would pass below and away from him, because the motorcade would be formed at Love Field Airport before proceeding to downtown Dallas and past the Depository; there would be no way in which the assassin could know in which car the President would be travelling. The Presidential limousine was to be, in fact, the third car in the motorcade, a pilot car proceeding the procession and a police car being in front of the limousine. In the front seats of the limousine there was a Secret Service driver with a Secret Service agent beside him. Behind the driver sat the wife of Governor Connally and on her right the Governor. Behind the wife of the Governor sat the wife of the President, to her right was the President, and in front of him the Governor, it being protocol that the Governor of a State would be seated in front of the President. When looking at the Presidential car below and going away from him, the assassin would be able to see only the top and the backs of the heads of four similarly dressed and hatless middle-aged men probably all with full heads of hair, and the top and the backs of the heads of the wives of the President and the Governor.

It was essential that identification of the Presidential limousine and the position of its occupants should be made as quickly as possible; from the window of the Depository it would be at first visible below for perhaps four seconds before it was obscured by the leafy branches of a tree, re-emerging into the 'execution stretch' and giving the assassin perhaps a further two or three seconds to identify the victims and commence firing. No risk of failure could be entertained for there could not be another attempt to assassinate the President.

When the limousine appeared on the other side of the tree, the eye of the assassin would already be close to if not on the telescopic sight which enlarged but limited vision to the small area occupied by the car in the sight; the constraints of time and vision would make *certain* identification of the car and the position of its occupants almost impossible. Furthermore, the sling around the Left arm of the assassin would have had to be already tightened, the rifle firm in its position on a carton and already directed at the place of execution before the car appeared from underneath the leafy branches.

After travelling through downtown Dallas the motorcade would emerge from the easterly end of Main Street, turn right and proceed northerly along Houston Street for about 60 yards directly towards the assassin at the window. If the colour of the dress of the President's wife was known, the assassin could identify the position of the car in the motorcade and the position of his victims during this northerly approach; by the time the motorcade completed a U-turn under his window and proceeded away from him under the tree, his twin problems would have been resolved. He could not, of course, fire at the easier targets approaching him from many persons — spectators, police, Secret Service agents and others in the motorcade — would be looking directly towards him; *he would have been unable to escape from the Depository after firing.* The skill employed by the assassin in avoiding detection at the window was considerable for, although the 14 Secret Service agents accompanying the Presidential and Vice Presidential cars were there for the purpose of observing the crowds and scanning the buildings, he was not detected by them before, during or after firing.

During 'late September and early October' 1963, Alfred Davidson was in Dallas to promote a radio show, 'The World of Fashion', on behalf of Oleg Cassini, couturier of New York. Cassini was the personal dressmaker to the wife of the President and had constructed the clothes, a luminous pink in colour, that she was to wear in Dallas on 22 November. Immediately upon Davidson's arrival in Dallas, Ruby became acquainted with him; their six week friendship is best described in the FBI report of an interview with Davidson in Los Angeles on 25 November, being the day after Ruby shot the assassin:

ALFRED DAVIDSON, JR., was personally contacted by the writer at his temporary residence, Hollywood Parkway Motel, 11034 Ventura Boulevard, North Hollywood, California, Room 7 (telephone 7638803) at which time he furnished substantially the following information.

During late September-early October, he was in Dallas, Texas, on business promoting a radio show. 'The World of Fashion'. He represented OLEG CASSINI, Women's Fashions, New York City. He was first introduced by phone to Jack Ruby by the Credit Manager of the Neiman-Marcus

Department Store in Dallas. He thereafter went over to see Ruby at his Carousel Night Club, and for approximately the next six weeks was befriended by Ruby. He saw him many times both during the day and at night at his night club.

Although he never met RUBY before, RUBY extended every hospitality to DAVIDSON, and RUBY refused to allow him to pick up any checks. DAVIDSON was toured about the city in RUBY's car from time to time. DAVIDSON stated that RUBY was apparently known by everyone in Dallas, was a friend of anyone who needed any help, knew everyone on the police force, treated them to free drinks, had a press pass on his car, had a police pass, and carried a revolver in the glove compartment of his car at all times although he did not have a permit. He claimed that he needed this revolver for protection inasmuch as he carried large sums of money with him from time to time, paying off his employees in cash, and not believing in the use of checking accounts. RUBY also indicated that he had friends and financial interest in Las Vegas, no details, and also had friends in Los Angeles, no details. As to the club itself, DAVIDSON always observed it was well run and proper. He considers RUBY as well fixed financially.

DAVIDSON characterizes RUBY as a glad-hander and a crusader for anyone who was wronged. As to the killing of OSWALD, he, DAVIDSON, was not surprised when RUBY was identified as the killer, and in fact had stated to a motel acquaintance when he had only been indicated on television as a night club owner, 'I'll bet that was JACK RUBY'.

It is DAVIDSON's opinion that RUBY, being of the nature that he is, and an admirer of President KENNEDY, took it upon himself to avenge what he considered to be a personal wrong. DAVIDSON stated that RUBY does not have the intelligence, education, or foresight to look ahead to the consequences of his act. DAVIDSON is certain, however, the RUBY cannot be considered insane.

Contrary to published reports, during his acquaintance with RUBY, he never saw any acts of violence or violent temper or any other abusive conduct on the part of RUBY.

DAVIDSON is not aware whether RUBY was acquainted with OSWALD.

RUBY telephonically contacted DAVIDSON at his current residence about four days ago merely for a social call. (Author's note: about 21 November.)

DAVIDSON will soon move into his own business to be known as Alfred Davidson and Associates, Suite 107, in a building next to the KLAC Building, 5800 block, Wilshire Boulevard, Los Angeles, California. In about two weeks, he will also move to another residence address on Rodeo Drive, Beverly Hills, specific address not at hand immediately. He can always be reached through the law firm of his ex-father-in-law, J. ARTHUR WARNER, New York Financier, which in Los Angeles is

Bautzer, Irwin, Schutzbank, and Schwab, 190 North Cannon Drive, Beverly Hills, California, telephone number CR 5-1212.

On 11/25/63   at North Hollywood, California   File No. Los Angeles 44-895

by SA JOHN P. ANDREWS: ps   Date dictated 11/26/63

It would not have occurred to FBI agent Andrews to ask Davidson whether during their six week friendship or during the telephonic 'social call' of about 21 November, Ruby had questioned him about the motorcade and the clothes that might or would be worn by the wife of the President in the motorcade. It is to be noted that Ruby had impressed Davidson with his admiration for Kennedy. Ruby's sentiments for the President are unknown but it is known that he 'hated' Attorney General Robert Kennedy; the killing of the President would mean a change of Attorney General.

The commercial and only purpose of the radio show was for Cassini to take advantage of the presence in Texas of his most illustrious client wearing his designs, and it would seem that there must have been a discussion of her clothes between Ruby and Davidson, however limited, and undoubtedly considered by Davidson to be of no importance and forgotten.

That Davidson should be friendly with Ruby is not surprising because the expensively dressed and expansive Ruby could be a charming and well-behaved companion, as some witnesses were to testify and others were to say in statements to the FBI.

During their investigation the Commission were to ask the FBI to supply a list of all known contacts of Ruby from 26 September 1963 to the time that he murdered the assassin. A list was supplied containing day-by-day the names of many persons who were known to have been in contact with Ruby during this period but, although on 25 November 1963 the FBI were aware of Ruby's six weeks friendship with Davidson, Davidson's name does not appear on the list in the Exhibits. It is unfortunate that the FBI should have omitted his name and that the probable purpose of Ruby's friendship with Davidson was apparently to elude the Commission.

Phase Four. Dallas. 3 October 1963 to 24 November 1963

After arriving in Dallas on the afternoon of 3 October 1963, Oswald went once more to the Dallas branch of the Texas Employment Commission where he filled in an unemployment claim and announced that he was again looking for work in Dallas. He spent the night at the Dallas YMCA where he registered as a serviceman, the Report speculating that he did this to avoid paying a fee.

On 4 October, he applied for a job as a typesetter trainee at Padgett Printing Co. He made a favourable impression, but the plant superintendent telephoned Jaggars-Chiles-Stovall and decided not to hire Oswald because of the unfavourable response which his inquiry produced, noting at the bottom of Oswald's application form: 'Bob Stovall does not recommend this man, and that he had been dismissed because of his record as a trouble maker, has Communistic tendencies'.

The Padgett printing Co. was not on the motorcade route and therefore it would seem unlikely that Oswald would genuinely have wished to work there. It is therefore interesting to look at Oswald's application form for Padgett's dated 4 October 1963, on which he gave his last but one employment as Jaggars-Chiles-Stovall from October 1962 to May 1963 which was approximately correct. Under the name of Jaggars-Chiles-Stovall he had written Louv-R-Pak Co. (another name for Leslie Welding Co.) as the place of his *last* employment, stating falsely that he had been employed there from May 1963 to September 1963 whereas he was there from July 1962 to October 1962. This lie obliterated the five months that he had spent in New Orleans, his employment at the coffee company and his visit to Mexico City; he stated neither verbally nor on the form that he had been a Marine.

He gave as referees on the application form for work at Padgett's the names of three members of the Russian emigré group: (1) Anna Meller, who was sympathetic to Marina, as she believed that Oswald was maltreating his wife. Her husband had telephoned the Dallas branch of the Texas Employment Exchange in October 1962 to ask the counsellor to assist Oswald in obtaining work, which had facilitated Oswald's entry into

JaggarsChiles-Stovall. When recommending Oswald to the counsellor, Mr. Meller had made a point of insisting that the counsellor should note that Oswald had been in Russia; as an emigré Russian he had not wished to involve himself with a man whom he regarded with suspicion. It is therefore probable that Anna Meller would have disclosed to Padgett's that Oswald had been in Russia. (2) George Bouhe, a Russian emigré who had met Oswald and Marina when they resided in Fort Worth after their arrival from Russia. He disliked Oswald and had been sympathetic to Marina over what he believed to be maltreatment by her husband, to the extent of endeavouring to persuade her to leave Oswald and live elsewhere. As a respected elderly member of the emigré community in Fort Worth and Dallas his adverse opinion of the one-time defector would have been noted by Pagett's. (3) George de Mohrenschildt (the Baron) who was in Haiti at that time, as Oswald knew. The plant superintendent of Padgett's, without even calling Jaggars-Chiles-Stovall, would perhaps have received adverse reports on Oswald from Mrs Meller and/or Bouhe and might then have examined Oswald's employment record as stated on his application form, and would have discovered his lies. During the last weeks of his employment at Jaggars-Chiles-Stovall, Oswald had made himself politically undesirable as an employee in a firm handling military secrets and knew full well what the firm would say of him – one of his last tasks there had been to execute photographic work for Padgett's; he probably discovered that Stovall and the plant superintendent at Padgett's were on friendly terms, and expected that the superintendent might telephone Stovall. If Oswald had been offered employment, he could have found a reason to refuse.

It is particularly to be noted that, although Marina was then living with Ruth Paine in Irving, Oswald did not give Ruth's name as a referee because she would have recommended him. It would seem to be clear that Oswald, inviting rejection, was only pretending to seek employment at Padgett's, thus making his employment at the Depository twelve days later appear not to have been obtained by sinister means. The Report indicates that Oswald's application for work at Padgett's was genuine, but does not analyse his application.

On the same day, 4 October, that Oswald had been rejected by Padgett's he telephoned Marina in Irving and asked her to request Ruth Paine to pick him up in downtown Dallas. Without asking Ruth who would have declined, Marina refused on the truthful ground that earlier that day Ruth had already been to Dallas to donate blood to a hospital; this attempt further to involve Ruth failed.

Later that day, 4 October, when Oswald arrived at Ruth's house in Irving he told Marina that he had hitch-hiked from Dallas; he said nothing about his application for work at Padgett's. Although Marina was to testify at one time that she believed that her husband's trip to Mexico was to enable him to enter and remain in Cuba, there were no expressions of delight such as 'Daddy loves us' when he, according to Marina, had unexpectedly turned up in Dallas; she reprimanded him for not telephoning her on 3 October. Although Ruth and Marina had not heard from Oswald from 23 September to 4 October, Ruth was to testify that they had never discussed him, his whereabouts or whether he might have succeeded in obtaining work in Houston, Philadelphia or elsewhere. She also said that neither Oswald nor Marina at any time disclosed to her that Oswald had been to Mexico, and that she had been allowed to continue in her belief that he had been looking for work in Houston or Philadelphia.

Oswald spent that weekend, 4, 5 and 6 October, at Ruth's house and he told Marina that if FBI agents should call at Ruth's house while he was not there, to note and let him have the registration number of their car. On 24 and 25 September he had left the address of Ruth's house as a forwarding address from his P.O. Box at the post office in New Orleans, and he therefore anticipated such a call. He gave Marina a silver bracelet on which her name was inscribed, and he bought a similar bracelet with his own name inscribed, both of which he had obtained in Dallas. Marina was to testify that she had asked Oswald to bring her a Mexican bracelet from Mexico as a present, that she had not liked the one he had bought but chose not to tell him; she thought he had bought it in New Orleans or Dallas. When Oswald was later arrested in Dallas he was wearing his own silver bracelet. Michael Paine was to testify that after Oswald came to Dallas from Mexico, his attitude to Marina changed from being harsh and cruel to one where 'They were not quarrelling. They billed and cooed. She sat on his lap and he said sweet nothings in her ear'.

On Monday, 7 October, Ruth drove Oswald to the bus station in Irving, and he returned to Dallas allegedly to look for work and a place to live. He left the YMCA and enquired about a room at 1026 North Beckley Avenue but there was no vacancy on 7 October, although there were 18 letting rooms. 1026 was about one mile as the crow flies from Ruby's apartment, both being in the Oak Cliff suburb of Dallas. He next responded to a 'For Rent' sign at Mrs. Bledsoe's roominghouse at 621 Marsalis Street, obtained a room for which he paid a week's rent of $7 in advance, moved in on the same day and registered in his correct name, L.H. Oswald. He then allegedly resumed his search for work, relying partially on referrals by the Employment Commission, and when not looking for work spent most of his time in his room. He telephoned Marina twice a day until a few days before 22 November, and she testified that he did this because he was worried about her wellbeing. In the light of subsequent events, it is probable that in addition to an interest in his family's wellbeing, Oswald was anxious to know if the FBI had called or were continuing to call at Ruth's house but, unknown to Oswald, the New Orleans FBI failed to find the forwarding address of Ruth's house until 25 October. He was, of course, unaware that the visits of the American male to the Russian Embassy in Mexico City in the name of 'Lee Oswald' had been discovered by the CIA and that the FBI had been told of this, although, like the CIA, wrongly believing the man to be the person they thought was ex-Marine Lee Harvey Oswald. He knew, however, that the report submitted by FBI agent Quigley would differ not only in his recorded height from the report of the FBI agents in Fort Worth but also in the information he had given about himself and Marina. His arrest in New Orleans had given him the opportunity to ask for an FBI agent to come to the police station in New Orleans and, for all he knew, the New Orleans FBI, the Dallas FBI or the Bureau in Washington had discovered and would act upon the discrepancies in the two FBI reports; he would, no doubt, have been able satisfactorily to explain the discrepancies by alleging that FBI agent Quigley had made mistakes. The false information he gave to Quigley may, perhaps, have been a yardstick to gauge FBI interest, and he may have thought he could avoid a confrontation with the Dallas FBI before the assassination of the President; in this he was to succeed with the assassistance of Ruth.

Oswald spent the next weekend of 12/13 October at Ruth's house when he told her that he had received the last of his unemployment cheques due to him and that it had been smaller than the previous one. Ruth was to testify that he appeared to be extremely discouraged because Marina was expecting a baby at a time when he had no job prospects and no longer a source of income.

Early on Monday *morning, 14 October*, Ruth, needing a repair to her Russian typewriter, drove Oswald to downtown Dallas and dropped him off within two blocks of the Depository.

On the same Monday *morning, 14 October*, a coffee party was held at the house of Mrs. Dorothy Roberts who lived next door to Ruth and Marina. Ruth, having now returned from downtown Dallas, went with the eight-month pregnant Marina to the party where the other guest was Mrs. Randle whose house was on the other side of Ruth's house. Mrs. Randle's younger brother, Wesley Frazier, had obtained work at the Depository on *13 September 1963*, this being the day on which the Dallas newspapers carried the first announcement that President Kennedy would shortly be visiting Texas on a one-day tour taking in Dallas, Fort Worth, San Antonio and Houston. Frazier had been living with Mrs. Randle only from the beginning of September, having arrived from Huntsville — 200 miles away — in order to look for work in Dallas.

After the coffee party the four women discussed the possibility of obtaining work for Oswald, several places being suggested but most of them apparently unsuitable for Oswald for he could not drive a car (II.245-251). Mrs. Randle tentatively suggested that there might be a job opening at the Depository, and Ruth asked if she would telephone the personnel manager to find out if there might be a position for Oswald. Mrs. Randle refused, saying that she did not know the manager, but when Ruth and Marina returned to Ruth's house after the party, Marina asked Ruth to telephone the Depository to ask if there might be work for Oswald. In reply to Ruth's call, the personnel manager, Roy Truly, said that he might have a temporary job for Oswald and that Ruth should tell Oswald to call to see him. Ruth was to testify that only the Depository had been mentioned.

On the *afternoon of 14 October*, which was *after* the coffee party and *after* Ruth's call to Truly, Oswald collected his belongings from Mrs. Bledsoe's roominghouse and returned to 1026 North Beckley where he was now allotted a room for $8 a week in the name of 'O.H. Lee'. This room was 'not usually let', did not have a room number, was on the ground floor leading off the lounge and adjoining the room of the elderly housekeeper, Mrs. Earlene Roberts. (Her sister, Mrs. Cheek, who lived elsewhere in Dallas and had, as did many others, a permanent pass card to 'The Carousel', was to be with Ruby from about 2.00 p.m. until about 4.30 p.m. on the afternoon of Monday 18 November. This was the day on which the President's motorcade route – finally fixed by the local authorities and the Secret Service on 16/17 November – was rehearsed during the morning by the Secret Service and the Dallas police from Love Field Airport through downtown Dallas and, passing the Depository, to a luncheon site at the Trade Mart. In testimony, no Commissioner being present, Mrs Cheek was to say that she had visited Ruby to discuss nightclub business, and said *inter alia*: 'Well, if I could do you any good, I would be happy to, but I don't know how I could be because I don't know Jack Ruby or Oswald very well. In fact, I didn't know Oswald at all, and I don't know Ruby well enough to help you.')

On the *evening of 14 October*, on telephoning Ruth's house Oswald was told by Marina that Ruth had made contact with Truly and that he had been asked to call at the Depository. It would seem that Oswald knew that the coffee party would take place and that, by registering at 1026 in a false name prior to hearing from Marina of the job prospect, he compromised Ruth as conspiring with him to arrange the coffee party; it is difficult to find a reason for the use of the false name 'O.H. Lee' other than an attempt further to implicate Ruth. It was somewhat dangerous to use this false name should the FBI call at 1026 to make enquiries or to interview him, although it would seem that this was a hurdle that he could clear by saying that the elderly housekeeper could not understand the name Oswald, so he had written Lee instead; the necessity to compromise Ruth had been of greater concern.

On 15 October, Oswald went to the Depository from 1026 and completed an application form for employment. On the form he gave his name as Lee Harvey Oswald and his height as 5' 9", stated that his last employment had been in the Marines, and gave Ruth's house in Irving as his address instead of 1026 North Beckley. Truly engaged him to commence work on 16 October, his duties being to fill book orders, and his hours of work being 8.00 a.m. to 4.45 p.m. at the rate of $1.25 an hour. As with his previous employments − apart from his apparently purposeful conversations with Ofstein at Jaggars-Chiles-Stovall − during his employment at the Depository Oswald kept to himself; most of his fellow employees knew him only by sight while those who spoke with him knew him only by the name of Lee. Soon after he had commenced work, Oswald became acquainted with Wesley Frazier who on three occasions was to drive him from the Depository to Irving on Friday evenings for Oswald to spend the weekend in Ruth's house.

Truly was to testify that Ruth had said to him on the telephone: 'Mr. Truly, you don't know who I am, but I have a neighbour whose brother works for you. I don't know what his name is. But he tells me his sister says that you are very busy. And I am just wondering if you can use another man ... I have a fine young man living here with his wife and baby, and his wife is expecting a baby − another baby in a few days, and he needs work desperately.' Truly said that this was his best recollection of the telephone conversation, that he had told the lady to send Oswald down to the Depository when he would talk to him, that he did not have anything in mind for him of a permanent nature but, if he was suited, they could probably use him for a brief time. When Oswald came to his office the next day for an interview he appeared to be quiet and well-mannered, and said that he had just served his term in the Marine Corps; 'He used the word "Sir", you know, which a lot of them don't do at this time.'

On 23 November 1963, which was the day after the

assassination, Truly was to swear an affidavit (XXIV.227), and this Exhibit shows that as Truly was beginning to describe Ruth's words to him, the Exhibit as printed must have been cut off at the words, 'she said she knew a nice young boy ... ', because immediately under the unfinished paragraph appears the signature of Truly and that of the Notary Public. Truly's affidavit was his first and probably best recollection of Ruth's words to him, and it would be interesting to know if Ruth – like Mrs. Latham to Graef at Jaggars-Chiles-Stovall – had continued her unfinished sentence with a mention of Oswald's service in the Marines.

It can now be seen how Oswald obtained his employment at Jaggars-Chiles-Stovall in October 1962 and at the Depository in October 1963. His employment was the result of a combination of his being neat in appearance, intelligent, respectful, a family man, having just left the Marines (preference for work being given to 'veterans') and Marina's friendship with two women, Anna Meller and Ruth Paine who were responsible for supporting telephone calls.

Both Wesley Frazier and his sister, Mrs. Randle, were to testify. Frazier said that while he was living with his sister he had been telephoned by an (unnamed) woman from an employment agency in Irving to suggest that he try to get a job at the Depository, and that in this he had at once succeeded.

It would seem unfortunate that – according to the Report and the Volumes of Testimony and Exhibits – neither the Commission, the FBI, the Secret Service or any other agency enquired more fully into Frazier's employment on 13 September 1963 at the Depository where there were only some 20 employees, how it had come about that the agency in Irving knew that Truly needed an employee, why an Irving agency – perhaps not unusual – was used by a Dallas firm, and as to the identity of the woman in the agency.

Oswald's ability to learn about possible employment at the assassination site having been obtained as the result of (a) Frazier's employment and (b) the coffee party, the creation of the party should also have been explored by the Commission. As previously mentioned, Ruth met Marina on 22 February 1963 at a party given by Everett Glover, and he was called to testify before the Commission. He was examined in detail (X.1-32) about his own background, his association with and knowledge of the Baron and Baroness, how he came to meet Oswald and Marina through them, how he came to meet Ruth through her husband, how he came to ask Ruth and the Oswalds to his party, some details of the conversations of Ruth, Marina, Oswald and others, and the identities of the other persons present and generally about the progress of the party. Mr. and Mrs. Ford had given a party on 28 December 1962 that was attended by the Oswalds, and they were examined in testimony in similar detail to Glover, although nothing of significance appears to have occurred at this gathering.

Nevertheless, neither in the Report nor in the Volumes of Testimony and Exhibits is there any evidence to show that Mrs. Dorothy Roberts either testified or was interviewed by the FBI, the Secret Service or any other agency; in the Report she is referred to only as 'a neighbour'. She could have been asked about her background, whether the coffee party was a spontaneous gathering or pre-arranged, and what places of possible employment for Oswald were mentioned at the party.

As stated at the beginning of this book, persons who have been named might have been manipulated by Oswald and the conspirators, and it must not be thought that Frazier or any of the four women attending the coffee party possessed foreknowledge of the assassination in five weeks time.

In 1965, one of the Commissioners, Gerald Ford, published a book entitled *Portrait of the Assassin*. On p.275 he says, 'Few questions the Commission had to deal with in its ten months of investigation required more thorough enquiry than "how did Lee Oswald get his job at the Texas School Book Depository?" No schemer could have chosen a better place from which to commit the crime. If there was an assassination plot thought out by masterminds, it was a place they might well have chosen for their trigger-man. Just at a point in the parade route where the motorcade would have to slow; just high enough above the street to make a perfect shot through a telescopic sight; even the sixth floor itself, piled high with cartons of books, made an ideal ambuscade for a gunman, and Lee Harvey Oswald was there at the right moment, rifle in hand. No writer of a T.V. suspense drama could have conceived a better setting. Creaking elevators, ceilings covered with grit and cobwebs, dusty windows that would screen the killer – it was simply too pat. It was a classical setting for a crime of this nature. Certainly one man, who according to public information was not noted for his intelligence, could not have planned and carried out this killing by himself. It just didn't seem possible.'

Ford might well have accentuated the ideality of the ambuscade by adding that to the assassin's immediate left was the solid brick outer wall of the Depository, and to his right and behind him he had piled high cartons of books shielding him from the sight of anyone who happened to be on the sixth floor prior to the assassination. In front of the assassin were two dirty windows, only the lower half of the Left window being raised and through which he watched and fired; he could be observed in the window only from a fraction of the area outside and, in fact, only a few persons saw a man in the window and only one of them saw him actually firing.

After saying on p.276, 'This was the most baffling real-life crime in history', on p.281 Ford says, 'Ruth Paine's account of how she helped Lee get the position at the Texas School Book Depository was verified by the witnesses concerned – Mr. Roy S. Truly, Mrs. Bill Randle, with whom her brother Wesley Frazier lived, and the other woman present at the coffee, the hostess, Mrs. Dorothy Roberts. *Each of these persons in turn was extensively investigated* (author's italics) for any motives he or she might have for altering the truth or covering up anything. They all proved to be loyal Americans whose normal pattern of life was like a typical housewife or business man in the United States. To doubt their word would be like doubting the word of your well-known neighbour. It just doesn't happen in Texas, or Michigan, or Indiana, that these neighbourhood housewives could be engaged in a plot to assassinate a President. Before the subject came up in the coffee-klatch, neither Lee or Marina Oswald could have had any knowledge of an opening at the building, nor is there any possibility Lee placed himself there with a foreknowledge that a Presidential motorcade would pass by there. The dates of the plans being made in Washington of the public announcements of the parade route, just don't check out with that possibility'.

Oswald could have known that the motorcade in all probability would pass the Depository. On 26 September – being the day on which he entered Mexico – the Dallas newspapers stated that the President would be visiting Dallas on 21 or 22 November. The site for the luncheon to which the motorcade would proceed would almost certainly be the Trade Mart and, according to retired Dallas Police Chief Curry (who appears to suspect conspiracy) on pp. 10 and 11 of his book published in 1969 revealing his *J.F.K. Assassination File*, 'In retrospect it is obvious that almost any route chosen would probably have passed directly under the School Book Depository at the assassination site. If the President came through town to go to a luncheon at the Trade Mart, any motorcade meant very simply that even tentative information given about the parade would have given conspirators every reason to believe that the President's open car would pass the site actually chosen for the assassination.'

It is difficult to believe that Ford would have written about the 'extensive investigation' of Mrs. Dorothy Roberts had he and the other Commissioners been properly informed by their investigators because, even if she was not asked to testify, she should have been interviewed by the FBI and the Secret Service. No report of the FBI and Secret Service interviews and investigations at Jaggars-Chiles-Stovall appears in the Exhibits, and it is only the testimony of Stovall and Ofstein that discloses these interviews occured; it may well be the same case with Mrs. Dorothy Roberts.

It would seem that the employment of Frazier at the Depository on 13 September and the organisation of the coffee party somewhere hold the key to Oswald's 'simply too pat' employment at the Depository.

On 20 October, a second daughter was born to Marina in Parkland Hospital, Dallas, the daughter being named Audrey Marina Oswald. Oswald was not at the hospital on the day of the birth, remaining at Ruth's house to look after his other little daughter, Jane, and Ruth's two children, while Ruth went in her car to the hospital for the birth. The next day Oswald went to the hospital to see Marina, and he then filled in two spaces on the birth certificate – reserved for the description of·work and place of employment of the father – with the words 'Laborer' and 'School Book Depository'. Another part of the certificate already filled up at the hospital gave the name of the new-born child as Audrey Marina Oswald, but Oswald squeezed in the name 'Rachel' at a slant after the name Marina. From the date of her birth, the new-born child was called and referred to as 'Rachel' by Ruth, Marina and Oswald.

Nevertheless, in Oswald's letter of 9 November 1963 despatched from Irving on 12 November to Consul Reznichenko at the Russian Embassy in Washington, Oswald referred in capitals to the new-born child as Audrey Marina Oswald. The purpose behind this is not apparent, but the omission of the call-name, Rachel, from his letter was perhaps a signal that would be understood by the recipient of the letter. The birth certificate does not appear in the Exhibits, but I obtained a copy from the authorities in Dallas.

On 1 November, Oswald rented P.O. Box No. 6225 at the Terminal Annex Post Office which was close to the Depository, and also near 'The Carousel' where during the daytime Ruby maintained his office, a room being reserved for that purpose. On Oswald's application for the Box he gave FPCC and ACLU as bodies entitled to receive mail.

It is necessary now to consider Ruby's activities at this time. On 1 November, he had taken to live with him in his apartment a 50 years old Jewish salesman, George Senator, who had lived in Dallas for ten years and had been acquainted with Ruby for eight or nine years. Ruby used him frequently in 'The Carousel' to collect the entrance fees at the door and to do other odd jobs. Also on 1 November, Ruby took 22 years old Curtis Crafard – known only as 'Larry' – into 'The Carousel', Crafard somewhat resembling Oswald in age, appearance and casual attire. Before his employment with Ruby, he had been employed for a short time up to 1 November in a side-show in which Ruby had a very small financial interest, at a fairground in Dallas. Prior to that time Crafard had been an itinerant casual worker in different parts of the United States. The fairground was frequented by Ruby, and shortly before leaving the fair for 'The Carousel' someone had struck Crafard so hard in the mouth that his four upper front teeth had been knocked out. The police were called and Crafard told them that the injury had been caused by his falling over a chair. When Crafard entered Ruby's employment on 1 November he was allowed to sleep at 'The Carousel', and was to act as an additional handyman and in particular to take telephone messages for Ruby. (Andy Armstrong was the permanent handyman at 'The Carousel', and there existed no apparent business necessity for Ruby to employ Crafard.) According to Crafard in testimony, he was allowed to take money out of the till for meals and other expenses that he might incur, and handled $300 or $400 nightly. This unusual arrangement continued from 1 November until he fled 'The Carousel' early on 23 November. If the plan had been for Oswald to make contact with Ruby or be in the vicinity of Ruby's apartment after the assassination, in the unlikely event of a casual observer noticing him in the area, Ruby might have been able to confuse the issue by indicating that the observer was mistaken and that it had been Crafard who on at least three previous occasions had visited him at his apartment. It is possible to believe that Crafard would, in view of his knowledge of Ruby, have chosen to support him in anything he said. Between 1 and 22 November, Ruby was to take Crafard around downtown and out to meals so frequently that he became known as 'Jack Ruby Junior' and 'Little Ruby'; the Commission were aware of this, and Counsel exhibited photographs of Crafard to Graef of Jaggars-Chiles-Stovall and asked Graef if Crafard bore a resemblance to Oswald. Graef said that although there was a resemblance anyone who knew Oswald would know that the photographs were not of him. The photographs were also shown to Ruth who said that although one of them bore a resemblance to Oswald, it was Crafard's attire in the photographs that created a similarity between the two men.

The Safe: All restauranters or club owners know or should know that the most satisfactory method of protecting a night's takings at the end of business is to install on the premises a small 'wall-safe' usually measuring about 7″ x 5″ and about 3″ deep, with an ordinary lock, inserted flush into a wall and secreted behind a piece of easily moveable furnishing. Ruby is not known to have installed a safe in any of his clubs at any time, but is known to have 'worked out of his pocket' and to have kept the nightly takings from 'The Carousel' and 'The Vegas' in the trunk of his car or in his pockets. It is known that in his apartment at 223 South Ewing there was no safe and that he always had large sums of money in the pockets of his suits or elsewhere in the apartment; according to Senator in testimony he appeared never to know where or how much it was.

In late October and early November, Ruby sought the advice of two detectives from the Theft Bureau at Dallas Police Station about a floor safe for 'The Carousel' and how it could be placed so that 'it would not be noticeable and yet it could easily be heard in the event burglars tried to get into it'. He asked one of the detectives to visit 'The Carousel' and advise him but, after inspecting the premises, the detective told Ruby that he would not be able to achieve the desired results (XXIII.344).

On the day that Ruby employed Crafard, 1 November, he and Crafard went to an electronics shop in Dallas to inspect electronic equipment, and about 7 November Ruby bought a safe standing about 18″ high, placing it on the floor of his office at 'The Carousel'. Prior to this, if on occasion the night's takings were not recovered by Ruby, the money had been hidden in a small drawer in a filing cabinet. Ruby did not obtain a similar or any other safe for 'The Vegas', although the takings were somewhat greater than at 'The Carousel'. It would seem that Ruby was expecting to receive a large sum of money at 'The Carousel' after 22 November, and which would be accommodated in the safe. If Ruby were to have received a reward after the escape of the assassin, he could not have risked placing it in one of the two deposit boxes that he kept together with small balances on his drawing account at banks in Dallas, the boxes not having been used for about a year. Ruby would not have dared to use a bank night-safe, for the cash contents of money pouches – the pouches being provided by the bank to drop in the safe – are counted next morning and credited to the customer's account. After 24 November, the safe was opened by the police and found to be empty, as might, perhaps, be expected.

On 3 October, a letter had been despatched from the FBI in New Orleans to the FBI in Dallas informing the latter that it had been discovered that Marina had left New Orleans on 23 September in a station-wagon with a Texas licence plate and that the car was being driven by a woman who could speak the Russian language. the letter went on to say that Oswald had remained behind but disappeared the following day; the Dallas FBI were requested to make attempts to trace both the Oswalds. The matter was now in the hands of Dallas FBI Agent Hosty who made some routine enquiries in Dallas but without success. The FBI in New Orleans had failed to check the New Orleans post office where they would have found that on 24 or 25 September Oswald had left Ruth's address in Irving as his change of address. Hosty had received a second letter from the FBI in New Orleans on 25 October, the letter containing information supplied by the CIA that a 'Lee Oswald' had been in contact with the Russian Embassy in Mexico City at the beginning of October; this was to cause Hosty to increase his efforts to find Oswald and Marina but still without success. On 29 October, Hosty had received a third letter from the FBI in New Orleans and at last they gave him Oswald's forwarding address. When dealing with this period between 24 September 1963 and 29 October 1963, the Report says that, 'Throughout this period the FBI had been aware of the whereabouts of the Oswalds (R.739)'. This statement is untrue for the FBI had lost track of them from 24 September, as is shown by Hosty when he came to testify that it was not until 29 October that he had been informed of the address of Ruth Paine's house.

On 1 November, after making pretext enquiries in the neighbourhood of Ruth's house regarding the Paines and the Oswalds, Hosty called at the house where he spoke to Ruth and Marina, Ruth acting as interpreter. Hosty was to testify that he had understood from Ruth that Marina and her little daughters were living with her, that Oswald was living at a roominghouse somewhere in Dallas but the address was unknown to either of the women, that Oswald was employed as a labourer in the Texas School Book Depository and – in response to Hosty's specific enquiry – that he was no longer actively engaged in FPCC activities. Hosty said that Marina was 'alarmed and upset' when he arrived, but that he calmed her by saying that he was not there to harm or harrass her and that it was the task of the FBI to protect people. When he came to leave, Marina was 'smiling and happy, and shook hands'; he had not mentioned Mexico City. He said twice and emphasised that Ruth had hesitated before telling him that Oswald was employed at the Depository, but she explained ·that she had hesitated because Oswald had told her that the FBI was the cause of him losing his jobs. In reply to Hosty's request, Ruth said that she would try to obtain the address of Oswald's roominghouse, but she did not tell Hosty that she had the telephone number of 1026 North Beckley in her telephone numbers book, nor did she tender the number to Hosty so that he could then and there ascertain the address where Oswald was now living. She was to testify and Hosty confirmed that she had told him that Oswald visited her house periodically at weekends. As Hosty was leaving, he wrote down on a piece of paper his name and business telephone number, and Ruth passed this information to Oswald later that day, Friday, when he came from the Depository to Irving for the weekend.

While Hosty was in or leaving Ruth's house, Marina mentally noted the licence number of his car which was parked some distance away but she misread one of the digits. When her husband came to Irving that evening she told him the number that she had recorded.

In Oswald's notebook (XVI.64) the name, *address* and telephone number of Hosty are written under date 1 November 1963. This entry includes the licence number of his car which is written *between* Hosty's name and his address. By the use of a bracket the entry in Oswald's notebook is made to appear that all this information was obtained at the same time from Ruth, and that it was she who had surreptitiously noted the licence number, and had looked up and added the address of the FBI office for Oswald to call there; she testified that he told her he had done so. If he did call at the office he did not see Hosty, for when Hosty was to arrive at Dallas police station shortly after Oswald's arrest, the latter said, 'So you're Hosty', and roundly abused him for 'accosting' Marina, saying that if Hosty had wanted to see him, he should have done so instead of approaching Marina. If Oswald did visit the FBI office, it would have been to involve Ruth further by suggesting that she had supplied him with the address and inspired the visit to the office. (It has recently been disclosed that a letter from Oswald was received by the Dallas FBI, apparently containing accusations of harrassment of Marina by Hosty; allegedly the letter was destroyed after the assassination and not shown to the Commission.)

On 4 November 1963, the Russian Embassy in Washington sent a communication to one or both of the Oswalds; the empty post-marked window-type envelope was discovered after the assassination. Marina was shown the envelope during her testimony and said that she did not know what it had contained but that Oswald had told her that she had received a congratulatory letter from the Russian Embassy commemorating the October Revolution, the dates coinciding. (The dates do coincide. The October Revolution was, under the old Russian calendar, on 25 October 1917 but with the advent of the new Russian calendar this became 7 November, the occasion commemorated each year with a Russian national holiday.) It is possible that the contents of the envelope contained a request from the Embassy for up-to-date information from Oswald about the extent of FBI interest in him since his return to Dallas from the Russian Embassy in Mexico City.

Oswald would have received the 4 November communication on 5/6 November and it must have been addressed to P.O. Box 6225 in Dallas because Oswald had sent a change of address card for Marina to Reznichenko giving the Dallas P.O. Box as her new address and operative as from 1 November 1963; this kept the communication from the eyes of Marina and Ruth.

On Tuesday 5 November, Hosty again called to see Ruth to ask if she had obtained Oswald's address in Dallas but, although Oswald had been at her house on the weekend of 1/2/3 November, she again told Hosty that she did not know the address of the roominghouse. It would seem either that she had forgotten to ask him or that he had refused to tell her, perhaps maintaining that a visit by the FBI to 1026 might cause him to be evicted. Ruth again failed to offer Hosty the use of her telephone to enable him to locate the roominghouse; Hosty was never to ascertain the address of the roominghouse nor was he to speak to Oswald prior to the assassination.

Hosty informed the FBI in New Orleans that he had traced Marina and partially traced Oswald, and that Oswald was employed in a non-sensitive industry. He testified that having checked with the Depository that Oswald was so employed and Oswald having ceased his FPCC activities, he had decided that he would see Oswald only after he received the complete file with up-to-date information from the FBI in New Orleans; this file was to be received by the FBI in Dallas on 21 November and was not to be studied by Hosty until after the assassination.

On 7 November, Ruby, who had never previously required a Post Office Box in Dallas, now rented P.O. Box No 5475 until 31 December 1964 at the same post office where Oswald had rented his Box a week previously. It was about eight feet from Oswald's Box and rented in the name of Earl Products — this being the name of a firm operated by Ruby and his three brothers in Chicago many years before, although the firm together with the right to use the name had been sold to a stranger in about 1959. During September, October and November 1963, Ruby had been engaged in trying unsuccessfully to promote a 'twist-board' exerciser and he was to testify that the acquisition of the Box was in connection with this promotion. After the assassination, postal authorities were able to ascertain that Oswald had received certain literature including Russian magazines at his Box but, as there was some dust on the floor of

Ruby's Box, it seemed to them that this Box may not have been used. Whether there was anything significant in the renting of the two Boxes is unknown, but it did supply Ruby and Oswald with a legitimate excuse to be in or near the Post Office if they wished to communicate in any way. From 7 through 22 November, the Boxes could have provided an opportunity for them to use the premises for a secret 'drop'. (A 'dead-drop' is a place where a message or other material may be secreted by one agent for another later to collect. A 'live-drop' is a physical 'brush' or verbal contact between agents for the purpose of transmitting information.) Ruby could have instructed Oswald about the times and route for escape from the Depository and from Dallas, and, with his police contacts, he could also have obtained some details of the motorcade and the time at which the President would pass the Depository.

The Report says, 'Although it is conceivable that Oswald and Ruby coincidentally encountered one another while checking their Boxes, the different daily schedules of the two men would render even this possibility unlikely. Moreover, Oswald's withdrawn personality makes it improbable that the two would have spoken if their paths had crossed (R.363)'.

This statement is not supported by the evidence, and it must be discussed because the Commission attempted to demolish any significance presented by the ownership of the Boxes.

In the first place, it can be established that the daily schedules of the two men did render it possible for them to meet. In testimony, Crafard said that during the time that he was employed by Ruby at 'The Carousel' – 1 through 22 November – Ruby had arrived at the club around 11.30 a.m. (XIII.421.435.497), and other evidence indicates that prior to 1 November Ruby's arrival at the club was usually later. Senator who lived with Ruby testified that for 'a few weeks' prior to 23 November, Ruby left the apartment at about 8.00 or 9.00 a.m. which was much earlier than usual; he said the early departure was in connection with the promotion of Ruby's 'twist-board' business. Oswald's lunch break at the Depository was from 12 noon to 12.45 p.m. and he finished work at 4.45 p.m. each day. Ruby, being his own master, could have crossed the path of Oswald for a 'live-drop' or a 'dead-drop' at any time of the day or night. The Commission's view that Oswald's 'withdrawn personality' would have made it improbable that the two men would have spoken if their paths had crossed is not substantiated by the evidence which makes it clear that Oswald could be withdrawn or outgoing, hostile or friendly, rude or polite, silent or talkative as the occasion required. The testimony of Ruth, Stuckey, the Murretts, the Jesuits and others establishes that Oswald could be warm, outgoing, friendly, polite or talkative, although some witnesses speak contrariwise when referring to other occasions.

If the window-envelope of 4 November contained a request from Reznichenko to Oswald for a present report on FBI interest in him, up to that time Oswald would have been unable to supply him with any information because, unaware of the failure of the FBI in New Orleans to locate his forwarding address of Ruth's house in Irving, he had been anticipating a visit from the FBI at her house at the beginning of October, and certainly before 1 November. He had been in no position to report the extent of FBI interest in him until he knew what it was, and he was not to know this until after Hosty's second visit to Ruth's house on Tuesday 5 November, when Hosty had remained for a moment and only to ask Ruth if she had ascertained the address of Oswald's roominghouse. Although the date for the assassination was approaching, it would have been advisable for Oswald to wait for another weekend to pass to see if the FBI would again visit Ruth's house; if they did not do so he could tell Reznichenko that the FBI was 'not now interested in my activities'.

He was therefore in no position to communicate with Reznichenko until after the weekend of 9/10 November.

On Saturday 9 November, Oswald was spending the weekend in Ruth's house, and Hosty had not called there since 5 November. During the morning of 9 November, Ruth, having advised Oswald that he should learn to drive and having given him some lessons and told him to obtain a driving licence, drove him to the Texas Drivers Licence Examining Station but, because it was an election day, the station was closed. Nevertheless, he partly filled in an application where he gave his height as 5' 9", the form was found after the assassination amongst his possessions. It would seem that the purpose of the visit was further to involve Ruth for, if he were to escape from the Depository and Dallas after the assassination, the authorities would suspect that he might have driven himself away in a car, having been taught to drive by Ruth.

During the afternoon of 9 November, using one of Ruth's typewriters (not the Russian one) Oswald typed a letter from himself and Marina to the Russian Embassy in Washington, the envelope being addressed to Reznichenko. He deliberately moved the typewriter so that Ruth could not see what he was typing, and he then left a handwritten but unaddressed draft (R.311) on her bureau. He had folded it so that the side on which he had written that the FBI were no longer interested in his activities, would be the first words Ruth would read and know it to be untrue. He knew that she would see these words, and curiosity might drive her to read it. She kept it, in fact, and gave it and a copy she had made to Hosty, but only after the assassination; her copy does not appear in the Exhibits. The weekend and the national holiday on the Monday (11 November) having passed without a further visit from Hosty, the letter was posted in Irving on Tuesday 12 November.

The letter is set out below as written and for convenience of reference the paragraphs are numbered:

FROM: LEE H. OSWALD, P.O. BOX 6225, DALLAS, TEXAS
       MARINA NICHILAYEVA OSWALD, SOVIET CITIZEN

TO: CONSULAR DIVISION
      EMBASSY U.S.S.R.
      WASHINGTON D.C.

      NOV. 9, 1963

Dear Sirs;
1. This is to inform you of recent events since my meetings with comrade Kostin in the Embassy of the Soviet Union, Mexico City, Mexico.
2. I was unable to remain in Mexico indefinily because of my mexican

visa restrictions which was for 15 days only. I could not take a chance on requesting a new visa unless I used my real name, so I retured to the United States.

3. I had not planned to contact the Soviet embassy in Mexico so they were unprepared, had I been able to reach the Soviet Embassy in Havana as planned, the embassy there would have had time to complete our business.

4. Of corse the Soviet embassy was not at fault, they were, as I say unprepared, the Cuban consulate was guilty of a gross breach of regulations, I am glad he has since been replced.

5. The Federal Bureau of Investigation is not now interested in my activities in the progressive organisation 'Fair Play For Cuba Committee', of which I was secretary in New Orleans (state Louisiana) since I no longer reside in that state. However, the F.B.I. has visited us here in Dallas, Texas, on November 1st. Agent James P. Hosty warned me that if I engaged in F.P.C.C. activities in Texas the F.B.I. will again take an 'interrest' in me.

6. This agent also 'suggested' to Marina Nichilayeva that she could remain in the United States under F.B.I. 'protection', that is, she could defect from the Soviet Uion, of course, I and my wife strongly protested these tactics by the notorious F.B.I.

7. Please inform us of the arrival of our Soviet entrance visa's as soon as they come.

8. Also, this is to inform you of the birth on October 20, 1963 of a DAUGHTER, AUDREY MARINA OSWALD in DALLAS, TEXAS, to my wife.

Respecfully,
Lee H. Oswald (Signed).

On November, a confidential informant of the FBI stationed at the Russian Embassy in Washington obtained a copy of the letter and sent it to the field office of the FBI in Washington who sent it to the Bureau on 19 November. The field office or the Bureau then communicated the contents of the letter to the field office in Dallas where it was to be received on the morning of 22 November but not to be seen by Hosty until shortly after the assassination.

As mentioned earlier, on 26 March 1964 the Commission were to submit a questionnaire to the Bureau of the FBI, one question being, 'What was the FBI evaluation of confidential information received on November 18, 1963, regarding Oswald's letter to the Soviet Embassy in Washington?'. The answer, contained in the letter dated 6 April 1964 and signed by J. Edgar Hoover was, ' ... the information received on November 18, 1963, concerning Oswald's contact with the Soviet Embassy tended to confirm his contact with the Soviet Embassy in Mexico City as reported by the CIA, and indicate the reasons for such contact, namely to secure visas to the Soviet Union'. When answering the question on 6 April, Hoover must have known that it was the American male who had twice visited the Soviet Embassy in Mexico City 'as reported by the CIA', and that these visits could hardly have been in connection with visas.

The alleged FBI evaluation of the letter is impossible to understand, because the letter gave the FBI information: (a) that Oswald had had 'meetings' with comrade Kostin at the Russian Embassy in Mexico City, in addition to the two visits to that Embassy of the American male on the first of which visits he had spoken with Kostikov and on the second had enquired about a reply to a telegram, (b) that Oswald had obtained a visa (intransit tourist card) and had travelled to Mexico not in his 'real name' – from the wording of paragraph 2 the use of a false name apparently was known to his masters – and could 'not take a chance' on requesting a new visa, (c) that his intention had been to reach the Soviet Embassy in Havana in a venture 'planned' with the Russians for the completion of 'our business' but had been prevented at the Cuban Consulate from so doing, (d) that he had attempted to reach Cuba, although travel to that country from the United States was then proscribed by law, (e) that unable to reach Havana he had turned to the Soviet Embassy in Mexico City where they were 'unprepared' for him, (f) that the FBI were 'not now interested' in his FPCC activities, (g) that he was requesting the Soviet Embassy in Washington to inform him of the arrival of visas – indicating that the business to be completed at the Russian Embassies in Havana or Mexico City could hardly have been in connection with visas, (h) that the inability to complete 'our business' was due to a time factor and resultant change in plans, and (i) that Oswald had somehow learned that the Cuban Consul in Mexico City 'has since been replaced'.

The Commission did not ask the FBI official who evaluated the letter to testify and explain the reasoning behind his conclusion that the letter was 'to secure visas to the Soviet Union'. Rejecting his opinion, the Commission themselves evaluated the letter: 'In the opinion of the Commission, based upon its knowledge of Oswald, the letter constitutes no more than a clumsy effort to ingratiate himself with the Soviet Embassy (R.310).'

It would seem that on 19 November the Bureau of the FBI should have realised that the visits to the Russian Embassy in Mexico City of the assassin and the American male could not have been to secure visas to the Soviet Union, since it must have been apparent to the Bureau not only from (g) above but from the fact that it would be improbable that a man would travel in a false identity to Mexico and attempt to reach the Soviet Embassy in Havana in order to secure visas for travel to Russia, when he had only to apply by letter to the Soviet Embassy in Washington, and needed no American male stand-in in Mexico City to help him obtain visas for Russia.

In addition the Bureau had the file of Oswald containing Hoover's memorandum of 3 June 1960, two different heights, contradictions, lies, evidence of Cuban and Russian interests, and evidence of a confederate American male. It would seem that someone in the Bureau when evaluating the letter had failed to read the prior entries in Oswald's file. (When the FBI informant in the Russian Embassy in Washington extracted the letter he had risked what is called 'blowing his cover', a step not lightly undertaken had he not considered the letter to be other than a request for visas.)

The Report displays odd logic (R.310) when it prefers to treat a draft of a letter (R.311) as representing what the sender intended to say. Even so, it does not point out that in the draft Oswald had spelt Kostin's name as Kostine, that the draft excludes paragraph 8 which omits the call name 'Rachel', and that all the words in capitals at the top of the letter were not in the draft. These words include 'P.O. Box 6225'; neither Ruth nor Marina knew of the Box rented by Oswald on 1 November 1963. (Oswald did have correspondence delivered to Ruth's address, and it would appear that he needed a post office box for clandestine purposes.) If Oswald had included in the draft, paragraph 8 of the letter, the omission of 'Rachel' might have increased Ruth's uneasiness and might have driven her to send the draft to Hosty. The purpose of leaving the draft appears to have been further to involve Ruth whose call to the Depository had assisted the assassin's employment in that building. It would seem that Oswald correctly judged Ruth's affection for Marina and rightly surmised that she would not risk alienating her by 'betraying' her husband to the FBI.

In clandestine operations much is left to the initiative of the agent, and in the letter Oswald did not have to explain why he and Albert Osborne rapidly departed from Mexico City, nor did he have to explain that he and Marina were living separately in Dallas and Irving, and that Hosty had not actually spoken to *him*. His words about Marina's rejection of Hosty's alleged suggestion of defection from the Soviet Union were to satisfy his masters that during the next ten days she would not disrupt his plans. In short, the letter was for consumption by the KGB in Russia and was, as it said, to inform them of 'recent events since my meeting with Comrade Kostin' at the Russian Embassy in Mexico City, i.e. the FBI were no longer interested in him, Marina was reliable and the assassination could proceed without interruption. It is profitless to speculate about 'the arrival of our Soviet entrance visas as soon as they come' in paragraph 7, except to say that it was not in the draft.

Page 310 of the Report says of the letter and the draft:

Some light on its possible meaning can be shed by comparing it with the early draft. When the differences between the draft and the final document are studied, and especially when crossed-out words are taken into account, it becomes apparent that Oswald was intentionally beclouding the true state of affairs in order to make his trip to Mexico sound as mysterious and important as possible. For example, the first sentence in the second paragraph of the letter reads, 'I was unable to remain in Mexico indefinily because of my mexican visa restrictions which was for 15 days only.' The same sentence in the draft begins, before the words are crossed out, 'I was unable to remain in Mexico City because I considered useless ... ' As already mentioned, the Commission has good evidence that Oswald's trip to Mexico was indeed 'useless' and that he returned to Texas with this conviction. The first draft, therefore, spoke the truth; but Oswald rewrote the sentence to imply that he had to leave because his visa was about to expire. This is false; Oswald's tourist card still had a full week to run when he departed from Mexico on October 3. The next sentence in the letter reads, 'I could not take a chance on requesting a new visa unless I used my real name, so I returned to the United States.' The fact is that he did use his real name for his tourist card, and in all dealings with the Cuban Embassy, the Russian Embassy and elsewhere. Oswald did use the name of 'Lee' on the trip but, as indicated below, he did so only sporadically and probably as the result of a clerical error. In the opinion of the Commission based upon its knowledge of Oswald, the letter constitutes no more than a clumsy effort to ingratiate himself with the Soviet Embassy.

A correct reading of the letter shows that Oswald said that he was unable to remain in Mexico *indefinitely* because of his Mexican visa restrictions which were for 15 days only; he did not imply that he had to leave 'because his visa was about to expire'. In the draft he said 'because I considered useless ... '; it was indeed useless as the draft says because there had been a change in plans and he could not stay in Mexico *indefinitely*, i.e. after the expiration of 15 days, the date of expiry having nothing to do with his and Albert Osborne's sudden departure from Mexico on 2 and 1 October 1963, seven days and nearly six months before their Mexican visas respectively expired. Oswald used the name 'Lee' for transit to Mexico City, for residence in that city and for return to Dallas solely to avoid the FBI. When he spoke to the two Australian girls on the bus trip he did *not* tell them his name. He used his real name at the Cuban Embassy (perhaps using his Russian name for 'meetings' with Kostin at the Russian Embassy in Mexico City from 27 September through 1 October) and *never* 'elsewhere' except on his application for the tourist card, the application being filed away and the vital travel card issued to 'Lee, Harvey Oswald'. His visit to the *Cuban* Embassy in the name of 'Lee Harvey Oswald' (no comma) was intended to be discovered but only after the assassination. The Report also indicates that the American male and the assassin were the same person when it says ' ... the Russian Embassy ... '. Had the authors of the Report known of the existence of the American male and of the placing in the National Archives of all material relating to his existence and presence in Mexico City, then the description in the Report of the most important document in the investigation as 'no more than a clumsy effort to ingratiate himself with the Soviet Embassy', would have been a deception.

In the Exhibits (XVI.33) the letter is reproduced legibly and measures 7.3″ x 5.2″, but in the Report the letter is reduced in size to 3.1″ x 2.2″. At the latter size and photographically reproduced it is difficult to decipher owing to the poor quality of the reproduction (R.311).

The Commission do not discuss the letter as a whole, but print and discuss it part by part in different sections of their Report, thus precluding an understanding of the letter. On page 309 of the Report, paragraph 1 of the letter is printed and discussed; on page 310 paragraph 2 is printed and discussed; *paragraph 3 is neither printed nor discussed thus omitting Oswald's attempt to reach the Soviet Embassy in Havana as planned*; on page 735 only the first part of paragraph 4 is printed thus omitting the 'replacement' of the Cuban Consul; on page 739 paragraphs 5, 6 and 7 are printed, 5 and 6 are discussed but there is no discussion of the request for information about visas in paragraph 7. *Paragraph 8 which omitted the name 'Rachel' is neither printed nor discussed.*

According to the foreword written by 'The Editors', just 80 hours after President Johnson released the Report, Bantam Books published a 'completely authoritive edition' of the Report including 'all the text and every single one of the vitally important Commission Exhibits necessary to an understanding of the Report'. The first printing by W.F. Hall Printing Company in Chicago of 700,000 copies of the Bantam edition of the Report established 'a new milestone in book publishing ... over 150 skilled men and women ... accomplished this gigantic task by working in eight-hour shifts around the clock. Since President Johnson felt it was of vital importance that the whole truth about President Kennedy's death be given to the world as quickly as possible, special arrangements were made to airlift the books all over the world. Thus, the Warren Commission Report in this edition will be read in London, Paris, Tokyo, Melbourne and other cities throughout the world almost as soon as it appeared in Los Angeles'.

The Bantam $1.00 paperback was cheaper than the Report, which sold at $2.50 paperback and $3.50 hardback, and the Bantam appeared under the imprimatur of *The New York Times*. The letter of 9 November 1963 – 'one of the vitally important Commission Exhibits necessary to an understanding of the Report' – was reproduced in the Bantam but reduced in size to $1'' \times 1\frac{1}{2}''$, and is illegible. Only a few thousand copies of the more expensive Report were sold, so that the vast majority of students of the assassination and of politicians throughout the world were never to read the whole letter.

On February 3 1964, Marina was called as the first witness to testify before the Commission and, the letter being verbally translated into Russian for her, she was asked to comment upon it. At the same time, the copy of the letter in the hands of Counsel was circulated to the six members of the Commission then present so that they could have 'a moment or two to examine it'. It would appear that they were not each supplied with a separate copy and, like Marina, had to rely upon memory of the letter while she was taken through it. She said that she had never seen the letter before and that it was 'a crazy letter', but that she did see the envelope because Lee had retyped it some ten times or so. When she was asked if she knew comrade Kostin she replied, 'I never wrote to him. I don't know. I don't know where he got that name from'. When asked if her husband had said anything about Kostin and his 'meetings' with him at the Embassy in Mexico City, she replied, 'He did not name him. He didn't tell me his name. But he told me he was a very pleasant, sympathetic person, who greeted him, welcomed him there'. She was not invited to give her views about paragraph 7 (visas) nor was she asked how her husband could have come to omit the call-name of his daughter, Rachel, from paragraph 8, although the Commissioners and Counsel knew that the child was named Rachel for they had learned in the first few minutes of Marina's testimony that this was her child's call-name. (I.2.)

When Counsel put paragraph 3 to Marina saying 'as I read the letter', he misquoted the paragraph by omitting the words 'as planned', by changing 'to complete our business' to 'to complete his business', and by adding after the word 'business' the words 'about the visa'. (I.47.) It is not surprising that the Commission believed that Oswald had visited Mexico City on 'his business' and had tried to visit Havana 'about the visa', and that the attempted visit to Havana had not been 'planned' by Oswald and the KGB.

The words of Counsel would appear in the published testimony of Marina and would mislead a student failing to read or decipher paragraph 3 into believing that the projected visit to the Russian Embassy in Havana had not been 'planned', and that the projected and accomplished visits respectively to the Russian Embassy in Havana and the Russian Embassy in Mexico City had been Oswald's private 'business' and only 'about the visa'.

The contents of the letter would have been encoded and radioed to the KGB officer in charge of the operation in Russia — Reznichenko probably being only the conduit; that the letter would not be interpreted in the United States but transmitted to Russia is suggested by the words 'New Orleans (State Louisiana)' instead of 'New Orleans, LA.'. Some six months earlier, Oswald had written, 'New Orleans, LA.' on his counterfeit vaccination certificate.

Marina was to testify that she had asked Oswald to stay in Dallas and not to visit Ruth's house in Irving for the weekend of 16/17 November, Saturday and Sunday, because he had been there for four days during the previous weekend (Friday through Monday), and she was worried that he might have outstayed his welcome on that occasion. It is not known what Oswald did on these two days in Dallas but it was on 16/17 November that the motorcade route was finalised by the authorities and on the morning of 18 November that it was rehearsed through downtown Dallas and past the Depository. Oswald and/or Ruby could have watched the precisely timed rehearsal.

On Sunday 17 November, Marina asked Ruth to telephone Oswald at the number that Oswald had given to Ruth, but when Ruth rang she was told by the person who answered the telephone that nobody with the name of Oswald lived there. Neither Ruth nor Marina had ever used the number before as it had not been necessary to do so because Oswald had telephoned Marina twice a day — in the middle of the day and in the evening. It is, perhaps, fortunate for Ruth and Marina that they called the number for it could not later be suggested that either or both were aware that Oswald was living under an assumed name. From the time Oswald arrived in Dallas from Mexico City, neither Ruth nor Marina had visited him at either of his roominghouses in Dallas, and only on 17 November — five days before the assassination — did they attempt to telephone him.

On Monday 18 November, Oswald telephoned Marina and, according to Marina, when she told him that she had been upset by the fact that he was not known at the number he had given Ruth, he became angry, telling her that he was living under a fictitious name and that she was not again to telephone him. According to Marina, he ordered her to erase the number from Ruth's notebook and, when Marina refused to do so, a quarrel developed. Marina's refusal to erase the number was to place Ruth in a difficult position, for her notebook would be seen by the authorities after the assassination and it would show that she had known but twice failed to give Hosty the telephone number of the roominghouse, 1026, where Oswald was living in the assumed name; it would also disclose her visits with Marina at the time of the Walker shooting, and her visit with Oswald and Marina on the day that the President's visit to Dallas was announced by Vice President Johnson, then himself in Dallas.

Nothing of importance is recorded for 20 November but on Thursday 21 November, Oswald asked Frazier to drive him to Irving after work that evening and to take him back to the Depository the following morning. Frazier agreed, understanding that Oswald was going down on Thursday instead of the usual Friday because he wished to pick up some curtain rods from Ruth's house to use in his own room in Dallas. The owners of 1026 North Beckley were to testify that no curtain rods were necessary, the windows in Oswald's room being adequately covered with material that did not require rods; there were two sets of curtain rods in Ruth's garage.

Both Ruth and Marina testified that they were surprised to see Oswald when he arrived on Thursday because he had always asked Ruth's permission to visit when he came to Irving but had not done so on this occasion nor – apart from his first visit to Ruth's house on 4 October after returning from Mexico – had he ever come to Irving other than at weekends.

Ruth testified that both she and Marina thought that Oswald had come to Irving to be reconciled with Marina after the quarrel on the telephone, and she said that Oswald had talked to Marina and played with his daughter June on the lawn before dinner. Marina testified that she would not talk to him because she was too angry about his use of a false name, but that they all had evening dinner in the house, and after the meal Ruth and she were busy with their children. At some point Oswald must have gone into the garage on the floor of which, according to Marina in testimony, he had kept his rifle wrapped in a blanket, and he then packed the rifle in a long paper bag which he had constructed from materials at the Depository. Marina testified that he went to bed at about 9.00 p.m. but that she did not follow him until about 11.00 p.m. In the morning, Oswald arose early and dressed while talking to Marina who was feeding the new baby. He left his wedding ring in a cup on Marina's dressing table and $170 in a wallet in the bedroom, retaining less than $14 for himself. He did not leave a note with instructions for Marina in the event of his being killed or arrested, as Marina said he had done before his alleged attempt to murder the General some eight months previously.

After drinking some coffee in the kitchen, he walked about 40 yards to Frazier's house carrying the paper bag.Frazier then drove him to the Depository where he saw Oswald enter the building carrying the package which Frazier thought contained curtain rods. It would seem that Oswald must have taken his rifle up to the sixth floor as soon as possible, there to secrete it amongst the hundreds of cartons of books on that floor and, so far as is known, he then carried out his normal duties in the building. At some time prior to 12.30 p.m. and after perfecting the 'sniper's nest' with cartons of books to his Right and behind him, and preparing a carton on which to sit and others upon which to rest the rifle, he lày in wait for the President to pass.

It may fairly be said at this point:

A. (1) That the conspiracy had its beginnings in October 1956 when the young Oswald wrote – if he did – to the Socialist Party of America saying that he was a Marxist, and a few days later joined the Marines; a young man who would appear to the Russians to be ideally suited for Marxist encouragement and later substitution. (2) That in July 1959, Khrushchev decided to use an impostor for the Marine, the latter being persuaded to go to New Orleans where he may or may not have met Jack Ruby, recently arrived from Cuba. If this occurred, Ruby could have shown him his passport with his one-day trip shown thereon, and intimating that he had received instructions from Castro. Thereafter, Oswald may or may not have proceeded to Russia.

B. That beyond reasonable doubt the man calling himself Lee Harvey Oswald was (1) a KGB agent and impostor, (2) trained in a spy school in or near Minsk, (3) the assassin of the President and the murderer of Tippit, and (4) possibly in conspiracy with Jack Ruby.

C. That a person or persons in Washington did not wish to be made public: (1) the physical differences between the Marine and the assassin, (2) Hoover's memorandum of 3 June 1960 warning about possible imposture, (3) the activities of Albert Osborne, (4) the existence of John Caesar Grossi, (5) the existence and identity of the American male, and his activities, (6) the existence of clandestine KGB officer Kostin, (7) the existence of Nosenko and what he had to say, (8) the 'sensitive' nature of Jaggars-Chiles-Stovall and the impostor's espionage, and (9) the possibility of conspiracy in the attempted murder of the General.

D. That reliance for disclosure of the facts cannot be placed either upon the Report of the Commission or upon the Volumes of Testimony of Exhibits.

E. That the National Archives and the grave of the assassin may furnish additional evidence of conspiracy.

The next Chapter will discuss the escape of the assassin and the activities of Ruby immediately prior to and after the assassination, and the behaviour of his two 'dependents', George Senator and 'Larry' Crafard after the assassination. The Chapter will establish beyond reasonable doubt that Ruby was a conspirator in the escape of the assassin from Dallas and that he had premeditated the murder of the assassin.

12

The events following the assassination and Oswald's arrest have been described earlier but his behaviour after leaving the Depository must shortly be repeated and augmented, and Ruby's behaviour and that of his two 'dependents' prior to and after Oswald's arrest must be more fully discussed.

Leaving the Depository by the main entrance Oswald walked seven blocks east before he found a southbound Marsalis bus travelling towards and passing the Depository. Immediately behind the Marsalis bus was the southbound Beckley bus which ran on a parallel course west of the Marsalis bus. If Oswald had intended to go directly to his roominghouse at 1026 North Beckley Avenue, he would have taken the Beckley bus which had a stopping point outside the roominghouse, whereas the Marsalis bus passed no nearer than seven blocks to the east of the house. The conclusion must be that Oswald preferred the Marsalis bus because he was not going to his roominghouse but to another destination – presumably near Jack Ruby's apartment as his 23c. ticket would have deposited him two short blocks west of that apartment although, of course, he could have left the bus before or after the 23c. stop but in so doing would have attracted attention, however slight.

After travelling on the bus for only two blocks, apparently dismayed by the presence of Mrs. Bledsoe he alighted and walked to a nearby Greyhound Bus Terminal where he took a taxi, requesting the driver to take him to the 500 block on Beckley Avenue. To arrive at the 500 block the taxi had driven some distance past the roominghouse and, after passing the house, Oswald asked the driver to stop in the 700 block. Oswald then walked back about four blocks to his roominghouse on the 1,000 block where, after hurrying into the house, he collected his revolver, and rapidly changed his trousers and put on a zip-up jacket. (It is unlikely that he would have taken the revolver with him to the Depository in the morning as the bulge in his trouser pocket would have made it noticeable either in the Depository or on the Marsalis bus where his outer clothing was only a shirt and trousers.) Rushing from the house, he walked rapidly southeast in the direction of the 23c. bus stop and Ruby's apartment, and when only two blocks short of the bus stop and four blocks short of the apartment killed officer Tippit at about 1.16 p.m. If Oswald had not encountered Tippit, he could have reached the 23c. bus stop at about 1.19 p.m. or Ruby's apartment at about 1.23 p.m.

Shortly after he had been arrested on 22 November, Oswald told the Dallas police that he had taken a bus to a stop near his home, changed his clothes and then walked to the cinema. The next day he was presented with evidence that this story was untrue, and he then admitted that he had been on the Marsalis bus, alleged that he got off because it was moving slowly and, the taxi driver having reported his fare to the police, then admitted that he had taken a taxi to his roominghouse. Oswald had at first hoped that the police might fail to discover that he had been on the Marsalis bus and had changed his route after encountering Mrs. Bledsoe, and had also hoped that the taxi driver might not be discovered.

It was Ruby's custom to visit the offices of the principal Dallas newspapers almost daily in connection with advertisements aimed at attracting customers for his business; he also advertised regularly for waitresses. He is known to have been in a newspaper office in downtown Dallas from about 12.20 p.m. until some time after 1.00 p.m. on 22 November, and that from a window in the room in which he was seated, he could have seen Dealey Plaza and the window from which the assassin fired. It is also known that from that office at about 1.00 p.m. he telephoned Armstrong, the permanent handyman at 'The Carousel' and apparently not distraught said that 'if anything happens we are going to close the club', and that he would be in the club in about half an hour. This could have given him sufficient time to go from the newspaper office to the vicinity of his apartment and, after assisting or observing Oswald commencing the next stage of his escape, then to return to the club arriving at the time that he had told Armstrong, 1.30 p.m. It would seem that when Ruby left the newspaper office he believed that Oswald was proceeding unhindered on the bus towards the 23¢. bus stop, and on Ruby's arrival in the vicinity of the 23c. bus stop or his apartment at about 1.20 p.m. he would have expected to observe the arrival of Oswald on the bus and/or his departure by car. (As will be discussed later, it is possible that the assassin would have travelled from the vicinity of Ruby's apartment to a nearby private airfield whence he could have been flown, perhaps to Mexico.) When Oswald did not appear, and realising from the sirens of police cars rushing to the site of Tippit's murder that something untoward had occurred. Ruby then waited a few minutes before departing for his downtown club which he was to enter distraught and 'mumbling' just before or just after it was announced on radio and television between 1.45 p.m. and 1.50 p.m. that a man had been arrested in Oak Cliff.

As the time of Ruby's departure from the newspaper office has not been satisfactorily determined except that it was after 1.00 p.m., an alternative to Ruby going from the newspaper office to the vicinity of his apartment might be for him to have remained in the office, having delegated the removal of the assassin from the vicinity of the apartment either to the assassin himself. or to another trusted person, who perhaps would not appreciate the gravity of his action until some hours after the assassination; he would be implicated and thereby silenced.

When Ruby was to testify to the Commission he did not volunteer where he went or what he did between 1.00 p.m. and about 1.45 p.m., nor did the Commission ask him.

Oswald had been walking east towards the vicinity of Ruby's apartment when he encountered and shot Tippit at 1.16 p.m., and from the location of this murder he would have been able to reach the vicinity around 1.20 p.m. After shooting Tippit, however, Oswald ran away west, was seen at about 1.20 p.m. but was not to be seen again until about 1.42 p.m. when entering the cinema. The distance from the point where Oswald killed Tippit to the cinema is 0.6 of a mile and Oswald could have covered that distance walking or running in a few minutes. There is no way of knowing what he did between 1.20 p.m. and 1.42 p.m. but it is possible that during the unaccounted 22 minutes he telephoned Ruby or another at the apartment to explain his failure to arrive, when it was decided that Oswald should take cover in a local cinema until such time as a further appointment for escape could be kept. It would seem to be something more than a coincidence that Oswald should have entered the cinema at about 1.42 p.m. and that Ruby should have entered his downtown club at about 1.45 p.m., i.e. Oswald 'disappeared' for 22 minutes and Ruby's movements for about the same time are unknown – approximately from 1.20 p.m. to 1.42 p.m. for Oswald, and some time after 1.00 p.m. to 1.45 p.m. for Ruby.

Ruby's two employees at 'The Carousel', Larry Crafard and Andy Armstrong, the latter having been employed by Ruby for some years and having a criminal record including a conviction for narcotics, were to testify that Ruby arrived at the club in a distraught condition, Armstrong believing that Ruby had arrived just before 1.45 p.m. 'mumbling and incoherent', his first coherent words being that the club would be closed for three days. Crafard believed that Ruby had arrived after the news of a man's arrest at 1.50 p.m. had been broadcast over the radio, Crafard adding that Ruby 'was much nervouser than Andy (Armstrong) or I'. In any event, on entering the club Ruby immediately embarked upon a series of local and long-distance telephone calls to relatives and acquaintances in Dallas, Detroit, Michigan, Chicago, Illinois and Los Angeles. At about 4.30 p.m. he left the club for his sister's apartment in Dallas, but shortly afterwards he was again at the club making more local and long-distance telephone calls, before again leaving for his sister's apartment after having thrice strenuously pressed Crafard to accompany him; Crafard, who now was alone at 'The Carousel', had not understood why Ruby so urgently had wanted to get him away, and had declined the invitation. On the way to his sister's apartment, Ruby purchased a great quantity of food which, according to his sister, was enough for 12 to 20 people.

He carried the food to his sister's apartment and it would appear that he intended to stay there for some days, but after a further series of local and long-distance telephone calls from his sister's apartment, by 7.30 p.m. and possibly as a result of one or more of these calls he changed his mind. While at his sister's apartment he ate sparingly, became ill and vomited, and it would seem that it was on the early evening of 22 November that either he was instructed or himself decided to silence the assassin. He left his sister's apartment at about 7.30 p.m. and, with Oswald in the forefront of his mind, engaged in a number of activities that were to culminate in the murder of the assassin. At least five people were to say that on the evening of 22 November they thought that they had seen Ruby in the police station before 9.00 p.m., one of them being a police detective who said that not only had he seen him in the early evening but again saw him on the third floor just before the midnight 'show-up' in the basement. Knowing that he could not deny being present at the 'show-up', Ruby was to testify that he did not arrive at the police station until 11.15 p.m., but the evidence indicates that he was not telling the truth, not wishing it to be known that so soon after his visit to his sister's apartment he had displayed such an interest in the assassin. It is not known what else Ruby may have done between 7.30 p.m. and 9.00 p.m., but it is known that he was back in his own apartment at 9.00 p.m. when he again made several long-distance calls. One of these calls was to his brother Hyman in Chicago and, according to Hyman, Ruby said that he was disturbed about the situation in Dallas, and that he might sell his business and return to Chicago.

Later that evening and probably shortly after 9.00 p.m., Ruby went to a synagogue arriving towards the end of the service to join in the post-service refreshments. A Rabbi who greeted him was to say that Ruby did not mention the assassination; Ruby may have had an assignment to meet someone there. Ruby testified that after leaving the synagogue he drove downtown and on the way heard a radio announcement that the police were working overtime. He stopped at a delicatessen and bought some sandwiches and soft drinks, but upon telephoning a detective in Fritz's 'Homicide' office to offer his refreshments he was told that the officers had eaten. It seems that he had hoped to enter Fritz's office, with the possibility of viewing the assassin. On leaving the delicatessen Ruby drove to the police station and by 11.30 p.m. he is known to have been on the third floor, where reporters had gathered near the homicide office in which Oswald was being interrogated. Although earlier in the evening the police had allowed newsmen into the building without questioning, they now had guards posted on the doors to prevent unauthorised entry. The detective who had seen Ruby earlier said that Ruby was carrying a notepad and professing to be a translater for the Israeli press. A newsman who knew Ruby gave the following description of his encounter with him at the police station: 'I saw Jack and two out-of-site reporters whom I did not know, leave the elevator door and proceed toward those television cameras, to go around the corner where Captain Fritz's office was. Jack walked between them. These two out-of-state reporters had big press cards pinned on their coats, great big red ones, I think they said 'President Kennedy's Visit to Dallas – Press', or something like that. And Jack didn't have one, but the man on either side of him did. And they walked pretty rapidly from the elevator area past the policeman, and Jack was bent over like this – writing on a piece of paper, and talking to one of the reporters, and pointing to something on the piece of paper, he was kind of hunched over.' It would appear that Ruby had employed a trick in a determined effort to avoid being refused admittance and that it had succeeded.

Films that were taken on the third floor show that Ruby was near the 'Homicide' office just before midnight, when Chief of Police Curry and District Attorney Wade made their announcement that Oswald would be shown to the Press in the basement. When Oswald was brought down to the basement for the midnight 'show-up' to the Press another film shows that Ruby, pencil and notepad in hand, was now in the basement and standing on a table at the back of the room with other reporters. After a brief appearance, Oswald was taken away but Ruby remained in the room to hear Wade answer questions from the Press, Wade saying that Oswald would probably be moved to the County jail at the beginning of the following week. When questioning was over, Ruby followed Wade out of the room and said to him, 'Hi! Henry, don't you know me. I am Jack Ruby. I run the "Vegas Club"'; Wade had never heard of Ruby. Ruby then obtained a night telephone number of radio station KLIF, telephoned KLIF and told them that he would like to bring them some sandwiches and cold drinks; he was invited to their premises. He then observed a reporter holding open a telephone line and trying to attract the attention of Wade; Ruby then directed Wade to the reporter who proceeded to interview him. Ruby again telephoned KLIF and offered to secure for them an interview with Wade and, by calling the latter to the telephone, KLIF were able to obtain a telephonic interview. Ruby then left the police station and drove to KLIF arriving at about 1.45 a.m. where he distributed some of his refreshments and remained in the studio for about 45 minutes making friends with some of the staff. On leaving KLIF, at about 2.30 a.m. Ruby went to a point near his Club where he met a police officer who was sitting in a parked car with another stripper from 'The Carousel'. All three were to testify that they talked for about an hour in the car and that they were all crying because of the assassination. Ruby then left them and drove to a newspaper office where he told some of the employees about his visit to the police station the previous evening and that he had set up a telephone interview of Wade by KLIF.

It would seem that Ruby had been ingratiating himself with Wade and the news media who might later be able to tell him exactly when Oswald would be moved from the police jail to the County jail. Wade was to testify that when he heard on his car radio on 24 November that Oswald had been murdered by a 'business man' but before Ruby's name was announced, Wade had said to himself, 'That must be Jack Ruby the way he looked (after the show-up). He looked kind of wild to me down there Friday night the way he was running everywhere, you know, and I said to myself that must be him.'

On the morning of 22 November there had appeared in one of the local newspapers a full page advertisement headed 'Welcome to Dallas Mr. Kennedy' and under which was asked a series of derogatory political questions of the President. At the bottom of the page appeared the name Bernard Weissman and under this name a Dallas P.O. Box No., the whole surrounded by *a thick black border*. On seeing this advertisement on the morning of 22 November, Ruby became greatly agitated by its hostile attitude, the black border and the Jewish name, because it indicated to Ruby that somebody in Dallas knew what was about to happen and that a Jew would be involved. This was an incipient threat to the secrecy of Ruby's involvement in the escape and with unpredictable consequences for Ruby, such as anonymous disclosure or blackmail. He telephoned his lawyer and questioned newsmen in an endeavour to find out if they had heard of Weissman, and when nobody could help him he checked the telephone directories, all to no avail.

The advertisement had been drawn up by Weissman and a group of young men, and had been approved and paid for by a few Dallas residents who, although opposed to the policies of Kennedy, knew nothing of the black border which Weissman was to testify had been added by himself only to draw attention to the advertisement.

That day or earlier, Ruby had noticed a billboard poster in a street, the poster being headed 'Impeach Earl Warren'. Ruby had never heard of Warren but now recollected that the poster had at the bottom a Massachusetts P.O. Box No.; he realised there existed a similarity between this Box No. and the one in the advertisement. Ruby thought that, if he could prove an association between the persons who had inserted the advertisement and the persons who were responsible for the poster, he could discover the identity of the person or persons who knew that he was implicated. He might then be able to incriminate others and possibly escape having to silence the assassin.

After leaving the policeman and the stripper outside 'The Carousel' at about 3.00 a.m., Saturday 23 November, Ruby returned to his apartment where his flatmate, George Senator, was in bed. He roused Senator, told him to dress and ordered him to drive downtown with him. He telephoned Crafard at 'The Carousel' and told him to bring the Polaroid instant camera from the club, and to meet him and Senator outside the club in a few minutes. After driving downtown and picking up Crafard they went in Ruby's car to the poster in the street, where Ruby instructed Crafard to take three flashlight photographs of the poster. The three men then drove to a coffee shop where for the next half-hour Ruby continued to discuss the advertisement and the poster. On leaving the coffee shop they all drove to the Dallas Post Office to find out if the Box No. in the advertisement existed and, if it did, to try to discover who had rented it. Ruby discovered that there was a Box of that number and found it to be full of mail. He rang the night bell and spoke to a postal employee through a 'little hole' asking for the name of the man who had rented the Box, but was advised to seek information next day from the man in charge. Ruby then dropped Crafard off at 'The Carousel' at about 6.00 a.m. and returned with Senator to their apartment. Crafard was to testify that at some point during this episode Ruby, referring to the Box Nos. in the advertisement and the poster, 'said something about the numbers were the same if turned around a little bit'.

During the episode or after returning to his apartment, Ruby wrote on an old envelope the Box No. of the poster in the top Left hand corner and the Box No. of the advertisement in the top Right hand corner, but underneath the Box No. of the advertisement he wrote a slightly different number; he could not have made a mistake because he had the advertisement in his pocket. He then wrote sideways on the envelope the word MON. As will be shown later, when Ruby was fruitlessly endeavouring to connect the Box Nos. on the unassociated advertisement and the poster, he was trying to use the same code that the assassin used to encode a certain telephone number in his notebook – turning numbers around and using the word MON. The envelope was found among Ruby's possessions after he had murdered the assassin; the Commission knew about the envelope but say in their Report that MON appeared to be a man's name.

Senator was to testify that on the morning of Sunday 24 November, Ruby – who had been increasingly distraught since early Saturday morning, was still 'mumbling' and more distraught about the assassination than anyone else known to Senator – left their apartment around 11.00 a.m., and that he himself went for coffee to the Eatwell Cafe opposite 'The

Carousel' and near the police station in downtown Dallas. Upon hearing that Oswald had been shot but *before* the name of the killer was announced, Senator telephoned a lawyer friend, visited his house and – Ruby in the meantime having been named on radio and television as the killer – then proceeded with the lawyer to the police station where Ruby was now incarcerated. When asked in testimony why he had rung the lawyer 'just to give him the local news' as Senator had testified, and why he had not rung up Ruby, who had told him before leaving the apartment that he was going to 'The Carousel', or crossed the road to speak to him, Senator replied that he did not think of ringing Ruby to tell him that Oswald had been shot. It would seem that Senator might have suspected that when Ruby left their apartment he would endeavour to kill the assassin; Senator would have been unable to prevent him.

On arrival at the police station Senator identified himself as Ruby's flatmate and was shortly interrogated by the police before being handed to the FBI for extensive questioning. He had volunteered to swear an affidavit for the police, and in the affidavit he said that he had been awakened by Ruby at about 3.00 p.m. on Saturday morning and that Ruby was crying – something Senator had never before seen – and 'too sad' about the assassination of the President to go to bed, with the result that Senator got up and after dressing drove to downtown Dallas with Ruby to visit the Southland Hotel Coffee Shop where, giving the lie the aspect of truth by adding irrelevant detail, he said that 'he had some coffee and Jack had some grapefruit juice' before returning to their apartment. (XXI.427-432.)

Senator had omitted from the affidavit that after Ruby had awakened him they had collected Crafard, that Crafard had photographed the poster, that they all then proceeded to the coffee shop where for half an hour they discussed the advertisement and the poster, that they all then went to the Post Office, and that Ruby and he had then dropped Crafard off at 'The Carousel' before returning to their apartment. After offering the affidavit, later that day, 24 November, Senator was interrogated at length by the FBI and gain omitted the 'Polaroid episode', following the form of his earlier affidavit.

When the FBI were interviewing him, they must have been

aware of most of the history of the assassin and his wife prior to the assassination two days before, and they must have known that Marina had obtained her entrance M.I. visa to the United States on 15 March 1962. Around that time Ruby had invited Senator to live with him in an apartment on Marsalis Street, and Senator was to remain there until some time in August 1962. The FBI report of their interview with Senator says, ' ... he (Senator) added he occasionally, when low on funds, would be asked by Ruby to come and stay a day or two with him until he got back on his feet, but he claimed that he never actually lived with him until about 1 November 1963 when he moved into the apartment of Ruby, Apartment 207, 223 South Ewing, Dallas, Texas'. (Apparently 207 was an FBI error for 206.)

It will be seen that Senator misled the FBI about his residence with Ruby on Marsalis Street, the truth being that Senator moved in to live with Ruby around 15 March 1962 and was to remain with him until some time in August 1962. In testimony, Senator was not asked to explain the deception of the FBI about his five months stay with Ruby. (It was in August 1962 that the FBI in Fort Worth had their second and final interview with Oswald and gave his file a 'closed status'. Also in August 1962, Senator, then out of work had obtained employment as a postcard and novelty vendor from a man who was a friend of Ruby. His tasks were to fill up postcard racks in stationery shops and to endeavour to sell novelties, and with this employment went a 'box-like' Volkswagon microbus with windows only at the back and in which Senator carried his postcards and novelties. When asked to explain in testimony to the Commission why he had left Ruby's Marsalis Street apartment in August 1962 he said that Ruby was 'not too clean' about the apartment and that as he now had a job he could afford to live away from Ruby; Senator did, in fact, join another man in another apartment. He testified that shortly after moving from Ruby's apartment on Marsalis Street in August 1962, *he* had noticed a new block of apartments being built at 223 South Ewing and, having told Ruby about this building, Ruby moved into apartment 206 and Senator with another man moved into apartment 207, the moves of Ruby and himself taking place at the end of November 1962. Ruby was, therefore, living alone from some time in August 1962 until the latter part of November 1962, the period during which Oswald left Leslie Welding in Fort Worth, and – his FBI file having a 'closed status' – obtained employment at Jaggars-Chiles-Stovall on 12 October 1962, presumably completing his 'Cuba Crisis' espionage before the latter part of November 1962. It was from the middle of October to early November 1962 that for two periods totalling 18 days Oswald lived at an address in Dallas that, according to the Report, the Commission were unable to discover.

When asked in testimony how he could have forgotten everything about the 'Polaroid episode' but had remembered the early morning visit to the coffee shop with the 'too sad' to go to bed Ruby where he, Ruby and Crafard had been seen by others, Senator explained that although the events of that early Saturday morning were unique in his association with Ruby, his omission of the 'Polaroid episode' to the police and the FBI were due to his being in a state of 'shock' on learning that his flatmate had murdered Oswald. 'Shock' could in no way explain his failure of memory about his five months stay with Ruby on Marsalis Street, and it would seem that Senator knew that this five months was significant, and wished to depreciate it.

It would seem that Senator was also aware of the significance of the 'Polaroid episode' and of Ruby's attempts to associate the P.O. Box Nos. by a method of decoding, and had wished at first to protect Ruby by eliminating the episode from the record. It is apparent that when he swore the false affidavit and shortly thereafter omitted the episode from his statement to the FBI, he knew that Crafard was on his way to hide in a remote part of Michigan some 800 miles from Dallas, and that he believed that Crafard – in Dallas known only as 'Larry' – would never be discovered. The omission of the episode from the affidavit and from the statement to the FBI both made on the afternoon of 24 November indicate not only that Senator knew of its significance *but knew that Crafard who could contradict him had fled Dallas some 22 hours earlier.*

A few hours after the episode and after returning to 'The Carousel', Crafard had indeed fled and had obtained a series of lifts to hide in his sister's cabin in the remote part of Michigan. His first long lift on the hitch-hike was given to him by a man from the fairground, known to him and possibly to Ruby. During his flight Crafard never told any of the many drivers who gave him lifts that he had been employed by Ruby even though during the three days of lifts he must have heard that Ruby had killed Oswald. ('Fled' is the word used by Commission Counsel in an Interrogatory about Ruby to the CIA, and Crafard is described therein as 'a close confidante of Ruby'.)

Crafard's name and whereabouts would never have been discovered had it not been for his oversight in leaving the address of a relative in the waste paper basket at 'The Carousel'. When discovered at the cabin and questioned by the FBI on 28 November 1963 he disclosed his employment with Ruby and the whole of the 'Polaroid episode', thereby disclosing the falsity of Senator's volunteered affidavit to the police and his signed statement to the FBI. (XIX.353-359.)

When Crafard's information to the FBI in Michigan was relayed to the FBI and the Secret Service in Dallas, the Secret Service interviewed Senator on 3 December 1963, and the FBI re-interviewed him on 20 December 1963. Senator was now forced to disclose the 'Polaroid episode' and his unbroken residence with Ruby for about five months on Marsalis Street. (XXI.433-440.)

Both Senator and Crafard testified at length but, in view of Senator's affidavit and statement to the FBI, reliance cannot be placed upon his testimony of his and Ruby's activities at any time before or after the assassination. The testimony of Crafard cannot be relied upon in its entirety for in testimony he tried to explain his flight by saying that he had for some time wished to visit his sister, and that another reason for leaving had been that he had telephoned Ruby about two hours after he had been dropped off at 'The Carousel' after the 'Polaroid episode' in order to ask Ruby about food for Ruby's dogs that were kept at the club. He testified that Ruby abused him on the telephone for waking him up, and that this had contributed to his leaving Dallas. He was unable to explain why before fleeing 'The Carousel' and Dallas he had not called Ruby on the telephone or left a note for him saying that he was about to depart, even though it was pointed out to him by Counsel how kind Ruby appeared to have been to him. Senator, then living with Ruby in Apartment 206, having moved from 207 on 1 November, testified that the telephone in the apartment shared by him and Ruby was near his room, that the extension cord would not reach into Ruby's bedroom, that he could have heard the telephone ringing if Crafard had telephoned Ruby, but that he had heard neither the telephone ringing nor Ruby abusing Crafard. Crafard volunteered a third excuse for his flight by alleging that Ruby had promised him a salary but had done nothing about it.

Neither Senator nor Crafard had ever been in trouble with the police, but both were penniless and dependent upon Ruby. Undoubtedly aware of Ruby's reputation and connections it would seem that they feared for their lives if they said anything – even in sworn testimony – that might show that the murder of the assassin had been premeditated by Ruby. It is interesting that in testimony Crafard said that it had appeard 'odd' to him that Ruby was more 'excited' over the advertisement and the poster than over the assassination, thus contradicting Senator's statements to the FBI and in testimony that Ruby was so progressively distressed by the death of the President that Senator feared that Ruby was becoming of unsound mind.

After Ruby had killed the assassin, according to the testimony of Senator and the statements and testimony of others, Senator feared for his own life and was afraid of being 'out after dark', but 'not as afraid in daylight' and afraid of being in 'an isolated place'. For ten days after the murder of the assassin he slept in a different bed every night and never returned to apartment 206. After this ten days he was accommodated by a married couple – whom he had known for some time and who understood his fear – until some five weeks later when, still fearful, he left Dallas forever. In testimony, he was unable satisfactorily to explain why he was immediately in fear for his life, as he had testified, he believed that Ruby had been emotionally activated when he slew the assassin, suggesting only that having lived with Ruby he might be killed by a 'crank'.

The 'Polaroid episode' together with the behaviour of Senator and Crafard thereafter is of importance because it indicates that (a) Ruby was premeditating the murder of the assassin in the early hours of Saturday morning, 23 November, after becoming ill and in his sister's apartment the night before and thereafter frequenting the police station, (b) Ruby ordered Crafard to disappear because he knew too much, and (c) Ruby and the impostor knew the same method of coding.

On Saturday, 23 November, Ruby appears to have remained in his apartment until about 12.30 p.m. before driving downtown to Dealey Plaza. There he introduced himself to a reporter from Radio Station KRLD who was working inside a mobile unit on the Plaza. The reporter mentioned to Ruby that he had heard of Ruby's help to KLIF in obtaining an interview with Wade the previous night, and Ruby then pointed out Captain Fritz and Chief of Police Curry who were in the vicinity, thus enabling the reporter to obtain an interview with and photographs of these officers. Ruby then discussed with the reporter the possible time for the transfer of Oswald from the police jail to the County jail.

During the afternoon of Saturday, 23 November, Ruby twice telephoned KLIF to ask the announcer if he knew when Oswald was being transferred and, when the announcer told him that he did not know, Ruby said that he would attempt to locate District Attorney Wade. Later that afternoon Ruby was again inside the police station and was again seen by at least five reporters, one of whom said that he saw Ruby enter an office in which the District Attorney was working.

Late on Saturday evening Ruby visited his sister at her apartment; she had always been the closest to him of all his relatives. From her apartment he made one more long-distance call to an old friend and, after bidding his sister farewell, left her to join Senator in apartment 206 arriving there at about 1.30 a.m. on Sunday morning 24 November. About one hour later, the threats – apparently from one man but with another man present – to kill the assassin were received at the office of the FBI and the Sheriff, and transmitted to the police. Later that morning and after allegedly accepting a toll call at 10.19 a.m. from 'Little Lynn', Ruby left the apartment to make his final unauthorised entrance to the police station, arriving in the basement one minute before the assassin arrived by elevator from the third floor.

It can be seen from the above facts that Ruby had frequented the police station from shortly after the arrest of the assassin until he killed him, and that the jury at the trial of Ruby in Dallas were right in finding beyond reasonable doubt that he had premeditated the murder of the assassin.

To kill the assassin, Ruby had taken into the basement the .38 Cobra revolver which he usually kept either in the glove compartment or in the trunk of his car. After the murder he was taken to the police jail where his clothes and possessions were removed; he had more than $2,000 in a pocket and was wearing an expensive suit, shirt, hat and other clothes including a 100% silk tie, a diamond Le Coultre wristwatch, a gold ring with three diamonds, a gold-plated tie clasp and a French Melville belt; a further $1,500 was later found in the trunk of his car.

At this point the reader may have accepted that Ruby was to assist the assassin to escape from Dallas, but he may wish to know how that escape from the vicinity of Ruby's apartment might have been effected.

Red Bird private airfield was about $4\frac{1}{2}$ miles and an almost direct drive from 223 South Ewing. This airfield was as large as the public airfield at Love Field and was surrounded by hangars for private planes. If it was intended that the assassin should escape from Dallas by plane, a simple method would have been for him to enter Senator's microbus without being seen in that somewhat deserted area and then, hiding in the back, being driven by someone to Red Bird and deposited at the back of a hangar. After a non-stop flight to Mexico a plane could land on a secret 'narcotics' or other landing strip; further arrangements would be made to remove the assassin from Mexico, perhaps with the aid of the American male. It would appear unlikely that the assassin would have driven himself as the 'escape' vehicle would be found abandoned and subsequently traced.

Immediately after the assassination, the Dallas police could not search the tens of thousands of houses and automobiles in Dallas, and could not ground every public and private plane at Love Field and Red Bird. As it was to transpire, from the time of the assassination at 12.30 p.m. until 2.00 p.m. on 22 November most of the 1,200 Dallas policemen and other security forces were searching the Depository and downtown areas, and at no time was Red Bird airfield – about 7 miles from the Depository – either watched or closed.

If this reconstruction is correct, the assassin would have arrived in the vicinity of Ruby's apartment before 1.30 p.m., by 1.40 p.m. he could have been at Red Bird, and by 1.45 p.m. en route for Mexico or elsewhere. (The aforementioned British spy, George Blake, escaped from England by plane but in his case not only did he have to scale the wall of a high security prison but left Britain on a regular airline service, accomplishing this before his escape from the prison was discovered.)

At 1.00 p.m. on a day in late December 1973, I travelled by taxi down the Marsalis bus route to the 23c. bus-stop, walked west to the site of the Tippit killing and then east to 223 South Ewing. I was first impressed by the fact that the apartment block comprised rather small apartments, was in a rather deserted area in the outskirts of Dallas, and was downgrade from the apartment that Ruby had been occupying in September 1959 and which I had already seen. Although I walked round the block and looked in many windows, I saw nobody and apparently was not observed. Between 1.20 p.m. and 1.30 p.m. on the day of the assassination, even less interest in a stranger would have been evinced for the occupants of the apartments would have been listening to their radios or watching television; it seemed to me unlikely that an undistinguished youth would have had difficulty in entering unobserved a strategically parked car. I was then driven for about ten minutes on an almost direct and somewhat deserted road to Red Bird airfield, and once there it appeared to me that 223 South Ewing had been selected in August 1962 as the escape point from Dallas – direct and slow Marsalis bus to the 23c. bus stop, direct and speedier transport to Red Bird airfield, and terminating in a flight by plane while the authorities would be searching the Depository and downtown Dallas for the assassin. This method of travel is not dissimilar to Oswald's (?) zig-zag journey from New Orleans in September 1959, first by slow freighter to Le Havre, then by the most rapid possible transport to London, and terminating in a plane flight to Helsinki and the Russian Embassy in that city.

It is possible that, as Ruby would not have chosen to take anyone into his confidence, the assassin might have entered or hidden in the vicinity of Ruby's apartment, Ruby himself driving him to Red Bird after dark. It is interesting in this connection that Senator was to testify that he was away from the apartment from the early morning of 22 November until after nightfall.

The speculation about escape by plane from Dallas is not without foundation because – as already mentioned – after the assassination the FBI and the New Orleans police were greatly interested in 'Captain' David Ferrie, the one-time aircraft tutor of the young Lee Harvey Oswald in the New Orleans Civil Air Patrol and who later was found dead the day before James Garrison, the District Attorney of New Orleans, was to arrest him on a charge of conspiracy to assassinate the President. The FBI also interviewed a friend of the young Oswald who was in the Air Patrol and knew Ferrie, and he was asked if he knew whether Ferrie ever made 'long flights'.

In testimony, Ruby was not to be asked to account for his movements between 1.00 p.m. and about 1.45 p.m. on the day of the assassination, Friday 22 November, but in testimony Senator was asked where he was when he first heard of the assassination. He answered that he had left Ruby's apartment early to go to work and before Ruby ' ... who was sleeping ... I was in a bar having a liquid lunch. I was uptown. I was in a bar and had a couple of beers for lunch instead of eating lunch, and some chap walked in, who I don't know and he drove up with his car and he had the radio on, and as he walked in he said, "The President was shot." And I hollered, "You're kidding." He says, "No; I am not kidding." So we got outside and this is all going on on this car radio we listen to'. Senator testified that he never saw Ruby at all on the day of the assassination, that Ruby had not attempted to contact him on that day and that Ruby could not have contacted him because he (Senator) was 'around'. When asked what he meant by 'around', he said he was ' ... around town, no particular place.' When asked whether he was going from bar to bar, he replied, 'No, not bar to bar. I had been at a couple of bars. I was with a friend of mine that night and we went out, we had a couple of beers and were so disgusted, if you can picture the overall picture of Friday night in the city of

Dallas after the occurrence, what happened that afternoon or late that morning, the city was, I don't know how to describe it, morgue like. They were brooding. Everybody was brooding, a sad affair'.

It is to be noted that Senator changed the subject from questions about his movements during the morning and early afternoon of 22 November, by saying, 'I was with a friend of mine that night ... '.

Although Senator testified that he got up early on Friday morning 22 November in order to go to work, he said only that he had been at a couple of bars around lunchtime. He did not identify the bars, the people he met or the people on whom he might have called in connection with his business from early morning 22 November until about 7.30 p.m. on that day, at which time he was able to recollect that he had met some named people; when interviewed they were not able to recollect seeing him at any time on the day of the assassination, but remembered meeting him on the following day. It would seem that the Commission should have asked for full details of his movements from early morning of Friday 22 November, and should have established the whereabouts of his microbus before about 1.30 p.m. on 22 November. While in no way suggesting that Senator would have been commissioned by Ruby to transport someone to Red Bird, if that airfield was to be the point of escape 'from Dallas, transport by unobtrusive 'box-like' microbus would have been suitable. After the assassination Senator did no more work for his 'postcard and novelty' employer, but the latter did not require the return of his microbus, Senator retaining it in his possession until he left Dallas five weeks later.

The method of coding employed by the assassin to encode telephone numbers in his notebook is described in Appendix E to this book, and it will show that the numbers were intended to be decoded after the assassination. The encoding was, apparently, for the purpose of compromising others and not for the use of the assassin.

The story is now told and it is for the reader to decide for himself who knew the truth and why it was concealed. In particular, he may wish to speculate as to the identity of the person who authorised to be placed in the National Archives the material identifying the approximately 35 years old American male, who ordered that no enquiry should be made to discover his identity, who instructed Helms to submit a second affidavit to the Commission, and who authorised the omission of his first affidavit from the Volumes of Testimony. In addition, he may wonder who authorised Hoover's warning against imposture to be withheld from the Commission − if it was − and why the Commission were not informed of the differing heights, the differing scars and the apparent absence of mastoidectomy. Furthermore, he may wish to know why the 'sensitive' nature of Jaggars-Chiles-Stovall is not mentioned in the Report nor why the assassin's espionage activities in that firm were not mentioned. The reader may be puzzled by the brevity with which the 75 years old Albert Osborne *alias* John Howard Bowen is treated in the Report and why John Caesar Grossi *alias* Jack Leslie Bowen is omitted from the Report, and he may wonder whether there existed any relationship between these two men other than the similarity of their aliases and their friendship with the assassin.

Whatever the reason may have been for the concealment of the truth, the events of the last eleven years indicate that some person or persons in the United States made an error of judgement that was to result in ever increasing international and domestic violence.

Had the truth of the murder of President Kennedy and its underlying aim been disclosed by the Report, it is my view that the events of these years − disastrous for the free world − would have been avoided, and that if the Americans and their allies are now alerted to their peril, world peace is within their grasp.

APPENDIX A

TESTIMONY OF BELMONT UNDER QUESTIONING BY COUNSEL HANKIN AND STERN (V.6-14):

COUNSEL:	We were getting, Mr. Belmont, to the question of whether you had been personally involved in the investigation since the assassination.
BELMONT:	I said I have indeed.
COUNSEL:	Yes. As a part of that you have reviewed in detail the investigation made prior to the assassination?
BELMONT:	Yes.
COUNSEL:	I show you a letter with attached memorandum which has been marked for identification Commission Exhibit No. 833. Can you identify this document, Mr. Belmont? (The document referred to was marked Commission Exhibit No. 833 for identification.)
BELMONT:	This is a letter transmitted on April 6, 1964, to Mr. Rankin by the FBI with enclosure answering a number of questions which the Commission posed to the FBI.
COUNSEL:	Did you supervise the preparation of this letter?
BELMONT:	Yes.
COUNSEL:	And you have reviewed it and are familiar with it?
BELMONT:	Yes.
COUNSEL:	We have covered in your answers to Mr. Dulles and Mr. McCloy a good deal of the material in here. (Author's note: McCloy's questions are not relevant to this testimony.) I would like briefly to touch upon several of the questions, the more important questions, regarding the nature of the FBI's interest in Lee Harvey Oswald at various times, and I would like you to refer to each question that I indicate but not read your answer. Paraphrase it. I think we have had a good deal of the specific detail but what I am interested in is a description from your examination of the investigation as it was carried on, of the nature of the FBI interest in Oswald.
	I would like to turn to the first question in which we asked-
	You mean by that you could get, we could get, a better

307

idea from paraphrasing the answer than we could get from the exact answer itself?

COUNSEL: I think he might be able to highlight the answer. We have the exact answer on the record, and I thought it might –

CHAIRMAN Well, highlight it, if there is anything in addition I would think that would be relevant and pertinent. But to ask him to paraphrase that which he has done with great meticulousness would seem to me to be abortive and would take a lot of our time, and I don't see what it would prove. If you have anything in addition that you want to ask him, if you want to ask him if there is anything in addition he has not put in there, that is all right. But to just ask him to paraphrase answers that have been done with great care would seem to me to be confusing the record, and serve no purpose.

COUNSEL: I might ask, Mr. Belmont, whether there is anything you would like to add or amplify in these questions?

BELMONT: I believe the answers speak for themselves, although in view of Mr. McCloy's questions a little while ago, I would be very happy to make clear our approach to this matter. For example, the fact that our interest in defectors, in this case, is shown by the fact that in early November 1959 we opened a file on Oswald based on the newspaper publicity as to his defection. And the fact that he had applied to renounce his citizenship. We checked our files then to see was this a man we had a record on, and found that we had a fingerprint record solely based on his enlistment in the Marines.

We had no other record on him but we placed a stop or a flash notice in our fingerprint files, at that time so that if he should come back into the country unbeknownst to us and get into some sort of trouble we would be immediately notified. That is our opening interest in the case with the thought in mind that should he come back to the country we would want to know from him whether he had been enlisted by Soviet intelligence in some manner.

That is our procedure because of our experience that these things have happened, and we consider it our responsibility to settle that issue whenever we can.

COUNSEL: Could you explain, Mr. Belmont, this procedure of placing a stop in the files that you just referred to?

BELMONT: We merely notified our indentification division to place what we call a flash notice in the man's fingerprint file, which means that should he be arrested and the fingerprints be sent to the FBI, that the appropriate division, in this case the domestic intelligence division, would be notified that the man had been arrested, for what and where he was arrested, thus enabling us to center our attention on him.

Our next interest in this man arose as a result of the fact that his mother had sent, I believe, $25 to him in Moscow, so we went to her in April 1960 and we talked to her. At that time she told us that he had told her that he would possibly attend the Albert Schweitzer College ' in Switzerland.

So as a follow up, we had our legal attache in Paris make inquiry to see whether he had enrolled in this college. The resultant check showed that while they had expected him and a deposit had been placed that he did not show up at the college.

COUNSEL: I think that is all covered in quite adequate detail in the answer to the first question.

DULLES: I have one question I would like to put to you on the first question and answer in your letter of April 6, in Exhibit 833 – the Bureau's letter of April 6. You refer, first, to the fact that the first news you got about Oswald was from a news service item, and then later on at the bottom of the second full paragraph you state, 'A file concerning Oswald was prepared and as communications were received from other U.S. Government agencies those communications were placed in his file.'

The record may show the other communications, I guess our record does show, but do you feel that you adequately were advised by the State Department as this case developed or by the CIA or other agencies that might have known about it?

BELMONT: Yes. We received a number of communications from other agencies, and we set up a procedure whereby we periodically checked the State Department passport file to be kept advised of his activities or his dealings with the Embassy in Moscow so that on a periodic basis we were sure we had all information in the State Department file.

We received communications from the Navy, and from other agencies.

DULLES: Is there any general procedure with respect to Americans abroad who get into trouble. Do you get informed so in case they come back you can take adequate precautionary measures? Is that established SOP?

BELMONT: Yes, Mr. Dulles. We do receive such information, and if we pick up the information initially as we did here, from press reports or otherwise, we go to the other agencies and ask them whether they have any information and establish

	an interest there so that if they have not voluntarily furnished us the information they will do so upon our request.
DULLES:	Thank you.
COUNSEL:	On page 3, Mr. Belmont, in the answer to question No. 3, the second paragraph, could you tell us why the FBI preferred to interview Oswald after he had established residence and why it was not preferable to interview him upon his arrival in New York?
BELMONT:	This is a matter of experience. Generally speaking when an individual such as Oswald arrives back in the country and the press is there, there is an unusual interest in him. Immigration and Naturalization Service has a function to perform, and we prefer, unless there is a matter of urgency, to let the individual become settled in residence. It is a much better atmosphere to conduct the interview, and to get the information that we seek. If it is a matter of urgency, we will interview him immediately upon arrival.
COUNSEL:	On page 5, Mr. Belmont, in your answer to question No. 6, was it ordinary procedure for Agent Fain to re-interview Oswald so soon after his first interview under the circumstances? Is there anything unusual about that?
BELMONT:	There is nothing unusual whatsoever. Agent Fain interviewed Oswald on June 16, 1963-1962, I believe it was, was in not?
CHAIRMAN	Yes; 1962.
BELMONT:	And was not satisfied that he had received all the information he wanted nor that it was a matter that should be closed at that time.
	Therefore, he set out a lead to re-interview Oswald, and after an appropriate period he went back and re-interviewed him. This is within the prerogative of the investigative agent, and certainly if he was not satisfied with the first interview it was his duty and responsibility to pursue the matter until he was satisfied.
COUNSEL:	In your answer to question No. 5, does the response of Oswald to the question why he went to Russia seem typical to you of the returned defector, or unusual?
BELMONT:	There is no such thing as a typical response. Each case is an individual case, and is decided on its merits and on the background of the individual, and the circumstances surrounding it.
COUNSEL:	Would it be usual for the defector to agree to advise you if he got a contact? Are they generally that cooperative?
BELMONT:	We ask them because we want to know, and the purpose of our interview with him was to determine whether he

had been recruited by the Soviet intelligence, and we asked him whether he would tell us if he was contacted here in this country. He replied he would. Whether he meant it is a question. However, you must bear in mind that this man, I believe it was when he was interviewed in July or 1961 in the American Embassy, the interviewing official there said it was apparent that he had learned his lesson the hard way, and that he had a new concept of the American way of life, and apparently had decided that Russia was not for him.

When we interviewed him likewise he told us that he had not enjoyed his stay in Russia. He likewise commented that he had not enjoyed his stay in the Marines. So that in direct answer to your question, it is customary for us in such a case as this, to ask the man if he will report a contact, and it is customary for him to say yes, because frankly, he would be putting himself in a rather bad light if he didn't say yes.

COUNSEL: Turning to —

DULLES: Could I ask a question there: Do I correctly read your report and those of your agents to the general effect that you had no evidence that there was any attempt to recruit Oswald in the United States?

BELMONT: No evidence whatsoever.

COUNSEL: Question 8, Mr. Belmont, on page 5, sets out the information from a report by Agent Hosty regarding alleged Fair Play for Cuba Committee activity by Oswald while he was still residing in Dallas. Have you found that an investigation was conducted to determine whether that was accurate and do you think it should have been investigated?

BELMONT: As to whether he was active with the Fair Play for Cuba Committee in Dallas? We did check. We have rather excellent coverage of such activities. There is no evidence whatsoever to indicate that he was active with the Fair Play for Cuba Committee in Dallas. And, as a matter of fact, I can go a step further and say that following his dissemination of pamphlets and his activities in New Orleans, our inquiry of our sources who are competent to tell us what is going on in the organizations such as Fair Play for Cuba Committee, advised that he was not known to them in New Orleans. So that his activities in New Orleans were of his own making, and not as a part of the organized activities of the Fair Play for Cuba Committee.

McCLOY: On that point, Mr. Belmont, where did he get his material, the printed material that he was distributing?

	Must he not have gotten them from some headquarters?
BELMONT:	It is my recollection that he had that printed up himself.
CHAIRMAN	That is right.
McCLOY:	All of it, so far as you know, was self-induced, so to speak?
BELMONT:	Correct.
COUNSEL:	Does your answer imply, Mr. Belmont, that there were Fair Play for Cuba activities in Dallas and New Orleans that you knew about?
BELMONT:	No; we do not have information of Fair Play for Cuba activities in Dallas nor any organized activity in New Orleans. So that this letter that you refer to, which was undated, was, as in so many things that Oswald wrote, not based on fact.
COUNSEL:	On page 7 in the answer to question 12, you refer to the inconsistencies and contradictions between the information Oswald gave to Agent Quigley when he interviewed him in the New Orleans jail and the facts as they were known to the FBI before that, and say that 'in the event the investigation of Oswald warranted a further interview, these discrepancies would have been discussed with him.'
	Can you explain why the fact of these inconsistencies and contradictions and perhaps outright lies to Agent Quigley was not itself reason for a further interview?
BELMONT:	Let me turn this just a little bit and say why should we re-interview him?
	Our interest in this man at this point was to determine whether his activities constituted a threat to the internal security of the country. It was apparent that he had made a self-serving statement to Agent Quigley. It became a matter of record in our files as a part of the case, and if we determined that the course of the investigation required us to clarify or face him down with this information, we would do it at the appropriate time.
	In other words, he committed no violation of the law by telling us something that wasn't true, and unless this required further investigation at that time, we would handle it in due course, in accord with the whole context of the investigation.
COUNSEL:	Do you know whether the fact of these contradictions was called to the attention of the Dallas office at the time of Oswald's return to Dallas?
BELMONT:	The entire file, of course, or the pertinent serials were sent to Dallas at the time that the case was transferred back to Dallas so they would have that information.
COUNSEL:	I gather what you are saying is they would note the

contradictions from the reports?

BELMONT: Yes.

COUNSEL: In the answer to question 14 on page 8, again in connection with these inconsistencies, the letter reads 'These inconsistencies were considered in subsequent investigation.'
Can you expand on that and tell us how they were considered?

BELMONT: That is right along the line of my previous explanation to you, namely, that they were recorded in the file. In the event it was desired to talk to him further at a future date, they would be considered as to whether we desired to have him further explain.

COUNSEL: On page 12, in response to question 22, which asked for an explanation of the reason for the investigation to ascertain his whereabouts, the letter reads, 'In view of Oswald's background and activities the FBI had a continuing interest in him.'
What was the nature of that continuing interest at that time?

BELMONT: On August 21, 1963, because of his activities in distributing these pamphlets, and his arrest in New Orleans, headquarters here in Washington sent a letter to the New Orleans and Dallas offices instructing them to pursue the investigation. In other words, in evaluating this information we felt it desirable that we further explore his activities to determine whether they were inimical to the internal security of the country. So that we had this continuing interest based on our evaluation, and so instructed our field offices.

COUNSEL: Mr. Chairman, I believe the answers to the other questions give us a complete enough record.

CHAIRMAN   Very well.

COUNSEL: May this exhibit which has been marked 833 for identification be admitted?

CHAIRMAN   It may be admitted in evidence under that number.
(The document referred to, previously marked Commission Exhibit No. 833 for identification, was received in evidence.)

McCLOY: Is there anything else, Mr. Belmont, that you may want to add? You have already been asked this question as you went through all these questions and answers, but is there anything else you would like to add in view of your answers this morning in further elaboration of the answers that have been given?

BELMONT: No, sir; unless the Commission has further questions at this

	point, I believe that the questions are answered properly and sufficiently.
McCLOY:	You think that if you are interviewing a defector which is something that provokes your interest, and I guess the mere fact of defection and return to the United States would do so, and if you found that defector was lying to you, you think that without something in addition to that there would be no further necessity of examining him. Is that a fair question? Let me put it another way.
BELMONT:	I have just a little difficulty following you.
McCLOY:	Here is my point. Here was a defector who comes within the category of interesting cases naturally.
BELMONT:	Yes, sir.
McCLOY:	And you question him and you find he is lying to you. At that stage, as I understand your testimony, you say without something more you don't necessarily go any further, is that right?
BELMONT:	No; that is not correct. We had talked to this man twice in detail concerning the question of possible recruitment by Soviet intelligence. We had checked his activities. He was settling down. He had a wife and a child. He had, according to what he had told us, in our interview with him, he had not enjoyed his stay in Russia. The State Department evaluation of him in Moscow was that he had learned his lesson and, as a matter of fact, he had made some statement to the effect that he now recognized the value of the American way of life, along those lines.

So that we had pretty well settled that issue. At the time that we interviewed him in the jail in New Orleans, we had again been following his activities because of his communications, his contacts with The Worker, and the Fair Play for Cuba Committee and our interest there was to determine whether he was a dangerou subversive. The interview in the jail was very apparently a self-serving interview in an attempt to explain his activities in the New Orleans area, and if I recall correctly, he took the position that the policy as directed against Cuba was not correct, and that the Fair Play for Cuba Committee was merely addressing itself to the complaints of Cuba, and was not in effect a subversive organization.

If, Mr. McCloy during those first two interviews where we were pursuing this matter of him being a defector and his recruitment, he had lied to us, and the agent was not satisfied we would have pursued it to the bitter end. Or if during any other time information came to our attention which indicated a necessity to pursue that further we

	would have pursued it to the bitter end.
McCLOY:	You speak of this as a self-serving interview. Do you think that he sought the interview with you, with Mr. Quigley eventually, because he had known of the prior contacts that he had had with the FBI, and he simply wanted to keep out of trouble?
BELMONT:	I don't know why he asked to see an agent. I simply do not know why.
McCLOY:	I think that is all.
COUNSEL:	Mr. Belmont, I show you a letter marked for identification Commission Exhibit No. 834. Can you identify that for the Commission, please?
	(The document referred to was marked Commission Exhibit No. 834 for identification.)
BELMONT:	This is a letter dated May 4, 1964, addressed to the Commission which sets forth in summary the contents of the headquarters file on Oswald prior to the assassination.
COUNSEL:	Do you have that file with you?
BELMONT:	Yes, sir.
COUNSEL:	Would you explain generally to the Commission what materials there are in that file that for security reasons you would prefer not to disclose?
BELMONT:	The file contains the identity of some of our informants in subversive movements. It contains information as to some of the investigative techniques whereby we were able to receive some of the information which has been made available to the Commission.
COUNSEL:	I think that is enough, Mr. Belmont, on that.
McCLOY:	You didn't have anything further to add to that, did you?
BELMONT:	No.
CHAIRMAN	I think as to those things if it is agreeable to the other members of the Commission, we will not pursue any questioning that will call for an answer that would divulge those matters that you have just spoken of.
BELMONT:	I would like to make it clear, Mr. Chairman, that – I think that is very kind of you – I would like to make it clear that Mr. Hoover has expressed a desire to be of the utmost help to the Commission, and to make any information available that will be helpful to the Commission. I think your observation is very much worthwhile.
COUNSEL:	Mr. Belmont, have you reviewed the actual file and this letter of May 4 which summarizes each document in the file?
BELMONT:	Yes, sir.
COUNSEL:	And to your knowledge, is this an accurate summary of each piece of information in the file?

BELMONT: Yes, sir.

COUNSEL: The file is available to the Commission?

BELMONT: Yes, sir.

COUNSEL: If they want to look at any item in it?

BELMONT: Yes, sir.

CHAIRMAN   The file does not include that security matter that you mentioned, or does it?

BELMONT: This file is as it is maintained at the Bureau with all information in it.

CHAIRMAN   With all information in it?

BELMONT: Yes, sir; this is the actual file.

CHAIRMAN   I see.

COUNSEL: Mr. Belmont, are you willing to leave the file a reasonable time in case any of the Commissioners desire to examine it personally?

BELMONT: Yes, sir.

COUNSEL: We will return it.

CHAIRMAN   I wonder if we do want it on those conditions. If we want to get anything from it don't you think, Mr. Rankin, that we ought to make it known here while the witness is here. I personally don't care to have this information that involves our security unless it is necessary, and I don't want to have documents in my possession where it could be assumed that I had gotten that information and used it, so I would rather, I would rather myself confine our questions to this file to the testimony of Mr. Belmont. Then if we want it, if we want any of those things, it then becomes a matter to discuss here in the open, and not just in privacy.

COUNSEL: Mr. Chairman, I felt it made a better record if the file is available only to the Commissioners in case they do want to examine it, and then it will be taken back and the staff will not examine it.

CHAIRMAN   I think he has stated that the file will be made available to us whenever we want it.

COUNSEL: Yes.

CHAIRMAN   If we do want it to read it that is one thing. For myself, I think we can get what we want from examining the witness, and then if there is any portion of it that comes into play why we can determine the question here, but I really would prefer not to have a secret file, I mean a file that contains matters of that kind in our possession.

COUNSEL: There is one factor that I wanted to get before the Commission and in the record, and that is that you had all the information that the FBI had in regard to this matter, and I thought that was important to your proceedings, so that we would not retain such a file, and we had an accurate summary but that it is available so that the Commission can be satisfied that nothing was withheld from it in regard to this particular question. That was the purpose of the inquiry.

DULLES: I assume, Mr. Belmont, if later other testimony arises that would make us desire to refer to this file we could consult it in your offices or you would make it available to us?

BELMONT: Yes, sir.

CHAIRMAN I think I would personally rather have it done on that basis. What do you think, Mr. McCloy?

McCLOY: I was just glancing at the file, and it seems to have the regular, the usual type of reports that we have seen. But there is a good bit of elaboration in those, in that file of the summary which is here. This summary I don't think can purport to be a complete description of the documents that are in here, as I glance through them here.

I just happened to see a good bit of detail in here which doesn't have anything to do with the security problem we talked about, but I would think that probably it would be wise for some member of the Commission or members of the Commission as a whole, to run through that file in order to be sure that we have seen the material elements of the file that we would not perhaps, might not, be able to get from this letter of May 4.

CHAIRMAN Well, there are so many of these questions in here that are obviously matters that we would have no more concern with than just to know about them.

Start from the very beginning, a news clipping from the Corpus Christi Times, dated October 2, 1959. Now if that excites any interest on the part of any member, why we could say, 'Well, could you show us that?' Then the next is the United Press release, dated October 31 at Moscow, and a great many of these.

Now, I wonder if it wouldn't be better for us to look over all of these various things, items that are in the file, and then if there are any that happen to excite our interest, we can ask Mr. Belmont about it. If it is a matter that involves security, we could then discuss it and make our determination as to whether we wanted to see it. I would think that when we are dealing with things that are as sensitive as the FBI has to deal with in that respect, that that would be adequate; that is my opinion of it.

But if the rest of the Commission feel that they want to see it notwithstanding the security measure, I would, of course, have no objection.

COUNSEL: Mr. Chief Justice, what I was trying to deal with was a claim by someone that the Commission never saw all there was in the hands of the FBI about Lee Harvey Oswald, and we recognize that some of these items should not be considered important by anyone, as we look at the matter, but we wanted you to be able to satisfy the public and the country that whatever there was that the FBI had, the Commission had it, and we didn't think that in light of the security problems the whole file should be a part of the files of the Commission. And we tried to present here a summary, even of items that did not seem important, but we did want the record in such condition that the Commission could say in its report, "We have seen everything that they have." I think it is important to the case.

McCLOY: I notice, Mr. Belmont, in running through this file, a note here that symbols are used in instances where the identities of the sources must be concealed.

BELMONT: That is correct, sir.

McCLOY: If that is so —

BELMONT: In some instances.

McCLOY: Only in some instances. There are other cases where that is not the case.

BELMONT: Yes; that is right.

McCLOY: There is a great deal of narrative in here about Oswald and his relations with the Embassy. Maybe it is elsewhere in the record.

BELMONT: I would presume that you have received that from the other agencies. Those are copies of communications that the other agencies sent to us.

CHAIRMAN Well, why couldn't we go over this list and see what items we would be interested in and then we can determine, can we not, whether we want —

McCLOY: I am not so sure, you can look through this yourself, I am not so sure if from reading just that short summary you get the full impact of all the narrative that is in the various reports. There is a good bit here. For example, one page I have here about this business of beating his wife and the drinking. There is a good bit of detail.

BELMONT: Mr. McCloy, you have that record.

CHAIRMAN We have the record, I have read the records myself.

McCLOY: Maybe we have that one.

BELMONT: Any investigative report you have.

McCLOY: Is there any investigative report in here that we have not got?

BELMONT: No, sir.

COUNSEL: We are trying to develop, Mr. Chief Justice and

Commissioners, that you have everything that the FBI had, this is their total file in regard to this matter of Lee Harvey Oswald so that there is nothing withheld from you as far as the FBI is concerned. That is part of what we are ,trying to develop this morning, in addition to the items themselves.

DULLES: I wonder if the staff, Mr. Rankin, could not go over this and check over those items we have from other sources and what the FBI has already furnished us so what we deal with with respect to this file are only items that are not in the Commission's records already. That would cut this down by half, I would imagine or more.

COUNSEL: Yes; we could do that for you.

DULLES: Then we could have this available possibly at a later date just to check over the other items against your files to see if there is any information there that we really need.

CHAIRMAN You could come back, couldn't you, Mr. Belmont?

BELMONT: I am at your disposal.

CHAIRMAN You could come back, couldn't you, Mr. Belmont?

BELMONT: I am at your disposal.

CHAIRMAN I think that would be better. I think, Mr. Rankin, your purpose is entirely laudable here, but I think we do have to use some discretion in the matter, and you say that you want it so we can say we have seen everything. Well, the same people who would demand that we see everything of this kind would also demand that they be entitled to see it, and if it is security matters we can't let them see it. It has to go back to the FBI without their scrutiny.

So unless, I would say, unless there is something that we think here is vital to this situation, that it isn't necessary for us to see the whole file, particularly in view of the fact that we have practically — we have all the reports, he says we have all the reports that are in that file, and it just seems like thrashing old straw to go over it and over it again.

McCLOY: Do we have copies of all these telegrams that are in here from the Embassy?

BELMONT: You are looking at —

McCLOY: Not Embassy; here is one from Mexico. Do we have that? We don't have these in our files, for example.

BELMONT· This is subsequent to the assassination. You see your area of interest at this point is information, all information we had prior to the assassination. I did not remove from this file the items that started to come in subsequent to the assassination, you see.

McCLOY: My feeling is that somebody on the Commission should examine that file. I can't come to any other conclusion after reading it all, because I don't know what is in it, what is in our record, and what is in that file. There is a good bit of material there that is narrative, which I think would be relevant. Certainly, I don't believe we can be possibly criticized for deleting or not producing a file which contains the type of information that you are speaking of. We are just as interested in protecting the security of your investigative processes as you are. But I don't think that when it is on the record that we have this file, that may contain material that was not in our files, and we are given the opportunity to examine it, without disclosing these confidential matters that we ought not to have somebody go through it.

DULLES: I agree with that but I think we could save time if we checked off first what we have already and that would cut out about half of that file probably.

McCLOY: I think in a rapid glance through it, I think just about half of it.

CHAIRMAN Well, suppose you do that then, get those and let's see. All right proceed, Mr. Stern.

CQUNSEL: I think perhaps we ought to leave the entire matter of the file then until we can give you the information.

CHAIRMAN That is right.

COUNSEL: May we admit for the purposes of the record this list at this time, Mr. Chief Justice, which has been marked No. 834?

CHAIRMAN Yes. There are no security matters in this?

BELMONT: No, sir.

CHAIRMAN It may be admitted as Exhibit No. 834.

APPENDIX B

By Compatriot

(27 November 1963)

MRS OSWALD OFFERED HOME

Fort Worth (AP) – Mrs. Maria Pultz arrived late last night in an effort to find Mrs. Lee Harvey Oswald, Russian-born wife of President Kennedy's alleged assassin.

All she wants to do is help, she said. She wants Mrs. Oswald to join her family in their three-bedroom house in San Antonio.

'I want her to live with us,' said Mrs. Pultz, who speaks fluent Russian and fast English, interspersed with American slang.

Says the talkative 36-year old woman, 'I feel sorry for her, living in America and not speaking the language. She needs some one who understands.'

You'd say Mrs. Pultz understands, all right. Her husband is an airline employee and she has three teenage children. But she finds time to sell real estate, too.

Came from Kiev

She came to the United States 15 years ago from Kiev in Russia's Ukraine. Asked if she were an American citizen, she replied, 'I think I much better citizen than most people in state, but sometimes I get screwed up in my talking.'

The attractive redhead told reporters in her plush motel room here: 'Mrs. Oswald can learn English by living with me. I can teach her things she might never learn.

'With two kids it's kinda rough in strange country. I need to get started some way to get hold of her. Before in the morning I find her one way or another ...' Shortly after midnight, her quest was still fruitless.

The Secret Service, newsmen in Fort Worth believe, is keeping Mrs. Oswald and her family out of sight.

Free country

Asked how she thought people would feel about her having Mrs. Oswald living with her family, Mrs. Pultz tossed her red hair and replied:

'I don't care what Americans think ... this is free country. I believe most Americans good. They understand.

'If I can talk with her I can make her stay with me in San Antonio. I have helped many people and many have helped me. I can talk with her; I give her, please, something nice to stay.

'I really want to do it out of my heart. I hear of it, I think, by golly, if I can get hold of that girl, she definitely don't want to go back to Russia.'

Two years ago, the determined talkative redhead spoke to Soviet Premier Nikita Khrushchev's son-in-law in New York City. 'I was able to get my mother in Russia to come to United States for five months.'

'I think I can do it now, too.' She said and newsmen present were inclined to believe her. (XVI.524.)

APPENDIX C

Historic Diary.
From Oct. 16 1959 Arrival –

Leaveing
1st Page

Oct. 16. Arrive from Helsinki by train; am met by Intourest Repre. and in car to Hotel "Berlin". Reges. as. "stedet" 5 day Lux. tourist. Ticket.) Meet my Intorist guied Rimma Sherikova I explain to her I wish to appli. for Rus. citizenship. She is flabbergassed, but aggrees to help. She checks with her boss, main office Intour; than helps me add. a letter to Sup. Sovit asking for citizenship, mean while boss telephons passport & Visa office and notifies them about me.

Oct. 17 – Rimma meets me for Intourist sighseeing says we must contin. with this although I am too nevous she is "sure" I'll have an anserwer soon. Asks me about myself and my reasons for doing this. I explaine I am a communist, ect. She is politly sym. but uneasy now. She tries to be a friend to me, she feels sorry for me I am someth. new.

Sun Oct. 18. My 20th birthday, we visit exhib. in morning and in the afternoon The Lenin-Stalin tomb. She gives me a present Book "Ideot" by Dostoevski.

Oct. 19 Tourism. Am anxious since my visa is good for five days only and still no word from auth. about my reqest.

Oct.20. Rimmer in the afternoon says Intourist was notified by the pass & visa dept. that they want to see me I am excited greatly by this news.

Oct.21. (mor) Meeting with single offial. Balding stout, black suit fairly. good English, askes what do I want?, I say Sovite citizenship, he ask why I give vauge answers about "Great Soviet Union" He tells me "USSR only great in Literature wants me to go back home" I am stunned I reiterate, he says he shall check and let me know whether my visa will be (extended it exipiers today)

Eve. 6.00 Recive word from police official. I must leave country tonight at. 8.00 P.M. as visa expirs. I am shocked! My dreams! I retire to my room. I have $ 100. left. I have waited for 2 year to be accepted. My fondes dreams are shattered because of a petty offial; because of bad planning I planned to much!

7.00 P.M. I decide to end it. Soak rist in cold water to numb the pain. Then slash my left rist. Than plaug wrist into bathtub of hot water. I think "when Rimma comes at 8. to find me dead it will be a great shock. somewhere, a violin plays, as I

31
2nd page   DIARY

Oct 21. (con.):wacth my life whirl away. I think to myself. "how easy to die" and "a sweet death, (to violins) about 8.00 Rimma finds me unconscious (bathtub water a rich red color) she screams (I remember that) and runs for help. Amulance comes, am taken to hospital where five stitches are put in my wrist. Poor Rimmea stays by my side an interrpator (my Russian is still very bad) far into the night, I tell her "go home" (my mood is bad) but she stays, she is "my friend" She has a strong will only at this moment I notice she is preety

Oct. 22. Hospital I am in a small room with about 12 others (sick persons.) 2 ordalies and a nurse the room is very drab as well as the breakfast. Only after prolonged (2 hours) observation of the other pat. do I relize I am in the Insanity ward. This relization disquits me. Later in afternoon I am visited by Rimma, she comes in with two doctors, as interr she must ask me medical questions; Did you know what you were doing? Ans. yes Did you blackout? No. ect. I than comp. about poor food the doctors laugh app. this is a good sign Later they leave, I am alone with Rimma (amonst the mentaly ill) she encourgest me and scolds me she says she will help me get trasfered to another section of Hos. (not for insane) where food is good.

Oct. 23. Transfered to irdinary ward, (airy, good food.) but nurses suspious of me.) they know).

Afternoon. I am visited by Rosa Agafonova of the hotel, tourist office who askes about my health, very beauitiful, excelant Eng., very merry and kind, she makes me very glad to be alive. Later Rimma vists

Oct. 24 Hospital routine, Rimma visits me in afternoon

Oct. 25 Hospital routine, Rimma visits me in afternoon

Oct. 26 An elderly American at the hospital grow suspious about me for some reason. because at Embassy I told him I had not registered as most tóurist and I am in general evasive about my presence in Moscow and at hospital. Afternoon Rimma visits.

Oct. 27 Stiches are taken out by doctor with "dull" scisor
   Mo

Wed Oct. '28 Leave hospital in intorist car. with Rimma for Hotel "Berlin" later I change hotels to "Metropole" all cloths packed, and money from my room (to the last kopeek) returned as well as watch, ring. Ludmilla Dimitrova (Intorist office head) and Rosa invite me to come and sit and take with them any time. I get lonesome at new hotel. They feel sorry for me.

Oct. 28(con.) Rimma notifies me that, pass & registration office whshes to see me about my future. Later Rimma and car pick me up and we enter the officies to find four offials waiting for me (all unknown to me) They ask How my arm is, I say O.K., They ask "Do you want to go to your homeland. I say no I want Sovite citizen. I say I want to reside in the Soviet Union. They say they will see about that. Than they ask me about the lone offial with whom I spoke in the first place (appar. he did not pass along my request at all but thought to simply get rid of me by not extending my Soviet visa. At the time I requested it) I desqribe him (they make notes) (what papers do you have to show who and what you are? I give them my dischare papers from the Marine Corps. They say wait for our ans. I ask how long? Not soon. Later Rimma comes to check on me. I feel insulted and insult her.

Oct. 29. Hotel Room 214 Metropole Hotel. I wait. I worry I eat once, stay next to phone worry I keep fully dressed

Oct. 31. I make my dision. Getting passport at 12″00 I meet and talk with Rimma for a few minutes she says: stay in your room and eat well, I don't tell her about what I intend to do since I know she would not approve. After she leaves I wait a few minutes and then I catch a taxi, "Amercian Embassy" I say. 12″30, I arrive American Embassy, I walk in and say to the receptionist 'I would like to see the Consular" she points at a large lager and says "If you are a tourist please register". I take out my American passport and lay it in the desk, I have come to dissolve my American citizenship. I saymatter-of-factly she rises and enters the office of Richard Snyder American Head Consular in Moscow at that time. He invites me to sit down. He finishes a letter he is typing and then ask what he can do for me. I tell him I have dicided to take Soviet citizenship and would like to leagly dissolve my U.S. citizenship. His assitant (now *Head* Consular) McVickers looks up from his work. Snyder takes down personall Information, ask questions

Sat. Oct 31 (con) warnes me not to take any steps before the soviets except me, say I am a "fool", and says the dissolution papers are along time in preparing (In other words refuses to allow me at that time to dissolve U.S. citiz. I state "my mind is make up" From this day forward I consider myself no citizen of the U.S.A. I spend 40 minutes at the Embassy before Snyder says 'now unless you wish to expound on your maxist belifes you can go." I wish to disolve U.S. citiz, not today he says in effect. I leave Embassy, elated at this showdown, returning to my hotel I feel now my enorgies are not spent in vain. I'm sure Russians will except me after this sign of my faith in them. 2:00 a knock, a reporter by the name of Goldstene wants an interview I'm flabbergassed "how did you find out? The Embassy called us" He said. I send him away I sit and relize this is one way to bring pressure on me. By notifing my relations in U.S. through the newspapers. Although they would say "ifs for the public record." A half hour later another reporter Miss Mosby comes. I answewer a few quick questions after refusing an interviwe. I am surprised at the interest. I get phone calls from "Time" at night a phone call from the States I refuse all calles without finding out who's it from. I feel non-deplused because of the attention 10:00 I retire.

Nov. 1 – more reporters, 3 phone calls from brother & mother, now I feel slightly axzillarated, not so lonly.

Nov -2-15 Days of utter loneliness I refuse all reports phone calls I remaine in my room, I am racked with dsyentary.

Nov 15 – I decide to give an interview, I have Miss Mosbys card so I call her. She drives right over. I give my story, allow pictures, later story is distorted, sent without my perrmission, that is: before I ever saw and O.K.'ed her story. Again I feel slightly better because of the attention

Nov. 16. A Russian official comes to my room askes how I am. Notifies me I can remain in USSR till some solution in found with what to do with me, it is comforting news for me.

34   Diary   Page 5

Nov 17 – Dec. 30 I have bought myself two self-teaching Russian Lan. Books I force myself to study 8 hours a day I sit in my room and read and memorize words. All meals I take in my room. Rimmĕa arranged that. It is very cold on the streets so I rarley go outside at all for this month and a-half I see no one speak to no-one accept every-now-and-than Rimmea, who calls the ministry about me. Have they forgotten?, During December I paid no money to the hotel, but Rimmer told Hotel I was expecting alot of money from USA. I have $28 left. This month I was called to the passport office and met 3 new offials who asked me the same questions I ans. a month before. They appear not to know me at all.

Dec 31. New Yearseve, I spend in the company of Rosa Agafoneva at the Hotel Berlin, she has the duty. I sit with her until past mignight, she gives me a small 'Boratin', clown, for a New Years present She is very nice I found out only recently she is married, has small sone who was born crippled, that is why she is so strangely tender and compeling.

Jan 1-4 No change in routine

Jan 4. I am called to passport office and finilly given a Soviet document not the soviet citizenship as I so wanted, only a Residence document, not even for foringners but a paper called 'for those *without* citizenship.' Still I am happy. The offial says they are sending me to the city of 'Minsk' I ask 'is that in Siberia? He only laughes. he also tells me that they have arranged for me to recive some money through the Red Cross. to pay my hotel bills and expensis.I thank the gentelmen and leave later in the afternoon I see Rimma 'she asks are you happy' 'yes'

Jan. 5. I go to Red Cross in Moscow for money with Interrupter (a new one) I recive 5000. rubles a huge sum!! Later in Mink I am to earn 70 rubles a month at the factory.

Jan. 7. I leave Moscow by train for Minsk, Belorussia. My hotel bill was 2200, rubles and the train ticket to Minsk 150 rubles so I have alot of money & hope. I wrote my brother & mother letters in which I said 'I do not wish to every contact you again.' I am beginning anew life and I don't want *any part* of the old'.

35   Diary   Page 6

Jan 7. Arrive in Minsk, met by 2 women Red Cross workers We go to Hotel "Minsk" I take room, and meet Rosa and Stellina two persons from intourist in hotel who speak English Stellina is in 40's nice married young child, Rosa about 23 blond attractive unmarried Excellant English, we attract each other at once.

Jan 8. I meet the city mayor, comrade Shrapof, who welcomes me to Minsk promisis a rent-free apartment "soon" and warns me about "uncultured persons" who somethimes insult foriengers. My interputer: Roman Detkof. Head For. Tech Instit. next door.

Jan. 10. The day to myself I walk through city, very nice.

Jan. 11 I vist Minsk radio factory where I shall work. There I meet Argentinian Immigrant Alexander Zeger Born a Polish Jew. Immi to Argen. in 1938 and back to Polish homeland (now part of Belo.) in 1955 speaks English with Amer. accent he worked for Amer. com. in Argen. He is Head of a Dept. a quialified Engenier, in late 40's mild mannered likable He seems to want to tell me somet. I show him my tempor. docu. and say soon I shall have Russ. citiz. Jan. 13-16 I work as a "checker" metal worker, pay: 700 rubles a month, work very easy, I am learning Russian quickly Now, Everyone is very freindly and kind. I meet many young Russian workers my own age they have varied personatities all wish to know about me even offer to hold a mass meeting so I can say. I refuse politly. At night I take Rosa to the thearter, movie or operor almost every day I'm living big and am very satisfied. I recive a check from the Red Cross every 5th of the month "to help." The check is 700 rubles. Therefore every month I make 1400. R. about the same as the Director of the factory! Zeger observes me during this time I don't like: picture of Lenin which watchs frome its place of honour and phy. training at 11.-11.10 each moring (complusery). for all. (shades of H.G. Wells!!)

March 16. I recive a small flat one-room kicten-bath near the factory (8 min. walk) with splendid view from 2 balconies of the river, almost rent free (60. rub. a mon.) it is a Russians dream.

March 17-April 31 — work, I have lost contact with Rosa after my house moving. I meet Pavil Golovacha. A yonuge man my age friendly very intelligent a exalant radio techniction his father is Gen. Golovacha Commander of Northwestenr Siberia. Twice hero of USSR in W.W.2.

May 1 – May Day came as my first holiday all factories Ect. closed after sptacular military parade all workers parad past reviewing stand waving flags and picutres of Mr. K. ect. I follow the Amer. custom of marking a Holiday by sleeping in in the morning. At night I visit with the Zegers daughters at an party throw by them about 40 people came many of Argentine origen we dance and play around and drink until 2 am. when party breaks up. Leonara Zeger oldest dau. 26 formally married, now divorced, a talanted singer. Anita Zeger 20 very gay, not so attractive but we hit it off. Her Boy-friend Alferd is a Hungarian chap, silent and brooding, not at all like Anita. Zeber advised me to go back to U. S. A. its the first voice of oppossition I have heard. I respect Zeger, he has seen the world. He says many things, and relats many things I do not know about the U. S. S. R. I begin to feel uneasy inside, its true! June-July Summer months of green beauty, pine forest very deep. I enjoy many Sundays in the enviorments of Minsk. with the Zegers who have a car "mos.vick" Alfred always goes along with Anita, Leonara seems to have no permanet Boy-friend, but many admirirs. She has a beautiful Spanish figure, long black hair, like Anita. I never pay much atten. to her shes too old for me she seemes to dislike my lack of attention for some reason. She is high strung. I have become habituatated to a small cafe which is where I dine in the evening the food is generally poor and always eactly the same, menue in any cafe, at any point in the city. The food is cheap and I dont really care about quiality after three years in the U.S.M.C.

Aug-Sept As my Russian improves I become increasingly conscious of just what sort of a sociaty I live in. Mass gymnastics, compulsary after work meeting, usually political information meeting. Complusary attendance at lectures and the sending of the entire shop colletive (except me) to pick potatoes on a Sunday, at a State collective farm. A "patroict duty" to bring in the harvest. The opions of the workers (unvoiced) are that its a great pain in the neck. They don't seem to be esspicialy enthusiastic about any of the "collective" duties a natural feeling. I am increasingly aware of the presence, in all thing, of Lebizen, shop party secretary, fat, fortyish, and jovial on the outside. He is a no-nonsense party regular.

Oct. The coming of Fall, my dread of a new Russian winter, are mellowed in splendid golds and reds of fall in Belorussia plums peachs appricots and cherrys abound for these last fall weeks I am a healthy brown color and stuffed with fresh fruit. (at other times of the year unobtainable)

Oct. 18 my 21st birthday see's Rosa, Pavil, Ella at a small party at my place Ella very attractive Russian Jew I have been going walking with lately, works at the radio factory also. Rosa and Ella are jelous of each other it brings a warm feeling to me. Both are at my place for the first time. Ella and Pavil both give ask-tray's (I don't smoke) we have a laugh.

Nov. Finds the approach of winter now. A growing lonliness overtakes me in spite of my conquest of Ennatachina a girl from Riga, studying at the music conservorie in Minsk. After an affair which last a few weeks we part.

Nov 15 in Nov. I make the acquaintaces of four girls rooming at the For. Ian. domitory in room 212. Nell is very interesting, so is Tomka, Tomis and Alla. I usually go to the institute domatory with a friend of mine who speaks english very well. Eraich Titov is in the forth year at the medical institute. Very bright fellow At the domatory we 6 sit and talk for hours in english

Dec

1 I am having a light affair with Nell Korobka.

Jan 1

New Years I spend at home of Ella Germain I think I'm in love with her. She has refused my more dishonourable advanis, we drink and eat in the presenec of her family in a very hospitable atmosfere. Later I go home drunk and happy. Passing the river homeward, I decide to propose to Ella.

Jan. 2. After a pleasent handin-hand walk to the local cinima we come home, standing on the doorstep I propose's She hesitates than refuses, my love is real but she has none for me. Her reason besides lack of love; I am american and someday might be arrested simply because of that example Polish Inlervention in the 20's. led to arrest of all people in the Soviet Union of polish oregen "you understand the world situation there is too much against you and you don't even know it" I am stunned she snickers at my awkarness in turning to go (I am too stunned too think!) I realize she was never serious with me but only exploited my being an american, in order to get the envy of the other girls who consider me different from the Russian Boys. I am misarable!

27   Diary   Page 9

Jan 3. I am miserable about Ella. I love her but what can I do? It is the state of fear which was alway in the Soviet Union.

Jan. 4. On year after I recived the residence document I am called in to the passport office and asked if I want citizenship (Russian) I say no simply extend my residental passport to agree and my document is extended untill Jan 4. 1962

Jan-4-31 I am stating to reconsider my disire about staying. The work is drab the money I get has nowhere to be spent. No nightclubs or bowling allys no places of recreation accept the trade union dances I have have had enough.

Feb. 1st Make my first request to American Embassy, Moscow for reconsidering my position, I stated "I would like to go back to U.S."

Feb. 28th I recive letter from Embassy. Richard E. Sneyder stated "I could come in for an interview anytime I wanted."

March 1-16 I now live in a state of expectation about going back to the U.S. I confided with Zeger he supports my judgment but warnes me not to tell any Russians about my desire to reture. I understade now why.

March 17 – I and Erich went to trade union dance. Boring but at the last hour I am introduced to a girl with a French hair-do and red-dress with white slipper I dance with her. than ask to show her home I do, along with 5 other admirares. Her name is Marina. We like each other right away she gives me her phone number and departs home with an not-so-new freiend in a taxi, I walk home.

March-18-31- We walk I talk a little about myself she talks alot about herself. her name is Marina N. Prosakoba

Apr: 1st-30 We are going steady and I decide I must have her, she puts me off so on April 15 I propose, she accepts.

April 3', after a 7 day delay at the marraige beaure because of my unusual passport they allow us to registra as man & wife two of Marinas girl friends act as bridesmaids. We are married at her aunts home we have a dinner reception for about 20 friends and neboribor who wish us happiness (in spite of my origin and accept) which was in general rather disquiting to any Russian since for. are very rare in the soviet union even tourist. after an evening of eating and drinking in which uncle Wooser started a fright and the fuse blow on an overloaded circite We take our leave and walk the 15 minutes to our home. We lived near each other. at midnight we were home.

26   **Diary**   Page 10

1st
May Day 1961. Found us thinking about our future. Inspite of fact I married Marina to hurt Ella I found myself in love with Marina.

May – The trasistion of changing full love from Ella to Marina was very painfull esp. as I saw Ella almost every day at the factory but as the days and weeks went by I adjusted more and more my wife mentaly. I'still haden't told my wife of my desire to return to US. She is maddly in love with me from the very start, boat rides on Lake Minsk walks throught the parks evening at home or at Aunt Valia's place mark May.

June – A continuence of May, except. that; we draw closer and closer, and I think very little now of Ella. in the last days of this month I revele my longing to return to America. My wife is slightly startled. But than encourages me to do what I wish to do.

July – I decived to take my two week vacation and travel to Moscow (without police permission) to the American Embassy to see about geting my U.S. passport back and make arrangements for my wife to enter the U.S. with me.

July 8 – I fly by plane to Minsk on a i1-20, 2 hrs 20m later after taking a tearful and anxiou parting from my wife I arrive in Moscow departing by bus. From the airfield I arrive in the center of the city. Making my way through heavy traffic I don't come in sight of the embassy until 3:00 in the afternoon. Its

Saturday what if they are closed? Entering I find the offices empty but mange to contact Snyder on the phone (since all embassy personal live in the same building) he comes down to greet me shake my hand after interview he advised he to come in first thing mon.

(see – July 8-13)

July 8. Interview July 9 recive passport; call Marina to Moscow also.

July 14. I and Marina returen to Minsk.

July 15. Marina at work, is shocked to find out ther everyone knows she entered the U. S. embassy. They were called at her place of work from some officials in Moscow." The boses hold a meeting and give her a strong browbeating. The first of many indocrinations.

| 25 | Diary | 11rd Page |

July 15 Aug 20. we have found out which blanks and certifikates are necessceary to apply – for a exit visa they number about 20 papers; Birth certificates affidavite photos ect. On Aug 20th we give the papers out they say it will be $3\frac{1}{2}$ months before we know wheather they'll let us go or not. In the meantime Marina has had to stade 4 different meeting at the place of work held by her Boss's at the direction of "someone" by phone. The young comm. leauge headquthers also called about her and she had to go see them for $1\frac{1}{2}$ hrs. The purpose (expressed) is to disaude her from going to the U.S.A., Net effect: Make her more stubborn about wanting to go Marina is pregnet, we only hope that the visas come through soon.

Aug 21-Sept 1 – I make expected trips to the passport & visa office also to ministry of for. affairs in Minsk, also Min. of Interal affairs, all of which have a say in the granting of a visa. I extracked promises of quick attention to US.

Sept-Oct 18. No word from Min. (They'll call us.") Marina leaves Minsk by train on vaction to the city of Khkov in the Urals to vist an aunt for 4 weeks. During this time I am lonely but I and Erich got to the dances and public places for enitanment. I havent done this in quite a few months now. I spend my birthday alone at the opera watching my favoriot "Queen of Spades." I am 22 years old.

Nov-2 Marina arrives back, radient, with several jars of preserses for me from her aunt in Khkov.

Nov-Dec. Now we are becoming anoid about the delay Marina is beginning to waiver about going to the US. Probably from the strain and her being pregrate, still we quarrel and so things are not to bright esp. with the approach of the hard Russian winter.

Dec 25th Xmas Day Tues. Marina is called to the passport & visa office. She is told we have been granted Soviet exit visa's. She fills out the completing blank and then comes home with the news. Its great (I think!) New Years, we spend at the Zeger's at a dinner party at midnight. attended by 6 other persons.

Jan.4. I am called to the passport office since my Residenceal passport expires today, since I now have a US. passport in my possition I am given a totly new resid. pass. called, "Pass for Forin," and since they have given US perrmission to leave, and know we shall, good to July 5, 1962.

24	Diary	Page 12

Jan 15.

Feb.15. Days of cold Russian winter. But we feel fine. Marina is supposed to have baby on March 1st.

Feb 15 – Dawn. Marina wakes me. Its her time. At 9:00 we arrive at the hospital I leave her in care of nurses and leave to go to work. 10:00 Marina has a baby girl. when I vist the hospital at 500 after work, I am given news. We both wanted a boy. Marina feels well, baby girl, OK.

Feb 23 Maria leaves hospital I see June for first time.

Feb.28 I go to registra (as prespibed by law) the baby. I want her name to be June Marina Oswald. But those Beaurcrats say her middle name must be the same as my first. A Russian custom support by a law. I refuse to have her name written as "June Lee". They promise to call the city ministry (city hall) and find out in this case since I do have an U.S. passport. Feb. 29. I am told that nobody knows what to do exactly, but everyone agrees "Go ahead and do it, "Po-Russki." Name: June Lee.

March. The last commiques are exchanged between myself and Embassy. letters are always arriving from my mother and brother in the U.S. I have still not told Erich who is my oldest existing aquaitance, that we are going to the State, he's o.k. but I'm afriad he is too good a young communist leage member so I'll wait till last min.

March 24 – Marina quits her job in the formal fashion.

March 26 – I recive a letter from Immigration & Natur. service at San Antonio, Texas, that Marina has had her visa petition to the U.S. (Approved!!) The last document. Now we only have to wait for the U.S. Embassy to recive their copy of the approval so they can officially give the go ahead.

March 27 I recive a letter from a Mr. Philles (a employ. of my mother, pleging to support my wife in case of need.

April –

(Author's note: It is known that the part of the Diary relating to the first two months in Moscow was not written until the diarist had arrived in Minsk. It can only be that the Diary was left in his residence in Dallas by the assassin for disinformation purposes.)

APPENDIX D

Albert Osborne alias John Howard Bowen

After the assassination the FBI made efforts to trace and identify *John Howard Bowen*, the man who sat beside Oswald on the bus journey to Mexico City, and the following is a condensation of the close printed pages of FBI reports relating to *Albert Osborne* alias *John Howard Bowen* (**XXV**.20-75), less pages 7 and 8 which are missing from the Exhibit. This Appendix also includes information obtained by this author in Grimsby, England, from relatives of the 75 years old Albert Osborne.

The FBI first obtained from the Mexican authorities details of the application form that *John Howard Bowen* had completed for his six-month tourist card for Mexico. On this Bowen had stated that he was married, aged 60 years, born in the United States and living and employed in Houston, Texas, the application being supported by a birth certificate. The FBI then found that they already had an 'Internal Security' file on Bowen. It had been opened in 1942, when he was in charge of a boys camp near Knoxville, Tennessee, and when he was reported to have 'torn down the American flag and stomped it into the ground'. He was thought by the man who reported the matter to have been an Italian who owned 'three large police dogs which were very dangerous'. The FBI instituted enquiries at that time and they must, it would seem, have interviewed Bowen; the missing pages 7 and 8 (**XXV**.28) would, apparently, have covered that period. It was believed by the FBI that he had been born on 14 January 1887, at Chester, Pennyslvania, and had once resided at Houston, Texas.

The FBI then discovered that over the years articles had appeared in the *Knoxville Journal* regarding Bowen, based on information sent to the Journal in letters signed by John H. Bowen, Alberto Osborne or Dr. Martin Hilldago. One article in December 1953, reported that Bowen resided in Laredo, Texas, and had established a missionary station and Baptist church in Mexico, with a Post Office Box address at Laredo, Texas.

In November 1954, the Journal had received a post card from Bowen advising them that he was mailing some photographs to them and stating that, although he had earlier announced that he was retiring from missionary work, he had decided to continue. In a letter dated April 1958, and signed Dr. Martin Hilldago, the journal was advised that Bowen had injured his left side while sweeping two school children from the path of a truck in Mexico. The

333

letter went on to say that Bowen had saved three children from a burning hut about eight years previously. The Journal had received a letter dated 11 September 1961 and signed, Alberto Osborne, reporting that Bowen had been injured in an accident near Mexico City. The letter reported that Bowen would be eighty-two years old in January but could easily pass for a man in his middle fifties. The letter went on to relate that Bowen, prior to his work in Knoxville during the 40's, had served as a missionary in India and had been active in missionary work since 1910. The newspaper files contained two photographs purporting to be pictures of *John Howard Bowen*, and in December 1963 the FBI obtained copies. They then made enquiries regarding birth records, school board records, credit bureau records, city directories, newspaper morgues and death records at Chester, Pennsylvania, but no information was developed to identify or trace John Howard Bowen; similar enquiries were made at Houston, Texas, but also without success.

On 7 January 1964, an *Albert Osborne* was found living in a native mud-walled hut at Texmelucan, Mexico, the address having been given in the letter signed Alberto Osborne to the *Knoxville Journal* in the letter of September 1961. He now told the FBI that he was a Canadian Baptist missionary working in Mexico. When questioned about *John Howard Bowen*, he said that Bowen was an ordained Baptist minister who, over the years, had collected funds for the construction of several churches in Mexico. He said that Bowen had not been in Mexico since late September or early October 1963, at which time he collected his mail at Osborne's hut, and told Osborne that he was thinking of giving up missionary work because many of his contributors who had helped him financially over the years were deceased. Osborne suggested that Bowen could possibly be located in New Orleans, where the latter recently had been employed and was making efforts to qualify for social security benefits. He claimed that he had no way of communicating with Bowen and that he did not know Bowen's exact address in the United States.

On 21 January 1964, the FBI attempted to re-interview *Albert Osborne*, but he had left the hut. The two photographs of *John Howard Bowen* were shown to the teenage Mexican caretaker of the hut and also to a Mexican minister in the same community. Both·identified the photographs as being identical with *Albert Osborne*. The caretaker said that Osborne was on a trip to an unknown part of the United States and he did not know when he would return.

The suspicion that Bowen and Osborne were the same men was confirmed when an enquiry in February 1964 by the FBI at the American Express Office in Mexico City revealed that the same man collected mail in both names. The office also revealed that *John Howard Bowen* had cashed numerous cheques in amounts of $25-$30 each over the previous eight years. The office said that on 15 November 1963, Bowen had requested them to forward his mail to the American Express Office in New York.

Mexican immigration authorities reported to the FBI that in 1958 they had understood that *Albert Osborne* was a Canadian missionary working in Mexico, and at that time they had asked the Royal Canadian Mounted Police to make enquiries regarding him. The authorities said that they were interested in detaining Osborne should he return to Mexico, as he had been ordered to leave Mexico in 1958 as an undesirable alien. The RCMP failed to develop any background information of value, except that the address in Canada that Osborne had given the Mexican authorities did not exist.

On 8 February 1964, *John Howard Bowen* was located and interviewed by the FBI at Florence, Alabama. He said that to the best of his knowledge he was born at Chester on 12 January 1885, and that his father's name was James A. Bowen and his mother was Emily Bowen. He had not known his parents but was brought up in an orphanage in Philadelphia. His grandmother, Sarah Hall, participated to a limited extent in giving him guidance and shelter during the early years of his life. His grandmother and his relatives were, so far as he knew, all deceased. He had attended elementary schools intermittently in Philadelphia and in the Pennsylvania area, but took correspondence courses and had completed the equivalent of about two years of college. He also took a correspondence course in theology, which he completed in about 1914. Also at that time, he had been ordained as a minister by the Plymouth Brethren Church in Trentham, New Jersey, and five years later had been ordained as a minister by the Northern Baptist Convention, and he currently considered himself associated with that church body. He was formerly a member of the First Baptist Church at Knoxville, and more recently was a member of the First Baptist Church at Laredo. He stated that he considered himself an itinerant gardener as well as a preacher.

He said that about thirty years previously he had applied for a job as a Juvenile Counsellor with the Tennessee Valley Authority at Knoxville, and recalled that he was fingerprinted on that occasion. From about 1929 to about 1934 he had worked with juvenile delinquents from the city of Knoxville. (He was working at the boys' camp in 1942, and possibly before and after that year.) For about fifty years he had travelled extensively in the United States, particularly in the Stanton, Virginia, area and in the southern parts of the United States as an itinerant Baptist minister, and that on these itinerant preaching tours he resided in the home of the host pastor but moved frequently from place to place. During the past twenty years he had made numerous trips as an itinerant Baptist minister throughout Mexico.

He said that he had never been to Canada, England of any other country, except in about 1939 when he visited Bermuda. He had no passport but carried for identification purposes the following cards: Social Security, Texaco Company Credit, Gold Star Insurance, and Laredo National Bank.

He said that in about 1958 he had been residing at the Reece Hotel, Oaxaco, Mexico and residing in the same hotel was *Albert Osborne*, a retiring itinerant Baptist minister from Canada. Osborne had an English or Scottish accent, and he agreed that Osborne was about his same size and age. He said that at that time a census of some type was being taken by the Mexican authorities, and he had been unable to locate his identification papers. He had therefore borrowed the identification papers of Osborne and had exhibited them to the Mexican authorities, thereafter returning the papers to Osborne. He next saw Osborne in about the spring of 1961 or 1962 at the Railway Express Company

Office, Mexico City, and although he had corresponded occasionally with him he had not seen him since that occasion. He recalled having heard through friends in Mexico that Osborne was travelling in that country as an itinerant Baptist preacher in December 1963 and January 1964, but that Osborne was trying to return to Canada, possibly taking up residence in the vicinity of Vancouver.

When he was shown the two photographs obtained from the *Knoxville Journal*, he identified one as of himself, taken about 20 years before at Vera Cruz, Mexico and the other as *Albert Osborne*. He explained that it was entirely possible that persons might confuse him with Osborne, because they were both itinerant Baptist preachers and had both travelled extensively in Mexico. He repeated that they were of the same size and age.

He was questioned about a bus trip he made to Mexico City from Laredo on 26 September 1963, and said that he had sat beside a young man whom he thought was either Mexican or possibly Puerto Rican, but that he did not speak to him. He had arrived in Mexico City at about 9.30 a.m. on 27 September, thereafter boarding another bus in Mexico City and going to St. Augustine Hotel in Puebla, Mexico. The next day he boarded a night train at Puebla and travelled to the Railroad Hotel at Jesus Caranga, north of Juchitan, Mexico. He remained in this area for about a week, contacting various native ministers, delivering bibles and preaching. He then returned to the area of Puebla, where he resided with various persons connected with Baptist churches in the vicinity, later travelling to Laredo in about the middle of November 1963. He stated that he had never taught school, he had never written a book and knew nothing about the Lisbon earthquake of 1775. He could not recall seeing any Americans on the bus to Mexico City and knew of nobody on the bus who might have talked to the young man sitting in the seat adjacent to his. He stated that he definitely was not identical to *Albert Osborne*. (Travelling on the bus carrying 'Lee' and 'Bowen' from Laredo to Mexico City were the English couple, Dr. and Mrs. McFarland, who had already been interviewed by the British police in Liverpool, England. They had identified the photographs of Oswald and Osborne as being the pair who had sat immediately behind them on the bus to Mexico City. They said that the older man had told them that he was a retired school teacher who had taught in India and Arabia, and was currently writing a book on the Lisbon earthquake of 1775. Also on the bus were the Misses Mumford and Winston from Australia, and in addition to 'Lee', 'Bowen', the doctor and his wife, they were the only English-speaking persons on the bus, which was occupied wholly by Mexicans, children and small animals. (The Australian girls had had a short conversation with 'Lee' during which he had shown them his 1959 passport.)

On 16 February 1964, *John Howard Bowen* was re-interviewed at Laredo and again he was questioned regarding the bus trip he took from Laredo to Mexico City on 26 September 1963. He said that there were no other Americans or English speaking persons on the bus, and to his knowledge none of the Mexican passengers spoke English. He sat near the front of the bus next to the window and there was a young man sitting next to him who appeared to be a Mexican. He did not talk to this man nor did this man speak to him or anyone else on the bus. He reiterated that after the bus had arrived in Mexico City, the same day he had taken another bus to Puebla, and boarded a train to Jesus Caranga, where he had stayed at the Railroad Hotel for two nights, returned to Laredo. He became very indignant when asked about his activities since 1 September 1963, saying that it was a free country and that he could travel whenever and wherever he pleased. He admitted returning from Mexico to the United States on 2 October 1963 and said that he remained in Laredo until the latter part of October when he went on a lengthy trip in the United States, visiting churches and collecting religious books. This trip covered the latter part of October, November and most of December, during which time he first went to Houston and then to Memphis, Tennessee, and from there to Charlotte, North Carolina, then on to Columbia, South Carolina and back to Laredo, arriving just before Christmas. (He flew, in fact, from New York probably in the name of Bowen to Scotland, England, and may have then gone to Spain before returning to the United States in early December 1963.) After Christmas he went on another trip and visited Houston, Lake Charles and Baton Rouge, Louisiana, and returned to Laredo. In February he had made a further trip to Birmingham, Alabama. He again denied ever having used a dual-identity or ever having been in any foreign country, and that he had never used the name of Albert Osborne. He said that he knew a man by that name who was also a preacher and missionary in Mexico. He had last seen *Albert Osborne* in Mexico City in the Midsummer of 1963 and that he and Osborne were last together in Oaxaco, Mexico in 1959. He added that he and Osborne looked very much alike and were often mistaken for each other in Mexico. He repeated that during his travels in Mexico he always stayed with pastors and Christian people, and sometimes did the same thing in the United States. He could not furnish the names of people in the United States with whom he had stayed, explaining that he just could not remember them. He said that he was well-known in Mexico, particularly in Vera Cruz and Oaxaco.

He was shown a photograph of Oswald, but said that he could not identify Oswald as being on the same bus on 26 September and that he had never seen him at any time. When confronted with the fact that other people on the bus had identified him and Oswald as having been seated beside each other, he said that he was only saying what he knew and that possibly other people were not truthful.

When questioned about his background, Bowen stated that he had organized the boys' club in Knoxville in 1934, and it was now known as the Boys Club of America; at this point Bowen declined to answer any further questions.

On 5 March 1964, *Albert Osborne* was rediscovered and reinterviewed by the FBI at his temporary place of residence at the Central YMCA, Nashville, Tennessee, where he had registered under the name of *John H. Bowen* and had given as his address, 'The Old Folks Home, Grimsby, England'. At the outset of the interview, he denied his true identity and claimed that his name was *John Howard Bowen*, but later admitted that his name was *Albert Osborne*. He then said that he was educated at St. James' Academy, Grimsby, England, until the eighth grade and that he had joined the British Army in 1908, serving in India, Arabia and Bermuda. He had purchased his discharge from the British Army in 1914 while in Bermuda and thereafter came directly to the United States, proceeding to Washington, D.C. where he obtained employment in several grocery stores in his correct name of Albert Osborne.

He said that while in Washington he had taken a correspondence course in religion from the University of Chicago, thereafter going to Philadelphia where he had attended the Philadelphia Bible College for approximately one year while living and working as a janitor at the YMCA in Philadelphia. In 1916, he had proceeded to Canada where he joined the Canadian Army, remaining until the cessation of hostilities in World War I. Thereafter he had returned to Washington, where he met a Syrian, whose name he did not recall, and went into the rug cleaning business with this individual. He indicated that the rug cleaning business was of an itinerant nature, and that he and the Syrian travelled throughout the United States in this venture. During this period and at the suggestion of the Syrian, he had adopted the name *John Howard Bowen* in order to obtain a more Americanized name and for the purpose of eventually obtaining American citizenship and an American passport, so that he might accompany the Syrian to the latter's native country. He indicated, however, that he did not try to obtain American citizenship or to obtain an American passport, and that he had taken no steps to have his name changed legally but had merely adopted the name Bowen. After leaving the rug cleaning business, he said that he had worked for several years as an itinerant gardener, primarily in the states of Virginia and North Carolina.

He said that in 1929 he went to Knoxville where he became affiliated with the YMCA in boys' work, and he indicated that in the name *John Howard Bowen* he had founded the organisation that subsequently became known as The Boys Club of America. He said that he had remained in Knoxville until about 1943, when he became an itinerant Baptist preacher throughout the south. He said that he had been ordained as a Baptist minister in 1916 in the Bethany Baptist Church, Philadelphia, immediately before going to Canada to join the Canadian Army. He said that he had first visited Mexico in 1939 as a tourist and had become interested in missionary work, and since then he had been in and out of Mexico on numerous occasions. He said that he was well known at Laredo as *John Howard Bowen* and was a member of the First Baptist Church in that city, and that he had used the name Bowen in the United States since about 1916, except when he had applied for and received a Canadian passport in New Orleans on 10 October 1963 in his correct name of Albert Osborne.

He was questioned concerning his missionary work in Mexico and replied that he had visited various evangelical churches in Mexico City and other places in Mexico, providing books and financial assistance to these churches. Questioned about his source of funds to provide the finanical assistance and the books, he replied that these funds came from various independent Baptist churches and members of Baptist churches with whom he was in contact. Regarding churches from whom he had first received financial support, he indicated that he received financial assistance from the First Baptist Church, Roanoke, Virginia, Isabelle Baptist Church, Laton. Alabama, and several other churches in that area as well as some churches in Florida, the identity of which he was unable to provide. He emphasized that he did not solicit these funds, but that the churches and individuals knew of his work and voluntarily sent him contributions from time to time.

He was specifically questioned concerning his activities during and since June 1962 (when the assassin entered the United States) and said that in June 1962 he had been at Laredo, but that since then he had travelled around considerably. When asked to make specific places, he said that he had spent some time in *New Orleans*, Baton Rouge and other Louisiana towns and cities, looking for old and rare books which he collected and was able to sell for a profit. (cf. Antique book dealer, Kroger, of the Portland spy case in Britain placed microdots in such books and sent them on a circuitous route to Russia. Osborne could have been Oswald's contact for microdots to be concealed and despatched to Russia in antique books.) He indicated that he stayed in roominghouses and cheap hotels, none of which was he able to identify. He was questioned concerning his contacts during this period but was unable to provide specifics.

Osborne maintained that on the trip to Mexico City on 26 September 1963, there were no other English speaking people, and specifically denied that Lee Harvey Oswald, whose picture he had viewed on several occasions, was a fellow passenger. He said that he was seated on the bus with a young Mexican or Spanish appearing person who apparently spoke no English, and that the only conversations he had with any person on the bus was with two elderly Mexican women who were holding a young baby. It was his present recollection that he had arrived in Mexico City at 9.30 a.m. on 27 September 1963 and took a bus to Puebla, where he remained for two or three days picking up some religious books at an evangelical book store. He then went to a residence in Texmelucan, maintained by missionaries who were native preachers who came and went from that residence. He said that he had returned to Laredo on 1 October 1963 by way of Vera Cruz, and thereafter, went to New Orleans, where he obtained a Canadian passport in his own name on 10 October 1963. He had remained in New Orleans for about three days and had then returned to Laredo, where he remained for a few days and then went to New York City by bus, leaving New York City for London, England. (He went to Scotland and then to Grimsby, England, before proceeding to London, and perhaps to Spain.)

He admitted that he had been untruthful in previous interviews concerning his identity and had furnished false information concerning John Howard Bowen, whom he had previously indicated was an acquaintance for whom he, Osborne, had been frequently mistaken. He said that the reason for his untruthfulness was that he had been caught up in his own web of furnishing false information years ago to the Mexican authorities, which established his dual-identity of Osborne and Bowen.

He was questioned concerning his means of livelihood over the past years, and replied that he was an expert gardener and, when funds were low, obtained jobs at various places as an itinerant gardener. When questioned for names of persons or concerns by whom he had been employed he was able to furnish only the name of Tyler Nursery Company, Tyler, Texas, as a place where he worked during the summer of 1963. He had worked in various places in other Texas cities including Austin, but could not recall the names of such employers, nor could he furnish the names of other cities where he had worked as a gardener.

He was advised that his photograph had been positively identified by other English-speaking people on the bus to Mexico City on 26 September 1963, and he again denied that he was on the bus with any other English-speaking people, and repeated that he spoke no English to anyone on the bus. He said that since he had finally revealed his true identity, he would have no purpose in being further untruthful and that, if he were a passenger on the bus with Lee Harvey Oswald and other English-speaking people, he would freedly admit it. However, he persisted in maintaining that he had never seen Oswald or had been a fellow passenger with him on the bus.

On 4 February 1964, the Royal Canadian Mounted Police Headquarters, Ottawa, Canada, reported to the FBI that they had developed no information regarding *Albert Osborne* or his alleged service in the Canadian Army.

The FBI interviewed several people who had sent *John Howard Bowen* money believing it would be used for Baptist missionary work and the purchase of bibles; some of them sent to Bowen at Laredo parcels of old clothes. These people said that, to ease the release of money, Bowen had told them various stories, such as that he had been a Baptist minister for twenty years and that his children had died in India. One said that Bowen had told her that he was a representative of the Pentecostal or Gospel Church and that he had several Evangelists working throughout Mexico. The Associated Registrar of the Baptist Annuity Board, Southern Baptist Convention, Dallas, told the FBI that he had no record of *John Howard Bowen* in the files of that office and that, from the information concerning Bowen's background and history of employment, he doubted that Bowen had ever been a Baptist minister or a regular appointed missionary. The pastor of the First Mexican Southern Baptist Church, Kansas City, Missouri, advised the FBI that he had made numerous contacts with people of Mexican extraction and people associated with the Baptist church without developing information concerning *John Howard Bowen* or *Albert Osborne*. He advised that whereas there were numerous conventions within the Baptist Church of the United States, the missionary work in Mexico during approximately the last twenty years had been consolidated into one organisation. The co-ordinator of the Language Department, Baptist General Convention, Dallas, the secretary of the Baptist Home Mission Board, Atlanta, Georgia, a retired missionary of the southern Baptist Convention of Panama and the Latin-American Associate of the South Baptist Convention in Dallas all advised the FBI that they had never heard of a missionary in Mexico whose name was either *John Howard Bowen* or *Albert Osborne*.

It is clear from the lies and contradictions in the stories told by Albert Osborne and John Howard Bowen that almost all of what 'they' said was untrue. On 26 September 1963, Osborne had produced to Mexican immigration officials a counterfeit birth certificate in order to support his application for a tourist card in the name of John Howard Bowen. On 10 October 1963, he had produced a true birth certificate and a false record of service in the Canadian forces, both in the name of Osborne, to the Canadian Consulate in New Orleans in order to support his application for a passport. The self-styled impecunious itinerant preacher had paid $3.00 for a six-month tourist card to Mexico for travelling on the bus with Oswald, but returned to the United States after five days; he could have obtained a 15-day card for 50c. A few days before the assassination, he had flown from New York to Scotland, and after travelling to England possibly went to Spain, all such travel covering about three weeks. He had at first endeavoured to conceal from the FBI that he had been out of the United States for the three weeks beginning shortly before and ending shortly after the assassination of the President.

The Commission did not call Albert Osborne to testify, and as a result his alias, frauds and counterfeit documents do not appear in their Report and the counterfeits do not appear in the Exhibits. Although it would seem that the FBI must have questioned Osborne about the source of the counterfeits, there is no record of this in the Exhibits, nor of any prosecution of Osborne for the offences he must, it would appear, have committed in forging and/or uttering counterfeit documents.

The son of a fisherman, Albert Osborne was born in 1888 at Grimsby, England, and at an early age he enlisted in the British Army. In 1908 his regiment was ordered to India and Albert asked an older sister, Emily, to write to his commanding officer to tell him that Albert was younger than his army record indicated and that he should not be sent to India. When the officer refused to accede to this request, Albert bought himself out of the army and emigrated to the United States. He returned to Grimsby for two short visits to his relatives in 1953 and November 1963. On the second visit which was about a week before the assassination, Osborne had left New York for Scotland by plane and, on arrival, he had entrained some 300 miles to Grimsby to stay with Emily and visit his brother in 'The Old Folks Home'.

Having talked incessantly about religion to Emily, after three days he left, telling her he was going to London. Postcards posted in Spain were later received in the United States from Osborne, but American intelligence agencies in France and Spain could find no evidence that Osborne or Bowen had been in either country.

Another older sister, Ada, who had emigrated to the United States with her husband at about the same time as Albert, when interviewed by the FBI in 1964 said that she had seen Albert only once in the last 55 years, when he had visited her in Gary, Indiana, for one night in about 1944. She had not troubled to keep in contact with him because of a minor disagreement over an unpaid loan she had made to him, explaining that he had written to her in the 1920's asking for money and she had sent some c/o *John Howard Bowen* in New York City. She said that Albert formerly lived in New York and Washington, and had then settled in the South, mostly in areas of Tennessee, the names of which she could not remember. In Albert's infrequent letters he told her that he often travelled to Mexico, crossing the border at Laredo and El Paso, but he did not mention having lived in Canada, or having served in the Canadian armed forces. She believed that he had married in the United States but she did not know his wife's name or whereabouts. She also believed that he had a son who had been killed in action in the American Army during World War II, and that he had a daughter-in-law and a grandson in the United States, their names and whereabouts being unknown to her. She understood that Albert's occupation was that of a preacher, but she did not know under what denomination. She believed that at some time he had been employed as an actor and also as a lecturer on India, and that in earlier years Albert had shown some talent as an artist and that he had spent some time sketching. She had not heard of Albert having any scientific or technical skill, or being involved in *oceanographic* or scientific projects. (When the FBI were questioning her about this matter, it would seem that they had in mind possible espionage in Jaggars-Chiles-Stovall who handled oceanographic matter for the armed forces of the United States, and were considering a possible relationship between Albert Osborne *alias* John Howard Bowen on the Mexican bus and John Caesar Grossi *alias* Jack Leslie Bowen who with the spy/assassin was employed at the same time by Jaggars-Chiles-Stovall. In early 1964, according to Gary Lawler, Grossi said that he was going from Dallas to New York and Mexico.)

After her interview with the FBI in 1964, Ada came to England to visit Emily and other relatives. She told Emily about the FBI interview and that she had been informed by the FBI that Albert had died, but that she did not know how, where or when his death had occurred. She also told Emily that from the line of questioning she had concluded that the FBI suspected that her brother had been a spy. According to Emily and her niece, they were interviewed by the FBI in Grimsby, but no record of the interview(s) appears in the Exhibits. The recently retired head of the FBI in London is reported to have said that one of his two most interesting assignments during his seventeen years in London had been the investigation in Britain following the assassination of President Kennedy. It would seem that these investigations must have included (a) Albert Osborne whose real name may not have been either Osborne or Bowen, and (b) the two political sabotage groups (New York and London) operated by London-based Russian intelligence officer, Eugene Ivanov.

APPENDIX E

This book has described how Oswald compromised Fidel Castro, Ruth and Michael Paine, ACLU, Heindel, Robert Oswald and his wife, Vada, who had promised to let the FBI know when the 'defector' arrived at their house from Russia on 14 June 1962 but failed to do so, no doubt at the request of the 'defector'. All other groups or persons who had occasion to be in contact with Oswald automatically came under suspicion.

It will now be demonstrated how Oswald through the use of his notebook and the encoding therein – the notebook having been left behind at his residence before he set out to assassinate the President – compromised Organised Crime (OC), the CIA and the FBI. The encoded telephone numbers in the notebook were not intended to be used by Oswald but were intended to be found and decoded after the assassination. The encoded number of Jack Ruby's apartment would embarrass OC because a rumour – perhaps fabricated by the conspirators – had been circulated that OC had offered a million dollar 'hit' on the President. Were the President to be eliminated, Robert Kennedy, the Attorney General and hostile to OC, would be replaced by the choice of the new President. The rumour would be believed because the Kennedy brothers had been planning an 'umbrella' agency that would co-ordinate the work of different agencies investigating OC. The encoded numbers of the CIA and the FBI would embarrass those agencies because they could not prove the negative, i.e. that they had not used Oswald as an informant or in some other way.

At 1.0 a.m. on the morning of 27 November 1963, the Dallas FBI telephoned Captain Fritz (of Homicide) at his home and requested him to deliver to them the notebook; this was then handed by Fritz to Hosty. The FBI were, no doubt, anxious to discover if the notebook contained any reference to Ruby for on 24 November he had, of course, been arrested. If Ruby had not become involved as a result of the frustrated escape of the assassin, the task of the decoders would have been more arduous but they would have achieved the same results.

Organised Crime

Cryptoanalysts are aware of a simple method of encoding that makes use of the letters or digits in the slots of the telephone dial plus scrambling figures ('turning numbers around a little bit', cf. Crafard). This method of encoding can be broken *only* if a decoder is already aware of some numbers that might have been encoded.

On a page of Oswald's notebook (XVI.58) appears the number PO 19106. Oswald intended the PO to look like the Russian DD in the 'masking' and partly illegible number immediately above, but he had lengthened the downward stroke of the first D making it look like a P, and he had partly eliminated the lengthened downward stroke of the second D, making it look like an O; an enlargement shows this more clearly. The FBI would know that the unlisted telephone number of Ruby's apartment which the assassin had twice been approaching, first by bus and later on foot, was WH.15601. In a slot of the telephone dial the digit 7 appears under the letter P, and the digit 6 appears under the letter O: $7 + 6 = 13$. Under W in a slot iis the digit 9 and under H is the digit 4: $9 + 4 = 13$. The FBI now guessed that they had succeeded in decoding PO into WH. They would then scramble 19106 by writing down the first digit, then the last digit, then the next to the first digit, then the next to the last digit, and so on. The number at which they would arrive would be 16901. They could reduce 16901 to the second part of Ruby's telephone number, 15601, only be deducting 1300. They had now decoded PO 19106 to WH.15601, the unlisted telephone number of Ruby's apartment at 223 South Ewing (XXV.237), and the 'catalyst' they had used was 1300, the block number of Ruby's club, 'The Carousel'.

Cryptoanalysts are aware that with this and other methods of encoding it is not unusual for the encoder to use as a catalyst a number or numbers that he cannot easily forget, e.g. block numbers of residences, offices etc. The FBI now knew that Oswald had encoded the telephone number of Ruby's apartment by using the block number of Ruby's club, and that it was possible that he used this and other block numbers for further encoding in the notebook.

The Central Intelligence Agency

Before they received the notebook from Fritz, the FBI knew (a) that a 'Lee Harvey Oswald' of New Orleans had visited the Cuban Consulate in Mexico City on 27 September 1963, (b) that the assassin had left at his residence considerable evidence that he had been in Mexico City, *inter alia, This Week-Este Semana*, for 28 September to 4 October 1963, (c) that Marguerite had stated publicly, to the Secret Service and to the FBI that she had always believed that her son went to Russia as an agent of the United States government, and (d) that stenographer Bates had received the impression from Oswald that he had gone to Russia as a United States' agent, and that Ofstein of Jaggars-Chiles-Stovall had received a similar impression.

The FBI would see on a page of the notebook (XVI.54) that Oswald, before, during or after his visit to Mexico City, had written under the heading 'Mexico City' the address of the Cuban Consulate, the address of the Russian Embassy, the address of Cuban Airlines *and* the address of the United States

Embassy in Mexico City where CIA agents were stationed. They knew that Oswald had been particularly active in New Orleans prior to his visit to Mexico City, and they would wonder if by chance the CIA had recruited Oswald for some purpose or if Oswald was trying to involve the CIA. They knew that the listed telephone number of the CIA in New Orleans was 522.8874, and they would have searched the notebook for a possible encoding of that number.

On a page of the notebook (XVI.39) Oswald had done a little multiplication sum, 185 x 10 = 1850, and that adjacent were written MON.2. and the number 1147. Realising that Oswald would not require to execute this multiplication, the FBI would wonder whether this was to draw attention to the adjacent writing which might contain some kind of code. They knew from the successful decoding of Ruby's telephone number that Oswald had used letters in the telephone dial slot, and they would see that MON were the same letters as MNO in a slot. Under MNO in the slot is the digit 6. Taking 7 for M, 6 for N and 6 for O the total is 3 x 6 = 18. Taking the 2 after MON as possibly indicating halving, the total would now be 9. The first part of the CIA telephone number was 522, the digits when added together totalling 9. The FBI now suspected that they were approaching the complete decoding of the encoded CIA number. Knowing Oswald's methods when encoding Ruby's telephone number, the FBI could simplify the encoding of the second part of the CIA number by *adding* 1300 to 8874: result 10174. Unscrambling (by reversing Oswald's scrambling method), they would arrive at 11470. The FBI would have seen that the 10 in the multiplication sum was written slightly thicker and apparently with a different pen to the 185 and the 1850, and that 1147 had been written similarly slightly thicker and apparently with the same pen as 10. They could now see that Oswald had intended to draw their attention to the use of the digits 1 and 0 in connection with 1147, and, the 0 being more heavily written than the 1, that Oswald had added 0 to the end of 1147; result 11470. By scrambling 11470 to 10174 and deducting 1300, the result is 8874 which is the second part of the CIA number.

The FBI would also have seen that on·three other occasions in the notebook – apparently unnecessarily but apparently to draw attention – Oswald had written his Russian residence permit number. On page (XVI.40) he had written MNO, 311479, on page (XVI.46) he had written M.311479, and on page (XVI.59) he had again written M.311479; these three entries would draw attention to the central digits, 1147. They could see that the 3 in front of the 1147 could indicate a three digit prefix, and that the 9 at the end of 1147 could indicate that the three digit prefix totalled 9. It would seem that the assassin was determined that the cryptoanalysts should not overlook the obvious. (The Russian P looks like an English M, but with a slightly curved cross-bar at the top.)

They now realised that, if Oswald had escaped and Ruby therefore not at once suspected, Oswald had led the FBI not only to the decoding of the CIA number but to the catalyst, 1300, which catalyst they would then have used to decode PO 19106. They would then have suspected that Ruby had been involved in the escape of the assassin, and that OC might have organised the assassination. Fortunately for the CIA, they had had informants inside and outside the Russian Embassy in Mexico City; on 10 and 18 October 1963 they had supplied the FBI with information about the visits of the American male to that Embassy, and on 22 and 23 November 1963 they had supplied the FBI with photographs of this man.

(During the 'Polaroid episode', Ruby spoke to Crafard about the Box Nos. on the poster and the advertisement being the same 'when moved around a little bit', and Ruby later tried to discover a connection between the Box Nos. When he wrote on the old envelope the Box No. of the poster, 1757, in one corner, and the Box No. of the advertisement, 1792, in the opposite corner with 'or 1772' written underneath, Ruby had had no need to write an alternative number for he carried the advertisement with him. Sideways on the envelope he had written MON and, as shown in the CIA encoded number, when halved MON can represent 9. It appears that Ruby knew about halving 18 to arrive at 9, for above the MON Ruby had written EM, being letters in the dial slots that had digits underneath of 3 and 6: total 9. Apparently trying to discover a connection he had written after EM, the number 11197, which number does bear a slight resemblance to the three numbers he had written at the top of the envelope, and also to 311479. He had also written another number, DA 10467, sideways on the envelope, but apparently this was not written in connection with his attempt to associate the Box Nos. (XXV.213).

Senator testified that before the episode, Ruby was 'excited' about the Box Nos. and Crafard testified that Ruby was 'more excited' about the Bos Nos. than about the assassination. Senator testified that after the episode and presumably after Ruby's written efforts to associate the Box Nos. Ruby did not again mention the Box Nos.)

The Federal Bureau of Investigation

Shortly after the assassination, a Houston reported, Hudkins, printed a story — alleged to be based on information received from the chief criminal deputy of the Sheriff in Dallas, Sweatt, — that Oswald had been an informant for the FBI with No. S179 and that he had been paid $200 a month commencing in September 1962.

Recruitment for secret informants is done verbally and payments are sometimes made to a bank account in order to avoid any observable contact between the FBI and their informant. Oswald is not known to have had a banking or savings account in any place, at any time or in any name, but on a page in the notebook (XVI.67) under Oswald's entry 'FINGER PRINTS' appear the words 'BANK ACC'. Oswald or another man is known to have cashed at least one small money order at a post office in Dallas prior to the assassination, the order having been delivered to the YMCA and the payee having made a point of being particularly objectionable apparently so that he would be remembered at the post office. He had been unable to produce any proof of identity to satisfy the paying clerk that he was entitled to the money order, but he left the building to obtain proof of identity, returning with a Marine identity card and a library card. At this time Oswald was not living at the YMCA but, having on two occasions stayed there, could have collected the money order(s).

On learning through Waggoner Carr and Wade of Hudkin's story, before hearing testimony the Commission held a secret session with these men to discuss the source of the rumour and to consider what ought to be done. The Commissioners were all present and, after suggestions were considered, it was finally decided that they would not accept affidavits from Hoover or other FBI agents that the assassin had not been an FBI informant, but that they would make their own enquiries. According to the Volumes of Testimony and Exhibits they did no more than accept the affidavits of Hoover and other FBI agents, and they called neither Hudkins nor Sweatt to testify. September 1962 would have been the appropriate time for Oswald to have been recruited as it was after the second FBI interview with Oswald in Fort Worth on 16 August 1962 that his file was given a 'closed status'; neither Hudkins nor Sweatt could have known about the 'closed status', and neither could have realised that the 'reformed' defector and his younger and pretty Russian wife would have appeared to the FBI to be 'tailor-made' to infiltrate – which they did – the extensive Russian emigre groups in Dallas and Forth Worth, in at least two members of which the FBI were interested. It would seem that there must have been some evidence of the assassin being an informant with the number, rate of payment and date of commencement as above, for Hudkins and Sweatt could not have invented their information; it may be that it was the conspirators who had somehow created evidence of this alleged and embarrassing FBI involvement.

In addition to (a) the words 'BANK ACC', (b) the cashing of the money order(s) and (c) the allegation of 'FBI informant', to add to the embarrassment of the FBI, Oswald had encoded their listed telephone number in New Orleans, using his method of encoding but in a somewhat complicated manner, although comparatively easy to discover once it was known that a block number had been used as catalyst. For the encoding of the FBI number, Oswald used as catalyst the block number of Wesley Frazier's home in Irving, 2400.

There is an interesting sidelight on coding. Some four years after the assassination, District Attorney James Garrison of New Orleans charged a prominent New Orleans businessman, Clay Shaw, with conspiracy to assassinate the President, and was proposing to charge 'Captain' David Ferrie who was found dead in his apartment the day before Garrison was to arrest him. The charges against Shaw were later dismissed.

Oswald had lived in New Orleans in the same district as Shaw from early

May to 25 September 1963 and, after visiting Mexico City, had returned to Dallas where seven weeks later he was to assassinate the President.

When Garrison arrested Shaw, the latter's notebook was seized, and it contained the handwritten entry: Lee Odum. P.O. Box 19106. Dallas, Tex. That the man arrested on a charge of conspiracy to assassinate the President should have this number in his notebook cannot be dismissed as a coincidence for, by extracting the words 'Odum' and 'Box', the result is Lee. P.O. 19106, Dallas, Tex. This entry in Shaw's notebook would appear to link Shaw both to 'Lee' (at one time in and later to return to Dallas, Tex.) and to Ruby's encoded telephone number in Dallas, i.e. the entry appeared to confirm the association of Oswald with Ruby, and therefore the complicity of OC at the least in the escape of the assassin. Ivan *Lee*, Bardwell and Hart *Odum* were three Dallas FBI agents active in the post-assassination investigations; the entry thus hinting at FBI involvement with Oswald and Ruby.

The telephone number of Shaw's residence in New Orleans was also encoded in Oswald's notebook, Oswald using his method of encoding but again in a slightly different manner and with a different catalyst, this time the block number of Oswald's apartment in New Orleans, 4900. To my knowledge Shaw was associated via Canada with the London political sabotage group itself linked.to the New York group (both mentioned in the foreword to this book) although I make no suggestion that Shaw was knowingly involved in any political sabotage. Curiously, when Oswald was televised on the street passing out leaflets, he was standing outside the International Trade Mart (import and export) and under Shaw's window in the building.

The Report says: 'All of Oswald's known writings or other possessions which might have been used for code or other espionage purposes have been examined by either the Federal Bureau of Investigation or the National Security Agency, or both agencies, to determine whether they were so used.' (R.244).

It would not be unreasonable to expect that the next paragraph should state whether or not coding had been discovered; the Report changes the subject.

The Exhibits disclose that the FBI knew that the assassin had cut single Russian letters out of a book, and extracted sentences and whole paragraphs from other printed material, in one case removing the handwritten word 'write' from a letter received by him. This is a method employed by spies to make up a message by using a conglomerate of items which cannot be traced back to them. As it is a fact that the assassin made these extractions, it is not unreasonable to believe that he must have made use of them and also his notebook for some irregular purpose.

The possibility of coding, the method and details were brought to my attention in the United States some years ago but, in view of the powerful evidence of conspiracy contained in this book, I would not have mentioned them had it not been for the fact that rumours have circulated that either the CIA or the FBI were in some manner involved with the assassin; the contents of this Appendix would appear to dissipate any such rumours.

IMPORTANT INFORMATION ADDITIONAL TO CHAPTER 9
(See Page 158)

Since writing the above, I have seen a document recently released from the National Archives. It is a letter written by Hoover and sent by courier service to the Special Counsel to the Commission, Rankin. It is dated 9 June 1964, which was two days *after* Ruby first testified and denied his one-day trip to Havana. Ruby was to testify again at a later date, but was never questioned about the trip nor about his role as FBI informant. The letter says:

'. . . Jack Ruby was contacted by Special Agent Charles W. Flynn of the Dallas Office on March 11, 1959, in view of his position as a night club operator who might have knowledge of the criminal element in Dallas. The purpose of this contact was to determine whether or not Ruby might have such knowledge, and if so, if he would be willing to furnish information to his Bureau. Ruby was advised of the FBI's jurisdiction in criminal matters, and he expressed a willingness to furnish information. A personal description of Ruby was obtained by Special Agent Flynn on the occasion of this contact on March 11, 1959, but no information or other results were obtained. Between March 11, 1959, and October 2, 1959, Ruby was contacted on eight other occasions but he furnished no other information whatsoever and further contacts with him were discontinued. . . .'

It was on 4 March 1959, that Marine Oswald, *who carried a high security clearance in radar*, had written to the college in Switzerland for enrolment in their April 1960 course. On 16 September 1959, he had left his mother's home in Fort Worth for New Orleans and booked into the Liberty Hotel in that city on 17 September 1959. On 20 September 1959 he had allegedly sailed from New Orleans for Russia. According to Delgado, he had been in touch with a Cuban Consulate during his last year in the Marines—November 1958 to September 1959—and had had a long meeting outside the gates of the camp with an unidentified civilian.

On 11 March 1959, Ruby had been in Dallas for 12 years, coming from Chicago where from the age of 15 he had been a 'street brawler' and associated with Al Capone. He had associated with many criminals from the time of his arrival in Dallas, and himself had committed almost every known crime. He had also become a man of extreme ferocity and was known to be powerful and 'very fast', using feet, knees, fists, black-jack, knuckle-dusters, and revolver, usually attacking his victims—including women—without warning. He had been arrested many times in Dallas but he had never been convicted. (After he killed the assassin by revolver, a pair of 'used' and a pair of 'new' knuckle-dusters were found in his car.) Prior to 11 March 1959, Ruby for years had considerable interests and a number of criminal friends in the gambling world in Havana, particularly in 'The Tropicana', the largest gambling complex in the world.

It might be speculated that Ruby was informed or that the FBI learned of Marine Oswald's sympathy for Castro and of his 4 March letter to the college in Switzerland, and that the FBI—perhaps at Ruby's suggestion—decided to enlist Ruby thereby placing him in a position to prevent Oswald from leaving the country for Cuba or elsewhere. The employment of Ruby as informant was on 11 March 1959, he appeared in New Orleans on 13 September 1959, and his employment with the FBI ceased on 2 October 1959, at which time someone calling himself Lee Harvey Oswald was on the freighter and half-way across the Atlantic en route to Russia. Ruby could have told the FBI that the Marine had evaded him, but in fact could have met him, shown him his passport with the one-day trip to Cuba marked thereon, told him that he had a message from Castro, and then given him money for the trip to Russia or killed him. In the alternative, the FBI may have known nothing of the Marine's interest in Cuba or of his intention to go to the college, in which case Ruby would have invited the FBI to employ him so as to give 'cover' for his possible contact with the Marine between 11 March and 20 September 1959—and the 'framing' of the FBI for the killing of the real Oswald if this, in fact, occurred.

That this speculation is not without foundation is shown by the fact that one of these interpretations must have occurred to the authors of the Report for not only does it fail to mention Ruby's role as FBI informant commencing on 11 March—about which Ruby was not asked in testimony—but makes it appear that Ruby was employed *before* the Marine's 'suspicious' application to the college, the Report saying on p. 688, that Oswald's 'application is dated 19 March'. This statement is untrue for Oswald's application was dated 4 March (XVI.625) although for some reason he made a second application that was dated 19 March (XVI.621).

The reader must decide for himself what, if anything, occurred between Ruby and the Marine between 17 and 20 September 1959, but he should bear in mind that the impostor must have been chosen long before Oswald left the Marines since it could only have been the impostor who paid the first visit to the American Embassy in Moscow on 31 October 1959, this being only 15 days after the real Oswald is alleged to have arrived in Moscow on 16 October 1959; the KGB could not have found and trained an impostor in 15 days. Furthermore, it would have been unwise for the KGB to take the risk of the real Oswald changing his mind about going to Russia while on the freighter or when in France, Britain, or Finland. It would have been wiser for the KGB to infiltrate the impostor into New Orleans in September 1959 and for the impostor, taking Oswald's clothes and identity upon the latter's arrival in New Orleans, to make the zig-zag journey to Russia.